MW01063689

Disruptive Technology and the Law of Naval Warfare

Disruptive Technology and the Law of Naval Warfare

JAMES KRASKA AND RAUL PEDROZO

OXFORD

UNIVERSITY PRESS

OXFORD
UNIVERSITY PRESS

Oxford University Press is a department of the University of Oxford. It furthers the University's objective of excellence in research, scholarship, and education by publishing worldwide. Oxford is a registered trade mark of Oxford University Press in the UK and certain other countries.

Published in the United States of America by Oxford University Press
198 Madison Avenue, New York, NY 10016, United States of America.

Library of Congress Cataloging-in-Publication Data
Names: Kraska, James, author. | Pedrozo, Raul, author.
Title: Disruptive technology and the law of naval warfare / James Kraska and Raul Pedrozo.
Description: New York, NY : Oxford University Press, [2022] | Includes bibliographical references and index.
Identifiers: LCCN 2021045563 (print) | LCCN 2021045564 (ebook) | ISBN 9780197630181 (hardback) |
    ISBN 9780197630204 (epub) | ISBN 9780197630198 (updf) | ISBN 9780197630211 (digital-online)
Subjects: LCSH: War, Maritime (International law) | Naval art and science—Technological innovations.
Classification: LCC KZ6563 .K73 2022 (print) | LCC KZ6563 (ebook) | DDC 341.6/3—dc23/eng/20211105
LC record available at https://lccn.loc.gov/2021045563
LC ebook record available at https://lccn.loc.gov/2021045564

DOI: 10.1093/oso/9780197630181.001.0001

1 3 5 7 9 8 6 4 2

Printed by Integrated Books International, United States of America

Note to Readers
This publication is designed to provide accurate and authoritative information in regard to the subject matter covered. It is based upon sources believed to be accurate and reliable and is intended to be current as of the time it was written. It is sold with the understanding that the publisher is not engaged in rendering legal, accounting, or other professional services. If legal advice or other expert assistance is required, the services of a competent professional person should be sought. Also, to confirm that the information has not been affected or changed by recent developments, traditional legal research techniques should be used, including checking primary sources where appropriate.

(Based on the Declaration of Principles jointly adopted by a Committee of the American Bar Association and a Committee of Publishers and Associations.)

You may order this or any other Oxford University Press publication
by visiting the Oxford University Press website at www.oup.com.

Contents

Acknowledgments

This book focuses on the application of the law of naval warfare to emerging technologies at sea. The study is a fusion of law and operations to provide a bridge between operational planners and legal thinkers. The law of naval warfare is only re-entering the lexicon of international law as great power competition among the United States, China, and Russia plays out at sea. Emerging technologies are quickly transforming the maritime battlespace, so this book is just a first salvo in what is certain to be a continuing discussion.

The book benefited from numerous engagements with professors James FitzSimonds, William S. Murray, and Craig M. Koerner of the U.S. Naval War College; Bill Rearick of Navy Warfare Development Command; and Tom Choinski of the Naval Undersea Warfare Center. We thank them for their thoughtful insights on parts of the monograph.

The book benefited from legal insights by the faculty of the Stockton Center for International Law at the U.S. Naval War College, and legal officers and advisers throughout the world, including Commander Koki Sato of the Japan Maritime Self Defense Force. We especially thank Professor Michael N. Schmitt and Lieutenant Colonel Elton Johnson for numerous ad hoc discussions that sharpened our analysis. We are especially indebted to Wing Commander Kieran Tinkler, Royal Air Force, for his conversations on international law applicable to outer space and his nuanced suggestions to improve Chapter 8 on the challenges of applying the law of armed conflict to outer space.

The book also benefited from editorial advice from Captain Ralph Thomas, U.S. Navy (ret.), who serves as Associate Editor of *International Law Studies*. Vishaka Ramesh and Vishesh Bhatia, who serve as research fellows in the Stockton Center, provided diligent assistance and careful copyedit of the manuscript. Heidi Garcia, Andrea Groce, and Julie Zecher at the U.S. Naval War College Library were exceptionally helpful and generous with their time in locating sources. We also thank the Harvard Law School library for providing copies of rare materials.

Despite all this support and assistance, we are, of course, responsible for any errors. The views presented are those of the authors and do not reflect the official policy or position of the U.S. Navy, the Naval War College, or the Department of Defense.

James Kraska
Chair and Charles H. Stockton Professor of International Maritime Law,
Stockton Center for International Law, U.S. Naval War College

Raul Pedrozo
Howard S. Levie Chair of the Law of Armed Conflict, Stockton Center for
International Law, U.S. Naval War College

Newport, Rhode Island

Authors

James Kraska is Chair and Charles H. Stockton Professor of International Maritime Law in the Stockton Center for International Law at the U.S. Naval War College and Visiting Professor of Law and John Harvey Gregory Lecturer on World Organization at Harvard Law School. He has served as a visiting professor of international law at the University of the Philippines and Gujarat National Law University, visiting scholar at Duke University Marine Laboratory, and fellow at Woods Hole Oceanographic Institution. A retired Navy Commander, he held numerous positions advising senior military and Defense officials, including Director of International Negotiations on the Joint Staff.

Raul Pedrozo is the Howard S. Levie Chair of the Law of Armed Conflict in the Stockton Center for International Law at the U.S. Naval War College and a retired Navy Captain. He served in numerous positions advising senior military and Defense officials, including Special Assistant to the Under Secretary of Defense for Policy, Principal Legal Adviser to U.S. Naval Special Warfare Command, and Principal Legal Adviser to Commander, U.S. Pacific Command. He has participated in numerous international negotiations, including the International Maritime Organization, Transnational Organized Crime Convention, International Civil Aviation Organization, and United States-China Military Maritime Consultative Agreement.

Introduction

Throughout history naval warfare has evolved as marine technology continuously changed mankind's relationship with the sea. In ancient Mediterranean civilizations, rowed galleys were used to project power. With little innovation, the galley dominated seapower for three millennia. Galley fighting at sea was akin to fighting on "land" with soldiers connecting with and boarding one another's ships in afloat infantry combat.[1] Reinforcing this quality of land warfare, in the early modern period galleys were outfitted with fortress-like towers from which archers could rain arrows down on enemy soldiers aboard nearby warships. A rudimentary naval ram constructed into the bow sometimes might sink an enemy galley but not without physical contact that imperiled one's own forces. The limited ability to project force from the ship ensured conflict would be hand to hand.

1. Propulsion by Oar: Rowed Galleys and Infantry Combat at Sea

Galleys are open to the air and have a low freeboard, so they lack endurance and are unstable in heavy seas. The Greek penteconter had a single row of oars and most of the space on the ship was used to accommodate the human rowers and store supplies of food and water, with little space available for weapons and cargo. These ships were equipped with an auxiliary sail, yet they rarely left sight of land. Crews typically slept on the beach, afraid to navigate in the dark.

The bireme, with two banks of rowers, generated even more power than the penteconter, which was especially important for maneuver and attack in combat. The Romans mastered the trireme with three banks of oars. Even

---

[1] The small and fast penteconter was used by Athens and Sparta during the Peloponnesian War; the Phoenicians and Assyrians used the bireme, which had two banks of oars. The trireme and quadrireme added additional rows of oars. CHESTER G. STARR, THE INFLUENCE OF SEA POWER ON ANCIENT HISTORY 3–14 (1989).

Disruptive Technology and the Law of Naval Warfare. James Kraska and Raul Pedrozo, Oxford University Press.
© James Kraska & Raul Pedrozo 2022. DOI: 10.1093/oso/9780197630181.003.0001

though the trireme had three times as many rowers as the penteconter, its speed was only 20 percent greater because wave resistance grows exponentially with the speed of the ship. The trireme, however, was much more maneuverable than the penteconter and could accelerate from standstill to half speed in just 8 seconds and reach a top speed in 30 seconds.

Warships changed little between the battle of Actium in 31 BC with the clash of the fleet of Octavian and the combined forces of Marc Antony and Cleopatra, and the Battle of Lepanto in 1571 AD, a contest for control of the Mediterranean Sea. The 200-ton Renaissance galley at Lepanto was not materially different from one used by the Greeks 2,000 years earlier.[2] The Battle of Lepanto pitted a hastily organized fleet under the Holy League against the Ottoman Empire, and it was the last naval engagement dominated by the rowed galley. The Holy League was comprised of the combined forces of Venice, Genoa, the Papal States, and Spain, and it defeated the Ottoman Turk advance in the Western Mediterranean Sea. The Ottoman force had some 250 galleys, manned in part by 15,000 Christian slaves chained to the bench.[3]

With 208 galleys, the Holy League was supplemented by eight powerful galleasses—innovative heavy barges bristling with firepower. A single galleass carried 180 cannons and 500 arquebusiers. The galleass was outfitted with a sail as well as oars, but it was so slow and cumbersome that it had to be towed into battle.[4] Despite these shortcomings, just a handful of galleasses provided the decisive advantage against the larger Ottoman fleet in the battle off the coast of western Greece. The artillery on board the new ships was overwhelming and sliced into the fragile Ottoman galleys. The massive engagement at Lepanto likely saw more men fall in battle in a single day than in any other conflict in history to that point.[5] The massive hybrid galleass foretold the superiority of firearms over arrows and crossbolts and the ascendancy of the all-sail warship.

Sail power meant ships required smaller crews, reducing the space needed for stores of food and water while freeing space for cargo, ammunition, and weapons. The higher freeboard and the invention of gun portals meant sailing ships were steadier than galleys in harsh conditions on the open sea. Thus, the emergence of the all-sail ship coincided with the integration of

---

[2] BERNARD & FAWN M. BRODIE, FROM CROSSBOW TO H-BOMB: THE EVOLUTION OF THE WEAPONS AND TACTICS OF WARFARE 64 (1962).

[3] *Id.* at 64.

[4] WILLIAM OLIVER STEVENS & ALLAN WESTCOTT, HISTORY OF SEAPOWER 61 (1920, rev. ed. 1937).

[5] Approximately 30,000 Turks and 7,500 Christians were killed in the melee. *Id.* at 66.

heavy cannons on board warships, opening the way for Western naval dominance and the age of imperialism. The design of the gun portal also increased firepower since multiple layers of cannon could be fired from below the main deck.

The deadly galleass also proved the value of firearms as the first effective stand-off weapons in naval warfare and led to the transition to galleons. The galleon was larger, stronger, and more seaworthy than the galley. By the time of the Napoleonic Wars, round shot projectiles fired from a ship of the line had a theoretical range of about 2,000 yards, although the effective range was just 500 yards.[6] Most engagements were still fought by exchanging close broadsides, but boarding action had become rare. The ship, rather than the complement of soldiers on board, had become the weapon (and the target) in naval warfare, transforming the law applicable to armed conflicts at sea. Whereas the law of armed conflict generally is focused on targeting or protection of individuals based on their status, the law of naval warfare looks to the status of the ships they occupy.

2. Propulsion by Sail: Carracks, Caravels, and the Age of Discovery

While the Battle of Lepanto was the last gasp of the rowed galley, the geopolitical shift began more than a century before with the development of the all-sail carrack and caravel. In the early modern period, Portuguese and Spanish seafarers wandered down the coast of Africa and westward into the Atlantic Ocean. The Iberian powers laid claim to vast oceans as sovereign territory. While the Ottomans seized Constantinople in 1453, on the western edge of the Mediterranean Sea, Portugal and Spain perfected the carrack and caravel for transatlantic travel, trade, and colonial power projection.

Carracks are three or four-masted ships developed by sailors in Genoa in the 14th century and used for trade because of their endurance and generous cargo capacity. These ocean-going ships are square-rigged on the fore and main masts and lateen-rigged on the mizzenmast. The caravel can tack into the wind and maneuver like a rowed ship. In the early 1400s, Spain and Portugal began operating caravels, using them to explore the West African coastline. Spain discovered the Canary Islands between 1402 and 1405, while

---

[6] ANGUS KONSTAM, BRITISH NAPOLEONIC SHIP OF THE LINE 33 (2001).

Portugal laid claim to Madeira in 1415, the Azores Islands in 1427, and Cape Verde in 1462. The Catholic monarchs of Castile and Aragon reached agreement with Afonso V and his son, Prince John of Portugal, to divide the islands of the eastern Atlantic Ocean along a north-south axis. With its focus on Africa and the Indian Ocean, Portugal valued the southern route and negotiated the Treaty of Alcáçovas-Toledo with Spain in 1479. Except for the Canary Islands, all territories in dispute remained in Portuguese hands, including the gold mines in Guinea, the island of Madeira, the Azores, and Cape Verde. Portugal also won the exclusive right to rule the Kingdom of Fez—present-day Morocco.

In 1492, Spain completed the reconquest of the Iberian Peninsula from Islam after a 600-year period of occupation. With the homeland secure, the Iberian powers looked West. The same year as the reconquest, the Catholic monarchs of Spain sponsored Italian explorer Christopher Columbus to sail two small caravels and a larger carrack in search of a western route to India. Upon returning from his encounter with the New World, Christopher Columbus was diverted to Portugal, where John II was convinced that the newly discovered islands fell under his dominion in accordance with the 1479 treaty.

The Spanish monarchs dispatched emissaries to Pope Alexander VI to stake their claim. Being originally from Valencia (the Kingdom of Aragon), the pope was suspected of being partial to Spain. Alexander VI mediated the dispute by issuing the Bull Inter Caetera ("among other works") on May 4, 1493, to replace the Treaty of Alcáçovas-Toledo. The edict altered the understanding between Spain and Portugal by dispensing with the horizontal boundary and dividing their claims on a vertical line that ran 100 leagues west of Cape Verde, with Portugal retaining everything to the east and Spain inheriting yet unknown lands to the west.[7]

Portugal was pleased with the recognition that waters off Africa fell within its domain but was incensed that it lacked maneuver space in the Atlantic Ocean to enable its ships to catch the southwestern pattern of the northeasterly trade winds across the equator. As ships pass the Intertropical Convergence Zone, they face into the southeasterly trade winds blowing them north and west, preventing progress east through the Gulf of Guinea and south, down the coast of Africa. In concession, the following year Spain and Portugal agreed to the Treaty of Tordesillas. The new agreement shifted

---

[7] A league was about 2.6 statute miles. The metric was abolished by Philip II in 1568.

the boundary line in Portugal's favor, westward to 300 leagues from Cape Verde. Portuguese ships could sail farther west and then swing back southeast to reach the Cape of Good Hope, the point where ships begin to travel eastward into the Indian Ocean. While "traveling west to reach the east," Portuguese navigator Pedro Álvares Cabral accidentally encountered Brazil in 1500, giving Portugal a vast new claim on the Spanish mainland of South America.

Portuguese explorer Bartolomeu Dias first rounded the cape in 1488, opening the Indian Ocean to maritime colonial conquest and trade. During a voyage from 1497 to 1499, Vasco da Gama became the first European to reach India by sea as he searched for a maritime route to the spice trade that would bypass the treacherous "silk road" through Ottoman lands. The maritime route also circumvented onerous taxes imposed on eastern imports by the Italian city states that controlled ports of entry for eastern trade into European markets. Portugal founded outposts at Cape Town, Muscat, Goa, Colombo, Malacca, Timor, and Macau, and made the first western landfall in Japan in 1543, establishing a trading port in Nagasaki. Meanwhile, the Spanish Empire began to rule in South America, with cities in Havana, Veracruz, Acapulco, Cartagena, Lima, Santiago, and Buenos Aires.

Portugal and Spain set in motion a contest at sea that would draw in the great powers of Europe. First challenged by the Dutch, and then by the British, Portugal and Spain slowly ceded command of the oceans. The development of more powerful shipboard artillery meant that opposing forces engaged at ever-increasing distances. Eventually ships were built around the gun rather than merely placing guns on ordinary ships. The entire platform became the weapon; defeating the enemy meant sinking the ship. The warship became the most sophisticated military machine of the age.

3. Propulsion by Steam: Firearms and the Industrial Era

Firepower at sea, coupled with a revolutionary form of propulsion, further advanced naval warfare. Harnessing wind power freed warships from the oar and harnessing steam freed them from the whims of the wind. The adoption of steam power in the 19th century transformed naval operations.[8] The

[8] BRODIE & BRODIE, *supra* note 2.

propelling screw replaced the paddlewheel allowing the engines to be placed below the waterline. With steam power, tactics were no longer dominated by the direction and velocity of the wind or exceptional seamanship.[9] Steam technology favored simple superiority in numbers, contributing to industrial competition.[10] At the same time, the cost of steam meant that only a handful of countries could compete in high-end naval conflict. When France constructed its first screw propeller driven ship of the line, the *Napoleon*, in 1850, the Royal Navy realized it had to convert its entire force to steam at enormous cost.[11] While steam power provided tactical advantage, it also created strategic dependence on coaling stations. Continuous presence and patrol in a single location became more difficult because of the need to take on coal. Distant coaling stations complicated the Royal Navy's operations beyond the home waters and favored its rivals, such as the United States and Japan.

The hot blast furnace, invented in 1834, reduced the cost of iron, making it possible to build stronger and lighter warships. Ships became armored and more survivable through the advent of cellular construction or compartmentalization. Larger ships could carry heavier guns with increased stability, and they also could be outfitted with heavier armor. Later, the regenerative furnace could inexpensively make high quality steel. In 1847, Alfred Krupp built the first steel gun, the greatest advance in naval gunfire in 300 years. The 1861 duel between the ironclads CSS *Merrimack* and the USS *Monitor* symbolized these changes. The Union *Monitor*, outfitted with a single turret with two 11-inch guns, presaged designs of the early 20th century. Naval guns increased in size and power, further extending the range of engagement. By the late 19th century naval guns were housed in revolving turrets. In response, ship armor became stronger and thicker, increasing to 24 inches at the waterline by 1880.

Progress in mines, torpedoes, and eventually submarines, also transformed naval warfare. During the U.S. Civil War, the Confederate submersible boat named *Hunley* sank the Federal corvette *Housatonic* with a spar torpedo, a bomb rigged to the end of the pole.[12] The first automatic torpedo entered service in 1873. As torpedoes became more reliable, navies developed torpedo boats—and torpedo boat destroyers to counter them. The modern

[9] *Id.* at 154.
[10] *Id.* at 157.
[11] *Id.* at 157.
[12] *Id.* at 165.

"destroyer" is a direct descendent.[13] The torpedo complemented the gun for fighting at extended range.

After 1905, the Imperial German Navy began to cautiously build diesel engine diving boats, but the first effective U-boat did not enter the force until 1913. The Germans began the First World War with superior U-boats and both sides perfected the torpedo. The German submarine war against Allied commerce was tactically successful but also drew the United States into the war, which delivered a strategic defeat to Germany. On February 4, 1915, the Kaiser approved U-boat attacks on commercial ships, eliciting a U.S. protest. The Kaiser stopped and then resumed unrestricted submarine warfare on August 1, 1916, only to retreat again after renewed American protests. When the Kaiser launched the unrestricted campaign in earnest on February 1, 1917, however, it was too late to save the German war effort. The submarine also played a dispositive role in naval combat during the Second World War, especially in the Pacific theater, as the United States conducted its own campaign of unrestricted submarine warfare.

4. Revolutions in Military Affairs

The United States adopted the First Offset Strategy during the 1950s to counter numerically superior Soviet forces in Europe by relying on tactical nuclear weapons. "Offset" means that the United States was not striving to match the Russian forces tank for tank or ship for ship, but instead used technology to offset the mismatch to counter Soviet numerical advantage. Instead of trying to counter the Soviet Army soldier for soldier, Eisenhower turned to nuclear weapons, where the United States had an advantage, to negate Moscow's superiority in conventional forces.

As early as 1954 the U.S. Navy had nearly 100 nuclear weapons afloat.[14] With the entry into service of the USS *Polaris* in 1960, the Navy acquired a strategic second-strike capability. Similarly, nuclear power transformed the naval order of battle. Onboard nuclear reactors replaced diesel engines, greatly extending surface ship and submarine endurance for the wealthiest and most advanced states. Even now nuclear power at sea is limited to

---

[13] *Id.* at 166.
[14] Hans Kristensen, *Declassified: US Nuclear Weapons at Sea*, FEDERATION OF AMERICAN SCIENTISTS (online), Feb. 3, 2016.

the five permanent members of the Security Council and India.[15] Although originally developed as a supplement to land-based ballistic missiles and nuclear armed bombers, because of their greater survivability nuclear powered submarines quickly became the most important nuclear deterrent.

Technology enabled miniaturization of nuclear components, shrinking a 5,000-pound bomb into the size of a 150-pound bomb, and making deployment at sea manageable. By the 1970s and 1980s, the United States had about one-fourth of its nuclear forces at sea.[16] As the Soviet Union reached nuclear parity with the United States, however, Flexible Response was no longer a credible deterrent to a massive conventional ground invasion of Western Europe by the U.S.S.R. With nuclear weapons off the table, the United States searched for another way to counter superior Soviet forces.

To meet the conventional military challenge, the United States initiated the Second Offset Strategy. This concept leveraged technological innovations to prevail on the conventional battlefield despite Soviet numerical superiority. Precision munitions, electro-optics, stealth technologies, advanced C4I, and other innovations countered the advantage in numbers. DARPA was created in 1973 as a factory for these ideas. Rather than expending a high number of rounds against enemy tanks, the United States sought to assign one round per enemy armored tank, precision weapons promised to negate the Soviet Union's quantitative advantage. These technologies were paired with new operational concepts.

In the late 1970s, General Bernard Rogers lead U.S. Army development of operational plans to attack the enemy in depth.[17] These efforts culminated in the AirLand Battle in 1982.[18] In 1984, NATO envisioned strikes against Soviet "follow-on" forces moving West to reinforce Moscow's initial assault, resulting in the doctrine of "follow-on forces attack" or FOFA.[19] Missile and aircraft deep strikes into the Soviet bloc would interdict armored columns before they reached contact with NATO forces in Western Europe. Throughout the 1980s and 1990s, a "revolution in military affairs" (RMA) unfolded by breakthroughs in sensors and weapons technologies that made FOFA possible, closing the kill chain long before the enemy came into contact with NATO forces. These technologies and concepts were applied by U.S. forces

---

[15] BRODIE & BRODIE, *supra* note 2, at 289–91.

[16] Kristensen, *supra* note 14.

[17] DEP'T OF THE ARMY, FIELD MANUAL 100-5 OPERATIONS 20-20 to 2-24 (July 1, 1976).

[18] DEP'T OF THE ARMY, FIELD MANUAL 100-5 OPERATIONS 7-1 (Aug. 1982).

[19] John F. Rybicki, *Follow-On Forces Attack*, THE MILITARY ENGINEER (Sept./Oct. 1989), at 12, 14–15.

in the First Gulf War in 1991 and the Air War in Kosovo in 1999 to identify, acquire, and destroy mobile targets throughout the war zone. The Second Offset Strategy was enormously successful.

The Third Offset Strategy is underway, motivated by the increase in quality and number of Russian and Chinese battle networks.[20] Using unmanned and autonomous platforms, artificial intelligence (AI), miniaturization, big data, and cyber capabilities, the Third Offset seeks to use emerging technology to circumvent adversary capabilities. This approach aligns with what futurist Alvin Toffler referred to as the Third Wave of human development, the information revolution.[21] The First Wave of warfare arose from agrarian societies and was based on agriculture.[22] The Second Wave began in Europe in the 1600s and was rooted in industrialization and mass production.[23]

Third Wave warfare is engaged by networked systems that utilize data to make self-regulated adjustments in real time. Information technology, autonomy, big data, and AI are the tools of Third Wave conflict. Data are collected by distributed sensors, communicated within systems, continually analyzed, and applied throughout the military enterprise.[24] Transformational technology is not based on adding new elements or components to existing systems, such as a better ship or a newer submarine, but focused on changing the game itself, including the platforms used to engage the adversary, the organization of the forces, and their doctrine and tactics—and indeed the rules by which they operate.[25]

Third Wave naval warfare involves a sophisticated network of platforms, sensors, and weapons forming a technological maritime ecosystem that reaches from the seabed to outer space. For example, while the U.S. Navy operates aircraft carrier strike groups, regarded as among the most mobile and lethal naval forces in the world, these legacy platforms risk being overmatched by Chinese missile forces. The consensus is growing that, in a future of networked technology warfare, the United States would be defeated in a contest at sea.[26] The historical preponderance in U.S. naval power

---

[20] Secretary of Defense Chuck Hagel, Reagan National Defense Forum Keynote Address at Ronald Reagan Presidential Library, Simi Valley, CA (online) (Nov. 15, 2014); Remarks by Deputy Secretary of Defense Bob Work, Third Offset Strategy (online) (Apr. 28, 2016).

[21] ALVIN TOFFLER, THE THIRD WAVE 9–12 (1980).

[22] ALVIN & HEIDI TOFFLER, WAR AND ANTI-WAR 35–40 (1993).

[23] *Id.* at 41–47.

[24] *Id.* at 93.

[25] *Id.* at 32.

[26] Sydney J. Freedberg, Jr., *US "Gets Its Ass Handed to It" in Wargames: Here's A $24 Billion Fix*, BREAKING DEFENSE (online), Mar. 7, 2019.

is vulnerable to Chinese asymmetric offsets in long-range, precision strike (LRPS) missiles and hypersonic weapons, autonomous weapons, and the application of AI, cyberattack, chemical and biological warfare, attacks in outer space, and lasers and other directed energy weapons.[27] Whether the United States can succeed in its own Third Offset Strategy, or China and Russia beat America at its own game, remains to be seen. The regulation of any potential conflict, however, will have to contend with a naval and joint force engaged in all-domain conflict that is profoundly shaped by emerging technology. The law of naval warfare has not adequately accounted for the integration of these new methods and means of naval warfare.

In recent decades, the pace of innovation and technology is increasing exponentially. For example, it took 64 years for 50 million people to use airplanes and 62 years for the same number to use automobiles. Fifty million people used Pokémon Go in 19 days.[28] While the laws of naval warfare are stable, the lesson from the world wars demonstrates that once conflict begins, legal norms quicky shift, or even evaporate.[29] The United States, for example, adopted unrestricted submarine warfare the day after the attack on Pearl Harbor. This approach was inconsistent with the prevailing legal regime of the time. Furthermore, it is virtually impossible to predict the nature of the future battlespace, which may be marked by biological contagion, cyber chaos, or electromagnetic pulse. The ability of experts to predict such change is at best random probability. Experts who spend their lives studying the state of the world are "poorer forecasters than dart-throwing monkeys."[30] Humans are especially ill-equipped to make predictions about disruptive or transformational change.[31]

---

[27] Office of the Under Secretary of Defense (Comptroller/Chief Financial Officer), U.S. Department of Defense Fiscal Year 2021 Budget Request, Program Acquisition Cost by Weapon System, February 2020, at Introduction and U.S. Government Accountability Office, Report to Congressional Committees, National Security: Long-Range Emerging Threats Facing the United States as Identified by Federal Agencies, GAO-19-204SP, Dec. 13, 2018, at 3.

[28] Leslie P. Norton, *The 20s are Ready to Roar* (Interview with Haim Israel), BARRON'S, Dec. 30, 2019, pp. 24, 25.

[29] D. P. O'Connell, *International Law and Contemporary Naval Operations*, 44 BRITISH YEARBOOK OF INTERNATIONAL LAW 19, 47–52 (1970).

[30] Louis Menand, *Everybody's an Expert: Putting Predictions to the Test*, THE NEW YORKER (online), Nov. 28, 2005 (Review of Philip E. Tetlock, Expert Political Judgment: How Good Is It? How Can We Know? (2005)).

[31] NASSIM NICHOLAS TALEB, THE BLACK SWAN: THE IMPACT OF THE HIGHLY IMPROBABLE 137–45 (2d ed. 2010).

5. The Rules of the Game

Contemporary naval warfare would arise in an unexpected international system. Twenty years ago, the United States and its friends and allies did not foresee that an ascendant and malign China and revanchist Russia would become principal drivers of the international system.[32] China has been a particularly stunning disappointment. Rather than becoming "more like us" as it became stronger, China has become more repressive at home and more coercive abroad.

The emergence of China and Russia as great powers has shifted attention from insurgencies and terrorism toward warfare at the higher end of the conflict spectrum.[33] The United States and its partners and allies are less likely to engage in large-scale ground combat, such as the wars in Vietnam or Iraq, than be involved in armed conflict throughout the global commons. These conflicts were unsuccessful, underscoring the inherent limitation democracies confront in fighting foreign civil wars. As world politics fragments into a multi-polar world, Russia and China seek to erode the rules-based international order and they have the resources to invest in developing and deploying the world's most technologically advanced weapons. By their nature, these weapons are capable of projecting power throughout the oceans and airspace, as well as into cyberspace and outer space of the global commons. Military technologies are also transforming the nature of naval warfare, making it more diffuse and lethal. Consequently, the United States is returning to a strategy of offshore balancing and selective engagement projected from the sea to maintain a decisive presence in strategic maritime regions while avoiding the political and material costs of land warfare.

Information is the currency of great power competition, and information technology is the defining feature of future war at sea. Any major international conflict will be fought mostly from and within the virtual arena of

---

[32] There were some analysts who warned of the impending confrontation, but they were largely marginalized. Aaron Friedberg's work was almost clairvoyant. *See generally* AARON L. FRIEDBERG, A CONTEST FOR SUPREMACY (2011).

[33] THE WHITE HOUSE, INTERIM NATIONAL SECURITY STRATEGIC GUIDANCE 8 (Mar. 2021); DEPARTMENT OF DEFENSE, SUMMARY OF THE NATIONAL DEFENSE STRATEGY OF THE UNITED STATES OF AMERICA 2018 at 2 (2018) [hereinafter INTERIM NATIONAL SECURITY STRATEGIC GUIDANCE]; NATO 2030: UNITED FOR A NEW ERA: ANALYSIS AND RECOMMENDATIONS OF THE REFLECTION GROUP APPOINTED BY THE NATO SECRETARY-GENERAL 5 (Nov. 25, 2020) [hereinafter NATO 2030]. *See also* Statement of the Honorable Thomas M. Modly, Acting Secretary of the Navy, Adm. Michael M. Gilday, Chief of Naval Operations, and Gen. David H. Berger, Commandant of the US Marine Corps on Fiscal Year 2021, Department of the Navy Budget Before the Senate Armed Services Committee (Mar. 5, 2020), p. 2.

cyberspace and the physical domains of outer space, airspace, and the oceans. Technology ties these domains together, and only naval forces operate seamlessly among them. Naval power from the sea ultimately affects geopolitical events on land but the risk of escalation and the specter of nuclear war mean that great power conflict involving the United States, Russia, or China are more likely to occur from the sea than on land territory.

Control of state territory is the ultimate object of warfare, yet ground combat is the most cumbersome and least agile form of military power. Land operations are the slowest and weakest in attack and most static and vulnerable in defense. In contrast, naval operations launched from the seabed, the water column, the surface of the water, the airspace, and outer space are inherently expeditionary. The speed, agility, and flexibility of maritime operations is evident in peacetime commercial transportation. Travel by rail is the most efficient means of moving large amounts of cargo on land, more efficient than travel by road. Both options are orders of magnitude less efficient than travel by sea. Similarly, naval forces are by nature mobile and maneuverable, versatile, scalable, persistent, and sustainable, and generally superior to land forces in power projection throughout the spectrum of conflict. Furthermore, the most advanced naval forces are increasingly networked among the physical domains and between them and cyberspace.

Emerging technology affects every aspect of naval operations, from mundane facets of unit maintenance and readiness to high-end conflict. For example, new composite materials can seal cracks in the superstructure of warships.[34] Drones equipped with lasers identify hull warping and corrosion so ships spend less time in the shipyard.[35] Likewise, autonomous ships and submarines may obviate the need for large crews and shoreside maintenance workers, enhancing force presence and endurance.[36] These systems may integrate features of AI during operations to find and attack enemy forces.

This book focuses on those aspects of technology that affect naval operations at the high end of the conflict spectrum involving the most advanced weapons. This focus is driven by changes in the international environment, from the threats posed by terrorist groups and rogue states in the past to the dangers presented by major powers in the present. China, along with Russia, Iran, and North Korea, pursue strategies to displace the American-led

---

[34] Michael Fabey, *High Maintenance*, JANE'S NAVY INTERNATIONAL 10–11 (Jan./Feb. 2020).
[35] *Id.*
[36] KELLEY M. SAYLER, CONGRESSIONAL RESEARCH SERVICE, EMERGING TECHNOLOGIES: BACKGROUND AND ISSUES FOR CONGRESS 2–10 (Nov. 10, 2020).

international order with a new coexistence that is more fractured, mercantilist, hierarchical, and less liberal. These states reject the rule of law in favor of a system in which the law is a tool used by the stronger to control the weaker.[37] To achieve their aims, China and Russia plan to overshadow U.S. and Allied forces with cutting-edge military technology, including nuclear weapons, cruise missiles, ballistic missiles, and hypersonic weapons, cyber operations and electromagnetic warfare, AI and autonomous weapons, directed energy weapons and lasers, outer space weapons, and undersea and seabed systems.

As the quality of their armed forces has been transformed over the past 20 years, China and Russia have demonstrated a growing contempt for regional stability and international law. Between the two states, China is the greater threat. Technologically, China's weapon technology is advancing quickly; in comparison, Russia is falling behind.[38] Beijing, with its enormous population and substantial economic, military, and political power, is a full spectrum systemic rival to the Indo-Pacific region and beyond.[39] China's military-civil fusion intentionally blurs the lines between commercial and civilian technologies on the one hand, and military technology on the other, and it has used this whole-of-society approach to vault to the top in AI, high-performance computing, quantum information sciences and communications, biotechnology, outer space, and advanced robotics.[40] Russia lacks global economic and political influence, but it uses its military forces to threaten states in Eastern Europe and intimidate Japan and NATO.[41] Enabled by Russia and China, Iran and North Korea are junior partners in challenging regional stability and the U.S.-led global security architecture.

Rogue states mix emerging technologies with asymmetric strategies or "gray zone" coercion to demoralize, disorient, and subdue their neighbors. While the revisionist powers are physically distant from the United States, they directly threaten American allies and the free and open international maritime order essential to security and prosperity.[42] The United States

---

[37] Jamie McIntyre, *Is War with China Just a Matter of Time*, WASHINGTON EXAMINER, Mar. 9, 2021, pp. 40, 41.

[38] John A. Tirpak, *DIA Says China's Weapon Technology Advancing Fast While Russia Falls Behind*, AIR FORCE MAGAZINE (online), Apr. 30, 2021.

[39] INTERIM NATIONAL SECURITY STRATEGIC GUIDANCE, *supra* note 33, at 8; NATO 2030, *supra* note 33, at 27.

[40] Tirpak, *supra* note 38.

[41] NATO 2030, *supra* note 33, at 25.

[42] MINISTRY OF FOREIGN AFFAIRS, GOVERNMENT OF JAPAN, JAPAN'S EFFORT FOR A FREE AND OPEN INDO-PACIFIC 2 (Jan. 2021); DEPARTMENT OF DEFENCE, AUSTRALIAN GOVERNMENT, 2020 DEFENCE STRATEGIC UPDATE 11–12 (Dec. 2020).

remains connected to its allies in Asia and Europe only through the oceans and airspace. American naval command of the oceans has been the defining element of its status as a global superpower.[43]

Since the Spanish-American War, the cornerstone of U.S. foreign policy and national security has been to prevent the rise of a hostile, hegemonic power in either Europe or Asia. Efforts to diminish navigational freedom and overflight or control of the sea lanes that connect the United States to these geopolitical centers of power poses virtually an existential threat and therefore could lead to confrontation and armed conflict. Beijing's strategy of ocean enclosure and control are reflected in its coercion and expansion in the East China Sea, the South China Sea, and the Taiwan Strait, and its effort to build a sphere of dominance that stretches from the Middle East to Oceania.[44] The key question is whether the global maritime system will remain free and open or evolve into a Sino-centric world.[45] If peacetime competition does erupt into armed conflict, the law of naval warfare will set the rules of the game.

[43] Barry R. Posen, *Command of the Commons*, 28 INTERNATIONAL SECURITY 5, 7 (Summer 2003); JAMES KRASKA & RAUL PEDROZO, THE FREE SEA: THE AMERICAN FIGHT FOR FREEDOM OF NAVIGATION 1–2 (2018); JAMES KRASKA, MARITIME POWER & LAW OF THE SEA: EXPEDITIONARY OPERATIONS IN WORLD POLITICS 88–94 (2011).

[44] Christopher Wray, Director, Federal Bureau of Investigation, Threat Posed by the Chinese Government, and the Chinese Communist Party to the Economic and National Security of the United States (online) (July 7, 2020).

[45] MICHAEL PILLSBURY, THE HUNDRED-YEAR MARATHON: CHINA'S SECRET STRATEGY TO REPLACE AMERICA AS THE GLOBAL SUPERPOWER 28 (2015).

1

The Law of Naval Warfare and Maritime Neutrality

1. Law of Naval Warfare

The law of naval warfare is comprised of three overlapping bodies of law: the conduct of hostilities and protection of victims (*jus in bello*), the law of prize or capture, and the law of maritime neutrality. *Jus in bello* concerns the use of force during armed conflict. The law of neutrality regulates the relationship between belligerent states and neutral states in order to protect neutral states and prevent an escalation of the conflict. Neutral states are obliged to protect their neutral status from parties to the conflict. Neutral vessels and aircraft may be attacked if they make an effective contribution to the military action of a belligerent. The law of prize permits seizure of enemy private property at sea as a form of economic warfare. Belligerents can condemn the assets in a prize court and convert them to state property.

The law of naval warfare has a relationship to the peacetime law of the sea, as reflected in the United Nations Convention on the Law of the Sea (UNCLOS) by States party to that agreement, via other treaties, such as the four 1958 Geneva conventions on the law of the sea, and through customary international law by non-parties.[1] While the law of naval warfare is *lex specialis* and displaces the law of the sea during armed conflict for belligerents, the law of the sea persists as between belligerents and neutral states and among neutral states.

---

[1] United Nations Convention on the Law of the Sea, Dec. 10, 1982, 1833 U.N.T.S. 397 [hereinafter UNCLOS]; Convention on the Territorial Sea and the Contiguous Zone, Apr. 29, 1958, 15 U.S.T. 1606, T.I.A.S. No. 5639, 516 U.N.T.S. 205; Convention on the High Seas, Apr. 29, 1958, 13 U.S.T. 2312, T.I.A.S. No. 5200, 450 U.N.T.S. 11; Convention of the Continental Shelf, Apr. 29, 1958, 15 U.S.T. 471, T.I.A.S. No. 5578, 499 U.N.T.S. 311; Convention on Fishing and Conservation of the Living Resources of the High Seas, Apr. 29, 1958, 17 U.S.T. 138, T.I.A.S. No. 5969, 559 U.N.T.S. 285. The United States is not party to UNCLOS but accepts that most provisions reflect customary international law. *See* President's Statement on United States Oceans Policy, Weekly Compilation of Presidential Documents, v. 19, No. 10, p. 383 (March 14, 1983), *reprinted in* 22 INTERNATIONAL LEGAL MATERIALS 464 (1983).

Disruptive Technology and the Law of Naval Warfare. James Kraska and Raul Pedrozo, Oxford University Press.
© James Kraska & Raul Pedrozo 2022. DOI: 10.1093/oso/9780197630181.003.0002

Furthermore, the law of the sea provides boundaries for the areas that naval warfare may be conducted. Naval warfare and belligerent operations may be conducted on the high seas, the exclusive economic zone (EEZ), and on the continental shelf of coastal states, and in international airspace.[2] The territorial sea of neutral states is inviolable, although belligerent warships do not lose their right of innocent passage (or "mere passage") and may be permitted entry into neutral ports under port state conditions.

1.1 Law of Naval Warfare Distinct from the Law of Armed Conflict

There are important distinctions between the law of armed conflict on land and the law of naval warfare. Unlike the law of land warfare, the law of naval warfare concerns mainly attacks on platforms rather than individuals. These platforms, namely aircraft, ships, and submarines, have special status in the law of naval warfare, including belligerent rights. The platforms are also considered themselves to be lawful targets regardless of the status of the persons on board. Additionally, the oceans are a more complex battlespace than ground combat. The area of conflict in naval warfare automatically includes most of the globe—all of the oceans outside of the territorial sea of neutral states, some 70 percent of the surface of the earth. This area is open to the shipping and aviation commerce of the world, so belligerent warships may be expected to interact with commercial and military ships and aircraft of numerous neutral states.

All commercial vessels outside of neutral territorial seas are subject to visit and search, and neutral ships attempting to aid a belligerent or break a blockade may be seized, or even attacked, if they resist. While civilians directly participating in hostilities on land may be targeted, so too may neutral and enemy commercial ships be targeted if they take a "direct part" in hostilities. All private property on land, including enemy and neutral property, is free from confiscation (although subject to requisition with reimbursement). The rule at sea, however, is that enemy private or commercial property and vessels are liable to capture. Every capture is adjudicated in court and the vessel may be condemned as prize and converted to state property of the belligerent that seized it.

---

[2] UNCLOS, *supra* note 1, arts. 58(1), 58(2), and 87.

Noncombatants are treated slightly differently in naval warfare and land warfare. In land warfare, noncombatants may not be made prisoners of war so long as they do not interfere in military operations. This is normally the rule at sea as well. Articles 5 and 6 of Hague Convention XI states that if enemy civilian seafarers surrender without fighting, and then they commit to not undertake hostilities and do not take any part in the armed conflict, they are to be set free. Similarly, article 4(5) of the Second Geneva Convention (GC II) states that masters and crew members of civilian vessels and the merchant marine may be lawfully imprisoned upon capture unless they benefit by more favorable treatment from "any other provision of international law."[3]

1.2 Law of Naval Warfare in IACs and NIACs

The rules governing the conduct of hostilities apply between parties to an international armed conflict. The law of naval warfare applies to international armed conflicts (IAC) at sea. It does not apply to incidents at sea during peacetime or maritime law enforcement operations. Yet, article 2 of GC II has a relatively low threshold for recognition of an IAC, stating that the convention applies in cases of declared war or "any other armed conflict" between the parties. Low-level incidents of coercion or use of force at sea raise questions about when the threshold for an IAC is crossed. The ICRC Commentary states that each individual use of force may serve as the basis for an IAC. This issue was obfuscated in the *Russia v. Ukraine Case*, when Russian state vessels used force against Ukrainian warships. The International Tribunal for the Law of the Sea, which only has jurisdiction over matters under the peacetime law of the sea and not the law of naval warfare, (mis)characterized the Russian action as a law enforcement operation and ordered Russia to release the detained Ukrainian warships and sailors, who were properly prisoners of war.[4]

There is uncertainty over the application of the law of naval warfare in non-international armed conflicts (NIACs) that extend beyond the territorial sea. If a nonstate armed group attacks ships beyond the territorial sea,

---

[3] Convention (II) for the Amelioration of the Condition of the Wounded, Sick, and Shipwrecked Members of Armed Forces at Sea art. 4, Aug. 12, 1949, 6 U.S.T. 3217, 75 U.N.T.S. 85 [hereinafter GC II].

[4] James Kraska, *Did ITLOS Just Kill the Military Activities Exemption in Article 298?*, EUROPEAN JOURNAL OF INTERNATIONAL LAW: TALK! (online), May 27, 2019.

they are considered private actors and pirates under article 101 of UNCLOS. If an armed group, such as insurgents, conducts attacks inside the territorial sea (inside the territory of a coastal state), they may fall under customary international law rules that apply during NIACs. The Tamil Sea Tigers, for example, were engaged in a conflict against the Sri Lankan government and foreign vessels. Attacks by the Sea Tigers beyond the territorial sea constituted piracy under article 101 of UNCLOS because they were conducted for private means, not on behalf of a government. This approach recognizes that private individuals may not serve as privateers and conduct warfare at sea.

1.3 Restatements of the Law of Naval Warfare

The U.S. Naval War College produced the United States Naval Code of 1900.[5] The Oxford Manual of Naval Warfare was adopted in 1913.[6] There has been no further codification of the law of naval warfare since 1949. In 1955, the U.S. Navy released NWP 10-2, *Law of Naval Warfare*, that restated the law of naval warfare.[7] This publication evolved, with publication in 1987 of *The Commander's Handbook on the Law of Naval Operations* (NWP-9), periodically updated and produced as NWP 1-14M (2017).[8] NWP 1-14M has been translated into numerous foreign languages and adopted by nations as a guide to the law of naval warfare.

In 1994, an international group of experts produced the *San Remo Manual* as a restatement of the law of naval warfare.[9] In 1998, the Committee on Maritime Neutrality, International Law Association, produced the *Helsinki Principles on the Law of Maritime Neutrality*.[10] The U.S. *Commander's Handbook* and the *San Remo Manual* have served as the most

---

[5] *The United States Naval Code of 1900*, *reprinted in* 3 INTERNATIONAL LAW STUDIES 103 (1904).

[6] Institute of International Law, The Law of Naval Warfare Governing the Relations between Belligerents (1913) (Oxford Manual of Naval Warfare), *reprinted in* DIETRICH SCHINDLER & JIŘÍ TOMAN, THE LAWS OF ARMED CONFLICTS 1123 (1988).

[7] OFFICE OF THE CHIEF OF NAVAL OPERATIONS, U.S. NAVY, LAW OF NAVAL WARFARE, NAVAL WARFARE INFORMATION PUBLICATION (NWIP) 10-2 § 500 (1955), *reprinted in* 50 INTERNATIONAL LAW STUDIES 359 (1955) [hereinafter NWIP 10-2].

[8] U.S. NAVY, U.S. MARINE CORPS, & U.S. COAST GUARD, NWP 1-14M/MCTP 11-10B/ COMDTPUB P5800.7A, THE COMMANDER'S HANDBOOK ON THE LAW OF NAVAL OPERATIONS (2017) (NWP 1-14M) [hereinafter NWP 1-14M].

[9] SAN REMO MANUAL ON THE LAW APPLICABLE TO ARMED CONFLICT AT SEA (Louise Doswald-Beck ed., 1995) [hereinafter SAN REMO MANUAL].

[10] *Helsinki Principles on the Law of Maritime Neutrality* (1998), *reprinted in* DIETRICH SCHINDLER & JIŘÍ TOMAN, THE LAWS OF ARMED CONFLICTS 1425 (4th ed. 2004).

influential restatements of the law of naval warfare. Indeed, for decades, the Commander's Handbook was the foremost reference for military operations and international law generally. It has been followed by numerous manuals, none of which focus primarily on the law of naval warfare.[11] Yoram Dinstein and Arne Willy Dahl led a group of 15 experts under the auspices of the Norwegian Defence University College to produce the *Oslo Manual* in 2020, which addresses some topics on the law of naval warfare.[12]

2. Principles of the Law of Armed Conflict

The law of naval warfare is part of the law of armed conflict (LOAC). LOAC "regulates the resort to armed force; the conduct of hostilities and the protection of war victims in both international and non-international armed conflict; belligerent occupation; and the relationships between belligerent, neutral, and non-belligerent States."[13]

Articles 48 to 67 of Additional Protocol I (AP I) set forth general principles of the law of armed conflict. AP I includes the principles of distinction (article 48);[14] indiscriminate attacks and direct participation in hostilities (article 51); the definition of a military objective (article 52(2); and precautions in attack (article 57). These rules apply to land, air, and sea warfare, which may affect the civilian population or civilian objects on land. Article 49(3), however, states that certain provisions do not apply to naval warfare proper, that is,

---

[11] Notably, the UNITED KINGDOM MINISTRY OF DEFENCE, THE MANUAL OF THE LAW OF ARMED CONFLICT (2004); MICHAEL N. SCHMITT, CHARLES H. B. GARRAWAY, & YORAM DINSTEIN, THE MANUAL ON THE LAW OF NON-INTERNATIONAL ARMED CONFLICT WITH COMMENTARY (2006); PROGRAM ON HUMANITARIAN POLICY AND CONFLICT RESEARCH AT HARVARD UNIVERSITY, MANUAL ON INTERNATIONAL LAW APPLICABLE TO AIR AND MISSILE WARFARE (2009); TALLINN MANUAL ON THE INTERNATIONAL LAW APPLICABLE TO CYBER WARFARE (Michael N. Schmitt gen. ed., 2013); TALLINN MANUAL 2.0 ON THE INTERNATIONAL LAW APPLICABLE TO CYBER OPERATIONS (Michael N. Schmitt gen. ed., 2017)

[12] Section III, Remote and Autonomous Weapons; Section IV, Unmanned Maritime Systems; Section V, Undersea Infrastructure, Systems, and Devices, and Section VI, Submarine Cables and Pipelines, YORAM DINSTEIN & ARNE WILLY DAHL, OSLO MANUAL ON SELECT TOPICS OF THE LAW OF ARMED CONFLICT: RULES AND COMMENTARY (2020).

[13] SAN REMO MANUAL, *supra* note 9, § 1.3; NWP 1-14M, *supra* note 8, § 5.2; HEADQUARTERS, DEPARTMENT OF THE ARMY, HEADQUARTERS, UNITED STATES MARINE CORPS, FM 6-27/MCTP 11-10C, THE COMMANDER'S HANDBOOK ON THE LAW OF LAND WARFARE §§ 1-4 to 1-6 (2019) [hereinafter FM 6-27].

[14] In its advisory opinion in the Nuclear Weapons case, the ICJ stated that the principle of distinction was one of the "cardinal principles" of international humanitarian law and therefore an "intransgressible principles of international customary law." Legality of the Threat or Use of Nuclear Weapons, Advisory Opinion, 1996 I.C.J Rep. 226, ¶ 78 (July 8) [hereinafter Nuclear Weapons Advisory Opinion].

they do not apply to naval engagements occurring sea-to-sea, air-to-sea, sea-to-air, and air-to-air. The provisions apply only to attacks conducted from sea-to-land and from land-to-sea. Consequently, engagements not affecting the land are governed by customary international law. The United States has signed but not ratified AP I, although it considers many of its provisions to reflect customary international law.[15] The *San Remo Manual* captures many of the rules concerning the principle of distinction, the definition of military objectives, indiscriminate attacks, and precautions in attack.[16]

The U.S. Department of Defense states that U.S. forces will comply with LOAC "during all armed conflicts, however such conflicts are character-ized, and in all other military operations."[17] This duty includes the obliga-tion to "respect and to ensure respect" for the 1949 Geneva Conventions.[18] Compliance with LOAC conditions military effectiveness, encourages rec-iprocity by the adversary, and builds political support and legitimacy at home.[19]

2.1 Necessity

Military necessity justifies the use of all measures needed to defeat the enemy quickly and efficiently, so long as the methods and means employed are not otherwise prohibited by the law of war.[20] Destruction, seizure of persons and property, and alternate means of subduing an enemy, such as propaganda

---

[15] Michael J. Matheson, *Remarks on the United States Position on the Relation of Customary International Law to the 1977 Protocols Additional to the 1949 Geneva Conventions at the Sixth Annual American Red Cross-Washington College of Law Conference on International Humanitarian Law* (Jan. 22, 1987), 2 AMERICAN JOURNAL OF INTERNATIONAL LAW & POLICY 419, 426 (1987).

[16] SAN REMO MANUAL, *supra* note 9, ¶ 39 (distinction), ¶ 40 (military objectives), ¶ 42(b) (indis-criminate attacks), and ¶ 46 (precautions in attack).

[17] U.S. Department of Defense, DoD Directive 2311.01E, DoD Law of War Program ¶ 4.1 (2006) [hereinafter DoD Directive 2311.01E].

[18] Common art. 1, Convention (I) for the Amelioration of the Condition of the Wounded and Sick in the Armed Forces in the Field, Aug. 12, 1949, 6 U.S.T. 3114, 75 U.N.T.S. 31; GC II *supra* note 3; Convention (III) Relative to the Treatment of Prisoners of War, Aug. 12, 1949, 6 U.S.T. 3316, 75 U.N.T.S. 135; Convention (IV) Relative to the Protection of Civilian Persons in Time of War, Aug. 12, 1949, 6 U.S.T. 3516, 75 U.N.T.S. 287.

[19] OFFICE OF THE GENERAL COUNSEL, U.S. DEPARTMENT OF DEFENSE, LAW OF WAR MANUAL § 18.2 (rev. ed., Dec. 2016) [hereinafter DoD LAW OF WAR MANUAL].

[20] *Id.*, § 2.2; NWP 1-14M, *supra* note 8, § 5.3.1; and FM 6-27, *supra* note 13, §§ 1-23 to 1-27. *See also* Nuclear Weapons Advisory Opinion ¶ 140 and 1 CUSTOMARY INTERNATIONAL HUMANITARIAN LAW Rule 70 (Jean-Marie Henckaerts & Louise Doswald-Beck eds., 2005). For historical context, *see* U.S. Department of War, Instructions for the Government of Armies of the United States in the Field, General Order No. 100, Apr. 24, 1863 (Lieber Code).

and intelligence gathering, are all justified during armed conflict, while causing unnecessary suffering is prohibited.

Combatants are entitled to inflict destruction, injury, and death on enemy combatants and lawful military targets.[21] The principle of humanity, however, forbids the infliction of suffering, injury, or destruction beyond what is necessary to accomplish a legitimate military purpose.[22] Elementary considerations of humanity may be regarded as the inverse of military necessity, since unnecessary actions are prohibited.[23] Generally, suffering is unnecessary if it is the inevitable result of the normal use and reasonably anticipated effects of military action that is needless, superfluous, or manifestly disproportionate in relation to the anticipated military advantage.[24]

2.2 Military Objects

In LOAC, only military objects are lawful targets. Military objects are those that by their nature, location, purpose, or use make an effective contribution to the enemy's military action, as reflected in article 52(2) of AP I and para. 40 of the *San Remo Manual*. The U.S. view is broader, however, and holds that any object that makes an effective contribution to the enemy's military action or war-sustaining effort may be targeted.[25] The U.S. position extends back to the Civil War and the Confederacy's reliance on cotton exports. It is also evident in targeting Iraq's electrical power grid during the 1990–91 Gulf War.[26] The law of naval warfare, however, provides a distinct and profound

---

[21] Exec. Order No. 13732, 3 C.F.R. § 13732 (2016) and Jennifer O'Connor, Department of Defense General Counsel, Applying the Law of Targeting to the Modern Battlefield , Address at NYU School of Law, *reprinted in* JUST SECURITY (online), Nov. 28, 2016. ("The citizen who does not participate in hostilities is to be spared in person, property, and honor as much as the exigencies of war will admit.").

[22] DoD LAW OF WAR MANUAL, *supra* note 19, § 2.3; NWP 1-14M, *supra* note 8, § 5.3.2; and FM 6-27, *supra* note 13, §§1-28 to 1-30. *See also* Military and Paramilitary Activities in and against Nicaragua (Nicar. v. U.S), Judgment, 1986 I.C.J. Rep. 14, ¶ 218 (June 27). For historical context, *see* L. OPPENHEIM, 2 INTERNATIONAL LAW §67, pp. 85 (Longman Greens & Co. 1921) (The principle of humanity "postulates that all such kinds and degrees of violence as are not necessary for the overpowering of the opponent should not be permitted to a belligerent.").

[23] Corfu Channel (U.K. v. Alb.), Judgment, 1949 I.C.J. Rep. 4, 22 (Apr. 9) and DoD LAW OF WAR MANUAL, *supra* note 19, § 2.3.1.1.

[24] DoD LAW OF WAR MANUAL, *supra* note 19, § 6.6; FM 6-27, *supra* note 13, §§ 1-28. *See also* MARCO SASSÒLI, INTERNATIONAL HUMANITARIAN LAW: RULES, SOLUTIONS TO PROBLEMS ARISING IN WARFARE AND CONTROVERSIES § 8.368 (2019).

[25] NWP 1-14M, *supra* note 8, § 5.3.1.

[26] DEP'T OF DEFENSE, FINAL REPORT TO CONGRESS: CONDUCT OF THE PERSIAN GULF WAR 612 (Apr. 1992); Ryan Goodman, *The Obama Administration and Targeting "War-Sustaining" Objects*

departure from targeting only military objectives, since the law of blockade permits infliction of economic warfare.

2.2.1 Effective Contribution

Article 52(2) of AP I and para. 40 of the *San Remo Manual* state that those objects that by their nature, location, purpose, or use make an effective contribution to the enemy's military action are lawful targets. Neutral merchant ships may be attacked if they fulfill this definition and make an effective contribution to the military action of a belligerent state.[27] An "effective contribution" means more than carrying ordinary exports, such as a neutral oil tanker carrying oil from a belligerent party.[28] In such case, the oil tanker may not be attacked as a military objective even though the export is essential to the war-sustaining effort.[29] The U.S. view is even broader, however, and states that any ship that makes an effective contribution to the enemy's war-sustaining effort (and not just military action) may be targeted.[30] However, U.S. practice on the issue has been somewhat circumspect.

During the Iran-Iraq War, for example, the United States was a neutral state. Iran could not legally attack U.S.-flagged Kuwaiti oil tankers carrying Iraqi oil as long as those vessels were not carrying oil exports directly from Iraq. In the "Tanker War," as Kuwait reflagged 11 of its oil tankers to sail under the American flag and escort, Secretary of Defense Casper Weinberger reported to Congress:

> The United States will be in full compliance with international law in providing escort to the reflagged tankers. International law clearly recognizes the right of a neutral state to escort and protect its flag vessels in transit to neutral ports. The tankers will carry Kuwaiti oil to neutral ports and will return in ballast; they will not carry contraband for either of the belligerents. If a belligerent seeks to exercise the right of visit and search for contraband, the U.S. escorts will certify its absence.[31]

---

in Non-international Armed Conflict, 110 AMERICAN JOURNAL OF INTERNATIONAL LAW 674–75 (Oct. 2016).

[27] SAN REMO MANUAL, *supra* note 9, ¶ 67(f).

[28] *Id.* ¶ 67(f).

[29] DINSTEIN, THE CONDUCT OF HOSTILITIES UNDER THE LAW OF INTERNATIONAL LAW OF ARMED CONFLICT 129, n. 738 (3d ed. 2016).

[30] NWP 1-14M, *supra* note 8, § 5.3.1; DoD LAW OF WAR MANUAL, *supra* note 19, § 5.17.2.3.

[31] CASPER W. WEINBERGER, SECRETARY OF DEFENSE, REPORT TO CONGRESS ON SECURITY ARRANGEMENTS IN THE PERSIAN GULF (1987), at 21.

"Whether this rule [targeting war-sustaining capabilities] permits attacks on war-sustaining cargo carried in neutral bottoms at sea, such as by Iraq on the tankers carrying oil exported by Iran during the Iran-Iraq War, is not firmly settled."[32] The U.S. administration explained:

> In providing this protection [to Kuwaiti vessels], our actions will be fully consistent with the applicable rules of international law, which clearly recognize the right of a neutral state to escort and protect ships flying its flag which are not carrying contraband. In this case, this includes the fact that U.S. ships will not be carrying oil from Iraq. Neither party to the conflict will have any basis for taking hostile action against U.S. naval ships or the vessels they will protect.[33]

Neutral vessels also may be attacked if they travel under escort of enemy warships.[34] However, neutral ships that are in a convoy of neutral warships (not necessarily belonging to the neutral state) and bound for a neutral port can neither be attacked nor subjected to visit and search.[35] These neutral vessels are inviolable if under escort from neutral warships of another neutral state even if there is no "genuine link" between the flag state of the merchant ship and the flag state of the warship.[36]

2.3   Proportionality

The principle of proportionality dictates combatants shall refrain from attacks on military objects in which the expected loss or injury to civilians and damage to civilian objects are excessive compared to the anticipated concrete and direct military advantage.[37] The principle of proportionality

---

[32] ANNOTATED SUPPLEMENT TO THE COMMANDER'S HANDBOOK ON THE LAW OF NAVAL OPERATIONS § 8.1.1, n. 11 (1999), *reprinted in* 73 INTERNATIONAL LAW STUDIES 403 (1999).

[33] Richard W. Murphy, Assistant Secretary of State for Near Eastern and South Asian Affairs, *Statement Before the Subcomm. on Europe and the Middle East of the H. Comm. on Foreign Affairs*, 100th Cong. (1987), *reprinted in* 87 DEP'T OF STATE BULL. 59, 60–61 (1987).

[34] SAN REMO MANUAL, *supra* note 9, ¶ 67(e)

[35] GEORGE P. POLITAKIS, MODERN ASPECTS OF THE LAW OF NAVAL WARFARE 560–61, 571–78 (1998).

[36] UNCLOS, *supra* note 1, art. 91(1).

[37] DoD LAW OF WAR MANUAL, *supra* note 19, §§ 2.4, 5.1.2.5; NWP 1-14M, *supra* note 8, §§ 5.3.3, 9.1.2; and FM 6-27, *supra* note 13, §§ 1-44 to 1-48. *See also* Protocol Additional to the Geneva Conventions of 12 August 1949 and Relating to the Protection of Victims of International Armed Conflicts, art. 51(5)(b), 57(2)(b), June 8, 1977, 1125 U.N.T.S. 3 [hereinafter AP I]; 1 CUSTOMARY

does not spare civilians from harm that results from attacks, but the harm to civilians or civilian objects, or collateral damage, must not be excessive in relation to the anticipated military advantage.

2.4   Distinction

Belligerents are prohibited from attacks against the civilian populations as such.[38] Distinction must be made at all times between persons taking part in the hostilities and members of the civilian population to the effect that the latter be spared as much as possible. Distinction is made between civilians and combatants, as well as civilian objects and military objects for purposes of targeting. Remember, however, that at sea enemy merchant ships are subject to seizure or attack if they resist. Furthermore, attacks on enemy warships and naval auxiliaries are based on the status of the platform and not the status of individuals who may be on board the ship or naval auxiliary. Belligerents are required to distinguish between warships and auxiliaries on the one hand, and civilian vessels, on the other, but are not required to make a separate distinction between individuals on board a warship, even if it carries noncombatants.

Distinction requires parties to a conflict to distinguish between the armed forces and the civilian population.[39] Methods and means of warfare must discriminate between military targets and protected persons and objects, and especially between combatants and civilians. The provisions of AP I indicate precautions in attack encompass a duty by defending belligerents to "endeavor to remove" the civilian population from the vicinity of military objectives, which overlaps with the principle of distinction.[40] Customary international law also requires parties to a conflict, "to the extent feasible," to remove civilian persons and objects under its control "from the vicinity of

---

INTERNATIONAL HUMANITARIAN LAW, *supra* note 20, 14; and Letter from Mr. Webster to Mr. Fox (Apr. 24, 1841), 29 BRITISH AND FOREIGN STATE PAPERS 1840–1841, at 1129 (1857).

[38] DoD LAW OF WAR MANUAL, *supra* note 19>, § 6.7 and AP I, *supra* note 37, art. 51(6) ("Attacks against the civilian population or civilians by way of reprisals are prohibited.").

[39] *Id.* § 2.5; NWP 1-14M, *supra* note 8, § 5.3.4; and FM 6-27, *supra* note 13, §§ 1-34 to 1-43. For historical context, *see* J. Fred Buzhardt, *General Counsel, Department of Defense, Letter to Senator Edward Kennedy, Sept. 22, 1972, reprinted in* 67 AMERICAN JOURNAL OF INTERNATIONAL LAW 122 (1973) and Ex parte Quirin, 317 U.S. 1, 30 (1942) ("By universal agreement and practice, the law of war draws a distinction between the armed forces and the peaceful populations of belligerent nations. . . .").

[40] AP I, *supra* note 37, art. 58 (Precautions against the effects of Attacks).

military objectives."[41] The law governing the conduct of hostilities focuses not just on protection of the sick and wounded, but also on shipwrecked sailors under GC II (Protection of victims). Soldiers, sailors, and crews of enemy merchant vessels are within the scope of article 13(5), GC II, but there is no explicit protection for crews of neutral vessels even though under some circumstances they may qualify as lawful targets. This is a gap in GC II, which may be filled through customary international law. The protection of shipwrecked sailors also applies as a matter of customary international law.

Generally, ruses of war—acts intended to mislead the enemy or induce him to act recklessly—are permissible so long as they do not infringe on any rule of LOAC.[42] Ruses include camouflage, decoys, mock operations, and misinformation. During the First World War, for example, Count Felix von Luckner, known as the Sea Devil, operated a three-masted windjammer named *Seeadler*, as an armed merchant raider. Although the ship appeared to be a civilian sailing ship it was outfitted with a secret auxiliary engine and offensive armament. Posing as a neutral trade ship, the *Seeadler* slipped through the unsuspecting British blockade and conducted a long cruise in the southern Atlantic Ocean and Pacific Ocean. When it came within range of enemy merchant ships through false signals or appeals for help or information, such as by innocuously requesting a time signal, it raised the German flag and fired shots. The *Seeadler* captured 14 enemy ships.

The law of naval warfare permits the use of certain ruses or deception, but perfidy is prohibited. Lawful deception also includes using electronic emissions to disguise a destroyer to look like an oiler or a cruiser to look like an aircraft carrier. Biomimetics imitate natural features of the marine environment, such as the U.S. Navy's GhostSwimmer unmanned underwater vehicle (UUV) made to look like a marine mammal.[43] Commercial ships are identified through the VHF-system, Automatic Identification System (AIS), or satellite-based Long-Range Identification and Tracking (LRIT) system pursuant to the Safety of Life at Sea Convention (SOLAS), as amended. These systems leverage the global positioning system (GPS). AIS is particularly

---

[41] 1 CUSTOMARY INTERNATIONAL HUMANITARIAN LAW, *supra* note 20, Rule 24.

[42] 1863 Lieber Code, art. 15; Hague Regulations (1899), art. 24, *reprinted in* DIETRICH SCHINDLER & JIŘÍ TOMAN, THE LAWS OF ARMED CONFLICTS 69-93 (1988); Convention (II) with Respect to the Laws and Customs of War on Land and its annex: Regulations concerning the Laws and Customs of War on Land, art. 24, 29 July 1899, *reprinted in* DIETRICH SCHINDLER & JIŘÍ TOMAN, THE LAWS OF ARMED CONFLICTS 69-93 (1988); AP I, *supra* note 37, art. 37(2. *See also* Ruses of War, 1 CUSTOMARY INTERNATIONAL HUMANITARIAN LAW, *supra* note 20, Rule 57.

[43] Huw Williams, *USN Trials of Biomimetic UUV*, JANE'S INT'L DEFENCE REV. 22 (Feb. 2015).

vulnerable to hacking or misuse, and GPS and presumably LRIT, while more secure, are also vulnerable to deception. The rule on ruses suggests that states may misrepresent their credentials or position in these systems.

2.5 Chivalry or Honor

Chivalry or honor is a core value of the U.S. armed forces and reflects a historic canon of fairness and observance of formalities and courtesies that forbid breaking trust with the enemy.[44] In particular, honor requires good faith on the part of belligerents to refrain from taking advantage of an opponent's adherence to the law by falsely claiming the law's protections, as in offering a false surrender in the hope of ambushing enemy forces.

This principle poses challenges in the context of fully autonomous weapons because they do not yet exist and there are competing visions for how they will operate during armed conflict. The debate over the legality of autonomous weapons systems (AWS) is driven by concern that such weapons must have a sufficiently rich human role in their design, production, and operation to ameliorate ethical concerns and ensure human accountability for compliance with LOAC. These issues are under discussion in meetings of a Group of Governmental Experts (GGE) under the auspices of the UN Convention on Certain Conventional Weapons (CCW).

2.6 Precautions in Attack

Combatants also must ensure feasible precautions are taken to reduce incidental harm to civilians, other protected persons, and civilian objects.[45] Feasible precautions are those that are practicable or practically possible, taking into account all circumstances prevailing at the time, including humanitarian and military considerations.[46] Such precautions are wide ranging. Depending on the weapon system and the operating environment,

---

[44] DoD LAW OF WAR MANUAL, *supra* note 19, § 2.6.2.2; NWP 1-14M, *supra* note 8, § 5.3.5; and FM 6-27, *supra* note 13, §§ 1-31–1-33. For historical context, *see* 2 LASSA OPPENHEIM, INTERNATIONAL LAW: A TREATISE §§ 67, 84–85 (Ronald F. Roxburgh ed., 3rd ed. 1921).

[45] DoD LAW OF WAR MANUAL, *supra* note 19, § 5.11; NWP 1-14M, *supra* note 8, § 8.3.1; and FM 6-27, *supra* note 13, §§ 1-44 to 1-45. *See also* AP I, *supra* note 37, art. 57.

[46] DoD LAW OF WAR MANUAL, *supra* note 19, § 5.14; NWP 1-14M, *supra* note 8, § 8.3.1; and FM 6-27, *supra* note 13, § 2-12.

precautions may require combatants to have an intimate grasp of how a weapon system functions and its relationship to the environment.

The law of naval warfare has some peculiarities concerning precautions in attack that make it a distinct body of law from precautions in land and air warfare. States have an obligation to take all feasible precautions to minimize the risk of injury to civilians from military operations in all domains.[47] The customary rule requires "all feasible precautions" must be taken to avoid, or at least minimize, incidental loss of civilian life, injury to civilians, and damage to civilian objects.[48] AP I states that those who "plan or decide upon attack" shall, "take all feasible precautions in the choice of means and methods of attack," and in air and naval warfare, it also requires that each Party shall "in conformity with its rights and duties under the rules of international law applicable in armed conflict, take all reasonable precautions to avoid losses of civilian lives and damage to civilian objects."[49] The CCW Protocols also incorporate the standard of "feasible precautions."[50]

The article 57(2(ii)) standard is widely accepted in customary law and is reflected in other treaties, such as article 3(10) of Protocol II of the CCW, which applies to mines, booby traps, and other devices. The protocol states "[a]ll feasible precautions shall be taken" to protect civilians. The article defines "feasible precautions" as those that are "practical or practically possible." Article 57(4), however, states that "in the conduct of military operations at sea or in the air" states "shall . . . take all reasonable precautions to avoid losses of civilian lives and damage to civilian objects."[51] The two standards are different, with the "feasibility" standard seeming to be a higher standard than the "reasonable" standard." Furthermore, article 49(3) excludes the applicability of article 57 to naval warfare proper. This means that in land warfare (or sea or air attacks from or to the land), belligerents must take all "feasible" precautions, whereas sea or air engagements that occur strictly in the oceans are subject to the lower, "reasonable" standard of precaution.

---

[47] Geoffrey Corn, *Precautions to Minimize Civilian Harm Are a Fundamental Principle of the Law of War*, JUST SECURITY (online), July 8, 2015.

[48] 1 CUSTOMARY INTERNATIONAL HUMANITARIAN LAW, *supra* note 20, ¶ 15 at 51.

[49] AP I, *supra* note 37, arts. 57(2)(ii) and (4).

[50] Protocol on Prohibitions or Restrictions on the Use of Mines, Booby-Traps and Other Devices as Amended on 3 May 1996, art. 3(10), May 3, 1996, 2048 U.N.T.S. 93; Protocol on Prohibitions or Restrictions on the Use of Incendiary Weapons, art. 2(3), Oct. 10, 1980, 1342 U.N.T.S. 171; Protocol on Blinding Laser Weapons, art. 4(2), Oct. 13, 1995, 1380 U.N.T.S. 370; and Protocol on Explosive Remnants of War to the Convention on Prohibitions or Restrictions on the Use of Certain Conventional Weapons which may be deemed to be Excessively Injurious or to have Indiscriminate Effects, arts. 5(1) and 6, Nov. 28, 2003, 2399 U.N.T.S. 100.

[51] AP I, *supra* note 37, art. 57(4).

3. Weapons Review

Parties to AP I must subject any new "weapon, means or method" of warfare to legal review to ensure that its employment is not prohibited by law.[52] The U.S. position is that only weapons (means) must be reviewed as a matter of customary international law.[53] The Department of Defense (DoD) tests, evaluates, and reviews weapons in accordance with their proposed use in physical and operational environments, anticipated rules of engagement, concepts of operation, and tactics, techniques, and procedures that would govern their use. Reviews must ensure new weapons or munitions do not cause suffering that is manifestly disproportionate to the military advantage reasonably expected from their use. States must determine whether a weapon can be controlled in such a manner that it is capable of being directed against a lawful target. In this regard, autonomous or semiautonomous weapons undergo special reviews by the armed services and DoD before they enter formal development.[54]

Although the United States is not a Party to AP I, it conducts a legal review of all new weapons to ensure they are in compliance with the applicable treaties, customary international law, and LOAC.[55] The review is one component of the DoD Law of War Program, which established U.S. policy to comply with LOAC during armed conflict and all other military operations.[56] The requirement is implemented through the uniformed judge advocates of the armed services.[57]

---

[52] *Id.* art. 36 (new weapons). It is debatable whether this rule has crystallized into customary international law. *See* Natalia Jevglevskaja, *Weapons Review Obligation under Customary International Law*, 94 INTERNATIONAL LAW STUDIES 186, 220–21 (2018).

[53] DOD LAW OF WAR MANUAL, *supra* note 19, § 6.2; NWP 1-14M, *supra* note 8, § 9.1; and FM 6-27, *supra* note 13, § 2-4.

[54] U.S. Department of Defense, DoD Directive 3000.09, Autonomy in Weapon Systems (2017), encl. 4, ¶ 8(b).

[55] U.S. Department of Defense, DoD Directive 5000.01, The Defense Acquisition System 9 (2020) [hereinafter DoD Directive 5000.01]. *See also* U.S. Department of Defense, DoD Instruction 5500.15, Review of Legality of Weapons under International Law (1974).

[56] U.S. Department of Defense, DoD Directive 2311.01, DoD Law of War Program § 1.2(a) (2020).

[57] *See* Headquarters, Department of the Army, AR 27-53, Legal Review of Weapons and Weapons Systems ¶ 4.f (2019) ("The Judge Advocate General's designee. TJAG's designee will--(1) Review weapons and weapon systems, including cyber weapons and cyber weapon systems, in accordance with this regulation to determine whether the weapons, weapon systems, cyber weapons, and cyber weapon systems and their intended use in combat are consistent with the international legal standards considered binding by the United States Government, whether derived from international agreements, customary international law, or a combination thereof."); *see also* Secretary of the Navy, SECNAVINST 5000.2F, Defense Acquisition System and Joint Capabilities Integration and Development System Implementation, encl. 3, ¶ 10(a) (2019) ("All potential weapons and weapon systems developed, acquired, or procured by the DoN will be reviewed by the Judge Advocate General (JAG) of the Navy to ensure that the intended use of such weapons or weapon systems is

Sometimes the lawfulness of a method or means of warfare is debatable. For example, during the Vietnam War, the United States coupled airpower with the widespread use of anti-personnel weapons, napalm, and cluster munitions; and it employed the new, small-caliber (5.56x45mm) M-16 rifle, conducted the Phoenix Program of political "assassination," and destroyed crops to deprive insurgents of food in the countryside.[58] While states may differ in their interpretation of the lawfulness of methods or means, the key is that those who develop and employ them have certain duties under LOAC.[59]

New weapons may require clarification of existing law or development of new law to ensure they balance considerations of humanity and military necessity.[60] New technologies, such as the introduction of artificial intelligence (AI) into AWS, may be completely lawful, whereas other technological innovations may be prohibited or restricted.[61]

4. Lasers and Directed Energy Weapons

Lasers may become a feature of future naval conflict, even though using them to blind the enemy violates CCW Protocol IV.[62] China has demonstrated a propensity to experiment with using lasers against U.S. military aircraft. In 2018, U.S. aircraft attempting to land at Camp Lemonier, the U.S. base in Djibouti in the Horn of Africa, were struck by military-grade lasers directed

consistent with domestic and international law."); Secretary of the Air Force, AFI 51–401, The Laws of War § 2.1.2 (2018).

[58] W. Hays Parks, *Means and Methods of Warfare*, 38 GEORGE WASHINGTON INTERNATIONAL LAW REVIEW 511, 512 (2006); Richard Falk, *Law and Responsibility in Warfare: The Vietnam Experience*, 4 INSTANT RESEARCH ON PEACE AND VIOLENCE 1, 4–8 (1974).

[59] WILLIAM H. BOOTHBY, WEAPONS AND THE LAW OF ARMED CONFLICT 283 (2009).

[60] AP I, *supra* note 37, art. 1(2) (general principles and scope of application).

[61] For example, the Russia Poseidon nuclear-armed underwater drone appears to be an unlawful weapon, per se, under the ENMOD Convention. Convention on the Prohibition of Military or Any Hostile Use of Environmental Modification Techniques art. 1(1), May 18, 1977, 31 U.S.T. 333, 1108 U.N.T.S. 151. *See* Dave Makichuk, *Russia to Test "Doomsday Drone" in High Arctic*, ASIA TIMES (online), May 26, 2020; Franz-Stefan Gady, *Russia (Once Again) Announces Start of Sea Trials of "Doomsday Weapon,"* THE DIPLOMAT (online), Dec 27, 2018. Russia (May 30, 1978), China (June 8, 2005), Japan (June 9, 1982), the United States (Jan. 17, 1980), and the United Kingdom (May 16, 1978) are parties as of the date indicated ENMOD.

[62] Additional Protocol to the Convention on Prohibitions or Restrictions on the Use of Certain Conventional Weapons Which May Be Deemed to Be Excessively Injurious or to Have Indiscriminate Effects, Oct. 13, 1995, 2024 U.N.T.S. 163 [hereinafter CCW Protocol IV].

at them from the nearby Chinese military base.[63] Two U.S. airmen suffered minor injuries. The United States protested four such incidents, which raised tensions between the two powers that operate military bases less than 10 miles apart.[64] Similarly, on February 17, 2020, a U.S. Navy P-8A Poseidon maritime patrol aircraft was lased by a Chinese Navy destroyer in international waters about 380 miles west of Guam.[65] These aerial laser incidents are unprofessional and unlawfully interfere with freedom of navigation, as well as the peacetime Code for Unplanned Encounters at Sea (CUES), a multilateral agreement concluded at the 2014 Western Pacific Naval Symposium to reduce incidents at sea. They are also inconsistent with the 2014 Memorandum of Understanding between the U.S. Department of Defense and the Ministry of National Defense of China Regarding Rules of Behavior for Safety of Air and Maritime Encounters.[66]

The use of laser weapons to injure or kill enemy combatants during armed conflict is permissible.[67] But, lasers have many other uses. The USS *Portland*, for example, successfully used a solid-state laser weapon to disable and bring down a target drone on May 16, 2020.[68] The test was the first successful demonstration of a directed energy weapon against a potential threat, and it presages their use in future naval conflicts. The United States has continued to install directed energy "dazzler systems" on Arleigh Burke-class guided missile destroyers to confuse or shoot down drones.[69]

If lasers are used as weapons, feasible precautions should be taken to avoid causing permanent blindness.[70] At sea the potentially lower standard of "reasonable precautions" would apply in cases involving only warships and aircraft.[71] Feasible precautions "include those that are practicable or

[63] Gordon Lubold & Jeremy Page, *Laser from Chinese Base Aimed at U.S. Military Pilots in Africa's Skies, Pentagon Charges*, WALL STREET JOURNAL, May 3, 2018 and *US Accuses China of Pointing Lasers at Its Pilots from Djibouti Base*, BBC NEWS (online), Mar. 4, 2018.

[64] Andrew Jacobs & Jane Perlez, *U.S. Wary of a Chinese Base Rising as Its Neighbor in Africa*, N.Y. Times, Feb. 26, 2017, at p. A1.

[65] Department of Defense Statement on People's Liberation Army Navy Lasing of U.S. Navy P-8A in Unsafe, Unprofessional Manner, (online), Mar. 6, 2020.

[66] Ankit Panda, *US Department of Defense: Guam Laser Incident "Unprofessional," Violates 2014 Code*, THE DIPLOMAT (online), Mar. 9, 2020 and James Kraska & Raul Pedrozo, *The US-China Arrangement for Air-to-Air Encounters Weakens International Law*, LAWFARE (online), Mar. 9, 2016.

[67] DoD LAW OF WAR MANUAL, *supra* note 19, § 16.5.

[68] *US Navy Warship Fires Laser Weapon, Downs Drone Off Pearl Harbor*, OPTICS.ORG (online), May 26, 2020; George Allison, *American Warship Fires Laser Weapon*, UK DEFENCE JOURNAL (online), May 26, 2020; and Megan Eckstein, *Video: USS Portland Fires Laser Weapon, Downs Drone in First At-Sea Test*, USNI NEWS (online), May 22, 2020.

[69] Megan Eckstein, *Navy Installing More Directed Energy Weapons on DDGs, Conducting Land-Based Laser Testing This Year*, USNI NEWS (online), Apr. 7, 2021.

[70] *Id.* §§ 5.2.3.4, 16.15.2, 19.21.5; CCW Protocol IV, *supra* note 62, art. 2.

[71] AP I, *supra* note 37, art. 57(4).

practically possible taking into account all circumstances ruling at the time, including humanitarian and military considerations."[72] Precautions also include training of the armed forces, promulgating doctrine, and rules of engagement.[73] Nonetheless, using an otherwise lawful laser weapon to blind an enemy combatant is not prohibited if militarily necessary and it is not feasible to avoid the harm.[74] For instance, it is not unlawful to use an otherwise lawful laser weapon to blind an enemy soldier in self-defense.[75]

The use of blinding lasers, however, is banned. Article 1 of Protocol IV to the CCW Convention prohibits the employment of laser weapons that are specifically designed, as a combat function, to cause permanent blindness to unenhanced vision.[76] "Unenhanced vision" excludes "vision through direct-view optics, such as binoculars, a telescopic sight, night-vision goggles, or similar devices used to increase vision beyond that of an ordinary person without such enhancement."[77] "Permanent blindness" is defined in article 4 as the "irreversible and uncorrectable loss of vision which is seriously disabling with no prospect of recovery."[78] "Serious disability" means the equivalent to visual acuity of less than 20/200 (Snellen eye chart) measured with both eyes.[79] Laser dazzlers designed to cause temporary loss of sight are therefore not prohibited by the Protocol.[80]

Several militaries use laser systems in a variety of roles, such as range-finding, target designation, jamming, dazzling, communications, and weapons guidance. These systems may inadvertently cause temporary loss of sight but are not prohibited by Protocol IV.[81] The United States successfully used laser devices in Iraq in ground combat, including convoys, mounted and dismounted patrols, and at vehicle checkpoints to warn or temporarily incapacitate individuals.[82] The use of an otherwise lawful laser system against optical equipment that causes blindness as an incidental or collateral effect is not covered by Protocol IV.[83] Therefore, laser weapons not specifically

---

[72] DoD LAW OF WAR MANUAL, *supra* note 19, § 6.15.2.
[73] *Id.*; CCW Protocol IV, *supra* note 62, art. 2.
[74] DoD LAW OF WAR MANUAL, *supra* note 19, § 6.15.2.1.
[75] *Id.*
[76] *Id.* § 6.15.1, 19.21.5; CCW Protocol IV, *supra* note 62, art. 1.
[77] DoD LAW OF WAR MANUAL, *supra* note 19, § 6.15.1.2.
[78] *Id.* CCW Protocol IV, *supra* note 62, art. 4.
[79] *Id.*
[80] DoD LAW OF WAR MANUAL, *supra* note 19, § 6.15.1.2.
[81] *Id.* § 6.15.1.1.
[82] DEFENSE SCIENCE BOARD, DEFENSE SCIENCE BOARD TASK FORCE ON DIRECTED ENERGY WEAPONS 13 (Dec. 2007).
[83] DoD LAW OF WAR MANUAL, *supra* note 19, § 6.15.1.1; CCW Protocol IV, *supra* note 62, art. 3.

designed to cause permanent blindness, but rather are intended to attack or destroy material or injure enemy personnel, which incidentally causes blindness, are permissible.[84]

Incendiary weapons are regulated by Protocol III to the CCW Convention. An "incendiary weapon" is defined as "any weapon or munition which is primarily designed to set fire to objects or cause burn injury to persons through the action of flame, heat, or combination thereof, produced by a chemical reaction of a substance delivered on target."[85] Some laser systems are specifically designed to set fire to objects or cause burn injuries. However, these systems are not considered incendiary weapons, and are therefore not regulated by Protocol III, because the injuries are not produced by a chemical reaction delivered on target.[86]

5. Law of Maritime Neutrality

The law of neutrality defines the legal relationship between belligerent states engaged in an international armed conflict and neutral states not taking part in the conflict. The law of armed conflict imposes duties and confers rights upon neutral and belligerent states. Neutral territory is inviolable, and belligerents have a duty to respect the inviolability of a neutral state. The principal duties of a neutral state are abstention—a duty to abstain from providing belligerents with war-related goods or services—and impartiality—exercising duties and rights in a nondiscriminatory manner toward all belligerents. Neutral states also have a duty to prevent belligerents from violating their neutrality—for example, preventing belligerent acts from neutral waters and airspace or using neutral ports and waters as a sanctuary or base of operations. A neutral state may legally use force to resist attempts to

---

[84] DoD Law of War Manual, *supra* note 19, § 6.15.1.1.

[85] Protocol (III) on Prohibitions or Restrictions on the Use of Incendiary Weapons, annexed to the Convention on Prohibitions or Restrictions on the Use of Certain Conventional Weapons Which May Be Deemed to be Excessively Injurious or to Have Indiscriminate Effects, art. 1 Oct. 10, 1980, 1342 U.N.T.S. 137.

[86] DoD Law of War Manual, *supra* note 19, § 6.14.1.1; Message From the President of the United States Transmitting Protocols to the 1980 Convention on Prohibitions or Restrictions on the use of Certain Conventional Weapons which may be deemed to be excessively injurious or to Have Indiscriminate effects: The Amended Protocol on Prohibitions or Restrictions on the Use of Mines, Booby-traps or other devices (Protocol II or the Amended Mines Protocol); The Protocol On Prohibitions or Restrictions on the Use of Incendiary Weapons (Protocol III or the Incendiary Weapons Protocol); and the Protocol on Blinding Laser Weapons (Protocol IV) 38, Treaty Doc. 105–1 (1997).

violate its neutrality. Nonetheless, neutrals are obligated to acquiesce in the exercise of lawful measures, such as visit and search, taken by belligerents against neutral merchant ships suspected of carrying contraband, breaching, or attempting breach of blockade, or performing unneutral service. Neutral states that fail to comply with their obligations may lose their neutral status.[87]

5.1 Neutral Territory

Neutral territory includes the land territory, internal waters (ports), roadsteads, territorial sea, archipelagic waters, and national airspace, but does not include the contiguous zone, the exclusive economic zone (EEZ) or the high seas.[88] If a neutral state is unable or unwilling to enforce its inviolability, the aggrieved belligerent may take necessary measures in neutral territory to counter the acts of the enemy force, employing a right of self-help. A belligerent may also act in self-defense if attacked or threatened with attack while in, or from, neutral territorial seas or territory.[89] Belligerents must not, however, violate a state's neutrality by using neutral ports and waters as a base of operations against their adversaries, or erect or use any apparatus to communicate with belligerent forces on land or sea.[90]

Neutral states may, but are not required to, close their ports and roadsteads to belligerent warships on a nondiscriminatory basis. At the outbreak of an armed conflict, a neutral state must provide belligerent warships in its ports or roadsteads, or in its territorial sea, a 24-hour notice to depart, unless local regulations stipulate a different time period.[91] If permitted by the neutral state, belligerent warships may visit neutral ports and roadsteads, but may only remain in port, a roadstead, or territorial sea for 24 hours, unless otherwise provided by local regulations or on account of damage or stress of

---

[87] Convention Concerning the Rights and Duties of Neutral Powers in Naval War, arts. 1, 2, 5, 6, 24 Oct. 18, 1907, 36 STAT. 2415 [hereinafter Hague XIII]; NWP 1-14M, *supra* note 8, § 7-1, 7-2; NWIP 10-2, *supra* note 7, § 230.

[88] DoD LAW OF WAR MANUAL, *supra* note 19, § 15.7.1. *See also* Vaughn Lowe, 14 SYRACUSE JOURNAL OF INTERNATIONAL AND COMPARATIVE LAW 657, 672 to 674 (1987–1988).

[89] NWP 1-14M, *supra* note 8, § 7-3; NWIP 10-2, *supra* note 7, § 441; DoD LAW OF WAR MANUAL, *supra* note 19, § 15.4.2.

[90] Hague XIII, *supra* note 87, art. 5; NWIP 10-2, *supra* note 7, § 442; Pan American Maritime Neutrality Convention, Feb. 20, 1928, arts. 3, 4 135 L.N.T.S. 187, 47 STAT. 1989, T.S. 845 [hereinafter Pan Am Convention], DoD LAW OF WAR MANUAL, *supra* note 19, §§ 15.5, 15.5.3.

[91] Hague XIII, *supra* note 87, art. 13; NWIP 10-2, *supra* note 7, § 443; Pan Am Convention, *supra* note 90, art. 5; NWP 1-14M, *supra* note 8, § 7.3.2; DoD LAW OF WAR MANUAL, *supra* note 19, § 15.7.3.1.

weather.[92] The warship must depart as soon as the cause of the delay is over.[93] The neutral state has a duty to enforce these time limits. If a warship refuses to leave, the neutral state may detain the ship and intern its crew.[94] These time limits do not apply to warships devoted exclusively to philanthropic, religious, or nonmilitary scientific purpose.[95]

Unless otherwise provided in local regulations, no more than three warships of any one belligerent may be present in the same neutral port or roadstead at any one time.[96] If warships of opposing belligerents are present in a neutral port or roadstead at the same time, not less than 24 hours must elapse between the departures of the respective enemy vessels. The warships will depart based on their order of arrival unless an extension of the stay is granted to the first vessel to arrive.[97] A belligerent warship may not leave a neutral port or roadstead until 24 hours after the departure of a merchant ship flying the flag of its adversary.

Belligerent warships in a neutral port or roadstead may only carry out such repairs as are absolutely necessary, as determined by the neutral state, to render them seaworthy.[98] Nor may belligerent warships make use of neutral ports, roadsteads, or territorial waters to replenish or increase their supplies of war materials or armaments, or complete their crews.[99] Nonetheless, belligerent warships may take on food "to the peace standard" and fuel "to enable them to reach the nearest port in their own country."[100] Alternatively, belligerent warships may take on bunker fuel if the neutral state has adopted

---

[92] Hague XIII, *supra* note 87, arts. 12, 14; NWIP 10-2, *supra* note 7, § 443; Pan Am Convention, *supra* note 90, art. 5; NWP 1-14M, *supra* note 8, § 7.3.2.1; DoD LAW OF WAR MANUAL, *supra* note 19 § 15.7.3.

[93] Hague XIII, *supra* note 87, art. 14; NWIP 10-2, *supra* note 7, § 443; Pan Am Convention, *supra* note 90, art. 5; NWP 1-14M, *supra* note 8, § 7.3.2.1.

[94] Hague XIII, *supra* note 87, art. 24; NWIP 10-2, *supra* note 7, § 443; Pan Am Convention, *supra* note 90, art. 6; NWP 1-14M, *supra* note 8, § 7.3.2.1; DoD LAW OF WAR MANUAL, *supra* note 19, § 15.9.2.

[95] Hague XIII, *supra* note 87, art. 14; Pan Am Convention, *supra* note 90, art. 5; NWP 1-14M, *supra* note 8, § 7.3.2.1.

[96] Hague XIII, *supra* note 87, art. 15; Pan Am Convention, *supra* note 90, art. 7; NWP 1-14M, *supra* note 8, § 7.3.2.1; DoD LAW OF WAR MANUAL, *supra* note 19, § 15.9.1.

[97] Hague XIII, *supra* note 87, art. 16; NWIP 10-2, *supra* note 7, § 443; Pan Am Convention, *supra* note 90, art. 8; NWP 1-14M, *supra* note 8, § 7.3.2.1; DoD LAW OF WAR MANUAL, *supra* note 19, § 15.9.3.

[98] Hague XIII, *supra* note 87, art. 17; NWP 1-14M, *supra* note 8, § 7.3.2.2; NWIP 10-2, *supra* note 7, § 443; DoD LAW OF WAR MANUAL, *supra* note 19, § 15.9.4.1.

[99] Hague XIII, *supra* note 87, art. 18; NWP 1-14M, *supra* note 8, § 7.3.2.2; NWIP 10-2, *supra* note 7, § 443.

[100] Hague XIII, *supra* note 98, art. 19; Pan Am Convention, *supra* note 101, art. 10; NWP 1-14M, *supra* note 8, § 7.3.2.2; DoD LAW OF WAR MANUAL, *supra* note 19, § 15.9.4.1.

this method for determining the amount to be supplied.[101] Once it has taken on fuel in a neutral port, a belligerent warship may not within the next three months replenish its fuel supply in a port of the same neutral power.[102] In practice, neutral states normally determine, on a nondiscriminatory basis, the conditions for the replenishment and refueling of belligerent warships.[103]

Hague XIII is silent on whether battle damage may be repaired in a neutral port or roadstead. Therefore, such repairs necessary to restore seaworthiness may be made if permitted by the neutral state. Some states have allowed the repair of battle damage, while others have not. Article 9 of the 1928 Pan American Maritime Neutrality Convention, however, specifically prohibits repairs of battle damage in neutral ports for those states that are parties to the convention.[104]

Since the adoption of Hague XIII in 1907, the breadth of the territorial sea has expanded from 3 to 12 nautical miles (nm).[105] Nonetheless, most states recognize that the law of neutrality applies in the expanded territorial sea and national airspace.[106] Any state may, on a nondiscriminatory basis, suspend temporarily innocent passage of foreign ships in specified areas of its territorial sea if such suspension is essential for the protection of its security.[107] Neutral states may, on a nondiscriminatory basis, suspend passage of belligerent warships, including submarines, through its territorial sea except as may be necessitated by distress or *force majeure*.[108]

Passage of foreign ships and belligerent warships may not, however, be suspended in international straits overlapped by neutral waters where the right of transit passage or non-suspendable innocent passage apply.[109] When transiting such straits in their normal mode of operation, belligerent forces shall proceed without delay and refrain from the threat or use of force against the sovereignty, territorial integrity, or political independence of neutral states bordering the strait.[110] Belligerent forces are also prohibited from

---

[101] *Id.*

[102] Hague XIII, *supra* note 87, art. 20; Pan Am Convention, *supra* note 90, art. 11; NWP 1-14M, *supra* note 8, § 7.3.2.2.

[103] NWP 1-14M, *supra* note 8, § 7.3.2.2.

[104] Pan Am Convention, *supra* note 90, art. 9; NWP 1-14M, *supra* note 8, § 7.3.2.2; DoD LAW OF WAR MANUAL, *supra* note 19, § 15.9.4.2.

[105] UNCLOS, *supra* note 12, art. 3.

[106] NWP 1-14M, *supra* note 8, § 7.3.4, 7.3.5.

[107] UNCLOS, *supra* note 12, art. 25.3.

[108] NWP 1-14M, *supra* note 8, § 7.3.4.

[109] *Id.* § 7.3.4, 7.3.5; UNCLOS, *supra* note 1, art. 37-44, 45; DoD LAW OF WAR MANUAL, *supra* note 19, § 15.8.1.

[110] NWP 1-14M, *supra* note 8, § 7.3.6; UNCLOS, *supra* note 1, art. 39.1.

using neutral straits as a place of sanctuary or a base of operations, and may not exercise the right of visit and search in such straits.[111]

Although the concept of archipelagic states did not exist in 1907, contemporary international law of the sea recognizes the right of qualifying island nations, like Indonesia and the Philippines, to establish archipelagic baselines enclosing archipelagic waters.[112] If the archipelagic state is neutral, the law of neutrality applies to these waters. Nevertheless, belligerent ships and aircraft, including submarines, retain the right of archipelagic sea lanes passage (ASLP) in the normal mode of operation through, under, and over all normal passage routes used for international navigation through the archipelago.[113] When engaged in ASLP through archipelagic waters (whether or not sea lanes have been formally designated), belligerent forces shall not engage in acts of hostility, or use archipelagic waters as a sanctuary or base of operations.[114]

5.2 The Exclusive Economic Zone and the High Seas

UNCLOS also created a new *sui generis* zone seaward of the territorial sea—the 200 nm EEZ where coastal states enjoy sovereign rights over the living and nonliving resources.[115] The EEZ of a neutral coastal state is not neutral waters. Rather, these waters have the character of high seas for the purpose of the law of naval warfare. Coastal state sovereign rights and jurisdiction in the EEZ do not modify the law of naval warfare. As a result, belligerents may conduct hostilities in the EEZ of neutral states.[116] Although not a binding instrument, the *San Remo Manual* purports to require belligerents to have due regard for the resource rights of the neutral state when conducting hostilities in the EEZ or on the continental shelf.[117] If a belligerent lays mines in

---

[111] NWP 1-14M, *supra* note 8, § 7.3.6. Note that special transit regimes apply in the Turkish Straits (1936 Montreux Convention), the Strait of Magellan (1881 Boundary Treaty between Argentina and Chile, 1984 Treaty of Peace and Friendship between Argentina and Chile), the Baltic Straits (1857 Treaty of Redemption of the Sound Dues and 1857 Convention on Discontinuance of Sound Dues between the United States and Denmark), and the Suez Canal, Panama Canal, and Kiel Canal.

[112] UNCLOS, *supra* note 1, arts. 46, 47, and 49.

[113] DoD Law of War Manual, *supra* note 19, § 15.8.2; NWP 1-14M, *supra* note 8, § 7.3.7; UNCLOS, *supra* note 1, art. 53.

[114] NWP 1-14M, *supra* note 8, § 7.3.7.

[115] UNCLOS, *supra* note 12, arts. 55–58, 60.

[116] NWP 1-14M, *supra* note 8, § 7.3.8.

[117] San Remo Manual, *supra* note 9, ¶ 34.

a neutral state's EEZ or continental shelf, the *San Remo Manual* requires it to notify the neutral state, as well as ensure that the size of the minefield and types of mines employed do not interfere with the neutral state's resource rights. Belligerents shall have due regard for the protection and preservation of the marine environment.[118] These requirements in the *San Remo Manual*, however, are progressive extensions of the law of naval warfare and therefore are not binding as a matter of law since the law of naval warfare is a special regime that displaces the law of the sea if the latter is inconsistent with the former.

The law of neutrality also regulates belligerent activities with respect to neutral commerce. Neutral commerce is all commerce between neutral states that does not involve "materials of war or armaments ultimately destined for a belligerent state, and all commerce between a neutral state and a belligerent that does not involve the carriage of contraband or otherwise contribute to the belligerent's war-fighting/war-sustaining capability."[119] The term "war-sustaining" is undefined, but the United States considers it to include maritime commerce that "indirectly but effectively" aids and sustains a belligerents war-fighting capability.[120] Some examples of war-sustaining goods include raw materials used to produce armaments and products that generate proceeds that a belligerent can use to purchase arms and armaments.[121]

Neutral states may legally engage in commerce with belligerent states but may not supply war materials or armaments (contraband) to them.[122] Contraband goods include commodities destined for a belligerent that may be used in an armed conflict against the enemy. Contraband is normally divided into two categories—absolute and conditional. Absolute contraband includes goods that are obviously intended for use in armed conflict, such as munitions, weapons, and uniforms. Conditional contraband, however, includes goods that can be used for either peaceful or warlike purposes, such as foodstuffs, construction materials, and fuel.[123] The distinction between absolute and conditional contraband fell into disuse during the Second World

---

[118] *Id.* ¶ 35.
[119] DoD LAW OF WAR MANUAL, *supra* note 19, § 15.12.1; NWP 1-14M, *supra* note 8, § 7.4.
[120] NWP 1-14M, *supra* note 8, § 7.4.
[121] *Id.*
[122] *Id.*
[123] DoD LAW OF WAR MANUAL, *supra* note 19, § 15.12.1.1; NWP 1-14M, *supra* note 8, § 7.4.1; NWIP 10-2, *supra* note 7, § 631.

War as the belligerents treated all goods directly or indirectly sustaining the war effort as contraband.[124]

At the beginning of hostilities, belligerents may declare contraband lists and notify neutrals of the type of goods considered contraband and those considered to be free goods that are exempt from capture.[125] If destined for the territory of, or occupied by, an enemy belligerent, contraband goods may be seized anywhere beyond neutral territory from the time the neutral vessel leaves a neutral port until it arrives in another neutral port. Enemy destination may be presumed if (1) the neutral vessel will "call at an enemy port before arriving at a neutral port"; (2) a neutral port serves as a port of transit for an enemy belligerent; or (3) "the goods are consigned 'to order' or to an unnamed consignee" in a neutral state that is located "in the vicinity of enemy territory."[126]

Belligerents may issue certificates of non-contraband carriage (navicert and aircert) to neutral vessels and aircraft to verify that the cargo on board has been inspected and is free of contraband. The use of navicerts and aircerts assist the belligerent's control of contraband goods without interference of neutral commerce.[127] Nonetheless, possession of a certificate does not guarantee that the vessel or aircraft will not be searched or that the cargo will not be seized. Moreover, a certificate issued by one belligerent does not affect the rights of opposing belligerents to visit and search.[128] The fact that a neutral merchant vessel or aircraft has been granted a navicert or aircert by one belligerent is not considered to be an act of unneutral service with regard to an opposing belligerent.[129]

During the Cuban Missile Crisis, the United States instituted a system of clearances (CLEARCERTS) to assist vessels transiting waters near Cuba and vessels bound for Cuban ports with cargoes containing no offensive weapons or associated material. CLEARCERTS could be obtained by merchant vessels departing U.S. and foreign ports. The purpose of the clearances was "to avoid unnecessary delays and other difficulties arising out of the stoppage, inspection, or possible diversion of

[124] DoD Law of War Manual, *supra* note 19, § 15.12.1.1; NWP 1-14M, *supra* note 8, § 7.4.1; NWIP 10-2, *supra* note 7, § 631.
[125] DoD Law of War Manual, *supra* note 19, § 15.12.1.3; NWP 1-14M, *supra* note 8, §§ 7.4.1, 7.4.1.1; NWIP 10-2, *supra* note 7, § 631.
[126] DoD Law of War Manual, *supra* note 19, §§ 15.12.2, 15.12.2.1, 15.12.2.2; NWP 1-14M, *supra* note 8, § 7.4.1.2; NWIP 10-2, *supra* note 7, § 63.
[127] DoD Law of War Manual, *supra* note 19, § 15.12.3; NWP 1-14M, *supra* note 8, § 7.4.2.
[128] DoD Law of War Manual, *supra* note 19, § 15.12.3; NWP 1-14M, *supra* note 8, § 7.4.2.
[129] San Remo Manual, *supra* note 9, ¶¶ 123, 133.

ships."[130] Nevertheless, like navicerts, possession of a CLEARCERT did not guarantee that a vessel would not be stopped, inspected, or diverted if necessary.[131]

Merchant vessels and civilian aircraft owned or controlled by a belligerent possess enemy character, even if they are operating under a neutral flag or bear neutral markings, and may be treated as such.[132] Neutral merchant vessels and civilian aircraft acquire enemy character and are subject to the same treatment as enemy warships and military aircraft if they (1) take a direct part in the hostilities on the side of the enemy, or (2) act in any capacity as a naval or military auxiliary to the enemy's armed forces.[133] Neutral merchant vessels and civilian aircraft acquire enemy character and are subject to the same treatment as enemy merchant vessels and civilian aircraft if they (1) operate directly under enemy control, orders, charter, employment, or direction; or (2) resist an attempt to establish their identity, including resistance to visit and search.[134]

Belligerents may exercise the right of visit and search against neutral merchant vessels and civil aircraft beyond neutral waters or airspace to ascertain their true character and nationality (enemy or neutral), as well as to verify the manner of their employment (innocent or hostile), whether they are carrying contraband or free goods, or have violated a blockade.[135] Belligerents may not, however, capture or destroy such vessels and aircraft that are engaged in legitimate commerce. If a neutral merchant ship does not stop after being hailed, fails to follow instructions, or resists visit and search, it may be stopped by force.[136]

Neutral warships and other government-owned or operated vessels engaged in noncommercial service are not subject to visit and search. Neutral merchant vessels under convoy of neutral warships of the same nationality may not be subjected to visit and search. However, the convoy commander may be required to provide to the commanding officer of the intercepting

<hr>

[130] *U.S. Acts to Avoid Delays for Ships Transiting Waters in Vicinity of Cuba*, Department of State Press Release 644, Oct. 27, 1962, DEPARTMENT OF STATE BULLETIN, Nov. 12, 1962, p. 747.

[131] *Id.*

[132] DoD LAW OF WAR MANUAL, *supra* note 19, § 15.14.1; NWP 1-14M, *supra* note 8, § 7.5; NWIP 10-2, *supra* note 7, § 501.

[133] DoD LAW OF WAR MANUAL, *supra* note 19, §§ 15.14.1, 15.14.2, 15.14.2.1; NWP 1-14M, *supra* note 8, § 7.5.1; NWIP 10-2, *supra* note 7, § 501.a.

[134] DoD LAW OF WAR MANUAL, *supra* note 19, § 15.14.2.2; NWP 1-14M, *supra* note 8, § 7.5.2; NWIP 10-2, *supra* note 7, § 501.b.

[135] NWP 1-14M, *supra* note 8, § 7.4, 7.6; Pan Am Convention, *supra* note 90, art. 1.

[136] DoD LAW OF WAR MANUAL, *supra* note 19, § 15.13.4.1; NWP 1-14M, *supra* note 8, § 7.6.1; NWIP 10-2, *supra* note 7, § 502; Pan Am Convention, *supra* note 90, art. 1.

warship information, in writing, as to the character of the vessels and their cargoes. If the convoy commander determines that a vessel in the convoy possesses enemy character or is carrying contraband goods, the commander shall withdraw protection to the offending vessel, making it liable to visit and search by the belligerent warship.[137]

A belligerent may impose restrictions on neutral vessels and aircraft, to include controlling their communications and prohibiting their entry into the immediate area of naval operations, to enhance battlespace management and ensure security of its forces. An international strait, however, may not be closed unless there is a route of similar convenience available to neutral ships and aircraft. Neutral merchant vessels and civilian aircraft that fail to comply with a belligerent's restrictions in the immediate area of naval operations risk being captured or fired upon. If a neutral vessel or aircraft transmits information to an opposing belligerent concerning military operations or military forces, it assumes enemy character and is liable to capture or destruction.[138]

In short, neutral merchant vessels and civilian aircraft that engage in any of the following acts are liable to capture by belligerent warships or military aircraft:

- carrying contraband;
- breaching or attempting to breach blockade;
- carrying military or public service personnel of an enemy;
- communicating information in the interest of an enemy;
- avoiding an attempt to establish identity, including visit and search;
- presenting irregular or fraudulent papers; lacking necessary papers; destroying, defacing, or concealing papers; or
- violating regulations established by a belligerent within the immediate area of naval operations.[139]

Captured merchant vessels and civilian aircraft may be diverted to a port or airfield under belligerent jurisdiction as a prize for adjudication by a prize court.[140] In such cases, belligerents may use forcible measures against

---

[137] DoD LAW OF WAR MANUAL, *supra* note 19, §§ 15.13.1, 15.13.2, 15.13.2.1, 15.13.2.2, 15.13.2.3, and 15.13.2.4; NWP 1-14M, *supra* note 8, § 7.6.

[138] DoD LAW OF WAR MANUAL, *supra* note 19, § 15.15.1; NWP 1-14M, *supra* note 8, § 7.8; NWIP 10-2, *supra* note 7, § 430.

[139] NWP 1-14M, *supra* note 8, § 7.10; NWIP 10-2, *supra* note 7, § 503.

[140] DoD LAW OF WAR MANUAL, *supra* note 19, § 15.15.2; NWP 1-14M, *supra* note 8, § 7.10.

neutral vessels or aircraft that resist capture.[141] If the commander of the capturing warship determines that the prize cannot be diverted to a belligerent port or airfield or properly released, the prize may be destroyed. In these circumstances, the commander must deliver the passengers and crew safely and preserve all documents and papers relating to the ship, as well as safeguard the passengers' personnel effects if practicable.[142] Persons on board a captured neutral merchant vessel or civilian aircraft, including officers and crew, who are not nationals of the neutral state are not considered prisoners of war (POW) and shall be repatriated to their state of nationality as soon as reasonably possible. However, the officers and crew can be held as POWs if the neutral vessel or aircraft assumed enemy character by taking a direct part in the hostilities on the side of the enemy or by serving as a naval or military auxiliary for the enemy.[143]

Whether the customary law of neutrality continues to apply completely in the UN Charter era is unsettled in situations where the Security Council has authorized collective action against an aggressor nation. The Security Council is primarily responsible for the maintenance of international peace and security and carries out its duties on behalf of the Member States.[144] Accordingly, Member States "agree to accept and carry out the decisions of the Security Council."[145] and shall give the UN "every assistance" in its actions, especially enforcement action.[146]

Under the Charter, Member States are required to "refrain in their international relations from the threat or use of force against the territorial integrity or political independence of any states. . . ."[147] If the Security Council determines that there has been a threat to the peace, breach of the peace, or act of aggression, it shall decide what measures to take to maintain or restore international peace and security.[148] Measures can include those not involving the use of armed forces, such as economic sanctions,[149] or action by air, sea, or land forces of Member States necessary to maintain or restore international peace and security.[150] This obligation, which is incompatible with the

---

[141] DoD Law of War Manual, *supra* note 19, § 15.15.2.1; NWP 1-14M, *supra* note 8, § 7.10.

[142] DoD Law of War Manual, *supra* note 19, § 15.15.3; NWP 1-14M, *supra* note 8, § 7.10.1.

[143] DoD Law of War Manual, *supra* note 19, § 15.15.4.1; NWP 1-14M, *supra* note 8, § 7.10.1.

[144] United Nations, *Charter of the United Nations*, art. 24(1), Oct. 24, 1945, 1 U.N.T.S. XVI [hereinafter UN Charter].

[145] *Id.* art. 25.

[146] *Id.* art. 2(5).

[147] *Id.* art. 2(4).

[148] *Id.* art. 39.

[149] *Id.* art. 40.

[150] *Id.* art. 41.

status of neutrality and the principle of impartiality, takes precedence over a nation's other international obligations, including the traditional law of neutrality.[151] Nonetheless, if the Security Council implements preventive or enforcement measures, any state that finds itself confronted with special economic problems arising from carrying out such measures has the right to consult with the Security Council regarding a solution to those problems.[152]

---

[151] DoD LAW OF WAR MANUAL, *supra* note 19, § 15.2.3.2; NWP 1-14M, *supra* note 8, § 7.2.2; NWIP 10-2, *supra* note 7, § 232.
[152] UN Charter, *supra* note 144, art. 50.

2

Merchant Ships

1. Introduction

The use of civilian forces during armed conflict is not new, but new technologies make it more likely they will become an important element of naval warfare. At sea, belligerents may use fishing vessels and merchant ships to support naval forces through logistics, to relay intelligence, sow mines, or even to engage in attack. Emerging technologies enable civilian ships, including fishing vessels, cargo ships, and oil tankers, to accomplish a much broader range of offensive and defensive naval missions. This includes serving as platforms for widely distributed targeting sensors and as missile launchers. The operation of civil shipping complicates the battle space and confounds enemy planning by expanding the area of operational maneuver, distributing and layering sensors and weapons in the "kill chain" to enhance defense, and multiplying strike options for offensive attack. While advanced warships are costly, merchant ships may serve as an inexpensive force multiplier.

The deliberate mixture of civilian and naval forces raises questions about the application of the law of naval warfare, the law of neutrality, and prize law. Neutral states may employ their merchant ships in a way that favors one belligerent over another, such as by carrying contraband or acting in the military or public service of the enemy. The overlay of complementary areas of law complicates legal and operational planning, places civilian ships and crews in greater danger, and risks widening a future conflict.

2. Rules That Apply to Neutral and Belligerent States

The peacetime law of the sea, reflected in the United Nations Convention on the Law of the Sea (UNCLOS), covers virtually every aspect of oceans

Disruptive Technology and the Law of Naval Warfare. James Kraska and Raul Pedrozo, Oxford University Press.
© James Kraska & Raul Pedrozo 2022. DOI: 10.1093/oso/9780197630181.003.0003

governance.[1] During armed conflict at sea, UNCLOS, associated rules from other agreements, and customary international law continue to apply among neutral states, and between neutral states and belligerent states. At the same time the law of naval warfare is a *lex specialis* regime that applies between or among belligerent states. That body of law is complemented by the law of neutrality and the law of prize that governs relationships concerning neutral rights and duties, and the capture of enemy merchant ships and deep-sea fishing vessels.

The international law of the sea reflects the rules for claiming areas under coastal state sovereignty—internal waters, archipelagic waters, and territorial sea—from those areas of the ocean lying outside of coastal state sovereignty.[2] These rules provide the parameters for the operation of ships, areas of belligerent operations, and neutral areas.[3] The law of the sea also underlies the law of naval warfare by setting forth fundamental flag state duties and responsibilities associated with the operation of ships.[4] Furthermore, UNCLOS states that the oceans are reserved for "peaceful purposes" only.[5] During armed conflict, the principle that the sea is reserved for peaceful purposes continues to apply among neutral states and between neutral states and belligerent states, as well as belligerent activities in self-defense or authorized by the UN Security Council.[6] The law of the sea principle of exclusive flag state jurisdiction also persists in peacetime and war among vessels flagged by neutral states and belligerent states.[7] Flag state jurisdiction identifies vessels that have neutral or belligerent status.[8] This is an important factor in the determination of the right of visit and search, capture and prize, and targeting in the law of naval warfare.

2.1 Flag State Responsibilities

All states, including landlocked states, have the right to sail ships flying their flag.[9] In addition to the duty to ensure activities at sea are pursuant only to

---

[1] United Nations Convention on the Law of the Sea, pmbl., *opened for signature* Dec. 10, 1982, 1833 U.N.T.S. 397 (entered into force Nov. 16, 1994) [hereinafter UNCLOS].

[2] *Id.* art. 2; SAN REMO MANUAL ON THE LAW APPLICABLE TO ARMED CONFLICT AT SEA Rule 14 (Louise Doswald-Beck ed., 1995) [hereinafter SAN REMO MANUAL].

[3] SAN REMO MANUAL, *supra* note 2, ¶¶ 10–12, 14–52, 59–61, 67–69.

[4] UNCLOS, *supra* note 1, art. 94.

[5] *Id.* art. 88.

[6] SAN REMO MANUAL, *supra* note 2, ¶¶ 1–2.

[7] UNCLOS, *supra* note 1, art. 94(1)–(2).

[8] SAN REMO MANUAL, *supra* note 2, ¶ 12.

[9] UNCLOS, *supra* note 1, art. 90.

"peaceful purposes," states that register ships must fulfill their responsibilities as a flag state. Flag states are required to maintain a register of ships that fly their flag and to ensure that the vessels are surveyed at the time they are launched and then periodically.[10] The registration requirement first arose in customary law and is reflected in the 1958 High Seas Convention, which requires each state to set conditions for the grant of its nationality to ships, ship registration, and common practices.[11] Later, the requirement was carried into UNCLOS.[12]

The scope of the responsibility entails an obligation to ensure ships have on board the appropriate navigational charts and instruments.[13] Officers and crews must be properly trained and qualified.[14] Flag states also must take such measures necessary to ensure safety at sea, especially to ensure the construction, design, equipment, manning, and seaworthiness of ships.[15] In taking these measures, flag states are required to "conform to generally accepted international procedures, practices," and enforcement.[16] States may conduct self-assessments of their compliance with the internationally accepted standards using guidance adopted by the member states of the International Maritime Organization (IMO).[17]

What standards exist for flag states? The IMO Secretariat suggests states are obligated to comply with agreements that reflect internationally accepted standards and therefore have entered the pantheon of customary law. Among these, the following agreements may relate to some aspects of conflict at sea:[18]

1. International Convention for the Safety of Life at Sea, 1974 (SOLAS 1974);[19]
2. Protocol of 1988 relating to the International Convention for the Safety of Life at Sea, 1974 (SOLAS Protocol 1988);

---

[10] *Id.* art. 94(2)(a).

[11] Convention on the High Seas art. 5, Apr. 29, 1958, 13 U.S.T. 2312, T.I.A.S. No. 5200, 450 U.N.T.S. 11 [hereinafter Convention on the High Seas].

[12] UNCLOS, *supra* note 1, art. 94(4)(a).

[13] *Id.* art. 94(4)(a).

[14] *Id.* art. 94(4)(b)–(c).

[15] *Id.* art. 94(3)–(4).

[16] *Id.* art. 94(5).

[17] IMO Res. A.921(22) (Nov. 29, 2001).

[18] The "Load Lines" and "Tonnage" agreements are also regarded as "internationally accepted": International Convention on Load Lines, 1966 (Load Lines 1966); Protocol of 1988 relating to the International Convention on Load Lines, 1996 (Load Lines Protocol 1988); and International Convention on Tonnage Measurement of Ships, 1969 (Tonnage 1969). *See* INTERNATIONAL MARITIME ORGANIZATION, IMPLICATIONS OF THE UNITED NATIONS CONVENTION ON THE LAW OF THE SEA FOR THE INTERNATIONAL MARITIME ORGANIZATION 15 (2014).

[19] International Convention for the Safety of Life at Sea, 1974, Nov. 1, 1974, 32 U.S.T. 47, 1184 U.N.T.S. 2 (as amended).

3. Convention on the International Regulations for Preventing Collisions at Sea, 1972 (COLREG 1972);[20]
4. International Convention on Standards of Training, Certification and Watchkeeping for Seafarers, 1978 (STCW 1978); and
5. International Convention on Maritime Search and Rescue, 1979 (SAR 1979).[21]

Several of these agreements apply to civilian ships involved in peacetime encounters at sea or during armed conflict. COLREG, for example, applies to private yachts, commercial ships, and public vessels, including warships and coast guard vessels.[22] Public vessels engaged only in government, non-commercial service, including naval and coast guard vessels, are immune from foreign state jurisdiction, however.[23] COLREG has 156 States Parties representing 98 percent of world tonnage.

COLREG requires states to ensure their vessels are operated safely, observing a detailed set of rules for safe navigation.[24] The rules apply on "the high seas and all waters connected therewith," regardless of maritime boundaries or associated disputes.[25] In complying with COLREG, the master of a ship shall exercise "due regard . . . to all dangers of navigation and collision. . . ."[26] In addition, "every vessel shall use all available means appropriate to the prevailing circumstances and conditions to determine if risk of collision exists. If there is any doubt such risk shall be deemed to exist."[27] Moreover, "any action taken to avoid collision shall be . . . positive, made in ample time and with due regard to the observance of good seamanship."[28] These rules require states to take affirmative steps to avoid collision, even when they believe they have the right of way.

---

[20] Convention on the International Regulations for Preventing Collisions at Sea, Oct. 20, 1972, 28 U.S.T. 3459, T.I.A.S. No. 8587, 1050 U.N.T.S. 16 [hereinafter COLREG].

[21] International Convention on Maritime Search and Rescue, 1979 (with annex), Apr. 27, 1979, T.I.A.S No. 11,093, 1405 U.N.T.S. 119.

[22] "These Rules shall apply to all vessels upon the high seas and in all waters connected therewith navigable by seagoing vessels." COLREG, *supra* note 20, r. 1.

[23] *See* UNCLOS, *supra* note 1, arts. 32, 96, 236; James Kraska, *Maritime Confidence-Building Measures for Navigation in the South China Sea*, 32 INTERNATIONAL JOURNAL OF MARINE & COASTAL LAW 268 (2017).

[24] COLREG, *supra* note 20.

[25] *Id.* art. 1(a).

[26] *Id.* art. 2(b).

[27] *Id.* art. 7(a).

[28] *Id.* art. 8(a).

If an incident occurs, such as a collision at sea, flag state administrations must investigate reports by other states that believe its exercise of flag state jurisdiction and control was inadequate.[29] Flag states also should investigate serious casualties to ships that fly their flag.[30] Finally, flag states are required to monitor, and if necessary, initiate proceedings, against ships that violate rules for marine environmental protection.[31] The contemporary regulatory framework for flag state responsibilities in UNCLOS is well developed, but its implementation is sometimes lacking.[32] Because the flag state has virtually plenary ("exclusive") jurisdiction, it also shoulders extensive duties and responsibilities. To ensure that these responsibilities fall appropriately on the state that registers the vessel, the law of the sea requires that there be a "genuine link" between the ship and the flag state that registers it.[33]

2.1.1 China Maritime Militia

In the South China Sea, People's Armed Force Maritime Militia (PAFMM) vessels enforce China's unilateral nine-dashed line claim that was unanimously rejected by the 2016 Philippine-China arbitration brought under UNCLOS, Annex VII.[34] Setting aside the merits and politics of the case, however, an analysis of numerous encounters between Chinese and Philippine vessels reveals equally troubling incidents that suggest Chinese disregard for the core IMO instruments. The South China Sea arbitration, for example, found that during several encounters in April and May 2012, Chinese public vessels violated COLREG, endangering Philippine ships.[35]

On April 28, 2102, the Chinese vessel FLEC-310 violated the COLREG when it passed within 200 yards of the Philippine-flagged SARV-002 and 600 yards of the Philippine-flagged SARV-003 at a speed of more than 20 knots.[36] Similarly, on May 26, 2012, Chinese public vessels CMS/MSV-71, FLEC-303, and FLEC-306 violated COLREG when they made multiple attempts to cross the bow of Philippine vessel MSC-3008 at a distance of only 100 yards and at speeds of up to 20 knots.[37] On March 9, 2014, two China Coast Guard (CCG)

---

[29] UNCLOS, *supra* note 1, art. 94(6).
[30] *Id.* art. 94(7).
[31] *Id.* art. 217.
[32] JOHN N. K. MANSELL, FLAG STATE RESPONSIBILITY 237 (2009).
[33] UNCLOS, *supra* note 1, art. 91.
[34] S. China Sea Arb. (China v. Phil.), Case No. 2013–19, Award, §§ 277–78 (Perm. Ct. Arb. 2016).
[35] *Id.* § 1123.
[36] *See also* Memorial of the Philippines, S. China Sea Arb. (China v. Phil.) 2014 Perm. Arb. Ct. Pleadings, Annex 239 (Mar. 19, 2014).
[37] *Id.*

ships intercepted a Philippine civilian-contracted resupply vessel AM700, preventing it from reaching a small detachment of Filipino Marines aboard the BRP *Sierra Madre*, a commissioned Philippine warship.[38]

The tribunal determined these actions were more than negligent. "Where Chinese vessels were under an obligation to yield, they persisted; where the regulations called for a safe distance, they infringed it."[39] China's actions were not borne from "occasional negligence" in failing to adhere to the COLREG, but rather point to a "conscious disregard."[40] Similarly, in the East China Sea, less than one month after the Philippine-China Award, China surged 14 CCG vessels to screen a fleet of some 230 Chinese fishing vessels unlawfully fishing in the waters off the Senkaku Islands.[41] The Chinese ambassador to Japan said the ships were there to "protect [China's] fishing boats."[42] Yet the right of freedom of navigation is a right of the flag state, rather than an individual right of the master or shipowner.[43] Consequently, infringements on this right are wrongful acts against a state. Breaches of UNCLOS and COLREG constitute an internationally wrongful act and give rise to state responsibility.[44]

3. Enemy Merchant Vessels

The use of merchant vessels during armed conflict intentionally puts civilians in harm's way and endangers all seafarers that may be present in the area of hostilities. States party to a conflict shall at all times distinguish between the civilian population and combatants and between civilian objects and military objectives and direct their operations only against military targets.[45] As a general rule, civilians shall not be the object of attack. An "attack" is "an act of

---

[38] S. China Sea Arb., *supra* note 34, § 1123. *See also* Jeff Himmelman, *A Game of Shark and Minnow*, N.Y. TIMES MAGAZINE, Oct. 27, 2013.

[39] S. China Sea Arb., *supra* note 34, § 1105.

[40] *Id.*

[41] Kana Inagaki & Lucy Hornby, *Chinese Vessels Raise Tension with Japan*, FINANCIAL TIMES (online), Aug. 8, 2016.

[42] Lucy Hornby, *Chinese Fishermen Caught Up in Asian Geopolitical Conflict*, FINANCIAL TIMES (online), Aug. 21, 2016.

[43] M/V Saiga (No. 2) (St. Vincent v. Guinea), Case No. 2, Judgment of July 1, 1999, ITLOS Rep. 1999 10, 45; *see also* PHILIPP WENDEL, STATE RESPONSIBILITY FOR INTERFERENCES WITH THE FREEDOM NAVIGATION IN PUBLIC INTERNATIONAL LAW 88 (2007).

[44] U.N. Doc. A/56/10, *Report of the International Law Commission on the Work of Its 53d Session*, 2 YEARBOOK OF THE INTERNATIONAL LAW COMMISSION 32 (2001).

[45] Protocol (I) Additional to the Geneva Conventions of Aug. 12, 1949, and Relating to the Protection of Victims of International Armed Conflicts, art. 48, June 8, 1977, 1125 U.N.T.S. 3 [hereinafter AP I]; ICRC IHL Database, Customary IHL, [hereinafter ICRC Customary IHL], Vol. I Rule 7.

violence against the adversary, whether in offense or defense."[46] Employing civilian vessels in the war effort disregards their special, protected status. It also makes it more likely that enemy merchant ships would resist the belligerent right of visit and search or capture—raising the likelihood of civilian casualties. All vessels operating under enemy flag, except those specifically exempt from attack or capture, possess enemy character. Enemy merchant ships shall not be attacked unless they become a military objective by their conduct or operation. Nonetheless, they are liable to capture and (after adjudication) condemnation as prize.[47] Using merchant ships as an auxiliary force upsets these rules, with potentially deadly consequences.

3.1 Prize Capture

Unlike the law of land warfare, at sea the decision to use force is not a binary choice between protected civilian objects and lawful military targets. A third option is available—capture of enemy merchant ships and goods to be adjudicated in admiralty court as a lawful prize. All enemy merchant ships, except those specifically exempt (below), are subject to capture as prize.[48] The term "prize" relates to those vessels or cargo that may be seized, with or without the consent of the captain or master of the vessel captured and detained, and then brought before a national prize court to be condemned for the use of the captor. These ships are still civilian objects and may not be attacked in ordinary circumstances unless otherwise warranted by their conduct or operation, even if they are subject to capture. Commercial ships may resist efforts at their capture, but if they resist, they may be attacked.[49]

Special categories of vessels are exempt from capture. These include:

a. hospital ships and small craft used for coastal rescue operations;
b. other medical transports, so long as they are needed for the wounded, sick and shipwrecked on board;

---

[46] AP I, *supra* note 45, art. 49(1).

[47] *Advisory Committee on Trade Questions in Time of War, A Handbook on Economic Warfare (1939), reprinted in* SEA POWER AND THE CONTROL OF TRADE: BELLIGERENT RIGHTS FROM THE RUSSIAN WAR TO THE BEIRA PATROL, 1854–1970 at 445, 465 (Nicholas Tracy ed., 2005).

[48] SAN REMO MANUAL, *supra* note 2, ¶ 116; YORAM DINSTEIN, THE CONDUCT OF HOSTILITIES UNDER THE LAW OF INTERNATIONAL ARMED CONFLICT 285 (2016) [hereinafter DINSTEIN, THE CONDUCT OF HOSTILITIES].

[49] SAN REMO MANUAL, *supra* note 2, ¶ 98.

   c. vessels granted safe conduct by agreement between the belligerent
      parties including;
       i. cartel vessels, e.g., vessels designated for and engaged in the trans-
         port of prisoners of war; and
       ii. vessels engaged in humanitarian missions, including vessels car-
         rying supplies indispensable o the survival of the civilian popula-
         tion, and vessels engaged in relief actions and rescue operations;
   d. vessels engaged in transporting cultural property under special
      protection;
   e. vessels charged with religious, non-military scientific or philanthropic
      missions; vessels collecting scientific data of likely military applications
      are not protected; and
   f. small coastal fishing vessels and small boats engaged in local coastal
      trade, but they are subject to the regulations of a belligerent naval com-
      mander operating in the area and to inspection.[50]

In order to maintain exemption from capture, such vessels must be innocently employed in their normal role; refrain from acts harmful to the enemy;
immediately submit to identification and inspection when required; and not
intentionally hamper the movement of combatants and obey orders to stop
or move out of the way when required.[51]

If enemy merchant ships refuse an order to stop for visit and search or actively resist capture as prize, they may be attacked. Belligerents have a "full
and perfect right" to capture enemy goods and articles going to their enemy
that are contraband of war.[52] Visit and search is the means of preventing and
enforcing neutral ships carrying contraband or breaking a blockade or rendering unneutral service to the enemy, and the exercise of the right of capture
of enemy ships.[53]

3.1.1 Armed Merchant Ships
In the age of sail, an armed merchant ship might fend off a privateer with
small arms. With the rise of steam-powered, steel-hulled warships in the

---

[50] *Id.* ¶ 136; *see also Resistance to or Evasion of Visit and Search*, 11 DIGEST OF INTERNATIONAL LAW
630–42 (1968).

[51] SAN REMO MANUAL, *supra* note 2, ¶ 137.

[52] The Nereide, 9 Cranch. 388, 427 (1815).

[53] C. JOHN COLOMBOS, INTERNATIONAL LAW OF THE SEA § 864 (6th ed. 1967).

mid-nineteenth century, however, these weapons became superfluous.[54] Consequently, merchant ships gradually lost their armament. In the First World War, British and then American merchant ships began to acquire armament for self-defense in response to Germany's effective U-boat campaign against allied shipping.[55] These merchant ships had concealed guns and would loiter in sea lanes, inviting U-boat attack. When ordered to stop, a false "panic party" would take to the lifeboats, apparently abandoning ship. When the submarine approached to sink the ship, however, the guns would be uncovered and manned, the naval ensign raised, and the ship would open fire on the submarine, sometimes with success.[56] These "Q-ships" would straggle behind allied convoys to entice German submarines to attack them, and then turn on their assailant.[57]

The use of civilian vessels in armed conflict raises the question of perfidy. Perfidy invites the confidence of the enemy to lead it to believe it is "entitled to, or obliged to accord," protection under the law of armed conflict.[58] Perfidious attacks include launching attack while feigning protected status, such as a civilian or neutral ship; or by feigning surrender or distress, such as crew taking to life rafts.[59] There is a view that Q-ships are not lawful during armed conflict.[60] The tactic of deception has been used during recent peacetime counter-piracy operations to run lights on a warship at night to make it appear like a merchant vessel to invite pirate attacks. Somali pirates have mistaken Dutch, American, French, and German warships for merchant vessels.[61]

---

[54] Bernard Brodie & Fawn M. Brodie, From Crossbow to H-Bomb: The Evolution of the Weapons and Tactics of Warfare 153–58 (1973).

[55] See generally E. Keble Chatterton, Q-Ships and Their Story: A History of Decoy Vessels (1922).

[56] Rodney Carlisle, Sovereignty at Sea: U.S. Merchant Ships and American Entry into World War I 26–27 (2009).

[57] 1 Samuel Eliot Morison, History of United States Naval Operations in World War II 281–85 (2010).

[58] Office of the General Counsel, U.S. Department of Defense, Law of War Manual § 5.22.1 (rev. ed., Dec. 2016) [hereinafter DoD Law of War Manual]; AP I, art. 37(1) ("Acts inviting the confidence of an adversary to lead him to believe that he is entitled to, or is obliged to accord, protection under the rules of international law applicable in armed conflict, with intent to betray that confidence, shall constitute perfidy.").

[59] San Remo Manual, supra note 2, ¶ 111.

[60] The Round Table commentary to the San Remo Manual is of the opinion that the practice of Q-ships is "no longer acceptable." Id.

[61] See, e.g., Pirates Hit Navy Ship in Error, BBC News (online), Oct. 7, 2019; David C. Scott, Somali Pirates Mistakenly Attack Dutch Warship. Oops., Christian Science Monitor (online), Mar. 18, 2010; Pirates Attack Wrong Ship, Are Captured, Sydney Morning Herald (online), Apr. 1, 2009; Somali Pirate Gets Life in Prison for Attack on US Navy Ship, Navy Times (AP) (online), Apr. 26, 2017.

3.2 Coastal Fishing Vessels Exempt from
Capture and Attack

Enemy coastal fishing vessels are exempt from capture (and attack).[62] For centuries, state practice has recognized that vessels used exclusively for fishing along the coast are exempt from capture or attack, unless they take part in hostilities.[63] The U.S. Supreme Court carefully recounts the 500-year emergence of this rule in the seminal 1900 case, *The Paquete Habana*.[64] The case is a landmark feature of U.S. foreign relations law because of the famous statement from Justice Gray's majority opinion: "International law is part of our law, and must be ascertained and administered by the courts of justice of appropriate jurisdiction as often as questions of right depending upon it are duly presented for their determination."[65] That holding profoundly connects U.S. foreign relations law to public international law.

In substantive international law, however, the case is best known for its decision in the field of the law of naval warfare concerning the protection of coastal fishing vessels during periods of armed conflict.[66] *The Paquete Habana* held that coastal fishing vessels, "pursuing their vocation of catching and bringing in fresh fish," are immune from capture or attack during armed conflict.[67] The findings of the court reflect customary international law.

The case of *The Paquete Habana* sprang from U.S. interdiction of Cuban shipping during the Spanish-American War. Two boats—*The Paquete Habana* and *The Lola*—were captured as prize and brought into Key West in 1898. *The Paquete Habana* was a 43-foot sloop displacing 25 tons and operated out of Cuba under a Spanish fishing license.[68] *The Lola* was an unlicensed

---

[62] SAN REMO MANUAL, *supra* note 2, ¶¶ 47(g), 136(f).

[63] Convention No. XI Relative to Certain Restrictions with Regard to the Exercise of the Right of Capture in Naval War, Oct 18, 1907, art. 3, 36 Stat. 2396, T.S. No. 544, [hereinafter Hague XI]; U.S. NAVY, U.S. MARINE CORPS & U.S. COAST GUARD, NWP 1-14M/MCTP 11-10B/COMDTPUB P5800.7A, THE COMMANDER'S HANDBOOK ON THE LAW OF NAVAL OPERATIONS § 7.5 (2017) [hereinafter NWP 1-14M]; OFFICE OF THE CHIEF OF NAVAL OPERATIONS, U.S. NAVY, LAW OF NAVAL WARFARE, NAVAL WARFARE INFORMATION PUBLICATION (NWIP) 10-2 § 503 (1955), *reprinted in* 50 INTERNATIONAL LAW STUDIES 359 (1955) [hereinafter NWIP 10-2].

[64] The Paquete Habana, 175 U.S. 677, 689–90 (1900).

[65] The importation of international law into U.S. law has been recognized after The Paquete Habana, most notably in Sosa v. Alvarez-Machain, 124 S. Ct. 2739, 2764 (2004), Banco Nacional de Cuba v. Sabbatino, 376 U.S. 398, 423 (1964), and Filartiga v. Pena-Irala, 630 F.2d 876, 880, 886–87 (2d Cir. 1980).

[66] Note, *Fishing Vessels Exempt from Capture*, 13 HARVARD LAW REVIEW 594, 594–95 (1900).

[67] The Paquete Habana, 175 U.S., *supra* note 64 at 686.

[68] *Id.* at 679.

51-foot schooner displacing 35 tons, also operating out of Cuba.[69] American naval forces seized *The Paquete Habana* on April 25, 1898, and *The Lola* on April 27, 1898. The vessels were sold upon auction for $490 and $800, respectively.[70] After dispensing with jurisdictional matters, the court addressed the issue of capture of the fishing "smacks." The court held, "By ancient usage among civilized nations, beginning centuries ago, and gradually ripening into a rule of international law, coastal fishing vessels, pursuing their vocation of catching and bringing in fresh fish, have been recognized as exempt, with their cargoes and crews, from capture as prize of war."[71] This rule applies so long as such vessels refrain from military activities.[72] The protection afforded to fishing vessels ceases to apply if they are operating for a "war like purpose," or if they give aid or information to the enemy.[73] The decision reinforces the principle of distinction to protect civilians and ameliorate the effects of warfare upon them.

In its 1996 advisory opinion on nuclear weapons, the International Court of Justice identified distinction as one of two "cardinal principles" constituting "the fabric of humanitarian law":

> The first [principle] is aimed at the protection of the civilian population and civilian objects and establishes the distinction between combatants and non-combatants; States must never make civilians the object of attack and must consequently never use weapons that are incapable of distinguishing between civilian and military targets.[74]

To better protect coastal fishing vessels, there is an obligation on parties to Hague XI not to misuse coastal fishing vessels so that they are not inadvertently targeted during an armed conflict. Specifically, contracting parties "agree not to take advantage of the harmless character of the said vessels in order to use them for military purposes while preserving their peaceful appearance."[75] Nonetheless, an otherwise protected fishing vessel becomes a legitimate military objective if by its "nature, location, purpose or use it makes

---

[69] *Id.*

[70] *Id.*

[71] *Id.* at 686.

[72] *Id.* at 708.

[73] *Id.*

[74] Legality of the Threat or Use of Nuclear Weapons, Advisory Opinion, 1996 I.C.J. 226, § 78 (July 8).

[75] Hague XI, *supra* note 63, art. 3.

an effective contribution to military action and whose total or partial destruction, capture or neutralization, in the circumstances ruling at the time,
offers a definite military advantage."[76]

If enemy fishing vessels fail to comply with Hague XI, they lose their
protected status. Such misuse would not necessarily amount to perfidy, but
it would increase the danger that an opposing belligerent might attack such
vessels on sight given their prior misuse. Moreover, once it is determined
that the vessel makes an effective contribution to the enemy's military action, it is immaterial in the law of targeting that the boat's crew is comprised
of civilian fishermen. Consequently, civilian vessels engaged in mine laying,
intelligence collection, and other actions that make such an "effective contribution" are subject to capture or attack.

Note that the protections afforded under international law apply only to
small coastal fishing vessels that are engaged in local coastal trade. Large,
deep-sea fishing vessels, like PAFMM fishing boats that operate far from
shore and on the high seas are treated like any other enemy merchant vessel.

3.3 Belligerent Service

Enemy merchant ships are civilian objects and therefore have a conditional
exemption from attack. The *San Remo Manual* accepts the following classes
of enemy shipping as having special protections:

a. hospital ships;
b. small craft used for coastal rescue operations and other medical
   transports;
c. vessels granted safe conduct by agreement between the belligerent
   parties including:
   i. cartel vessels, for example, vessels designated for and engaged in the
      transport of prisoners of war;
   ii. vessels engaged in humanitarian missions, including vessels car-
       rying supplies indispensable to the survival of the civilian popula-
       tion, and vessels engaged in relief actions and rescue operations;
d. vessels engaged in transporting cultural property under special
   protection;

[76] SAN REMO MANUAL, *supra* note 2, ¶ 40.

e. passenger vessels when engaged only in carrying civilian passengers;

f. vessels charged with religious, non-military scientific or philanthropic missions; vessels collecting scientific data of likely military applications are not protected;

g. small coastal fishing vessels and small boats engaged in local coastal trade, but they are subject to the regulations of a belligerent naval commander operating in the area and to inspection;

h. vessels designated or adapted exclusively for responding to pollution incidents in the marine environment;

i. vessels that have surrendered;

j. life rafts and lifeboats.[77]

These vessels retain their status as exempt from attack only if they are innocently employed in their normal role, submit to identification and inspection when required, and do not intentionally hamper the movement of combatants and obey orders to stop or move out of the way when required.[78]

Enemy merchant ships generally may be attacked only if by their conduct or operation they become a military objective.[79] Unlike in the law of armed conflict on land, however, public or private enemy property at sea, including merchant ships, is liable to capture and condemnation in court as prize.[80]

Enemy warships, naval auxiliaries, and military aircraft may be attacked and destroyed anywhere beyond the territory or territorial waters of neutral states.[81] Enemy merchant ships are civilian objects and therefore may be not be attacked.[82] They are, however, subject to capture anywhere beyond the territory or territorial waters of neutral states.[83] Captured enemy merchant ships may be condemned as prize after adjudication.[84] Merchant ships that have been captured may be destroyed without adjudication in case of military necessity when the capturing force is unable to escort the vessel into

---

[77] *Id.* ¶ 47.

[78] *Id.* ¶ 48.

[79] *Id.* ¶ 59.

[80] *See* ANNOTATED SUPPLEMENT TO THE COMMANDER'S HANDBOOK ON THE LAW OF NAVAL OPERATIONS § 8.2.2.1, *reprinted in* 73 INTERNATIONAL LAW STUDIES 408 (1999); Robert W. Tucker, 50 INTERNATIONAL LAW STUDIES 74–75 (1955); NWIP 10–2, *supra* note 63, § 503b(l); TENTATIVE INSTRUCTIONS FOR THE NAVY OF THE UNITED STATES GOVERNING MARITIME AND AERIAL WARFARE, May 1941 § 67; INSTRUCTIONS FOR THE NAVY OF THE UNITED STATES GOVERNING MARITIME WARFARE, June 1917, § 62.

[81] NWIP 10–2, *supra* note 63, § 503a; NWP 1-14M, *supra* note 63, § 8.6.1.

[82] SAN REMO MANUAL, *supra* note 2, ¶¶ 13(i), 59.

[83] NWIP 10–2, *supra* note 63, § 503b; NWP 1-14M, *supra* note 63, § 8.6.2.1.

[84] SAN REMO MANUAL, *supra* note 2, ¶ 116.

port.[85] In such case, however, the safety of the passengers and crew must be provided for.[86]

Enemy merchant vessels may be attacked and destroyed, either with or without warning, for actively resisting the belligerent right of visit and search or capture as prize or for refusing to stop after being duly summoned; serving as a naval auxiliary or incorporated into the enemy's intelligence system; sailing under convoy of enemy warships; and carrying armament of which there is a reasonable belief that it is intended for offensive use against the enemy.[87] The officers and crew of captured enemy merchant ships and aircraft may be made prisoners of war.[88] Other enemy nationals on board captured enemy vessels are subject to the discipline of the captor.[89] The officers and crew who are nationals of a neutral state, however, normally are not made prisoners of war unless they participate in acts of resistance.[90]

Enemy merchant ships become military objectives and may be attacked outright in certain circumstances:

a. engaging in belligerent acts on behalf of the enemy, for example, laying mines, minesweeping, cutting undersea cables and pipelines, engaging in visit and search of neutral merchant vessels, or attacking other merchant vessels;

b. acting as an auxiliary to an enemy's armed forces, for example, carrying troops or replenishing warships;

c. being incorporated into or assisting the enemy's intelligence gathering system, for example, engaging in reconnaissance, early warning, surveillance, or command, control and communications missions;

d. sailing under convoy of enemy warships or military aircraft;

e. refusing an order to stop or actively resisting visit, search or capture;

f. being armed to an extent that they could inflict damage to a warship; this excludes light individual weapons for the defense of personnel, for example, against pirates, and purely deflective systems such as chaff; or

g. otherwise making an effective contribution to military action, for example, carrying military materials.[91]

---

[85] *Id.* ¶ 139.
[86] *Id.* ¶ 139(a).
[87] NWIP 10-2, *supra* note 63, § 503b(3); SAN REMO MANUAL, *supra* note 2, ¶ 60.
[88] SAN REMO MANUAL, *supra* note 2, ¶ 165(d).
[89] NWP 1-14M, *supra* note 63, § 8.6.2.1.
[90] NWIP 10-2, *supra* note 63, § 512.
[91] SAN REMO MANUAL, *supra* note 2, ¶ 60.

Russia, for example, uses fishing trawlers to gather intelligence.[92] The Russian fishing vessel *Kapitan Man* was searched in 1993 by U.S. officers, who discovered sonobuoys capable of tracking submarines and expendable bathythermographs on board the ship.[93] If such a vessel were tracking submarines during an armed conflict, it would be liable to immediate attack and destruction. There is ample historical precedent for placing merchant ships into the zone of conflict at sea.

3.3.1 First and Second World Wars

The Royal Naval Patrol Service (RNPS) was part of the Royal Navy from 1914 to 1919 and 1939 to 1945 to directly leverage Britain's large fishing fleet and experienced seamen in the war effort. Consisting of all manner of rust-stained, coal-burning fishing trawlers, herring drifters, and whalers, it grew to a force of 6,000 weather-beaten vessels and 66,000 men during the Second World War.[94] The Patrol Service engaged in minesweeping and protection of the fishing flotilla. They operated to safeguard convoys in the Atlantic Ocean from the United States and in the Arctic Ocean bound for Murmansk and Archangel.[95] The ships also patrolled along the east coast of the United States, the Mediterranean Sea, off the coast of Africa, the Indian Ocean, and the Far East.[96] The vessels evacuated troops from Dunkirk and supported the invasion on D-Day.[97] A single herring boat, *Fisher Boy*, ferried 1,350 troops from the beaches and waters of Dunkirk and brought them safely to Britain.[98] The Dunkirk evacuation was aided by a menagerie of craft, from yachts to paddlewheel steamers and rusty cargo ships. In another action two weeks later on June 17, 1940, *Cambridgeshire*, with a crew of 16 men on board, saved 1,009 shipwrecked soldiers from the 16,000-ton troopship *Lancastria* that was sunk by German bombers.[99] In another action off Scotland, three patrolling trawlers, the *Arab*, *Gaul*, and *Stoke City*, banged away with depth charges at a U-boat hiding on the seabed until the boat broke up, evidenced by debris floating to the surface.[100] In another engagement, two trawlers operating in

---

[92] DoD Law of War Manual, *supra* note 58, § 15.14.2.1; NWIP 10-2, *supra* note 63, § 501.

[93] *Russian Merchant Ships Used in Spying*, Washington Times (online), Nov. 6, 2000.

[94] Paul Lund & Harry Ludlam, Trawlers Go to War 10 (1971).

[95] *Id.* at 9, 178.

[96] *Id.* at 9.

[97] *Id.* at 54–64, 227.

[98] *Id.* at 65.

[99] *Id.* at 66–67.

[100] *Id.* at 31.

tandem with a small destroyer ran a U-boat aground on the South Goodwin Sands.[101] The ships were part of the war effort, armed with Lewis guns, depth charges, and mines.[102] They faced attacks by enemy warplanes, warships, U-boats, fast-attack E-boats, mines, and monstrous storms. The RNPS lost more vessels than any other branch of the Royal Navy.[103]

During the war, the French also armed trawlers—three escaped across the channel and were armed with 100mm and antiaircraft guns.[104] These vessels carried on the fight with mixed French and British crews after the fall of France.

3.3.2 Vietnam War
North Vietnam made extensive use of civilian fishing vessels in the Vietnam War, using them to send supplies and forces into South Vietnam. These vessels, which ranged in size from small junks and sampans to large, self-pro-pelled barges, were dubbed "waterborne logistic craft" by the Americans— shortened to WBLCs and pronounced "WEE-bliks."[105] North Vietnam also used fishing vessels to report the position of U.S. warships in the Gulf of Tonkin.

The use of civilian fishing vessels as intelligence platforms and military transports made them military objects, subject to attack. In 1966, the United States initiated Operation Sea Dragon to interdict WBLCs on their north-to-south voyage. Destroyers were assigned to stations, disabling, boarding, and destroying logistics craft and hitting targets on the beach with naval gunfire. In its first year, Sea Dragon destroyed 382 WBLCs, damaged another 325, and struck shore batteries and radar sites along the coast. Sea Dragon also hampered the movement of forces and supplies into the South and forced lo-gistics movements back into the congested land routes and inland waterways, where they were subject to attack from the air.

One of the most remarkable occasions involving WBLCs was instru-mental in bringing the United States into the war. In September 1964, North Vietnam used its fishing vessels to report the position of U.S. warships in the Gulf of Tonkin. A declassified National Security Agency report of the

---

[101] *Id.*
[102] *Id.* at 10.
[103] *Id.*
[104] *Id.* at 75.
[105] THE VIETNAM WAR: AFTER ACTION REPORTS, LESSONS LEARNED DOCUMENTS, BATTLE ASSESSMENTS 49–52 (2009).

incident notes that a message was sent from "an unidentified vessel to an un-identified shore-based shipping net control station" while the *USS Maddox* passed two fishing vessels at 2,000 yards.[106] Soon thereafter the *Maddox* engaged in a naval battle with three North Vietnamese gunboats. The ensuing naval battle, the "Gulf of Tonkin Incident," resulted in a congressional resolution championed by President Lyndon Johnson authorizing American entry into the Vietnam War.[107] The Gulf of Tonkin resolution later was criticized as the "blank check" that opened the door to a decade of U.S. combat operations in Indochina.[108]

3.3.3 Falklands War

Civilian vessels were also used by both sides during the Falkland War. The Royal Navy utilized SS *Atlantic Conveyor*, a container cargo ship, as an air-craft carrier to ferry 20 Royal Air Force Harrier jets into the warzone. The ship was struck by two Exocet missiles and abandoned.[109] Britain also converted the 45,000-ton liner *Canberra* into a hospital ship and the 67,000-ton *Queen Elizabeth 2* as a troopship. The *Irishman* and *Yorkshireman*, both 690-ton tugboats, were the smallest civilian vessels to support the Royal Navy during the conflict.

These ships had a mixture of civilian crews and Royal Navy detachments. Altogether, Argentina damaged 49 British merchant vessels supporting the Royal Navy during the conflict. Likewise, the Royal Navy bombed and strafed the Argentine fishing trawler ARA *Narwhal*, which was shadowing British naval movements and passing electronic intelligence to Argentine forces. The *Narwhal* was captured by British forces and sank from damage incurred in the attack.

3.3.4 China's Maritime Militia

In recent time, no state has utilized merchant ships for naval purposes as extensively as China. The People's Liberation Army-Navy (PLAN) and PAFMM are improving interoperability to support combat missions during

---

[106] National Security Agency, Role of the Desoto Patrol 118 (1964).

[107] Gulf of Tonkin Resolution, Pub. L. No. 88-408, 78 Stat. 384 (1964) (repealed 1971).

[108] *U.S. Reaction to Events in the Gulf of Tonkin, August 1-10, in* 1 Foreign Relations of the United States, 1964-1968, Vietnam, 1964, at 589-664 (Edward C. Keefer & Charles S. Sampson eds., 1992); *The Gulf of Tonkin, the 1964 Incidents: Hearing before the S. Comm. on Foreign Relations*, 90th Cong. (1968) (Statement of Robert S. McNamara, Secretary of Defense).

[109] Drew Middleton, *British Merchant Vessels Are Playing Vital Role in Support of Combat Fleet*, N.Y. Times, May 28, 1982, at A8; Drew Middleton, *In Falkland Fighting, Harrier Jump-Jets and Exocet Missiles Won New Regards*, N.Y. Times, June 19, 1982, at 4.

armed conflict, even though most PAFMM boats are indistinguishable from purely civilian Chinese fishing boats.[110] This distributed network, estimated to number as many as 20,000 vessels and hundreds of thousands of militia, constitutes a maritime reconnaissance complex that complicates force planning for a potential adversary.[111] In June 2012, He Jianbin, the chief of the state-run Baosha Fishing Corporation in Hainan province, explained:

If we put 5,000 Chinese fishing ships in the South China Sea, there will be 100,000 fishermen. . . . And if we make all of them militiamen, give them weapons, we will have a military force stronger than all the combined forces of all the countries in the South China Sea. . . . Every year, between May and August, when fishing activities are in recess, we should train these fishermen/militiamen to gain skills in fishing, production and military operations, making them a reserve force on the sea, and using them to solve our South Sea problems.[112]

The most capable units of the PAFMM are prepared to wage a guerilla style "people's war at sea," armed with sea mines and antiaircraft artillery and missiles.[113] The supplemental civilian force "allows China to 'flood the zone' with activity, confusing and complicating opponents' intelligence collection and targeting capacity."[114] The PAFMM ships are also used to conduct intelligence, surveillance, and reconnaissance (ISR) and potentially relay data to facilitate the PLAN kill chain.[115] Massing large numbers of civilian ships may mask PLAN operations and divert attention from the main effort. During the 2009 harassment of the USNS Impeccable, for example, the PLAN was conducting naval exercises in the South China Sea when two fishing trawlers engaged in unsafe maneuvers, interfering with Impeccable's lawful military survey activities.[116]

[110] OFFICE OF THE SECRETARY OF DEFENSE, MILITARY AND SECURITY DEVELOPMENTS INVOLVING THE PEOPLE'S REPUBLIC OF CHINA 2020 69–72 (2020) [DoD CHINA REPORT 2020]; Interview by Yoshinari Kurose with Randall Schriver, Assistant Secretary of Defense, Not Much Distinction Between China's Navy and Militia Fishing Boats, JAPAN-FORWARD.COM (online), Dec. 13, 2018.
[111] James Kraska, China's Maritime Militia Vessels May Be Military Objectives During Armed Conflict, THE DIPLOMAT (online), July 7, 2020.
[112] Miles Yu, Inside China: Armed Fishermen, WASHINGTON TIMES (online), July 18, 2012.
[113] Edward Wong, Chinese Civilian Boats Roil Disputed Waters, N.Y. TIMES, Oct. 5, 2010, at A6.
[114] Dennis J. Blasko, Chinese Strategic Thinking: People's War in the 21st Century, 10 CHINA BRIEF 5 (Mar. 18, 2010).
[115] Andrew S. Erickson & Conor M. Kenned, Meet the Chinese Maritime Militia Waging a "People's War at Sea," WALL STREET JOURNAL (online), Mar. 30, 2015.
[116] DoD CHINA REPORT 2020, supra note 110, at 71.

Given its training, equipment, aggressive peacetime posture and operations, and integration with the PLAN, the PAFMM is likely to be a core element of Chinese naval power during armed conflict. China's maritime militia apparently participated in armed conflict during the 1974 seizure of the Western Paracel Islands from South Vietnam.[117] At that time, the islands were unoccupied but hosted periodic rotations of soldiers from South Vietnam. On January 15, 1974, South Vietnamese warships encountered armed Chinese fishing vessels near the islands and ordered them to leave. The Chinese ships began aggressive maneuvers, including directing guns at the South Vietnamese ships and cutting in front of the bows of the four ships comprising the Paracels Task Group.[118] A Chinese landing force captured Robert Island and Duncan Island. South Vietnamese forces unsuccessfully tried to dislodge Chinese forces on January 19. During the engagement nearly every Chinese and South Vietnamese warship was damaged by naval gunfire.

The U.S. Seventh Fleet reported to South Vietnam that a Chinese formation of 17 ships, including four submarines, was advancing from the northeast.[119] On January 20, a Chinese force of six companies (about 500 men) disembarked from fishing trawlers and landed on the four largest islands (Pattle, Robert, Duncan, and Drummond). Supported by MiG-21 and MiG-23 jet fighters, Chinese forces captured the islands.[120] They detained 47 South Vietnamese soldiers (and one accompanying American) on Pattle Island, releasing them to the Red Cross in subsequent weeks. In all, South Vietnam sank one ship and damaged three more, losing 74 men killed in action and 48 captured. Four Chinese ships were damaged, one went aground, and 18 Chinese soldiers were killed and 64 wounded.[121]

Distracted by Watergate and winding down its role in Vietnam, the United States did not protest the seizure of the Paracel Islands. Beijing learned that using fishing vessels to conduct the invasion was less likely to bring the United States into the conflict, even when a U.S. ally was threatened.[122] At the

---

[117] *See* Ho van Ky-Thoai, *Naval Battle of the Paracels, in* VOICES FROM THE SECOND REPUBLIC OF SOUTH VIETNAM (1967–1975) 153 (K. W. Taylor ed., 2014); Toshi Yoshihara, *The 1974 Paracels Sea Battle,* 69 NAVAL WAR COLLEGE REVIEW 1, 6–8 (2016).

[118] Ky-Thoai, *supra* note 117, at 155.

[119] *Id.* at 157.

[120] David K. Simpler, *Saigon Says Chinese Control Islands, but Refuses to Admit Complete Defeat,* N.Y. TIMES, Jan. 21, 1974, at 2.

[121] Ky-Thoai, *supra* note 117, at 157.

[122] *U.S. Cautioned 7th Fleet to Shun Paracels Clash,* N.Y. TIMES, Jan. 22, 1974, at 3; Derek Grossman & Logan Ma, *A Short History of China's Fishing Militia and What It May Tell Us,* RAND CORPORATION (Apr. 6, 2020).

outset of any future conflict involving China, the maritime militia may replicate the model of the Battle of the Paracel Islands, employ coercive tactics, such as ramming vessels, to goad an adversary into striking back, while overwhelming CCG and PLAN forces wait over the horizon to rush to the scene and "teach a lesson."[123] This tactic exemplifies China's "Three Warfares" asymmetric strategy to use disorienting psychological warfare, media warfare, and legal warfare to circumvent traditional and especially Western notions of armed conflict.[124]

Some more specialized PAFMM vessels are designed or outfitted to facilitate PLAN operations. These frontline forces have weapons and ammunition stores and are integrated into the PLAN order of battle.[125] During armed conflict, the ships may be directly targeted as de facto naval auxiliaries based on their status and regardless of their conduct.

Vessels of this subtype are not warships but auxiliaries. Auxiliaries may be targeted during armed conflict, although only warships are entitled to conduct belligerent operations. Warships must belong to the armed forces of a state, bear marks of nationality, be under command of a commissioned naval officer, and manned by a crew subject to military discipline.[126] Even though naval auxiliaries may not lawfully conduct belligerent acts, they are always military objects and may be targeted during armed conflict even if unarmed.[127] The United States has warned China that it will not treat hostile acts committed by PAFMM fishing boats differently from those of the PLAN. In 2019, then Chief of Naval Operations Admiral John Richardson informed Chinese Vice-Admiral Shen Jinlong that the U.S. Navy would respond to belligerent acts by the PAFMM in the same way it would respond hostile acts by the PLAN.[128]

Discerning among the varying missions and categories of fishing boats requires adequate intelligence collection and analysis to evaluate the

---

[123] Bernard D. Cole, *The People's Liberation Army in 2020–30 Focused on Regional Issues*, in THE CHINESE PEOPLE'S LIBERATION ARMY IN 2025, 165, 193 (Roy Kamphausen & David Lai eds., 2015).

[124] DoD CHINA REPORT 2020, *supra* note 110, at 87, 155; STEFAN HALPER, CHINA: THE THREE WARFARES (2013); TIMOTHY A. WALTON, CHINA'S THREE WARFARES (2012).

[125] CONOR M. KENNEDY & ANDREW S. ERICKSON, CHINA'S THIRD SEA FORCE, THE PEOPLE'S ARMED FORCES MARITIME MILITIA: TETHERED TO THE PLA 10 (2017).

[126] Convention No. VII Relating to the Conversion of Merchant Ships into Warships, arts. 2–5, Oct 18, 1907, 205 Consol. T.S. 319; Convention on the High Seas, *supra* note 11, art. 8; UNCLOS, *supra* note 1, art. 29.

[127] W. J. Fenrick, *Legal Aspects of Targeting in the Law of Naval Warfare*, 29 CANADIAN YEARBOOK OF INTERNATIONAL LAW 238–82 (1992).

[128] Shirley Tay, *US Reportedly Warns China Over Hostile Non-Naval Vessels in South China Sea*, CNBC (online), Apr. 29, 2019.

PAFMM in terms of the law of naval warfare.[129] The use of small coastal fishing vessels as a maritime militia during armed conflict runs counter to the protected status such craft enjoy in customary international law.[130] Given that the central purpose of the principle of distinction is to protect civilians and ameliorate the effects of warfare upon them, China's maritime militia risks blurring beyond recognition the line between fishing vessels pursuing peacetime commerce and naval functions during war.

While the legal principle of inviolability of small coastal fishing vessels endures in the contemporary law of naval warfare, China's maritime militia poses a special set of quandaries. The fleet-support missions being undertaken by the PAFMM may make the fishing vessels lawful targets during armed conflict, with potentially tragic consequences for legitimate fishermen from China and nearby states. The customary rule in the *Paquette Habana* case exerts great pressure on the United States and its allies to give wide effect to the inviolable status of China's fishing vessels. The principle of distinction is afforded tangible weight in numerous historical precedents that have solidified into customary international law, and the norm is therefore binding on all states. American naval forces have a legal obligation to avoid the use of force against China's maritime militia so long as they are not integrated into the order of battle and are engaged solely in local trade and coastal fishing. Yet distinguishing between legitimate fishing vessels and maritime militia boats supporting the PLAN will be virtually impossible because of the large number of vessels, the vast expanse of ocean space, and the lack of sensors on the U.S. side. While the law has long removed the exemption of inviolability from fishing vessels that contribute to an adversary's war effort, the problem of distinction between legitimate civilian craft and those engaged in military support is challenging in practice. With the combination of advanced communications and electronics, including mounted radar and sonar, and extensive paramilitary training, the maritime militia effectively circumvents the meaning and intent of the law of naval warfare by making distinction virtually impossible.

During any conflict China, Beijing is almost certain to exploit as a force multiplier the thousands of fishing vessels engaged in paramilitary activities. These forces will serve as the "eyes and ears" of China's burgeoning naval fleet and land-based force structure, and augment PLAN operations and

---

[129] Kraska, *supra* note 111.
[130] Edward Wong, *Chinese Civilian Boats Roil Disputed Waters*, N.Y. TIMES, Oct. 5, 2010, at A6.

intelligence activities, including support to complement the warship "kill chain" from target acquisition to putting ordnance on target. The militia will form part of China's network of ISR, "hiding in plain sight." While China's naval forces operate within a broadly enhanced sensor network to more efficiently and accurately target U.S. assets, the American fleet would struggle against detection by an omnipresent paramilitary force throughout the battlespace. In order to avoid being overwhelmed by the sheer number and scope of the maritime militia, the U.S. Navy and allied and friendly forces in the region will have to hone tactics, techniques, and procedures (TTP) to address the new threat of a massive, distributed network of civilian fishing vessels that are equipped and ready to participate in hostilities.

These circumstances make it likely that vessels of the maritime militia that are destroyed in naval combat will be the centerpiece of political and public diplomacy efforts by China to undermine U.S. and allied resolve. Even non-kinetic responses, such as electronic jamming of fishing vessel transmissions, would be incorporated into China's propaganda campaign to attempt to generate sympathy, particularly among other states in East Asia.

3.3.5 Deception and Ruses

Ruses include camouflage, decoys, mock operations, and misinformation. Generally, ruses of war—acts intended to mislead the enemy or induce him to act recklessly—are permissible in naval warfare so long as they do not infringe on any rule of the law of armed conflict.[131] This rule is in contrast to land warfare, where the use of false flags and markings are not legitimate. Perfidy is forbidden.

During the First World War, for example, Count Felix von Luckner known as the Sea Devil, operated a three-masted windjammer named *Seeadler*, as an armed merchant raider.[132] Although the ship appeared to be a civilian sailing vessel, it was outfitted with a secret auxiliary engine and fitted with armament.

---

[131] U.S. Department of War, Instructions for the Government of Armies of the United States in the Field, General Orders No. 100, art. 15, Apr. 24, 1863; Convention No. II with Respect to the Laws and Customs of War on Land, art. 24, July 29, 1899, 32 Stat. 1803, T.S. No. 403; Regulations Respecting the Laws and Customs of War on Land, annexed to Convention No. IV Respecting the Laws and Customs of War on Land, arts. 37(2), 39(3), Oct. 18, 1907, 36 Stat. 2227, T.S. No. 539; SAN REMO MANUAL, *supra* note 2, ¶ 109, *et seq. See also* 1 CUSTOMARY INTERNATIONAL HUMANITARIAN LAW r. 57 (Ruses of War) (Jean-Marie Henckaerts & Louise Doswald-Beck eds., 2005); C. JOHN COLOMBOS, INTERNATIONAL LAW OF THE SEA § 520 (6th ed. 1967).

[132] Dieter Fleck, *Ruses of War and Prohibition of Perfidy*, 13 MILITARY LAW & LAW OF WAR REVIEW 269, 293 (1974); Wolff Heintschel von Heinegg, *The Law of Armed Conflict at Sea* § 17.18, 17.19, *in* THE HANDBOOK OF INTERNATIONAL HUMANITARIAN LAW (Dieter Fleck ed., 4th ed. 2021).

Posing as a British vessel or neutral trade ship flying the Norwegian flag, the *Seeadler* slipped through the unsuspecting British blockade and conducted a long cruise in the southern Atlantic Ocean and Pacific Ocean. When it got within range of enemy merchant ships through false signals of help or for information, such as by innocuously requesting a time signal, it raised the German flag and fired shots. The *Seeadler* captured 14 enemy ships.

Sailing under a false flag is permitted; firing under false colors, however, is perfidy and violates international law because it invites the confidence of the enemy to "lead them to believe that they are entitled to, or are obliged to accord, protection under the law of war, with intent to betray that confidence."[133]

The rules governing ruses or deception are also potentially affected by new technologies, especially at sea. Today, ships are identified through Automatic Identification System (AIS) or Long-Range Identification and Tracking (LRIT) systems pursuant to amendments to the Safety of Life at Sea Convention (SOLAS). These systems leverage the global positioning system (GPS). AIS is particularly vulnerable to hacking or misuse, and GPS and presumably LRIT, although more secure, are vulnerable to ruse or deception. The rule on ruses suggests that states may misrepresent their credentials or position in these systems.

4. Neutral Merchant Vessels

While enemy ships have enemy character and are subject to attack (in the case of warships and auxiliary vessels) and capture (in the case of merchant ships), ships from neutral states generally are exempt from attack or capture.[134]

4.1 Exempt from Attack

Generally, neutral ships and goods are inviolable. Merchant vessels flying the flag of neutral states may not be attacked unless they:

    a. are believed on reasonable grounds to be carrying contraband or breaching a blockade, and after prior warning they intentionally and

---

[133] DoD Law of War Manual, *supra* note 58, § 5.22.1.
[134] San Remo Manual, *supra* note 2, ¶ 67.

clearly refuse to stop, or intentionally and clearly resist visit, search or capture;

b. engage in belligerent acts on behalf of the enemy;

c. act as auxiliaries to the enemy's armed forces;

d. are incorporated into or assist the enemy's intelligence system;

e. sail under convoy of enemy warships or military aircraft; or

f. otherwise make an effective contribution to the enemy's military action, for example, by carrying military materials, and it is not feasible for the attacking forces to first place passengers and crew in a place of safety. Unless circumstances do not permit, they are to be given a warning, so that they can re-route, off-load, or take other precautions.[135]

Although neutral ships are exempt from attack, the right of freedom of navigation is subject to the belligerent right of visit and search.[136] A merchant ship flying the flag of an enemy is conclusive evidence of its enemy character, whereas a ship flying a neutral flag is prima facie evidence of its neutral character.[137] Belligerent warships are entitled to visit (board) and search neutral ships to confirm the enemy character of the ship, whether it carries contraband, is attempting to breach a blockade, or is otherwise rendering unneutral service to the enemy.[138] Neutral merchant ships have a legal obligation to submit to the right of visit and search by belligerent warships everywhere outside of neutral internal waters, archipelagic waters, or neutral territorial seas.[139] Neutral ships may be attacked if they resist a belligerent's right of visit and search to determine the enemy character of the ship or contraband nature of the cargo.[140] Neutral ships also may be attacked if they attempt to breach a blockade.[141] These exceptions to freedom of navigation and exclusive flag state jurisdiction exist only during armed conflict.[142]

---

[135] Id. ¶ 47.

[136] See Wolff Heintschel von Heinegg, Visit, Search, Diversion, and Capture in Naval Warfare: Part I, The Traditional Law, 29 CANADIAN YEARBOOK OF INTERNATIONAL LAW 283–328 (1991); Wolff Heintschel von Heinegg, Visit, Search, Diversion, and Capture in Naval Warfare: Part II, Developments since 1945, 30 CANADIAN YEARBOOK OF INTERNATIONAL LAW 89–136 (1992).

[137] SAN REMO MANUAL, supra note 2, ¶¶ 112–13.

[138] Id. ¶¶ 114–16.

[139] Id. ¶ 67(a).

[140] Id.

[141] Id.

[142] The corresponding exceptions to exclusive flag state jurisdiction that underlie the peacetime law of the sea are set forth in UNCLOS, supra note 1, art. 110, and articles 42 and 51 of the Charter of the United Nations. See James Kraska, Broken Taillight at Sea: The Peacetime International Law of Visit, Board, Search, And Seizure, 16 OCEAN & COASTAL LAW JOURNAL 1 (2010).

In short, the purpose of visit and search is to determine the enemy character of the ship or its cargo (contraband). The right of visit and search may be exercised anywhere outside neutral internal waters, archipelagic waters, or territorial seas.[143] Neutral merchant ships that carry contraband acquire enemy character and may not be attacked (unless they resist), but they may be captured and adjudicated in court as prize.[144]

Neutral ships may acquire the character of enemy merchant ships by operating directly under the control, orders, charter, direction, or employment of a belligerent force, or by resisting attempts to establish their identity, including the right of visit and search.[145] These vessels may not be targeted, unless through their conduct, they become military objectives.[146] They are nonetheless subject to capture anywhere outside neutral waters as lawful prize.[147]

Historically, visit and search entailed presentation of documentation to a boarding officer of certificate of registry; crew and passenger lists; logbook; bill of health; clearance; charter party, if any; invoices of cargo manifest and bills of lading; and a consular declaration certifying the innocence of the cargo.[148] A vessel on international sea-going voyages is required to carry some 50 to 70 documents and certifications, many of them easy to forge in their current form. In a future conflict, some or perhaps all of this voluminous shipping documentation may be electronically acquired without resort to a physical boarding of the ship. For example, if bills of lading and cargo manifests were available through blockchain verification, it may obviate the need for traditional visit, board, search, and seizure (VBSS) operations. Blockchain allows data to be shared with substantially improved trust and security. The Internet permits efficient connection, displacing fax or mail or physical inspection. All of the information that is on the Internet is available by some other means, such as books or newspapers. The electronic exchange of information begins to lose value when you cannot trust and guarantee the quality of the data. Blockchain offers greater levels of trust, making data more reliable and therefore more valuable. In the case of visit and search, distributed ledgers will reduce the need for physical visits of ships.

---

[143] SAN REMO MANUAL, *supra* note 2, ¶ 114.
[144] *Id.* ¶¶ 146–52.
[145] NWIP 10–2, *supra* note 63, § 501.
[146] SAN REMO MANUAL, *supra* note 2, ¶ 41; NWP 1–14M, *supra* note 63, § 8.2.5.
[147] SAN REMO MANUAL, *supra* note 2, ¶135.
[148] NWIP 10–2, *supra* note 63, § 502.

4.1.1 "Missile Merchants"

Neutral vessels may be attacked if they engage in belligerent acts on behalf of the enemy or if they operate as auxiliary components of a belligerent armed force.[149] For example, in 2010, Russia unveiled the covert "Klub K" missile system that could be placed in a standard 40-foot shipping container, potentially turning any neutral (or enemy) container ship or port into a cruise missile shooter, mobilizing civil ships for armed conflict.[150] At a cost of about $15 million, the satellite-guided missile is inexpensive and highly accurate.[151] There exist numerous variants of the Klub K, which was demonstrated in a 2012 test. In 2016, China debuted its YJ-18C container missile that has an estimated range of 1,000 miles.

Russia may not be the only state looking to merchant ships to fill a capability gap. U.S. planners have likewise considered converting merchant ships into missile barges to fill the shortage of U.S. warships—especially to increase the number of vertical launch system (VLS) missile tubes deployed at sea.[152] Nearby aircraft and warships could provide command and control, radar, and targeting data to complete the kill chain. The attractions are obvious—enormous cost savings while distributing missiles and sensors to confound enemy planning. A double hull cargo ship costs between $25 to $50 million, but vessels already in use can be had for as little as $1 million.[153] Missiles could be launched directly from shipping containers on deck, or the vessels could be outfitted with vertical launch tubes, like those on a destroyer, in as fast as three to six months. Spreading missiles throughout a converted merchant fleet of 10 to 15 cargo ships, each carrying 30 to 50 cruise missiles, limits the loss if a single ship were damaged or sunk in action, while significantly augmenting fleet firepower.[154]

The United States is studying such a concept that would distribute missiles throughout a fleet of merchant ships. A fleet of 15 to 20 merchant ships armed with missiles would cost the same as one destroyer, yet it would support 30

[149] SAN REMO MANUAL, *supra* note 2, ¶ 60(a).

[150] Michael Stott, *Deadly New Russian Cruise Missile Hides in Shipping Container*, REUTERS (online), Apr. 26, 2010; Thomas Harding, *A Cruise Missile in a Shipping Box on Sale to Rogue Bidders*, THE TELEGRAPH (online), Apr. 25, 2010.

[151] CONGRESSIONAL BUDGET OFFICE, NATIONAL CRUISE MISSILE DEFENSE: ISSUES AND ALTERNATIVES 15, 29 (Feb. 2021).

[152] R. Robinson Harris et al., *Converting Merchant Ships to Missile Ships for the Win*, PROCEEDINGS OF THE U.S. NAVAL INSTITUTE (online), Jan. 2019.

[153] Alex Hollings, *"Missile Barges" Could Be America's Secret Weapon in the Pacific*, SANDBOXX (online), Aug. 18, 2020.

[154] *Id.*

missiles per merchant ship, or 450 to 600 missiles versus just 90 on a single destroyer.[155] The merchant vessels would also present 15 to 20 targets for the enemy instead of just one. Missiles in the vertical launch system can be used for antiaircraft roles, anti-submarine warfare, strike, naval surface fire support, and ballistic missile defense. The modular merchant fleet puts many missiles into numerous "baskets" in contrast to the "arsenal ship" concept that concentrates weapons on a single platform.

Containerized weapon systems present a legal quandary. Under international law, merchant vessels flying the flag of a neutral state but may be attacked if they carry war matériel that makes an effective contribution to the enemy's military action, even where "it is not feasible for the attacking forces to first place passengers and crew in a place of safety."[156] Attacking forces must generally give warning prior to attacking neutral merchant vessels to enable them to "re-route, off-load, or take other precautions"—but only where circumstances permit doing so.[157] And, although it is true that "[t]he mere fact that a neutral merchant vessel is armed provides no grounds for attacking it," it is nevertheless also the case that "engag[ing] in belligerent acts on behalf of the enemy" may effectively transform a neutral merchant vessel into a military objective.[158] In short, under certain circumstances, belligerent forces may attack neutral merchant vessels without prior warning and without first placing passengers and crew in a place of safety.[159] This rule preceded the development of containerized weapon systems, and fails to contemplate a scenario wherein the passengers and crew of a neutral merchant vessel are unaware that they are carrying military materials, as might be the case with the Russian Klub-K. The missiles can not only be disguised in a standard shipping container but can also be controlled by satellite. Containerized weapon systems therefore expose a dangerous gap in the current international legal framework. Any neutral merchant vessel is now a potential military objective that may be attacked without warning and without first placing passengers and crew in a place of safety—even where passengers and crew are unaware that they carry the weapon. The Klub-K raises additional issues. Hague VII requires that merchant ships used for belligerent

[155] Brian Wang, *A Missile Container Navy Would Be Six Times More Cost Effective*, NEXT BIG FUTURE (online), Jan. 11, 2019.
[156] SAN REMO MANUAL, *supra* note 2, ¶ 67(f).
[157] *Id.*
[158] *Id.* ¶ 69; *but see id.* ¶ 67(b).
[159] *Id.* ¶ 67(f).

acts must first be converted into and properly designated as warships prior to use in belligerent acts. Also, if a Klub-K system is placed surreptitiously on a neutral commercial container ship, it would be inconsistent with the inviolability of the neutral flag state.

4.1.2 "Direct Part in Hostilities"

Neutral merchant vessels (and aircraft) acquire enemy character and may be treated as enemy warships (and military aircraft) when they take a direct part in hostilities or act in any capacity as a warship or naval auxiliary.[160] The rule against merchant ships taking a "direct part in hostilities" is related to, but different than, the rule in the law of armed conflict that civilians may be targeted "for such time" as they directly participate in hostilities (DPH).[161]

In land warfare, civilians who DPH lose their immunity from attack and if captured, may be subject to criminal prosecution and punishment under the domestic law of the detaining state. The term "direct participation in hostilities" is not defined in any treaty. Consequently, in 2009 the ICRC published an *Interpretative Guidance* that decodes the law of armed conflict "relating to the notion of direct participation in hostilities."[162] The ICRC guidance examines three questions: (1) Who is considered a civilian for the purposes of the principle of distinction?; (2) What conduct amounts to DPH?; and (3) What modalities govern the loss of protection against direct attack?[163]

---

[160] NWIP 10–2, *supra* note 63, § 501a1.

[161] AP I, *supra* note 45, arts. 51(3), 52; Geneva Convention (I) for the Amelioration of the Condition of the Wounded and Sick in Armed Forces in the Field art. 3, Aug. 12, 1949, 75 U.N.T.S. 31; Geneva Convention (II) for the Amelioration of the Condition of Wounded, Sick and Shipwrecked Members of Armed Forces at Sea, art. 3, Aug. 12, 1949, 75 U.N.T.S., 85; Geneva Convention (III) Relative to the Treatment of Prisoners of War, art. 3, Aug. 12, 1949, 75 U.N.T.S. 135; Geneva Convention (IV) Relative to the Protection of Civilian Persons in Time of War, art. 3, Aug. 12, 1949, 75 U.N.T.S. 287; Protocol (II) Additional to the Geneva Conventions of 12 August 1949 and Relating to the Protection of Victims of Non-International Armed Conflict, art. 13, Jun. 8, 1977, 1125 U.N.T.S. 609; ICRC Customary IHL, *supra* note 45, Vol. I Rules 1 and 6.

[162] NILS MELZER, INTERPRETIVE GUIDANCE ON THE NOTION OF DIRECT PARTICIPATION IN HOSTILITIES UNDER INTERNATIONAL HUMANITARIAN LAW (2009) [hereinafter DPH Guidance]. The DPH rule is broadly regarded as reflecting customary international law. *See* Michael J. Matheson, Deputy Legal Adviser, Department of State, *Remarks on the United States Position on the Relation of Customary International Law to the 1977 Protocols Additional to the 1949 Geneva Conventions at the Sixth Annual American Red Cross-Washington College of Law Conference on International Humanitarian Law (Jan. 22, 1987)*, 2 AMERICAN UNIVERSITY JOURNAL OF INTERNATIONAL LAW & POLICY 419, 426 (1987) ("We also support the principle that the civilian population not be used to shield military objectives or operations from attack, and that immunity not be extended to civilians who are taking part in hostilities. This corresponds to provisions in articles 51 and 52 [of AP I].").

[163] DPH Guidance, *supra* note 162.

The guidance reflects the views of the ICRC, not of states, and is therefore not legally binding.

While the concept of DPH provides a useful standard for protecting civilians on land, efforts to apply it to the law of naval warfare are misplaced. Targeting considerations in armed conflict at sea are platform-based: warships and naval auxiliaries are lawful military targets.[164] Once an enemy warship or naval auxiliary has been identified, it may be targeted without determining whether civilians are on board the vessel and trying to distinguish individually among them who is DPH. The law of naval warfare has a related concept under which neutral ships (or protected enemy merchant ships, such as coastal fishing vessels) that take a direct part in hostilities, lose their protected status and may be targeted. This rule is separate from the DPH rule of customary international law concerning members of the civilian population that have taken up arms, as reflected in Additional Protocol I.

The naval rule is reflected in the 1909 *London Declaration* and the 1913 *Oxford Manual*. The *London Declaration* states: "A neutral vessel will be condemned and, in a general way, receive the same treatment as would be applicable to her if she were an enemy merchant vessel: (1) if she takes a *direct part* in the hostilities; (2) if she is under the orders or control of an agent placed on board by the enemy Government; (3) if she is in the exclusive employment of the enemy Government."[165]

Enemy vessels and aircraft innocently employed in certain activities are exempt from attack, destruction, or capture: ships designated for or engaged in exchange of prisoners; properly designated hospital ships medical transports, and medical aircraft; vessels with scientific, philanthropic, or religious missions; vessels or aircraft guaranteed safe conduct by prior arrangement; vessels or aircraft exempt by proclamation, operation, order or directive; and small coastal (not deep-sea) fishing vessels in local coastal trade.[166]

---

[164] Declaration concerning the Laws of Naval War, art. 46, 208 Consol. T.S. 338 (1909) [hereinafter Declaration of London]; *See also* Institute of International Law, The Laws of Naval War Governing the Relations Between Belligerents, art. 60, Aug. 9, 1913 (Oxford Manual of Naval Warfare), *reprinted in* THE LAWS OF ARMED CONFLICTS 858–75 (Dietrich Schindler & Jiří Toman eds., 4th ed. 2004) ("When a public or a private ship has directly or indirectly taken part in the hostilities, the enemy may retain as prisoners of war the whole personnel of the ship, without prejudice to the penalties he might otherwise incur."). *See also* SAN REMO MANUAL, *supra* note 2, ¶ 65.

[165] NWP 1–14M, *supra* note 63, § 7.5.

[166] NWIP 10-2, *supra* note 63, § 503b(3).

4.2 Exempt from Capture

In addition to being exempt from attack, neutral merchant ships and aircraft are generally exempt from capture as well, unless they:

a. are believed on reasonable grounds to be carrying contraband or breaching a blockade, and after prior warning they intentionally and clearly refuse to stop, or intentionally and clearly resist visit, search or capture;

b. engage in belligerent acts on behalf of the enemy;

c. act as auxiliaries to the enemy's armed forces;

d. are incorporated into or assist the enemy's intelligence system;

e. sail under convoy of enemy warships or military aircraft; or

f. otherwise make an effective contribution to the enemy's military action, for example, by carrying military materials, and it is not feasible for the attacking forces to first place passengers and crew in a place of safety. Unless circumstances do not permit, they are to be given a warning, so that they can re-route, off-load, or take other precautions.[167]

Neutral merchant ships are liable to capture if they carry contraband for a belligerent party to a conflict; break or attempt to break, blockade; carry personnel in the military or public service of an enemy; transmit information in the interest of an enemy; avoid attempts to establish or clarify their identify, such as resistance to visit and search; are missing necessary papers or present irregular or fraudulent papers; or violate regulations established by the belligerent on-scene commander in the area of naval operations.[168]

The officers and crew of neutral merchant ships and aircraft who are nationals of a neutral state should not be made prisoners of war.[169] Enemy nationals, however, found on board neutral ships who are part of the enemy armed forces or employed in the public service of the enemy may be made prisoners of war.[170]

---

[167] San Remo Manual, *supra* note 2, at 154–61 (Rule 67).
[168] NWIP 10-2, *supra* note 63, § 503d.
[169] San Remo Manual, *supra* note 2, ¶ 166(c).
[170] NWIP 10-2, *supra* note 63, § 513.

4.3 Armed Neutral Ships

The fact that a neutral vessel is armed is not justification to attack it.[171] The 1909 Declaration of London codified the international law that passengers and crew aboard civilian (merchant) ships carrying contraband should be "placed in safety" before a ship is destroyed.[172] Historically, merchant vessels enjoyed the right to carry small arms for self-defense, but these weapons were not intended to resist belligerent warships' demands for visit and search or to otherwise engage in the conflict.

As a neutral state at the outset of the First World War, the United States pushed the boundaries of merchant ship armament. In 1914, President Wilson urged U.S. citizens to be neutral in thought and deed.[173] The U.S. Neutrality Board determined that neutral armed ships could carry "an armament and ammunition for the sole purpose of defense without acquiring the character of a ship of war."[174] The presence of armament created a rebuttable presumption that the ship was armed for offensive purposes, a presumption the owners could overcome by showing that the ship had guns less than six inches, that the weapons were not mounted forward on the vessel, that it carried limited ammunition, that the vessel plied regular trade routes, and that it carried commercial cargo. This policy deviated from the Dutch approach, which held that all armed vessels were treated as warships.[175]

Both Germany and the United Kingdom violated American neutral rights. U.S. neutrality was viewed as extreme, requiring that every American on board any merchant ship be removed to a place of safety. Great Britain's blockade of the continent interfered with American neutral rights to trade freely, whereas Germany's unrestricted submarine warfare against the British Isles sank both enemy and neutral ships without warning. The United States asserted the right of its citizens to travel safely on British armed merchant ships, unwilling to accept that Germany could sink the vessel without first ensuring the safety of the

---

[171] SAN REMO MANUAL, *supra* note 2, ¶ 69.

[172] Declaration of London, *supra* note 164, art. 50.

[173] Proclamation of Aug. 4, 1914, With Regard to the War Between Austria-Hungary and Serbia, *in* FOREIGN RELATIONS OF THE UNITED STATES SUPPLEMENT 547–51 (1914).

[174] Letter from the Acting Secretary of State to the Diplomatic Representatives of Belligerent States (Sept. 19, 1914), *in* FOREIGN RELATIONS OF THE UNITED STATES Supplement 611–12 (1914).

[175] *Correspondence with the Netherlands Government Respecting Defensively Armed British Merchant Vessels, reprinted in* 12 AMERICAN JOURNAL OF INTERNATIONAL LAW SUPPLEMENT: OFFICIAL DOCUMENTS 196, 196–203 (July 1918).

passengers and crew.[176] Under the cruiser rules of customary international law, Germany had a duty to remove and place into safety the passengers and crew of any enemy merchant ship. But the introduction of the submarine into the naval war upset this long-standing rule. Submarines had to surface to launch torpedoes, and with unarmored hulls, they were vulnerable to even the slightest surface fire. Unlike a surface warship, submarines also lacked the space to take on board a merchant crew and passengers before sinking their ship. This created an impasse as Germany adopted a strategy of unrestricted U-boat warfare and British merchant ships fought back against Germany submarines, with U.S. citizens caught in the middle. President Wilson protested numerous incidents in which Americans were killed while traveling on armed British-flagged ships or unarmed ships that resisted the German right of visit and search.[177]

On February 15, 1915, Germany notified the United States that Britain was arming British merchant ships to repel its submarines and had offered a high bounty for the first destruction of a German submarine by an English merchant ship. Because submarines on the surface were vulnerable to naval guns, Berlin warned, U-boats would have to strike first, in defiance of the cruiser rules. The British Government also admitted to the misuse of neutral flags. Accordingly, Germany could offer "no further assurance" of the safety of neutral ships in the war zone.[178] What followed was a series of German submarine strikes on merchant ships, sometimes killing Americans, including the sinking of the *Lusitania*, in which 128 Americans perished.[179] After Germany's vacillation between observing and then rejecting the cruiser rules, the United States was drawn into the war.[180]

---

[176] *President Woodrow Wilson's Letter to Senator Stone Announcing His Stand on Armed Liner Issue*, N.Y. TIMES, Feb. 25, 1916, at A1.

[177] CARLISLE, *supra* note 56, at 19–20.

[178] Letter from Ambassador Bernstorff to the Secretary of State (Feb. 15, 1915), *reprinted in* FOREIGN RELATIONS OF THE UNITED STATES 104–05 (Supplement 1915).

[179] *Submarine Raid Killed American; Leon Chester Thrasher, an Engineer, Lost on the Falaba, Admiralty Announces*, N.Y. TIMES, Mar. 31, 1915, at 1; Letter from Ambassador James W. Gerard to the Secretary of State (June 1, 1915), *reprinted in* FOREIGN RELATIONS OF THE UNITED STATES 439–40 (Supplement 1915); 1, *300 Die as Lusitania Goes to Bottom; 400 Americans on Board Torpedoed Ship*, N.Y. TRIBUNE, May 8, 1915, at 1; *Loss of the Lusitania Fills London with Horror and Utter Amazement*, N.Y. TIMES, May 8, 1915, at 1; Letter from Ambassador W. H. Page to the Secretary of State (Aug. 19, 1915), *reprinted in* 10 AMERICAN JOURNAL OF INTERNATIONAL LAW SUPPLEMENT 165 (1916); Letter from the German Ambassador to the Secretary of State (Sept. 1, 1915), *reprinted in* 10 AMERICAN JOURNAL OF INTERNATIONAL LAW SUPPLEMENT 166–67 (1916).

[180] *Breaking Diplomatic Relations and War Declarations*, 17 INTERNATIONAL LAW STUDIES 222–23 (1918).

3

Unmanned Maritime Systems

1. Introduction

This chapter explores unmanned systems (UxS), their projected missions and tasks during naval warfare, and the rules that apply to them during such conflicts. Numerous states are developing and experimenting with UxS, which are sometimes called "drones" and include unmanned surface vessels (USVs), various submersible unmanned underwater vehicles (UUVs), and unmanned aerial systems or vehicles (UAS/UAVs).[1] UAVs may be launched from land, ships, submarines, or even from containers on the seabed. These systems enhance survivable, persistent presence in high threat environments near an adversary's coast at lower cost and with decreased risk to human life, so they are becoming the preferred alternative to manned platforms for certain dull, dirty, or dangerous missions. Unmanned systems free the warfighter for more critical operations while increasing resilience, connectivity, and real-time awareness through distributed network nodes.[2] In future conflicts, robotic combat systems will be everywhere—on the land, in the air, at sea, and in outer space. A Chinese White Paper, for example, envisions a "multi-dimensional, multi-domain unmanned combat 'system of systems' on the battlefield."[3]

The United States, China, and Russia are developing larger and more sophisticated unmanned maritime systems (UMSs) that displace the role of traditional platforms—warships and submarines—for tedious or dangerous maritime security and naval warfare missions. This trend means that traditional platforms may play the role of a "mother ship" and exercise command and control of a vast network of UMS.

---

[1] DEPARTMENT OF THE NAVY, UNMANNED CAMPAIGN FRAMEWORK 2 (Mar. 16, 2021) [hereinafter UNMANNED CAMPAIGN FRAMEWORK].

[2] U.S. DEPARTMENT OF DEFENSE, PUBLICATION NO. 14-S-0553, UNMANNED SYSTEMS INTEGRATED ROADMAP: FY2013–2038, at 20 (2014) [hereinafter DoD INTEGRATED ROADMAP]; UNMANNED CAMPAIGN FRAMEWORK, *supra* note 1, at 10.

[3] ELSA B. KANIA, BATTLEFIELD SINGULARITY: ARTIFICIAL INTELLIGENCE, MILITARY REVOLUTION, AND CHINA'S FUTURE MILITARY POWER 22 (Nov. 2017).

For more than two decades, observers have predicted that unmanned systems would transform maritime operations.[4] In the United States, institutional resistance to unmanned systems has stymied their advancement.[5] The traditional U.S. fleet force architecture is constructed around small numbers of large, gold-plated, and technologically exquisite platforms that are too valuable to risk in combat. China, however, has built a multiplying menagerie of inexpensive but lethal missiles to target and destroy the small number of American trophy warships. In East Asia, for example, the U.S. Seventh Fleet operates a single aircraft carrier and 10 to 14 destroyers and cruisers at any one time, all vulnerable to Chinese anti-ship ballistic missiles. To overmatch this force (and without putting a single warship to sea), China fields 200 intermediate-range ballistic missile launchers and more than 200 missiles linked to a battle network of reconnaissance satellites that can conduct precision strikes against U.S. warships.[6] The only way out of this "numbers game" is to multiply assets, and unmanned platforms are the only feasible route for doing so.[7] The United States has to move from a platform-centric approach to a capability-centric approach.[8] Yet the United States has moved slowly toward that conclusion, although the unsustainable costs of manned platforms and the comparative advantages of autonomous systems are too evident to ignore. The MQ-9 Reaper (Predator B), for example, costs about $14.5 million, compared to $94.6 million for a manned F-35 Joint Strike Fighter, without considering the costs of training and maintaining the aircraft. China has cut costs even further by copying U.S. systems. China's CH-4B, for example, is a virtual clone of the U.S. drone, just as its J-20 fifth-generation fighter looks strikingly like the F-35.[9]

Advances in marine and information technologies raise expectations that a distributed force with some elements capable of operating with a level of

---

[4] James Kraska, *The Uninhabited Future of Military Operations*, 6 NATIONAL SECURITY STUDIES QUARTERLY 81–92 (1998).

[5] CHRISTIAN BROSE, THE KILL CHAIN: DEFENDING AMERICA IN THE FUTURE OF HIGH-TECH WARFARE 43 (2020) (Similarly, in an earlier era, U.S. Air Force General Curtis LeMay tried to stop missile development because it threatened manned aircraft); Tyler Rogoway, *The Alarming Case of the USAF's Mysteriously Missing Unmanned Combat Air Vehicles*, THE DRIVE (THE WAR ZONE) (online), June 9, 2016.

[6] DEPARTMENT OF DEFENSE, MILITARY AND SECURITY DEVELOPMENTS INVOLVING THE PEOPLE'S REPUBLIC OF CHINA 2020: ANNUAL REPORT TO CONGRESS vii (2020) [hereinafter DoD ANNUAL CHINA REPORT 2020].

[7] *Unmanned Assets to Play Growing Role in Great Powers Numbers Game*, WARSHIP TECHNOLOGY 5 (Oct. 2020).

[8] UNMANNED CAMPAIGN FRAMEWORK, *supra* note 1, at 24.

[9] BROSE, *supra* note 5, at 36.

autonomy will become commonplace. UxS are being integrated into the naval force structure with manned warships to form a hybrid fleet. The pervasive use of unmanned systems will accelerate in all domains as new technologies make them stealthier, more mobile, and more versatile. A naval force built around unmanned systems operating independently or tethered to warships offers greater survivability and distributed lethality.

Shifting to a more distributed force promises key advantages for the navies that make the transition. First, spreading sensors and weapons among greater numbers of platforms complicates an adversary's targeting by multiplying the number of enemy units to detect, identify, track, and engage. The distributed force increases the complexity that confronts an adversary in prioritizing targets, given the fixed number of weapons. Second, widely distributing the force reduces the aggregate loss from the destruction of a single platform. Third, the large number of deployed UAVs, USVs, and UUVs in armed conflict facilitates missions that are tactically advantageous but too risky for manned ships. Commanders are emboldened to press advantage. Fourth, a widely distributed force can help to increase the modularity and configurability of the fleet, accelerating adaptive change.[10] Fifth, the cost curve favors unmanned systems, which are orders of magnitude less expensive than exquisitely outfitted manned warships and submarines. Sixth, unmanned systems are smaller and easier to hide and therefore usually more difficult to find and target.

The deployment of unmanned systems requires development of new operational concepts, raises issues about their legal status and sovereign immunity, and requires consideration of the rights and duties that inure to such craft for navigation at sea, and belligerent rights under the law of naval warfare.[11] The legal status of UMSs is governed by the law of the flag state, customary international law, and is reflected in the instruments of the International Maritime Organization (IMO). The navigational rights and duties these systems enjoy in the ocean and airspace during peacetime are also reflected in the United Nations Convention on the Law of the Sea (UNCLOS) and the Convention on International Civil Aviation (Chicago Convention).[12] UxS

[10] KELLEY SAYLER, A WORLD OF PROLIFERATED DRONES: A TECHNOLOGY PRIMER 6–7 (2015) [hereinafter CNAS PRIMER].

[11] James Kraska, *Unmanned Naval Systems and International Law*, 5 JOURNAL OCEAN TECHNOLOGY 44–68 (2010); James Kraska, *Autonomous and Expendable Marine Instruments in U.S. and International Law*, 26 OCEAN DEVELOPMENT & INTERNATIONAL LAW 311–55 (1995).

[12] United Nations Convention on the Law of the Sea, Dec. 10, 1982, 1833 U.N.T.S. 397 [hereinafter UNCLOS]; Convention on International Civil Aviation, Dec. 7, 1944, 61 Stat. 1180, T.I.A.S. No. 1591, 15 U.N.T.S. 295 [hereinafter Chicago Convention].

that conduct belligerent operations are subject to the laws of naval warfare, especially as the systems acquire greater levels of autonomy. Lethal autonomous weapons systems or LAWS, which are the focus of Chapter 4, have generated international discussions under the auspices of the Convention on Certain Conventional Weapons on how (or whether) their operations can be consistent with the law of armed conflict (LOAC).

2. Legal Characterization and Status

The legal character of UxS determines the extent they enjoy navigational rights in the water and through the air and whether they have sovereign immunity as distinct sovereign immune platforms as opposed to merely enjoying sovereign immunity because they are government property or an appendage or extension of a manned platform. The Chicago Convention and instruments adopted by the International Civil Aviation Organization (ICAO) define the legal status of UAS. ICAO is the specialized UN agency for global governance of rules associated with the operation of aircraft. Military manuals reflect some evidence of state practice, and they also address UAS. These sources of international law generally treat UAS as "aircraft" in international law. The characterization and status of UMSs as "ships" or "vessels" under international law, however, is crystallizing into customary law. The member States of the International Maritime Organization (IMO) have not adopted instruments that specifically refer to unmanned systems as "vessels" or "ships," although state practice is unmistakably headed in that direction and the IMO has acknowledged (as will be discussed) that many of its instruments could apply to unmanned vessels.

2.1 Unmanned Aerial Systems (UAS)

Some 150 different military UAS, ranging in size from the Black Hornet, with the dimensions of a hummingbird, to the 15,000-pound RQ-4 Global Hawk, are in operation by 47 other countries. While UAS are scalable from very large to micro-sized, there is a convergence in which it is difficult to distinguish between those that are actual aircraft, and those that are mere sensors or weapons. By 2025, worldwide military UAS production will more than triple from $2.8 billion to $9.4 billion. The United States accounts for more than 50 percent of this figure, as well as over 77 percent of global spending for military UAS research, development, test, and evaluation (RDT&E). By 2035, over 70 percent of Department of Defense (DoD) aviation assets will be unmanned systems.[13] More than 90 countries and nonstate actors, including the Islamic State of Iraq and Syria (ISIS), operate unmanned systems in military exercises or combat.[14] Since the United States first used armed UAS in combat in 2001, 27 nations currently have weaponized unmanned aircraft. Azerbaijan, Iran, Iraq, Israel, Nigeria, Pakistan, Turkey, and the United Kingdom also have used armed UAS in combat.[15]

The U.S. Navy developed the first UAV to be launched and recovered from an aircraft carrier—the X-47. The aircraft was so effective at dropping its tailhook at the exact same spot on the flight deck that it damaged the deck and had to be programmed to land in different locations.[16] The U.S. Navy is also developing the MQ-25 Stingray as part of the Unmanned Carrier Aviation program for delivery to the fleet in FY 2024. The Stingray will embark as part of the carrier air wing to provide aerial refueling and intelligence, surveillance, and reconnaissance (ISR) capabilities to the carrier strike group.[17] In June 2021, an MQ-25 successfully refueled a manned F/A-18 Super Hornet, providing the fighter with over 325 pounds of fuel. Carrier-based F/A-18s are currently refueled by other F/A-18s. The historic test demonstrates the ability of a drone to take on these duties, thereby freeing up F/A-18s for combat missions.[18]

China's DR-8 supersonic drone is believed to play an important role in delivering targeting solutions to China's "carrier killer" anti-ship ballistic missiles.[19] China also developed the Gonji-11 or Sharp Sword, a stealthy, combat UAV with an internal weapons bay, which also looks like a copy of the X47B.

Many UxS will acquire autonomous traits and be teamed with manned systems. The American AI company Psibernetix created ALPHA, which employs "fuzzy logic" to navigate questions without empirical answers and

---

[13] Jon Walker, *Unmanned Aerial Vehicles (UAVs): Comparing the USA, Israel, and China*, EMERJ. COM (online), Feb. 3, 2019.

[14] CNAS PRIMER, *supra* note 10, at 5.

[15] *Id.*

[16] Walker, *supra* note 13; BROSE, *supra* note 5, at 15.

[17] DEPARTMENT OF DEFENSE, DoD PROGRAM ACQUISITION COST BY WEAPON SYSTEM 1–12 (Feb. 2020); UNMANNED CAMPAIGN FRAMEWORK, *supra* note 1, at 14.

[18] Caitlyn M. Kenney, *Navy Drone Refuels Fighter Jet, a Key Step Toward Adding UAVs to Carrier Wings*, DEFENSE ONE (online), June 7, 2021.

[19] BROSE, *supra* note 5, at 98.

suggest optimal outcomes. The system routinely beats highly trained human pilots in simulated aerial combat scenarios. The Chinese military UAV manufacturer Ziyan is developing the Blowfish A2 that can autonomously perform complex combat missions, such as fixed-point timing detection, fixed-range reconnaissance, and targeted precision strikes. The aircraft may be equipped with either missiles or machine guns.[20] Similarly, China's BZK-005 high-altitude long-endurance (HALE) UAV used for ISR has a high degree of autonomy, able to track targets and take off and land independently.[21] Another Chinese HALE UAV, Caihong-5 ("Rainbow," CH-5) combat drone, could have the capacity to combine with other UAVs for multi-drone swarms.[22]

2.1.1 Unmanned Aerial Systems Are "Aircraft"

UAS are regarded as "aircraft" in international law. The term "aircraft" is defined in Annex 1 of the Chicago Convention as "any machine that can derive support in the atmosphere from the reactions of the air other than the reactions of the air against the earth's surface."[23] The Chicago Convention also refers to pilotless aircraft:

> No aircraft capable of being flown without a pilot shall be flown without a pilot over the territory of a contracting State without special authorization by that State. . . . Each contracting State undertakes to ensure that the flight of such aircraft without a pilot in regions open to civil aircraft shall be so controlled as to obviate danger to civil aircraft.[24]

Unmanned aircraft systems are further defined in ICAO Circular 328 as "aircraft and its associated elements which are operated with no pilot on board."[25] The Chicago Convention does not contain a "manning" or "pilot-in-command" requirement for state aircraft, although a predecessor treaty, the 1919 Paris Convention, included such a requirement. Article 31 of the Paris Convention provided that "Every aircraft commanded by a person in

---

[20] Gregory C. Allen, Understanding China's AI Strategy: Clues to Chinese Strategic Thinking on Artificial Intelligence and National Security (2019).

[21] Kania, *supra* note 3, at 22.

[22] *Id.*

[23] Chicago Convention, *supra* note 12, § 1.1.

[24] *Id.* art. 8.

[25] ICAO Circular No. 328 (AN/190), Unmanned Aircraft Systems (UAS) (2011) [hereinafter ICAO Circ. 328].

military service detailed for the purpose shall be deemed to be a military aircraft."[26]

The Chicago Convention and ICAO rules apply to civil aircraft, not state aircraft.[27] State aircraft include "aircraft used in military, customs, and police services."[28] State aircraft are entitled to sovereign immunity and are not required to comply with normal ICAO flight procedures. The only requirement is that states that operate state aircraft, including UAS, with "due regard for the safety of navigation of civil aircraft." This standard of "due regard" means that states owe one another the consideration called for by the circumstances and by the nature of the rights that each has as against the other.[29]

The United States defines "military aircraft" to include both manned and unmanned aircraft.[30] DoD guidelines provide that ICAO flight information region (FIR) rules and procedures that apply to civil aircraft "do not apply as a matter of international law to State aircraft, including U.S. military aircraft."[31] As a matter of policy, U.S. military aircraft normally follow ICAO flight procedures when conducting routine point-to-point flights.[32] Some tactical military flights, however, do not lend themselves to ICAO procedures, and in such cases military aircraft do not adhere to ICAO rules and procedures and instead fly with due regard for other aircraft. Flights to support combat and military contingencies, classified missions, politically sensitive missions, routine aircraft carrier operations, and some training activities do not participate in ICAO FIR protocols established for commercial and civil aircraft. Instead, tactical military missions are conducted with "due regard for the safety of all other aircraft," a mode of navigation that is in accordance with the Chicago Convention for such aircraft.[33]

---

[26] Convention Relating to the Regulation of Aerial Navigation art. 31, Oct. 13, 1919, 11 L.N.T.S. 173.

[27] Chicago Convention, *supra* note 12, art. 3(a).

[28] *Id.* art. 3(b).

[29] *Id.* art. 3(d). *See also* The Permanent Court of Arbitration (PCA) Case No. 2011-03 in the matter of The Chagos Marine Protected Area Arbitration before an arbitral tribunal constituted under Annex VII to the 1982 United Nations Convention on the Law of the Sea between the Republic of Mauritius and the United Kingdom of Great Britain and Northern Ireland, Award of Mar. 18, 2015, at 519, 534–36; Ioannis Prezas, *Foreign Military Activities in the Exclusive Economic Zone: Remarks on the Applicability and Scope of the Reciprocal "Due Regard" Duties of Coastal and Third States*, 34 INTERNATIONAL JOURNAL OF MARINE & COASTAL LAW 97, 106–07 (2019).

[30] U.S. Department of Defense, Publication No. 4540.01, Instruction: Use of International Airspace by U.S. Military Aircraft and for Missile and Projectile Firings 11 (2015) [hereinafter DoDI 4540.01]; *see also* OFFICE OF THE GENERAL COUNSEL, U.S. DEPARTMENT OF DEFENSE, LAW OF WAR MANUAL § 14.3.3 (rev. ed., Dec. 2016) [hereinafter DoD LAW OF WAR MANUAL].

[31] DoDI 4540.01, *supra* note 30, at 3.

[32] *Id.* at 8.

[33] *Id.* at 9.

To fly with due regard, the aircraft commander, or a visual observer in communication with the aircraft commander, must maintain continuous and direct line-of-sight visual observation airspace surrounding the aircraft.[34] UAS must also be equipped with a Military Department-certified electronic system that is sufficient to provide separation between them and other aircraft.[35] This "Identification, Friend or Foe" (IFF) system is a command-and-control mechanism carried on board the aircraft to both transmit and interrogate other aircraft to recognize friendly aircraft.

Like their crewed or manned counterparts, UAS are aircraft in international law, entitled to the navigational rights recognized in UNCLOS and the Chicago Convention. Principally, this conclusion means that UAS may exercise the right of overflight beyond the territorial sea of any state, as well as the associated rights of transit passage and archipelagic sea lanes passage through straits used for international navigation and archipelagic sea lanes, respectively. Moreover, UAS must comply with rules applicable to manned flight, such as consideration of "due regard" for other aircraft.

2.2 Unmanned Maritime Systems (UMSs)

The U.S. Navy established Unmanned Undersea and Surface Development Squadrons, UUVRON 1 and SURFDEVRON 1 in 2017 and 2019, respectively. SURFDEVRON and UUVRON will provide rapid feedback to developers to help incorporate unmanned systems into the fleet.[36] UUVs and USVs will be used to augment manned platforms and perform high-priority missions, including inshore port and harbor defense, mine countermeasures (MCM) in contested waters, and penetration into denied ocean space for ISR, offensive mining, anti-submarine warfare (ASW), anti-surface warfare (ASuW), and Time Critical Strikes (TCS).[37] UMSs may be especially effective at neutralizing enemy submarines because a single UUV or USV may be dedicated to trailing individual adversary submarines.[38] The continuous

---

[34] *Id.*
[35] *Id.*
[36] UNMANNED CAMPAIGN FRAMEWORK, *supra* note 1, at 25.
[37] BRADLEY MARTIN ET. AL, ADVANCING AUTONOMOUS SYSTEMS 4 (2019); David Blagden, *What DARPA's Naval Drone Could Mean for the Balance of Power*, WAR ON THE ROCKS (online), July 2, 2015.
[38] *DARPA Hands Over ACTUV Sea Hunter for Further Development*, WARSHIP TECHNOLOGY 13, 15 (Mar. 2018).

trailing of each underwater contact over extended ranges would negate the principal advantage of underwater stealth and present a strategic advantage to the defense. USVs may also aid in maritime interdiction operations (MIO) to facilitate the belligerent right of visit and search.[39]

UMS include USVs and UUVs, and the greatest issue with medium and large variants of these platforms is whether they are "ships," and if so, can they be considered "warships" entitled to belligerent rights. UMSs can operate effectively in bad weather and low visibility, serving as a force multiplier for conventional warships. These qualities enable UMSs to perform a range of functions from ISR and mine sweeping to precision strikes. These missions can be accomplished at a reduced cost; with minimal risk to personnel; and with greater persistence, range, accuracy, and speed. While the transition to unmanned and autonomous systems is well underway, systems capable of reacting to unexpected changes in the operational environment are still in development.

2.2.1 Unmanned Surface Vehicles (USV)

Naval forces are moving to leverage the cost and operational advantages of UMS. Cost-effective USVs are on the horizon to augment the manned surface fleet, enhancing naval and joint warfighting capabilities in the full range of missions throughout the spectrum of naval conflict. These UxS are situated along a spectrum, from remotely piloted UAVs to human-supervised operations (Littoral Battlespace Sensing-Gliders) to human-machine teaming (MQ-25) to nearly full autonomy, like the Large USV *Sea Hunter*. The cost advantages are staggering. The *Sea Hunter* Large USV (LUSV) costs $20 million compared to $1.6 billion for an Arleigh Burke-class destroyer, and the operating costs for the unmanned platform are just $15–20,000 compared to $700,000 for the destroyer. A more-effective future-force architecture will form a battle network comprised of a smaller number of large, legacy crewed surface combatants (cruisers and destroyers) and an increased number of smaller crewed surface combatants (frigates and littoral combat ships), and a significantly greater number of UMSs of various sizes. Future LUSVs will be 200 to 300 feet in length and displace 1,000 tons or more.[40] USVs may

[39] Unmanned Campaign Framework, *supra* note 1, at 31; U.S. Department of the Navy, The Navy Unmanned Surface Vehicle (USV) Master Plan xi, 1–3 (2007).

[40] Congressional Research Service Publication No. R45757, Navy Large Unmanned Surface and Undersea Vehicles: Background and Issues for Congress 8 (2021) [hereinafter CRS Report Large USVs/UUVs]; Brose, *supra* note 5, at xxv.

become the most numerous vessels in the fleet. To put USVs into the fleet in large numbers, however, naval forces will have to develop concepts of operation that integrate them into the future force.[41]

The U.S. Navy seeks to develop large USVs that are capable of long-range, ocean operations. These ships would be equipped with vertical launch systems and other payloads. The U.S. Marine Corps is developing a Long-Range USV (LRUSV) to enhance maritime ISR and long-range precision fires support in support of sea control and sea denial.[42] By 2045, the U.S. Navy may include 382 to 446 manned ships and 119 to 166 LUSVs and Medium USVs (MUSVs), and 24 to 76 Extra Large Unmanned Underwater Vehicles (XLUUVs).

The U.S. Defense Advanced Research Projects Agency (DARPA) has set aside $41 million to work on a revolutionary new program called No Manning Required, Ship (NOMARS). The unmanned warships could operate autonomously or under remote human control for up to 12 months without maintenance. The program aims to design a ship without having to account for supporting or supplying a human crew, including a controlled atmosphere, food, water, and space.[43] By eliminating design considerations associated with a crew, NOMARS will optimize hydrodynamic efficiency, further reducing the costs of operation and enhancing stealth characteristics.[44] Eliminating the human element from ship design will also have other advantages, such as a smaller size, reduced procurement and operations footprint for sustainability, and greater endurance and survivability.[45]

2.2.2 Unmanned Underwater Vehicles (UUV)

Like USVs, UUVs and Autonomous Underwater Vehicles (AUVs) are force multipliers that can help maintain maritime superiority, enhancing the combat capabilities of friendly forces while dividing enemy forces.[46] UUVs

---

[41] Jordan Wolman, *Pacific Fleet Unmanned Exercise Expected to Contribute to New CONOPS*, INSIDE THE PENTAGON, May 3, 2021.

[42] UNMANNED CAMPAIGN FRAMEWORK, *supra* note 1, at 15.

[43] U.S. DEFENSE ADVANCED RESEARCH PROJECTS AGENCY, NO MANNING REQUIRED, SHIP (NOMARS) PROPOSERS DAY (DARPA) (online), Jan. 13, 2020; Gregory Avicola, No Manning Required Ship (NOMARS) (DARPA) (online), undated; Mallory Shelbourne, *DARPA Testing the Limits of Unmanned Ships in New NOMARS Program*, USNI NEWS (online), Oct. 27, 2020; UNMANNED CAMPAIGN FRAMEWORK, *supra* note 1, at 33.

[44] Shelbourne, *DARPA Testing the Limits of Unmanned Ships in New NOMARS Program*, *supra* note 43.

[45] *Id.*

[46] *Autonomous Systems "Can Help Sustain Undersea Advantage*," WARSHIP TECHNOLOGY 10, 12–13 (Oct. 2020).

are employed in situations "where they increase performance, lower cost, enable missions that cannot be performed by manned systems, or reduce the risk to manned systems."[47] UUVs will conduct high-priority missions, including ISR, MCM, ASW, ASuW, and TCS.[48]

Like their unmanned aircraft and surface naval counterparts, UUVs range in size from Man-Portable to Light-Weight Vehicle to Heavy-Weight Vehicle to Large Vehicle.[49] Boeing has developed the XLUUV, Orca. The Orca is 51-feet long and can travel underwater autonomously for up to 6,500 nautical miles, roughly the distance from Los Angeles to Seoul, South Korea.[50] A 34-foot payload module can be added to the submersible to enable it to "drop things out of the bottom or launch things out of the top."[51] Even with advanced sensors and weapons, the $55 million Orca costs just a fraction of the $3.2 billion for the Navy's Virginia-class manned submarine. While the capabilities between a Virginia-class submarine and an Orca are vast, the cost savings for the XLUUV are evident. In 2019, the U.S. Navy awarded a contract to Boeing to build, test, and deliver five Orcas—the first two by Fiscal Year 2023.[52] The Orca may be used for MCM, ASW, ASuW, EW, and TCS missions.[53] Initially, however, the Navy announced that Orca will most likely be used for offensive mining operations.

2.2.3 Naval Mines

Naval mines provide a "low-cost battlespace shaping and force protection capability," which can be used to "deny an enemy access to specific areas or channelize the enemy into specific areas."[54] During the Second World War, the U.S. Navy laid more than 12,000 mines in Japanese shipping lanes and harbor approaches, sinking 640 Japanese ships and disrupting their maritime shipping operations.[55] Orca could be used to lay mines in critical chokepoints

---

[47] U.S. DEPARTMENT OF THE NAVY, THE NAVY UNMANNED UNDERSEA VEHICLE (UUV) MASTER PLAN 5 (2004) [hereinafter NAVY UUV MASTER PLAN]; UNMANNED CAMPAIGN FRAMEWORK, *supra* note 1, at 33.

[48] UNMANNED CAMPAIGN FRAMEWORK, *supra* note 1, at 33.

[49] *Id.*

[50] BROSE, *supra* note 5, at 142–43.

[51] *Id.*

[52] CRS REPORT LARGE USVS/UUVS, *supra* note 40, at 16–18.

[53] *Id.* at 16; David Axe, *Here Come the Robot Submarines: Meet Boeing's 4 Huge Robotic Subs*, NATIONAL INTEREST (online), Mar. 11, 2019; UNMANNED CAMPAIGN FRAMEWORK, *supra* note 1, at 14–16.

[54] U.S. DEPARTMENT OF THE NAVY, FACT FILES, *U.S. Navy Mines* (online), Dec. 28, 2018 [hereinafter FACT FILES, *U.S. Navy Mines*]; BRYAN CLARK, ET AL., SUSTAINING THE UNDERSEA ADVANTAGE: DISRUPTING ANTI-SUBMARINE WARFARE USING AUTONOMOUS SYSTEMS 54 (2020).

[55] FACT FILES, *supra* note 54.

along the First Island Chain running from Japan through Taiwan and the Philippines, thereby restricting China's ability to project naval power into the Western Pacific. Orca could also lay mines in Chinese shipping lanes or harbor approaches to keep People's Liberation Army Navy vessels and submarines bottled up in port.

There are currently two types of naval mines in the U.S. inventory—the Quickstrike mine (Marks 62, 63, and 65) and the Submarine Launched Mobile Mine (SLMM) (Mark 67). The Quickstrike mines are converted general-purpose bombs. They are shallow-water, air-delivered mines that are not suitable for employment by an undersea platform like the Orca. The SLMM—a modified MK37 torpedo with a mine target detection device—is a submarine deployed mine that can be used in areas that are not accessible to other mine deployment techniques or for covert mining. SLMMs could be deployed by the Orca, "but given that they can be safely deployed from manned platforms at standoff range," they would likely not be deployed by the Orca.[56]

The U.S. Navy is developing new mines to enhance its mine-laying capabilities. The Clandestine Delivered Mine (CDM) is a small, standard bottom mine, 4.5 feet in length and 1.5 feet in diameter, which can be deployed in very shallow water or the surf zone. While the Orca is designed for deepwater mining it could be used in CDM operations.[57] Purpose-built for deployment from the Orca, the Hammerhead mine is a moored, encapsulated torpedo that includes sensors, a high-density energy module, and acoustic communications.[58] Hammerhead mines can be deployed to the seabed for weeks or months at a time and later remotely activated at the outbreak of hostilities to engage enemy shipping and submarines. A Hammerhead minefield could also be employed as an underwater wireless sensor network for distributed ISR or Distributed Maritime Operations.[59]

Naval mines are lawful weapons, but given their potential for indiscriminate effects, their use is regulated by international law, primarily to protect neutral shipping. Modern naval mines can be armed or detonated by physical contact, acoustic or magnetic signature, or sensitivity to changes in water pressure generated by passing

---

[56] Id.
[57] Hammerhead, Orca, SSGN, STRIKE SYSTEMS (online), June 1, 2021; Megan Eckstein, U.S. Naval Offensive Mining Updates Will Focus on Sub Community Tactics, Smart Mines, USNI NEWS (online), Nov. 5, 2019.
[58] Hammerhead, Orca, SSGN, supra note 57.
[59] Id.

vessels.[60] In general, naval mines are classified as armed or controllable mines. Armed mines can be deployed with safety devices withdrawn or can be armed following deployment to detonate if predetermined parameters are met. Controllable mines must be affirmatively activated by some form of arming order before they are considered armed.[61] The Hammerhead mine is a "controlled mine" given its acoustic communication capability, which allows the warhead to be remotely activated or deactivated.

To be lawful, mining during an armed conflict must comply with the following requirements, and the presence of a minefield in international waters containing armed mines should also be announced to the international community as soon as military exigencies allow:[62]

1. The presence of a minefield in international waters that contains armed mines must be announced to the international community as soon as military exigencies allow.
2. Mines may not be emplaced by belligerents in neutral waters.
3. Anchored mines must become harmless as soon as they break loose of their moorings.
4. Unanchored (free-floating) mines must become harmless within an hour after loss of affirmative control over them by the belligerent that laid them.
5. The location of minefields must be carefully recorded to ensure accurate notification and to facilitate subsequent removal and/or deactivation at the conclusion of the conflict.
6. Although naval mines may be used to channelize neutral shipping, they may not be used to deny transit passage of international straits or archipelagic sea lanes passage of archipelagic waters by neutral shipping.
7. Naval mines may not be emplaced off the enemy's coast or ports with the sole objective of intercepting commercial shipping, but they may be employed in a strategic blockade of the enemy's ports, coast, and waterways.
8. A belligerent may not mine areas of indefinite extent in international waters, but it may deploy naval mines to establish reasonably limited

[60] U.S. Navy, U.S. Marine Corps & U.S. Coast Guard, NWP 1-14M/MCTP 11-10B/COMDTPUB P5800.7A, The Commander's Handbook on the Law of Naval Operations § 9.2.1 (2017) [hereinafter NWP 1-14M]; DoD Law of War Manual, *supra* note 30, ¶ 13.11.1.
[61] NWP 1-14M, *supra* note 60, ¶ 9.2; DoD Law of War Manual, *supra* note 30, ¶ 13.11.3.2.
[62] NWP 1-14M, *supra* note 60, ¶ 9.2; DoD Law of War Manual, *supra* note 30, ¶ 13.11.3.2.

barred areas, provided neutral shipping has an alternate route around or through such an area with reasonable assurance of safety.[63]

3. Are Unmanned Maritime Vessels "Ships"?

There is not a bright-line test for whether UMS are "ships" or "vessels" under international law. Although "ship" and "vessel" are not defined in UNCLOS, it envisions the use of UMS in the marine environment. Article 19, for example, provides that ships engaged in innocent passage may not launch, land, or take on board any military device. Military devices include UAS and UMS. Similarly, Article 20 requires submarines and "underwater vehicles" to navigate on the surface and show their flag when transiting the territorial sea in innocent passage.[64] The term "underwater vehicles" includes UUVs.

The line between a "vessel" and a mere "device" is subjective. Some states purport to regulate gliders, floats, and other attached or free-navigating marine instruments. The Intergovernmental Oceanographic Commission has developed guidelines for Argo profiling floats that are not ships, which direct that "concerned coastal States" must be informed in advance, of any profiling floats that "might drift into waters under their jurisdiction."[65] In practical terms, this standard is often unworkable.

The oceans are becoming more crowded. The U.S. Navy envisions an "Ocean of Things" (OoT), a DARPA program that is the maritime analogue to the "Internet of Things" that raises some of the same questions concerning navigational rights of marine instruments. The OoT will arise from thousands of low-cost drifting floats and marine instruments to maintain persistent maritime domain awareness through a distributed sensor network over expansive ocean areas. Each drifter will contain sensors to collect data about the natural marine environment, as well as nearby human activity,

---

[63] NWP 1-14M, *supra* note 60, ¶ 9.2.3; DoD Law of War Manual, *supra* note 30, ¶ ¶ 13.11.3, 13.11.4; Convention (VIII) relative to the Laying of Automatic Submarine Contact Mines, arts. 1–3, 5, 36, Oct. 18, 1907, Stat. 2332, T.S. 541, 1 Bevans 669.

[64] UNCLOS, *supra* note 12, art. 20.

[65] IOC Circ. Ltr. No. 2271, Implementation of IOC Res. EC-XLI.4, Guidelines for the Implementation of Resolution XX-6 of the IOC Assembly Regarding the Deployment of Profiling Floats in the High Seas within the Framework of the Argo Programme (Dec. 8, 2008), Annex. For the Navy's analogue, the Ocean of Things, see Unmanned Campaign Framework, *supra* note 1, at 33; James Kraska, *Oceanographic and Naval Deployments of Autonomous and Expendable Marine Instruments in U.S. and International Law*, 26 Ocean Development & International Law 311, 337–38 (1995).

such as the movement of vessels and aircraft. The constellation of small floats operates as a distributed sensor network and will transmit data via satellite or acoustically through the water column. This data will be sent to a cloud network for storage and analysis, potentially for real-time application by the warfighter.

The OoT devices and sensors, like their civilian counterparts, are not "ships." If these autonomous or expendable marine instruments are released from a ship or aircraft, they retain the sovereign immune status of the platform of origin. If they are released from shore, they still enjoy the status of state property and remain protected by sovereign immunity. If such property is found by a seafarer or another state it should be returned. As § 3.9 of *the Commander's Handbook on the Law of Naval Operations* states:

> The property of a State lost at sea remains vested in that State until title is formally relinquished or abandoned. Aircraft wreckage, sunken vessels, practice torpedoes, test missiles, and target drones are among the types of U.S. Government property which may be the subject of recovery operations. Should such U.S. property be recovered at sea by foreign entities, it is U.S. policy to demand its immediate return.

The proliferation of objects in the water arises in a regulatory environment in which UNCLOS states ships should be manned by a crew and under the charge of a master. Flag states are required to take necessary measures to ensure safety at sea regarding their flag vessels, to include the "manning of ships ... and the training of crews, taking into account the applicable international instruments."[66] Such measures shall include those necessary to ensure, inter alia:

- that each ship is in the charge of a master and officers who possess appropriate qualifications, in particular in seamanship, navigation, communications, and marine engineering; and that the crew is appropriate in qualification and numbers for the type, size, machinery, and equipment of the ship; and
- that the master, officers and, to the extent appropriate, the crew are fully conversant with and required to observe the applicable international regulations concerning the safety of life at sea; the prevention of

---

[66] UNCLOS, *supra* note 12, art. 94.

collisions; the prevention, reduction, and control of marine pollution; and the maintenance of communications by radio.[67]

In taking these measures, the flag state "is required to conform to generally accepted international regulations, procedures, and practices and to take any steps which may be necessary to secure their observance."[68] Such standards are reflected in IMO instruments. There is nothing in UNCLOS, however, that specifically requires that the master or crew be physically present on board the ship. It is common for UAS to be remotely piloted by personnel that are, in some cases, on a different continent thousands of miles away.[69]

The UAVs used to conduct counterterrorism operations in the Middle East and Africa, for example, are operated by Air Force pilots sitting in a building at Creech Air Force Base, Nevada.[70] It is therefore conceivable that a UMS could be remotely operated by a crew and under control of a master that is shore-based, far removed from the area of operations, or embarked on a warship or naval auxiliary in the vicinity of the UMS.[71] There is nothing to prevent a flag state from ensuring that the master, officers, and crew that are remotely manning and operating a UMS are fully competent to observe the applicable international regulations in the Safety of Life at Sea Convention (SOLAS), Collision Regulations (COLREG), Marine Pollution Convention (MARPOL), and maintain radio communications. Furthermore, flag states have the right to set conditions for vessels that fly their flag.[72]

Regulation V/2 of SOLAS defines "ships" as "any ship, vessel or craft irrespective of type and purpose."[73] The Convention for the Prevention of Pollution from Ships (MARPOL) is a bit more precise, defining "ship" in article 2 as "a vessel of any type whatsoever operating in the marine environment and includes hydrofoil boats, air-cushion vehicles, submersibles,

---

[67] Id.

[68] Id.

[69] Ed Pilkington, Life as a Drone Operator: "Ever Step on Ants and Never Give it Another Thought?," THE GUARDIAN (online), Nov. 19, 2015.

[70] Andrew Craft, Drone Pilots Fight Foreign Wars from Remote Nevada Desert, FOX NEWS (online), June 20, 2018.

[71] UNCLOS, supra note 12, art. 94, uses the term "charge" of a master.

[72] The Muscat Dhows Case (Fr. v. Gr. Brit.), Hague Ct Rep. (Scott) 93, 96 (Perm. Ct. Arb. 1916) (every sovereign decides "to whom he will accord the right to fly his flag and to prescribe the rules governing such grants.")

[73] IMO Res. MSC.99(73), Adoption of Amendments to the International Convention for the Safety of Life at Sea, as amended (Dec. 5, 2000); International Convention for the Safety of Life at Sea, Nov. 1, 1974, 32 U.S.T. 47, T.I.A.S. 9700 [hereinafter SOLAS].

floating craft and fixed or floating platforms."[74] Similarly, Rule 3 of COLREG provides a more expanded definition of the term "vessel" to include "every description of water craft, including non-displacement craft, WIG (wing-in-ground) craft and seaplanes, used or capable of being used as a means of transportation on water."[75] A broader definition is found in the London Convention, which provides in article 1 that the term "vessels" means "waterborne . . . craft of any type whatsoever . . . [and] includes air-cushioned craft and floating craft, whether self-propelled or not."[76] Finally, article 1 of the Convention on the Suppression of Unlawful Acts Against the Safety of Maritime Navigation (SUA) defines a "ship" as "a vessel of any type whatsoever not permanently attached to the sea-bed, including dynamically supported craft, submersibles, or any other floating craft."[77]

The differences between manned platforms and UMS—such as the means of propulsion, type of platform, capabilities, durability, persistence, human versus autonomous control, and potential mission sets—are not essential characteristics of what constitutes a "vessel," "ship," or "craft." Accordingly, lacking a definitive statement to the contrary in an international instrument, most, if not all, UMS can be characterized as a "ship," "vessel," or "craft" under domestic and international law. This assumption is supported by the work of the Comité Maritime International (CMI), which has stated that:

> existing international conventions that define the term "ship" do not include references to crewing and at national level . . . the definition of a ship is usually disconnected from the question of whether or not the ship is manned. It would . . . seem unjustified that two ships, one manned and the other unmanned, doing similar tasks involving similar dangers would not be subject to the same rules that have been designed to address those dangers.[78]

[74] International Convention for the Prevention of Pollution from Ships, art. 2, Nov. 2, 1973, 12 I.L.M. 1319; Protocol of 1978 Relating to the International Convention for the Prevention of Pollution from Ships, Feb. 17, 1978, 17 I.L.M. 546.
[75] Convention on International Regulations for Preventing Collisions at Sea, r. 3, Oct. 20, 1972, 28 U.S.T. 3459, T.I.A.S. 8587 [hereinafter COLREG].
[76] Convention on the Prevention of Marine Pollution by Dumping of Wastes and Other Matter, art. 1, Dec. 29, 1972, 26 U.S.T. 2403, 1046 U.N.T.S. 120.
[77] IMO Doc. LEG/CONF. 15/21, Adoption of the Final Act and Any Instruments, Recommendations and Resolutions Resulting from the Work of the Conference, Protocol of 2005 to the Convention for the Suppression of Unlawful Acts Against the Safety of Maritime Navigation (Nov. 1, 2005) [hereinafter SUA Convention].
[78] Comité Maritime International, CMI International Working Group Position Paper on Unmanned Ships and the International Regulatory Framework 3 [hereinafter CMI Position Paper].

CMI also concluded that the requirements of article 94 of UNCLOS can "arguably be met in case of remotely operated ships."[79]

In 2017, states proposed at the IMO Maritime Safety Committee (MSC) that the relationship between maritime autonomous surface ships (MASS) and IMO instruments should be explored.[80] The member States of the IMO agreed at the MSC's 98th session to include the issue of autonomous UMS on its agenda.[81] At its 100th session in December 2018, the Committee adopted a framework for a regulatory scoping exercise for MASS operations.[82] For purposes of the scoping exercise, MASS is defined as "a ship which, to a varying degree, can operate independently of human interaction."[83] The degrees of autonomy considered by the Committee during the exercise included:

- *Ship with automated processes and decision support*: Seafarers are on board to operate and control shipboard systems and functions. Some operations may be automated.
- *Remotely controlled ship with seafarers on board*: The ship is controlled and operated from another location, but seafarers are on board to take control if necessary.
- *Remotely controlled ship without seafarers on board*: The ship is controlled and operated from another location. There are no seafarers on board.
- *Fully autonomous ship*: The operating system of the ship can make decisions and determine actions by itself.[84]

Subsequently, at its 101st session in June 2019, the MSC approved Interim guidelines for Maritime Autonomous Surface Ships (MASS) trials.[85] At its 103rd session in May 2021, the MSC approved the *Outcome of the Regulatory Scoping Exercise for the Use of Maritime Autonomous Surface Ships (MASS)*,

---

[79] *Id.* at 6.

[80] IMO Doc. 98/20/2, Maritime Autonomous Surface Ships: Proposal for a regulatory scoping exercise Submitted by Denmark, Estonia, Finland, Japan, the Netherlands, Norway, the Republic of Korea, the United Kingdom, and the United States (Feb. 27, 2017).

[81] IMO Doc. MSC 98/20/2, Maritime Autonomous Surface Ships Regulatory Scoping Exercise (MASS RSE) (Feb. 27, 2017).

[82] IMO Doc. Report of the Maritime Safety Committee on its One Hundredth Session, at annex 2, ¶ 1 (Dec. 7, 2018).

[83] *Id.* ¶ 3.

[84] *Id.* ¶ 4.

[85] IMO Doc. MSC.1/Circ.1604, Interim Guidelines for MASS Trials (June 14, 2019).

which assessed the degree to which existing IMO treaties and instruments under the purview of the MSC might be affected by MASS operations. For example, the Scoping Exercise determined that, depending on the degree of autonomy, many IMO instruments could apply to unmanned vessels through "equivalences" or interpretation, while others would require amendment of the instrument or development of a new instrument altogether.[86]

In support of this effort, the CMI Executive Council established an International Working Group to study the current international legal framework and consider what amendments, adaptions, or clarifications were required in relation to unmanned ships to ensure the operation of such vessels is consistent with international law. To this end, CMI developed a questionnaire for the IMO asking nations whether UMS are considered "ships" under their national laws. Of the 19 nations responding to the CMI questionnaire, 17 indicated that UMS could be a ship under their national laws.[87]

3.1 U.S. State Practice

In the United States, all policies and regulations of the relevant governmental authorities are taken into consideration during the initial planning stages of an unmanned systems program. New technologies are "tested for safety and verified by the appropriate regulatory authority."[88] The Navigation Safety Advisory Council, which was established by Congress "to advise the Secretary of Transportation, via the Commandant, U.S. Coast Guard, on matters relating to the prevention of collisions, ramming, and groundings," requires that UMS comply with the safety of navigation rules applicable to international and inland waters.[89] In addition, "UMS must comply with other rules and regulations, such as for RF communication equipment operation and environmental restrictions covering the operation of sonars and underwater acoustic instruments."[90]

---

[86] IMO Doc. MSC.99/WP.9, Regulatory Scoping Exercise for the Use of Maritime Autonomous Surface Ships (MASS); Report of the Working Group (May 23, 2018). *See also* IMO Doc. MSC/99/22, Report of the Maritime Safety Committee on its Ninety-Ninth Session (June 5, 2018); IMO Doc. MSC.1/Circ.1638, Outcome of the Regulatory Scoping Exercise for the Use of Maritime Autonomous Surface Ships (MASS) (3 June 2021).

[87] IMO Doc. MSC 99/20, Report of the Maritime Safety Committee on its Ninety-Ninth Session, at annex 1 (Feb. 13, 2018).

[88] DoD INTEGRATED ROADMAP, *supra* note 2, at 82.

[89] *Id. See also* COMDTINST M16672.2D (Navigation Rules).

[90] *Id.*

DoD requires that all UMS be tested to certify compliance with the applicable regulations and demonstrate safe operations. In this regard, UMS "must meet the same requirements of a manned craft or boat that is intended to be put into service."[91] The Naval Surface Warfare Center Carderock, Detachment Norfolk, "has developed a guide for testing UMS and drafted an approach to certifying UMS."[92]

UNCLOS also makes clear that domestic law rather than international law governs ship registration—"every State shall fix the conditions for the grant of its nationality to ships, for the registration of ships in its territory, and for the right to fly its flag," and provide documents to that effect.[93] The only additional international law obligation is that "there must exist a genuine link between the State and the ship."[94] In the United States, Chapter 46, Part 67, of the Code of Federal Regulations, governs the documentation of U.S. flagged vessels. For the purposes of registration, the term vessel "includes every description of water-craft or other contrivance capable of being used as a means of transportation on water but does not include aircraft."[95] "Any vessel of a least five net tons wholly owned by a citizen or citizens of the United States is eligible for documentation" in the United States.[96] The regulations make no distinction between manned and unmanned vessels. Therefore, unmanned vessels that meet the ownership and tonnage requirements can be documented in the United States.

American courts have a liberal notion of what constitutes a "ship" or a "vessel." "Vessels" are considered "transportation" that involves movement of people or things from one place to another. Yet the U.S. Supreme Court held in *Lozman v. City of Riviera Beach* that not everything that floats is a "vessel." "[A] washtub, a plastic dishpan, a swimming platform on pontoons, a large fishing net, a door taken off its hinges, or Pinocchio (when inside the whale) are not 'vessels,' even if they are 'artificial contrivance[s] capable of floating, moving under tow. . . .' "[97] In *Lozman*, a houseboat that floats but could not be navigated was not regarded as a "vessel" although the lack of propulsion was not dispositive.[98]

[91] *Id.* at 83.
[92] *Id.*
[93] UNCLOS, *supra* note 12, art. 91.
[94] *Id.*
[95] 46 C.F.R. § 67.3 (2020).
[96] 46 C.F.R. § 67.5 (2020).
[97] Lozman v. City of Riviera Beach, 568 U.S.115, 121 (2013). *See also* Maritime Law Association of the United States, Response of the Maritime Law Association to the Comité Maritime International Questionnaire re: Ship Nomenclature 6 (Dec. 20, 2017).
[98] Lozman v. City of Riviera Beach, *supra* note 97, at 121.

3.2 Can UMSs Be Warships?

Assuming a UMS qualifies as a "ship" or "vessel," the next question is whether such a craft employed in the naval service can be characterized as a "warship" as that term is defined in international law. This is a very important issue given that warships are the only vessels that can exercise belligerent rights—offensive attacks or the belligerent right of visit and search of neutral ships—under the law of naval warfare.[99]

UNCLOS defines "warship" as "a ship belonging to the armed forces of a state bearing the external marks distinguishing such ships of its nationality, under the command of an officer duly commissioned by the government of the state and whose name appears in the appropriate service list or its equivalent, and manned by a crew which is under regular armed forces discipline."[100] Although article 29 is qualified by the phrase "for the purposes of this Convention," the rule emerged from the 1907 Hague VII negotiations concerning the conversion of merchant ships into warships.[101] This rule is accepted as customary international law.[102] The U.S. Navy and DoD doctrine recognize this definition as authoritative—warships need not be armed but must be under the command of a duly commissioned officer and manned by a qualified crew subject to armed forces discipline.[103]

Certainly, a UMS can belong to the armed forces of a state and can bear external markings regarding its nationality. Is a UMS, however, capable of being "under the command" of a commissioned officer and "manned" by a crew subject to armed forces discipline? Since DoD classifies UAS as military aircraft, it must adopt a similar position regarding the status of UMS as warships if it expects them to enjoy belligerent rights. At the time of publication in early-2022, however, U.S. Navy doctrine regards military UMS engaged exclusively in government, noncommercial service as "sovereign immune craft," rather than "warships."[104]

[99] Paris Declaration Respecting Maritime Law, Apr. 16, 1856, *reprinted in* 46 BRITISH & FOREIGN STATE PAPERS 26–27 (1865); Convention No. VII Relating to the Conversion of Merchant Ships into Warships, Oct 18, 1907, 205 Consol. T.S. 319 [hereinafter Hague VII]; INTERNATIONAL INSTITUTE OF INTERNATIONAL LAW, MANUAL OF THE LAWS OF NAVAL WAR art. 12 (1913); NWP 1-14M, *supra* note 60, § 2.2.1.

[100] UNCLOS, *supra* note 12, art. 29.

[101] A. PEARCE HIGGINS, THE HAGUE PEACE CONFERENCES AND OTHER INTERNATIONAL CONFERENCES CONCERNING THE LAWS AND USAGES OF WAR: TEXTS OF CONVENTIONS WITH COMMENTARIES 316–20 (1909); Hague VII, *supra* note 99.

[102] C. JOHN COLOMBOS, INTERNATIONAL LAW OF THE SEA § 270 (6th ed. 1967).

[103] NWP 1-14M, *supra* note 60, § 2.2.1; DoD LAW OF WAR MANUAL, *supra* note 30, § 13.4.1.

[104] NWP 1-14M, *supra* note 60, § 2.3.6.

The definition of "warship" originated in 1907, at the dawn of the era of all-big-gun dreadnought battleships. Since then, the submarine and aircraft carrier have transformed naval warfare, and unmanned systems and autonomous ships are profoundly shaping contemporary conflict at sea. Hague VII, which governs the conversion of merchant ships to warships, requires that the converted merchant ship (1) be "placed under the direct authority, immediate control, and responsibility of the Power whose flag it flies"; (2) "bear the external marks which distinguish the warships of their nationality"; (3) be under the command of a duly commissioned officer in the service of the state whose "name must figure on the list of the officers of the fighting fleet"; and (4) be manned by a crew "subject to military discipline."[105] The drafters of Hague VII did not envision unmanned systems, and the definition should be re-examined and reinterpreted in light of current and emerging technologies. That said, there is nothing in UNCLOS or any other instrument that requires the commander and crew to be physically on board a warship. UAVs are remotely piloted and still qualify as a military aircraft; we take a similar position with UMS. UMS can be remotely manned by a crew and under the command of a commissioned officer that is not physically present on the platform. Given that UMS have similar characteristics of manned combatants, they can be considered "warships" in international law.

All UMS are not warships, however. As UMS mission sets expand to include offensive operations, states should adjust their policy concerning the status of UMS. Under current U.S. Navy doctrine, naval auxiliaries, merchant vessels, and presumably UMS are not warships and therefore may only defend themselves from enemy attacks—they may not engage in offensive combat operations in an international armed conflict.[106] Yet, one of the nine priority mission areas for UMS is TCS, which calls for the delivery of ordnance on a target from an UMS or UMS-delivered weapon cache.[107] Thus, state practice and doctrine have moved in advance of the law; the lawyers should catch up.

A UUV's stealth, long-standoff distance and endurance features allow for clandestine weapon delivery and remote launch, making the unmanned underwater vehicles the weapon platform of choice for many TCS missions.[108]

---

[105] Hague VII, *supra* note 99, arts. 1–4.
[106] These limitations do not apply to non-international armed conflicts. NWP 1-14M, *supra* note 60, § 2.2.1.
[107] NAVY UUV MASTER PLAN, *supra* note 47, p. 15.
[108] *Id.*

Underwater weapons caches or buoyant missile launch capsules delivered by an UUV can "loiter in place awaiting launch instructions, or the UUV itself could carry the weapons and loiter."[109] Legal purists might suggest that in order to lawfully execute this capability, the UUV must be designated as a warship. Instead, we conclude that UUVs, like torpedoes, may serve as weapons or launch weapons, but the designation of a "warship" provides greater clarity on its status as a sovereign immune vessel and reinforces belligerent rights.

In the United States, the Chief of Naval Operations (CNO) has authority to register, classify, and designate naval water-borne craft as warships.[110] Warship classification applies to any ship built or armed for naval combat that the service maintains on the Naval Vessel Register. In this regard, the CNO is responsible for entering vessels into the battle force ship inventory and the Naval Vessel Register. Battle force ships are commissioned as United States Ship (USS) warships capable of contributing to combat operations, which could include some UMS currently under development.[111] Neither U.S. Navy Regulations nor Secretary of the Navy Instructions distinguish between manned and unmanned vessels. Consequently, there is nothing that prohibits the CNO from designating a UMS as a warship so long as he or she complies with applicable fiscal law requirements,[112] and determines that the manning and command requirements can be satisfied remotely and that the UMS can be operated safely.

With the abolition of privateers, only warships that fulfill the elements of the definition in article 29 of UNCLOS are entitled to belligerent rights, which include enforcement of a blockade, capture of vessels in prize law, and attacks against the enemy. Among all vessels, only warships may exercise belligerent rights during an international armed conflict under the law of naval warfare. This limitation on the authority to exercise belligerent rights was reaffirmed in the 1907 Hague VII Convention, which governs the conversion of merchant ships to warships.[113] If a belligerent converts a merchant ship into a warship, it must place the vessel "under the direct authority, immediate

---

[109] *Id.* at 48.

[110] U.S. DEPARTMENT OF THE NAVY, UNITED STATES NAVY REGULATIONS art. 0406 (1990); 10 U.S.C. § 6011 (2018).

[111] U.S. DEPARTMENT OF THE NAVY, SECRETARY OF THE NAVY INSTRUCTION 5030.8C, GENERAL GUIDANCE FOR THE CLASSIFICATION OF NAVAL VESSELS AND BATTLE FORCE SHIP COUNTY PROCEDURES (2016) [hereinafter SECNAVINST 5030.8C].

[112] 10 U.S.C. §§ 231, 8667 (2018).

[113] Hague VII, *supra* note 99. The United States is not a party to Hague VII.

control, and responsibility" of the flag state.[114] Additionally, the converted merchant vessel shall bear "external marks" that distinguish nationality.[115] The converted vessel shall be placed "under the command of a duly commissioned officer in the service of the state whose name must figure on the list of the officers of the fighting fleet" and shall be "manned by a crew subject to military discipline."[116] If a merchant vessel is converted, the belligerent state must also publicly announce the conversion in the list of warships as soon as possible.[117]

Although the United States is not a party to either the Paris Declaration or the 1907 Hague VII Convention, U.S. practice confirms that only warships and military aircraft can exercise belligerent rights at sea.[118] The *Department of Defense Law of War Manual* and *Commander's Handbook on the Law of Naval Operations* reiterate that during international armed conflict at sea, warships are the only vessels that may exercise belligerent rights, which include the right to conduct offensive attacks.[119] Thus, naval auxiliaries and merchant vessels, as well as UMS that are otherwise considered vessels but have not been designated as "warships," may not conduct attacks during an international armed conflict. Such vessels may only defend themselves.

3.2.1 Sovereign Immunity

As a matter of customary international law, all manned and unmanned vessels and aircraft owned or operated by a state, and used, for the time being, only on government noncommercial service are entitled to sovereign immunity. Moreover, the sovereign immunity of a UMS is not dependent on the status of its launch platform, but rather is inherent in the craft itself.[120] Accordingly, military UAS and naval UMS, wherever located, are immune from arrest, search, inspection, and foreign taxation. Additionally, the flag state has the authority to protect the identity of stores, weapons, or other property on board the craft.[121]

---

[114] *Id.* art. 1.
[115] *Id.* art. 2.
[116] *Id.* arts. 3, 4.
[117] *Id.* art. 6.
[118] OFFICE OF THE CHIEF OF NAVAL OPERATIONS, U.S. NAVY, LAW OF NAVAL WARFARE, NAVAL WARFARE INFORMATION PUBLICATION (NWIP) 10-2 § 500 (1955), *reprinted in* 50 INTERNATIONAL LAW STUDIES 359 (1955).
[119] DoD LAW OF WAR MANUAL, *supra* note 30, § 13.3.3; NWP 1-14M, *supra* note 60, § 2.2.1.
[120] NWP 1-14M, *supra* note 60, § 2.3.6.
[121] *Id.* § 2.1.

The principle of sovereign immunity is reflected in various provisions of UNCLOS. Article 32, for example, specifies that nothing in the treaty "affects the immunities of warships and other government ships operated for non-commercial purposes."[122] Similarly, articles 95 and 96 make clear that warships and government owned or operated ships used only on government noncommercial service operating on the high seas have complete immunity from the jurisdiction of any state other than the flag state.[123] Article 58 applies the immunities described in articles 95 and 96 to the EEZ—"Articles 88 to 115 and other pertinent rules of international law apply to the exclusive economic zone. . . ."[124] Thus, regardless of whether a UMS is considered to be a warship, a government craft, or a vessel operated for noncommercial purposes, it is entitled to all the rights, privileges, and immunities enjoyed by such vessels under international law.

3.2.2 Remote Civilian Operators and Targeting

Both the 1907 Hague Regulations and the 1949 Third Geneva Convention acknowledge that civilians can support and accompany the armed forces in times of armed conflict.[125] Additional Protocol I (AP I), article 50, further recognizes that these individuals, although affiliated with the armed forces, are still considered to be "civilians" for purposes of targeting, and article 51 specifies that civilians "shall not be the object of attack."[126] The Fourth Geneva Convention, article 27, similarly provides that "protected persons . . . shall at all times be . . . protected . . . against all acts of violence."[127] Accordingly, as long as these civilians do not directly participate in hostilities, they are not subject to direct attack by the enemy.

Civilians lose their protected status under AP I, however, if they directly participate in the hostilities (DPH).[128] Consequently, civilian contractors or government employees who participate in the conduct of offensive strikes against military objectives are directly participating in hostilities and

---

[122] UNCLOS, *supra* note 12, art. 32.
[123] *Id.* arts. 95–96.
[124] *Id.* art. 58.
[125] Regulations Respecting the Laws and Customs of War on Land, annexed to Convention No. IV Respecting the Laws and Customs of War on Land, art. 13, Oct. 18, 1907, 36 Stat. 2227; Convention Relative to the Treatment of Prisoners of War, art. 4A(4), Aug. 12, 1949, 6 U.S.T. 3316, 75 U.N.T.S. 135, [hereinafter GC III].
[126] Protocol Additional to the Geneva Conventions of 12 August 1949, and Relating to the Protection of Victims of International Armed Conflicts, art. 51, June 8, 1977, 1125 U.N.T.S. 3, [hereinafter AP I].
[127] GC III, *supra* note 125, art. 27.
[128] AP I, *supra* note 126, art. 51.

can be lawfully targeted by the enemy. Nevertheless, neither the Geneva Conventions nor the Additional Protocol define DPH. To fill this gap, the International Committee of the Red Cross (ICRC) issued non-binding, albeit somewhat controversial, interpretive guidelines concerning DPH. The ICRC proposes constitutive elements of DPH.[129] In order to constitute DPH, an act must meet the following three criteria:[130]

- Threshold of Harm. An act likely to adversely affect the military operations or military capacity of a party to an armed conflict or to inflict death, injury, or destruction on protected persons or objects.
- Direct Causation. There must be a direct causal link between the act and the harm likely to result from that act or from a coordinated military operation of which that act constitutes an integral part.
- Belligerent Nexus. The act must be specifically designed to directly cause the required threshold of harm in support of a party to the conflict and to the detriment of another.

Conducting offensive strikes with unmanned systems qualifies as DPH.

Opponents to the use of unmanned systems to conduct strikes argue that civilian operators are unlawful combatants and may not participate in hostilities.[131] This view is contrary, however, to the majority opinion expressed by most LOAC scholars, that it is not a war crime for civilians to participate in hostilities, but if they do, they are not entitled to combatant immunity under domestic law for their belligerent acts.[132] The Human Rights Council confirmed the majority view in 2010 in a report from the Special Rapporteur for Extrajudicial, Summary or Arbitrary Executions. The report indicates that "civilians . . . are not prohibited from participating in hostilities," and that DPH is not a war crime, but there are consequences that flow from such participation.[133]

[129] INTERNATIONAL COMMITTEE OF THE RED CROSS, INTERPRETIVE GUIDANCE ON THE NOTION OF DIRECT PARTICIPATION IN HOSTILITIES UNDER INTERNATIONAL HUMANITARIAN LAW 46 (Nils Melzer ed., 2009).
[130] Id.
[131] Mary Ellen O'Connell, When Is a War Not a War? The Myth of the Global War on Terror, 12 ILSA JOURNAL OF INTERNATIONAL & COMPARATIVE LAW 4, 12, 13, 22, 24 (2005); Mary Ellen O'Connell, Drones and the Law: What We Know, INTLAWGRRLS BLOG (online), Dec. 7, 2009.
[132] Rise of the Drones: Unmanned Systems and the Future of War: Hearing Before the Subcomm. on National Security and Foreign Affairs of the H. Comm. on Oversight and Government Reform, 111th Cong. 11 (2010) (statement of David W. Glazier, Professor of Law, Loyola Law School Los Angeles).
[133] U.N. Doc. A/HRC/14/24/Add.6, Report of the Special Rapporteur on Extrajudicial, Summary or Arbitrary Executions, at addendum ¶¶ 70–73 (2010).

The United States avoids this issue by prohibiting DoD civilian employees and contractors from engaging in functions that are inherently governmental, including combat operations.[134] Pursuant to DoD guidelines, civilians may not participate in combat operations if the planned use of disruptive and/or destructive combat capabilities is an inherent part of the mission.[135] Combat operations include actively seeking out, closing with, and destroying enemy forces, including employment of firepower and other destructive and disruptive capabilities on the battlefield.[136] Consistent with this guidance, only U.S. military personnel may conduct offensive strikes with unmanned systems against enemy military objectives.

4. Navigational Rights and Freedoms

Unmanned systems are entitled to all the navigational rights and freedoms enjoyed by manned ships and aircraft. ICAO regulations provide that civilian UAS "will operate in accordance with ICAO Standards that exist for manned aircraft as well as any special and specific standards that address the operational, legal and safety differences between manned and unmanned aircraft operations."[137] However, if the UAS is going to integrate into nonsegregated airspace or at a nonsegregated aerodrome, a pilot must be responsible for the UAS operation, and "under no circumstances will the pilot responsibility be replaced by technologies in the foreseeable future."[138]

CMI suggests a similar approach for UMS. Assuming that UMS are "ships" or "vessels" within the meaning of UNCLOS, "they are subject to the same rules of the law of the sea as any ordinarily manned ship."[139] UMS and their flag states have an obligation to comply with the same international rules

---

[134] Federal Activities Inventory Reform Act of 1998, Pub. L. No. 105–270, 112 Stat. 2382 (1998); Office of Management & Budget, Circular No. A-76: Performance of Commercial Activities, Aug. 4, 1983 (rev. ed. 1999); Deputy Secretary of Defense, Department of Defense Directive 1100.4, Guidance for Manpower Management ¶ 3.2.3 (Feb. 12, 2005); Under Secretary of Defense for Personnel and Readiness, Department of Defense Instruction 1100.22, Policy and Procedures for Determining Workforce Mix ¶ 4.c, encl. 4 ¶ 1.c (Apr. 12, 2010) [hereinafter DoDI 1100.22]; Under Secretary of Defense for Acquisition, Technology and Logistics, Department of Defense Directive 3020.41, Contractor Personnel Authorized to Accompany the U.S. Armed Forces ¶ 6.1.5 (Oct. 3, 2005).

[135] DoDI 1100.22, *supra* note 134 encl. 4 ¶ 1.c.

[136] *Id.*

[137] ICAO Circ. 328, *supra* note 25, ¶ 3.1.

[138] *Id.*

[139] CMI Position Paper, *supra* note 78, at 3.

that apply to manned vessels, and "they also enjoy the same passage rights as other ships and cannot be refused access to other states' waters merely because they are not crewed."[140] In this regard, 70 percent of states responding to the previously mentioned CMI questionnaire indicated that unmanned ships would enjoy the same rights and duties as manned ships under UNCLOS.[141] Similarly, the U.S. Maritime Law Association stated that under U.S. law a "ship" is defined without regard to manning and that unmanned ships are probably subject to the same rights and obligations under the law of the sea.[142]

Accordingly, UMS may exercise the right of innocent passage in foreign territorial seas and archipelagic waters.[143] UMS also may be deployed from another military platform that is engaged in innocent passage as long as their employment is consistent with UNCLOS, article 19 (employment not prejudicial to the peace, good order or security of the coastal state) and article 20 (no submerged transit in innocent passage).[144] However, while USVs and UUVs enjoy the right of innocent passage there is no reciprocal right of innocent passage for UAS through national airspace. The Chicago Convention prohibits state aircraft from flying over the territory of another state without its consent or authorization by special agreement or otherwise, and "territory" is defined in the Convention to include the "territorial waters adjacent thereto"[145]

UAS and UMS likewise enjoy the right of unimpeded transit passage, in the normal mode (on the surface, in flight, or submerged), through straits used for international navigation between one part of the high seas or an exclusive economic zone (EEZ) and another part of the high seas or an EEZ, and their approaches.[146] Similarly, UAS and UMS may exercise the right of archipelagic sea lanes passage (ASLP), in the normal mode, while transiting through, under, or over archipelagic sea lanes, which include all routes normally used for international navigation and overflight.[147] Beyond the

[140] Id.
[141] IMO Doc. MSC 99/INF.8, *Work conducted by the CMI International Working Group on Unmanned Ships*, annex 1 (Feb. 13, 2018).
[142] Id.
[143] NWP 1-14M, *supra* note 60, § 2.5.2.5.
[144] Id.; UNCLOS, *supra* note 12, arts. 19–20.
[145] Chicago Convention, *supra* note 12, arts. 1–3.
[146] NWP 1-14M, *supra* note 60, §§ 2.5.3.2, 2.7.1.1; UNCLOS, *supra* note 12, art. 38; DoDI 4540.01, *supra* note 30, p. 2.
[147] NWP 1-14M, *supra* note 60, §§ 2.5.4.1, 2.7.1.2; UNCLOS, *supra* note 12, art. 53; DoDI 4540.01, *supra* note 30, p. 2.

territorial sea, UAS and UMS possess the full range of high seas freedoms of navigation and overflight, and other internationally lawful uses of the sea guaranteed to all ships and aircraft—manned or unmanned—by international law.[148]

4.1 Duties and Obligations

With these navigational rights and freedoms come corresponding duties and obligations that UAS and UMS must observe. First, concerning innocent passage of UMS, passage is considered prejudicial to the peace, good order, or security of the coastal state if a ship engages in one of any number of proscribed activities, including:

- using force (or threatening the use of force) against the sovereignty, territorial integrity or political independence of the coastal State, or in any other manner in violation of the principles of international law embodied in the UN Charter;
- exercising or practicing with weapons of any kind;
- collecting information to the prejudice of the defense or security of the coastal State;
- engaging in acts of propaganda aimed at affecting the defense or security of the coastal State;
- launching, landing, or taking on board of any aircraft or military device;
- carrying out of marine scientific research or hydrographic survey activities; and
- conducting acts aimed at interfering with any systems of communication or any other facilities or installations of the coastal State.[149]

UUVs engaged in innocent passage must also navigate on the surface and show their flag.[150] That is not to say that submerged transit of a UUV in a foreign territorial sea is necessarily a violation of the international law of the sea. While submerged transit may violate the sovereignty of the coastal

---

[148] NWP 1-14M, *supra* note 60, §§ 2.6, 2.7.2; UNCLOS, *supra* note 12, arts. 58, 86–87; DoDI 4540.01, *supra* note 30, at 2.

[149] UNCLOS, *supra* note 12, art. 19.

[150] *Id.* art. 20.

state and make the UUV ineligible for the rights and privileges of innocent passage, its conduct is not per se unlawful under UNCLOS.[151] The United States takes the position that, in order to enjoy the right of innocent passage, submarines and other underwater vehicles are required to navigate on the surface and show their flag.[152] However, UNCLOS does not ban passage that is noninnocent.[153] The Convention merely sets "forth conditions for the enjoyment of the right of innocent passage in the territorial sea," but it does not prohibit or otherwise affect activities or conduct that is inconsistent with that right and therefore "not entitled to that right," such as intelligence collection and unprivileged submerged transits by submarines.[154]

SOLAS and UNCLOS allow coastal states to designate traffic separation schemes (TSS) and sea lanes in the territorial sea or international straits to regulate shipping, if such measures are necessary to ensure safety of navigation.[155] Warships, naval auxiliaries, and other government owned or operated ships used only on government noncommercial service, including UMS, however, are not legally required to comply with such sea lanes or TSS. SOLAS Regulation V/1 exempts such vessels from compliance.[156] Sovereign immune vessels, including UMS, that elect not to comply with IMO-approved, designated sea lanes and TSS must still exercise due regard for the safety of navigation of other ships in the area. Similarly, while exercising high seas freedoms of navigation and overflight and other internationally lawful uses of the seas in the EEZ, UAS and UMS must do so with due regard to the rights and duties of the coastal state.[157]

Although UMS are sovereign immune craft, if they do not comply with the laws and regulations of the coastal state concerning innocent passage (e.g., intelligence collection) and disregard any request for compliance therewith, the coastal state may require the UMS to leave the territorial sea immediately.[158] Likewise, the flag state bears international responsibility for any loss

[151] James Kraska, *Putting Your Head in the Tiger's Mouth: Submarine Espionage in Territorial Waters*, 54 COLUMBIA JOURNAL OF TRANSNATIONAL LAW 164, 212–28 (2015–16).

[152] NWP 1-14M, *supra* note 60, § 2.5.2.1.

[153] *Id.*

[154] S. Exec. Rep. No. 108–10, United Nations Convention on the Law of the Sea, 108th Cong., 2d Sess. (Mar. 11, 2004), pp. 8–9.

[155] UNCLOS, *supra* note 12, art. 22; SOLAS, *supra* note 73, Reg. V/10-V/12.

[156] SOLAS, *supra* note 73, reg. V/1.

[157] UNCLOS, *supra* note 12, art. 58.

[158] *Id.* art. 30.

or damage to the coastal state resulting from the noncompliance by a warship or other government ship operated for noncommercial purposes, including UMS, with coastal state laws and regulations concerning passage through the territorial sea or with the provisions of UNCLOS or other rules of international law.[159]

---

[159] *Id.* art. 31.

4

Lethal Autonomous Weapons

1. Autonomous Weapons in the "Kill Chain"

The development of a distributed, networked, unmanned force is accompanied by a convergence in software technologies that will produce lethal autonomous maritime systems (LAMS).[1] The emergence of surface, subsurface, and aerial autonomous weapons in naval warfare depends on a well-defined operational environment and access to rich, accurate, extremely large data sets, such as GPS, fed by distributed sensors, plus improved machine learning algorithms and high-performance processors that will fuse artificial intelligence (AI) into the kill chain.[2] The "kill chain" refers to the end-to-end sequence of events required to understand what is occurring in the battlespace, deciding what to do about it, and taking action that achieves a warfighting effect.

The kill chain process combines multispectral sensors to understand the warfighting environment; positively identify, track, and select targets; and engage them with the most appropriate effects.[3] The Soviet Union referred to this process as the "reconnaissance strike complex," while in the 1990s, John Boyd in the United States popularized the term, "OODA loop," in which armed forces race to "observe, orient, decide, and act" before their adversary.[4] AI is designed to facilitate this adaptive, multi-domain, high velocity decision-making model, and, in doing so, it is expected to provide a decisive military advantage.

---

[1] Hitoshi Nasu & David Letts, *The Legal Characterization of Lethal Autonomous Maritime Systems: Warship, Torpedo, or Naval Mine?*, 96 INTERNATIONAL LAW STUDIES 79, 80–82 (2020).

[2] David Hambling, *Drones May Have Attacked Humans Fully Autonomously for the First Time*, NEW SCIENTIST (online), May 27, 2021; CHRISTIAN BROSE, THE KILL CHAIN: DEFENDING AMERICA IN THE FUTURE OF HIGH-TECH WARFARE xviii (2020).

[3] RICHARD S. DEAKIN, BATTLESPACE TECHNOLOGIES: NETWORK-ENABLED INFORMATION DOMINANCE 473–75 (2010).

[4] Christian Brose, *The New Revolution in Military Affairs*, FOREIGN AFFAIRS (May/June 2019), 122, 122–23 (Russian "strike-reconnaissance complex"); Perrett, Bradley, *China's Growing Ability to Drive Away U.S. Forces*, 180 AVIATION WEEK & SPACE TECH. 56 (2018) (China's lethal kill chain); BARRY SCOTT ZELLEN, THE ART OF WAR IN AN ASYMMETRIC WORLD: STRATEGY FOR THE POST-COLD WAR ERA 81–82 (2012) (describing the "OODA loop").

Disruptive Technology and the Law of Naval Warfare. James Kraska and Raul Pedrozo, Oxford University Press.
© James Kraska & Raul Pedrozo 2022. DOI: 10.1093/oso/9780197630181.003.0005

Autonomous ships that may leverage AI are in the early stages of development. The U.S. Navy's *Sea Hunter* unmanned surface vessel, for example, can patrol without a human on board, using optical guidance and radar to avoid obstacles or watercraft. Future models will be capable of anti-mine warfare and anti-submarine warfare missions at a fraction of the cost of a destroyer. The demonstration model was obtained for $20 million, compared to about $1.1 billion for a frigate with comparable capabilities. The 145-ton *Sea Hunter* has an endurance of 10,000 nautical miles, able to operate 70 days autonomously, and can plow through rough seas. Lethal warships are just on the horizon, as the U.S. Navy grapples with how to contend with a Chinese Navy that already includes some 360 warships compared to fewer than 300 for the United States.

Lethal autonomous weapons appear to have already been used in combat. In the civil war in Libya, forces of the Government of National Accord apparently used the Turkish quadcopter STM Kargu-2 and other loitering munitions to attack Haftar Affiliated Forces (HAF). Retreating HAF forces and convoys were remotely engaged by the unmanned combat aerial vehicles (UAVs), which are programmed to attack targets without requiring data connectivity between the operator and the munition.[5]

In the late 1990s, the U.S. Air Force developed a loitering attack "smart munition" called the Low-Cost Autonomous Attack System (LOCAAS). LOCAAS was a broad area search and detect-to-kill weapon guided by GPS. While LOCAAS was successfully tested and operationally effective, it was canceled after Air Force leaders insisted a data link be added to maintain human monitoring and intervention. The desire to keep a human "in the loop" was based on ethical motivations rather than operational imperative.

The U.S. Department of Defense (DoD) defines "autonomous weapons" as those that, "once activated, can select and engage targets without further intervention by the human operator."[6] This definition includes

---

[5] UN Doc. S/2021/229, Letter dated 8 March 2021 from the Panel of Experts on Libya established pursuant to resolution 1973 (2011) addressed to the President of the Security Council, ¶ 64, at p. 17; Annex 30, p. 148; Histoshi Nasu, *The Kargu-2 Autonomous Attack Drone: Legal and Ethical Dimensions*, ARTICLES OF WAR (online), June 10, 2021; James Marson & Brett Forrest, *Armed Low-Cost Drones, Made by Turkey, Reshape Battlefields and Geopolitics*, WALL STREET JOURNAL (online), June 3, 2021.

[6] U.S. Department of Defense, DoD Directive 3000.09, Autonomy in Weapon Systems (May 8, 2017), Part II, p. 13.

part II (2012); U.N. Doc. CCW/GGE.1/2017/WP.7, Group of Governmental Experts of the High Contracting Parties to the Convention on Prohibitions or Restrictions on the Use of Certain Conventional Weapons Which May Be Deemed to Be Excessively Injurious or to Have Indiscriminate Effects, Characteristics of Lethal Autonomous Weapons Systems ¶ 12 (2017).

human-supervised autonomous weapons that are designed to allow human operators to override the processes of the weapon but can select and engage targets without further human input after they are activated.[7] The Pentagon has operated semi-autonomous (or more accurately, "automated") systems for decades.

The DoD defines "semi-autonomous weapon systems" as:

A weapon system that, once activated, is intended to only engage individual targets or specific target groups that have been selected by a human operator. This includes:

> Semi-autonomous weapon systems that employ autonomy for engagement-related functions including, but not limited to, acquiring, tracking, and identifying potential targets; cueing potential targets to human operators; prioritizing selected targets; timing of when to fire; or providing terminal guidance to home in on selected targets, provided that human control is retained over the decision to select individual targets and specific target groups for engagement.[8]

The Navy's Phalanx or "Close in Weapons System" (CIWS, or "SEE-wiz") is one such semi-autonomous weapon system. The CIWS is part of the Aegis Combat System that integrates vertical-launch missiles and the Phalanx point defense gatling gun into a comprehensive anti-air warfare and anti-ballistic missile suite that can automatically track, target, and destroy incoming missiles and aircraft.[9] Aegis integrates computer and radar technology that can be configured to independently detect, control, and engage inbound enemy targets for anti-air warfare and ballistic missile defense functions.[10] Humans are too slow to sort the large amounts of data and make a timely decision. The system is emblematic of automatic or semi-autonomous systems in that humans control the production, programming, and application of the weapon.[11] Once activated, however, Aegis can run without humans

---

[7] DoD Directive 3000.09, *supra* note 6, Part II, p. 13.

[8] *Id.* part II.

[9] The Aegis Combat System is used by naval forces of the United States, Japan, Spain, Norway, Korea, and Australia, and is part of Japan's and NATO's European missile defense system. U.S. DEPARTMENT OF THE NAVY, UNITED STATES NAVY FACT FILE: MK-15 PHALANX CLOSE-IN WEAPON SYSTEM (CIWS) (online), 2019.

[10] Joseph T. Threston, *The Story of AEGIS*, NAVAL ENGINEERS JOURNAL 109, 111 (2009); Kelsey D. Atherton, *Are Killer Robots the Future of War? Parsing the Facts on Autonomous Weapons*, N.Y. TIMES (online), Nov. 15, 2018.

[11] PETER W. SINGER, WIRED FOR WAR: THE ROBOTICS REVOLUTION AND CONFLICT IN THE 21ST CENTURY 124–27 (2009).

"in the loop" of decision-making, subject to an operator turning the system on or off—a human "on the loop." Semi-autonomous weapons also include "fire and forget" or "lock-on-after-launch" homing munitions that rely on established tactics, techniques, and procedures to maximize the probability of striking only targets within the seeker's "acquisition basket" that have been preselected by a human operator.[12] The Aegis system is in use by naval forces of the United States, Japan, Spain, Norway, Korea, and Australia, and is part of NATO's European missile defense system. Time compression will become even more imperative as hypersonic missiles enter the inventory of not only China, Russia, and the United States, but middle powers, like France, Germany, Japan, and India as well.[13] We expect LAWS to become more important as hypersonic weapons enter service.

2. Compliance with LOAC

The use of all weapons must adhere to the principles of proportionality, necessity, distinction, and precaution. These principles need to be identified as requirements and designed into LAWS systems. Engineers are not accustomed to this type of work so integration will require interdisciplinary teams, to include lawyers, as well as new forms of developmental and operational testing for verification and validation. Furthermore, civilian operators may exercise some level of control or direction over LAWS to conduct offensive strikes, adding an additional layer of complexity. The LOAC applies throughout the targeting cycle, particularly during the target development, validation, nomination, and prioritization phases, as well as the mission planning and force execution phases. The law recognizes that military forces often cannot realistically engage in hostilities without some degree of incidental injury to protected persons and collateral damage to protected objects.[14] The goal of the commander, therefore, is to minimize incidental injury to civilians and collateral damage to civilian objects consistent with mission accomplishment and the law.

---

[12] DoD Directive 3000.09, *supra* note 6, part II, p. 14.

[13] KELLEY M. SAYLER CONGRESSIONAL RESEARCH SERVICE PUBLICATION NO. R45811, HYPERSONIC WEAPONS: BACKGROUND AND ISSUES FOR CONGRESS 16 (2020).

[14] SAN REMO MANUAL ON INTERNATIONAL LAW APPLICABLE TO ARMED CONFLICTS AT SEA ¶¶, 13(c), 46(c)-(d), 51(d), 52(d), 57(d) (Louise Doswald Beck ed., 1995); U.S. NAVY, U.S. MARINE CORPS & U.S. COAST GUARD, NWP 1-14M/MCTP 11-10B/COMDTPUB P5800.7A, THE COMMANDER'S HANDBOOK ON THE LAW OF NAVAL OPERATIONS § 4.4.1 (2017) [hereinafter NWP 1-14M].

There is a debate over whether unmanned and autonomous systems are able to take such precautions into consideration before engaging a target. Debate is made more complex by the variation among such systems and their capabilities. The debate over the legality of LAWS is driven by concern that such weapons must have a sufficiently rich human role in their design, production, and operation to ameliorate ethical concerns and ensure human accountability for compliance with the LOAC. These issues are playing out at discussions held under the auspices of the UN Convention of Certain Conventional Weapons (CCW) through the discussions of a Group of Governmental Experts (GGE).

2.1 CCW Group of Governmental Experts (GGE)

The CCW effort is focused on identifying concerns and developing general principles associated with human-machine interaction, applicability of international law, and examining how those principles may be operationalized. To address these issues, the High Contracting Parties of the CCW decided in 2013 to convene an informal meeting of experts in 2014 to consider LAWS and their potential compatibility and compliance with LOAC, in particular, the principles of international humanitarian law, the 1949 Geneva Conventions, the Martens Clause, and customary law.[15] The CCW already regulates certain conventional weapons, with protocols that prohibit the use of non-detectable fragments (Protocol I), regulate employment of landmines and booby-traps (Protocol II) and control incendiary weapons (Protocol III), prohibit the use of blinding lasers (Protocol IV), and regulate explosive remnants of war (Protocol V).[16]

[15] U.N. Doc. CCW/MSP/2013/10, Meeting of the High Contracting Parties to the Convention on Prohibitions or Restrictions on the Use of Certain Conventional Weapons Which May be Deemed to Be Excessively Injurious or to Have Indiscriminate Effects, Final Report (Dec. 16, 2013); [hereinafter Meeting of the High Contracting Parties]; U.N. Doc. CCW/MSP/2014/3, Chairperson, Report of the 2014 Informal Meeting of Experts on Lethal Autonomous Weapons Systems (LAWS) ¶ 26 (June 11, 2014); *see also* Convention on Prohibitions or Restrictions on the Use of Certain Conventional Weapons Which May be Deemed to be Excessively Injurious or to Have Indiscriminate Effects, Oct. 10, 1980, 1342 U.N.T.S. 137.

[16] Protocol on Non-Detectable Fragments, Oct. 10, 1980, 1342 U.N.T.S. 168 (Protocol I); Protocol on Prohibitions or Restrictions on the Use of Mines, Booby-Traps and Other Devices, Oct. 10, 1980, 1342 U.N.T.S. 168 (Protocol II); Protocol on Prohibitions or Restrictions on the Use of Mines, Booby-Traps and Other Devices, as Amended on 3 May 1996 May 3, 1996, 2048 U.N.T.S. 93 (Protocol II, amended); Protocol on Prohibitions or Restrictions on the Use of Incendiary Weapons, Oct. 10, 1980, 1342 U.N.T.S. 171 (Protocol III); Protocol on Blinding Laser Weapons, Oct. 13, 1995, 2024 U.N.T.S. 163 (Protocol IV); Protocol on Explosive Remnants of War to the Convention on Prohibitions or

From 2014 to 2016, informal meetings of experts were convened to explore these questions within the framework of the CCW.[17] In 2015, Germany, as chair, submitted a "Food for Thought" paper that outlined many of the military, technological, ethical, and legal issues associated with the use of LAWS.[18] In 2016, the chairperson of the meeting, Ambassador Michael Biontino of Germany, prepared for submission to the CCW Review Conference a paper in his personal capacity containing recommendations for establishment of a CCW Group of Government Experts (GGE) to begin meeting in 2017 to address options relating to emerging technologies and LAWS.[19]

Accountability has been central to the debate over autonomous weapons at the GGE.[20] Meeting in 2017, the GGE held discussions on LAWS technology, military effects, and ethical and legal issues based on the chairperson's 2015 "Food for Thought" paper.[21] The GGE met twice in both 2018 and 2019, and discussions continue.[22]

The lines of argument have coalesced around whether LAWS should be subject to a new CCW protocol.[23] Some states propose negotiation of Protocol VI to the Convention to regulate or even ban LAWS—the latter option is supported by some NGOs.[24] Although the ICRC has not joined the call for a ban, it is moving in the direction of support for drafting a new

Restrictions on the Use of Certain Conventional Weapons which may be deemed to be Excessively Injurious or to have Indiscriminate Effects, Nov. 28, 2003, 2399 U.N.T.S. 100 (Protocol V).

[17] U.N. Doc. CCW/MSP/2015/WP.1/Rev.1, Revised Annotated Programme of Work for the Informal Meeting of Experts on Lethal Autonomous Weapons Systems (2015) [hereinafter U.N. Doc. CCW/MSP/2015/WP.1/Rev.1].

[18] U.N. Doc. CCW/GGE.1/2017/WP.1, Chairperson, Food-for-Thought Paper (Sept. 4, 2017).

[19] U.N. Doc. CCW/CONF.V/2, Chairperson, Report of the 2016 Informal Meeting of Experts on Lethal Autonomous Weapons Systems (LAWS), annex, Recommendations to the 2016 Review Conference (June 2, 2016).

[20] U.N. Doc. CCW/GGE.1/2018/3, Report of the 2018 Group of Governmental Experts on Emerging Technologies in the Area of Lethal Autonomous Weapons Systems ¶ 22 (Oct. 23, 2018); U.N. Doc. CCW/GGE.1/2017/3, Report of the 2017 Group of Governmental Experts on Lethal Autonomous Weapons Systems (LAWS) ¶¶ 21(b), 23(a) (Dec. 22, 2017); Carrie McDougall, *Autonomous Weapon Systems and Accountability: Putting the Cart Before the Horse*, 4 MELBOURNE JOURNAL OF INTERNATIONAL LAW 58, 74–76 (2019).

[21] U.N. Doc. CCW/GGE.1/2017/CRP.1, Report of the 2017 Group of Governmental Experts on Lethal Autonomous Weapons Systems (LAWS) ¶ 12 (Nov. 20, 2017); U.N. Doc. CCW/GGE.1/2017/3, *supra* note 20.

[22] U.N. Doc. CCW/GGE.1/2018/3, *supra* note 20; U.N. Doc. CCW/GGE.1/2019/3, Report of the 2019 session of the Group of Governmental Experts on Emerging Technologies in the Area of Lethal Autonomous Weapons Systems (Sept. 25, 2019).

[23] U.N. Doc. CCW/GGE.1/2017/3, *supra* note 20, ¶ 10.

[24] Matthew Bolton, Membership Secretary, International Committee for Robot Arms Control, Closing Statement to the 2015 U.N. CCW Expert Meeting, ICRAC (Apr. 17, 2015); CAMPAIGN TO STOP KILLER ROBOTS, KEY ELEMENTS OF A TREATY ON FULLY AUTONOMOUS WEAPONS 3 (2019).

protocol, at least to clarify the scope of human control in LAWS.[25] The GGE participants have split into four different camps.[26]

2.1.1 "Ban Killer Robots"

The most vocal group proposes negotiating a legally binding instrument that prohibits and regulates lethal autonomous weapons systems. Nearly 30 nations support banning LAWS. Austria and Brazil are among the most vocal, but the list also includes Algeria, Bolivia, Cuba, Costa Rica, Cuba, Ecuador, Egypt, Ghana, Guatemala, the Holy See, Mexico, Nicaragua, Pakistan, Panama, Palestine, Peru, Venezuela, and Zimbabwe.[27] The European Parliament seeks a binding treaty to stop the development, production, or use of LAWS.[28] The Non-aligned Movement supports that outcome as well, viewing a new protocol essential to ensuring autonomous functions remain under the "direct control and supervision of humans at all times."[29] The group believes that the only viable option is to negotiate a "legally-binding instrument . . . that comprehensively prohibits the development, production, and use of fully autonomous weapons . . . and . . . that requires meaningful human control over critical combat functions."[30]

This group argues that it would be difficult for fully autonomous weapons to comply with the principles of distinction and proportionality because LAWS "lack the human judgment necessary to determine whether expected civilian harm outweighs anticipated military advantage in ever-changing and unforeseen combat situations."[31] Furthermore, they argue the use of fully autonomous weapons would create a gap in individual criminal responsibility for war crimes because it "would be legally challenging, and

---

[25] International Committee of the Red Cross, Statement to the Group of Governmental Experts on Lethal Autonomous Weapons Systems on Possible Options for Addressing the Humanitarian and International Security Challenges Posed by Emerging Technologies in the Area of Lethal Autonomous Weapon Systems in the Context of the Objectives and Purposes of the Convention Without Prejudicing Policy Outcomes and Taking into Account Past, Present and Future Proposals (Apr. 11, 2016).

[26] U.N. Doc. CCW/GGE.1/2018/3, *supra* note 20.

[27] Campaign to Stop Killer Robots, *Country Views on Killer Robots* (Mar. 11, 2020).

[28] European Parliament Doc. 2014/2567(RSP), Resolution on the Use of Armed Drones, ¶ I.2(d) (2014).

[29] U.N. Doc. CCW/GGE.1/2017/WP.10, General principles on Lethal Autonomous Weapons Systems ¶ 9 (Nov. 13, 2017).

[30] Steve Goose, Director of Arms Division, Human Rights. Watch, Statement on Options for Future Work, CCW meeting on lethal autonomous weapons systems (Mar. 27, 2019).

[31] Bonnie Docherty, Senior Researcher, Human Rights Watch, Statement on International Humanitarian Law, CCW meeting on lethal autonomous weapons systems (Mar. 26, 2019) [hereinafter Docherty Statement].

unfair, to hold commanders liable for the unforeseeable actions of a machine operating outside their control."[32] Finally, they suggest the use of fully autonomous weapons would violate the Martens Clause[33] because LAWS are "unable to apply compassion or human judgment to decisions to use force."[34] By requiring "meaningful human control,"[35] a legally binding instrument "would ensure humans can apply judgment to the selection and engagement of targets, be held accountable for their actions, and uphold the principles of humanity and dictates of public conscience."[36] China purports to support a ban, but it defines LAWS exceedingly narrowly, to include only systems with the an "impossibility for termination" and that operate with "indiscriminate effect."[37] Such weapons are unlawful anyway, so the Chinese proposal to "ban" them is entirely specious. The wayward Chinese definition of LAWS underscores that there is no agreement on how to meaningfully and accurately characterize what it encompasses.

2.1.2 Political Declaration

A second group calls for the negotiation of a political declaration that would outline important principles, to include human control in the use of force, human accountability, transparency, and technology review. France and Germany call "for a political declaration, which should affirm that State parties share the conviction that humans should continue to be able to make ultimate decisions with regard to the use of lethal force and should continue to exert sufficient control over lethal weapons systems they use."[38] This group

---

[32] Id.

[33] The Martens Clause provides: "Until a more complete code of the laws of war is issued, . . . in cases not included in the Regulations . . ., populations and belligerents remain under the protection . . . of the principles of international law, as they result from the usages established between civilized nations, from the laws of humanity, and the requirements of the public conscience." Hague Convention (II) on the Laws and Customs of War on Land, July 29, 1899, 32 Stat. 1893, T.S. 403 [hereinafter Hague Convention (II)].

[34] Docherty Statement, *supra* note 31.

[35] Meaningful human control could encompass different elements, including but not limited to: (1) necessary time for human deliberation and action; (2) sufficient access to information about the context in which force might be used and the machine's process for selecting and engaging target objects; and (3) predictable, reliable, and transparent technology. *Id.*

[36] Id.

[37] U.N. Doc. CCW/GGE.1/2018/WP.7, Position Paper from China to the Group of Governmental Experts of the High Contracting Parties to the Convention on Prohibitions or Restrictions on the Use of Certain Conventional Weapons Which May Be Deemed to Be Excessively Injurious or to Have Indiscriminate Effects ¶ 3 (Apr. 11, 2018); *see also* COMMENTARY ON THE ADDITIONAL PROTOCOLS OF 8 JUNE 1977 TO THE GENEVA CONVENTIONS OF 12 AUGUST 1949, ¶ 1463 (Yves Sandoz, Christophe Swinarski & Bruno Zimmermann eds., 1987).

[38] Statement by France and Germany to the Meeting of the Group of Governmental Experts on Lethal Autonomous Weapons Systems, Geneva (Apr. 9-13, 2018). *See* WILLIAM H. BOOTHBY, WEAPONS AND THE LAW OF ARMED CONFLICT 342 (2d ed. 2016).

acknowledges that the rules of LOAC fully apply to the development and use of LAWS, and that "only new weapons that have been tested, legally reviewed and that could be employed in compliance with LOAC are acceptable means of warfare."[39] Additionally, with regard to human/machine interaction, this group believes that humans should maintain overall responsibility over weapons, and that weapon systems should be subordinated to a chain of command.[40]

2.1.3 Improve Compliance with AP I

Another group focuses on applying existing international law to the human-machine interface, as well as the need to identify best practices and measures to improve compliance with international law, underlining the importance of legal weapons reviews under article 36 of AP I. This group is led by Argentina, Australia, and the United Kingdom, and it advocates that a ban on LAWS is not necessary if states apply a system of control over all aspects of a weapon system from design through engagement to ensure the system operates in a lawful and regulated manner.[41] This group argues that the key consideration in the LAWS debate should be the level and nature of control over critical functions across the life cycle of the system, rather than the technology.[42] A key feature of this system of control is implementation of a robust legal weapons review mechanism under article 36 of AP I.

2.1.4 Apply Existing LOAC

The fourth group believes that existing LOAC is fully applicable to potential lethal autonomous weapons systems and that, therefore, there is no need to discuss further legal measures to regulate such systems. Russia's position is

---

[39] Statement by France and Germany to the Meeting of the Group of Governmental Experts on Lethal Autonomous Weapons Systems, Geneva (Apr. 9–13, 2018).

[40] *Id.*

[41] U.N. Doc. CCW/GGE.1/2019/WP.2/Rev.1, Australia's System of Control and Application for Autonomous Weapons Systems (Mar. 26, 2019); U.N. Doc. CCW/GGE.2/2018/WP.1, Human Machine Touchpoints: The United Kingdom's Perspective on Human Control Over Weapon Development and Targeting Cycles (Aug. 8, 2018).

[42] U.N. Doc. CCW/GGE.1/2019/WP.6, Questionnaire on the Legal Review Mechanisms of New Weapons, Means and Methods of Warfare to the Group of Governmental Experts on Emerging Technologies in the Area of Lethal Autonomous Weapons Systems, (Mar. 29, 2019); U.N. Doc. CCW/GGE.1/2018/WP.2, Fortalecimiento de los Mecanismos de Revisión de una Nueva Arma, o Nuevos Medios o Métodos de Guerra, Elaborado por Argentina (Strengthening the Mechanisms for the Review of a New Weapon, or New Means or Methods of Warfare, Submitted by Argentina) (Mar. 28, 2018); U.N. Doc. CCW/GGE.2/2018/WP.6, The Australian Article 36 Review Process (Working Paper for the 2018 Group of Governmental Experts of the High Contracting Parties to the Certain Conventional Weapons—Lethal Autonomous Weapon Systems) (Aug. 30, 2018).

that each state should set their own standards.[43] The United States opposes a ban.[44] Thus far, no NATO state has supported a ban. Russia and the United States maintain that existing international law, including the LOAC principles of "distinction, proportionality, and precaution, provide[s] a comprehensive framework to govern the use of . . ." LAWS.[45] Moreover, national processes and procedures for reviewing and testing LAWS, including legal reviews of new weapon systems required by article 36 of AP I, are essential to implementing these LOAC requirements.

Emergent technologies could strengthen the application of LOAC by reducing the risk of civilian casualties, facilitating the investigation of unanticipated incidents, enhancing the ability to implement corrective actions, and automatically generating data on unexploded ordnance. Proponents of this position argue that practical measures can be applied to ensure future use of autonomous weapon systems are used consistent with LOAC. Some of these measures include the following: (1) rigorous testing to assess whether the weapon systems' performance and reliability is consistent with LOAC requirements; (2) developing doctrine, training, and procedures for use of LAWS consistent with LOAC principles; and (3) conducting legal reviews of LAWS prior to their use, taking into consideration LOAC issues, to include precautions to reduce collateral damage and civilian casualties.

The CIWS capability highlights the lack of salience that some of these legal factors have over LAWS in naval and air warfare. Even if arguments calling for a ban of autonomous weapons may be considered in the context of urban warfare or ground operations, they become much less relevant in armed conflict at sea. In a purely maritime context, targeting in naval warfare is based on platforms—ships and aircraft that belong to the enemy or that have acquired enemy character. Enemy warships may be attacked as lawful targets. The electronic technologies available for a LAWS to discern a warship as a lawful target from a civil sailing vessel or merchant ship that enjoys protected

[43] U.N. Doc. CCW/GGE.1/2018/WP.6, Russia's Approaches to the Elaboration of a Working Definition and Basic Functions of Lethal Autonomous Weapons Systems in the Context of the Purposes and Objectives of the Convention ¶ 9 (Apr. 4, 2018).

[44] U.N. Doc. CCW/GGE.1/2018/WP.4, Humanitarian Benefits of Emerging Technologies in the Area of Lethal Autonomous Weapon Systems (United States) ¶ 40 (Apr. 3, 2018).

[45] U.N. Doc. CCW/GGE.1/2019/WP.5, Implementing International Humanitarian Law in the Use of Autonomy in Weapons Systems (United States) (Mar. 28, 2019); U.N. Doc. CCW/GGE.1/2019/WP.1, Potential Opportunities and Limitations of Military Uses of Lethal Autonomous Weapons Systems (Russia) (Mar. 15, 2019); U.N. Doc. CCW/GGE.1/2018/WP.4, supra, note 44; U.N. Doc. CCW/GGE.1/2017/WP.6, Autonomy in Weapons Systems (United States) (Nov. 10, 2017).

status already exists (and indeed exceeds human capabilities). This is a much easier analysis than distinguishing between human individuals on the battlefield or identifying a peasant farmer employed in gainful agriculture from another farmer who is directly participating in hostilities. In naval warfare, not only are the targets easier to identify and discriminate, but the likelihood of collateral damage is vastly reduced since vessels, unlike buildings, ground vehicles, and people, tend not to congregate in close proximity because of navigational safety. Thus, it is relatively easy to program a fully autonomous weapon to only attack enemy warships or submarines during an engagement at sea and doing so is unlikely to raise issues of distinction or collateral damage that recur in land warfare.

3. Levels of Control

It is impractical to satisfy the most aspirational desires to ban such LAWS; indeed, semi-autonomous weapons already exist and include a variety of automated weapons that have been employed by over 30 countries for over 30 years.[46] In great power competition, the logic of deterrence means major powers must develop AI systems, if only to deter potential adversaries. In this sense, systems that use AI will become essential to strategic stability and security. Consequently, talk of banning them is simply unrealistic, particularly since the CCW makes decisions by consensus. Most states agree there is a need for some form of human involvement in the design, development, and use of LAWS but stand against new regulation. A new CCW protocol that regulates LAWS without banning them is viewed as a middle ground, although even that may not materialize.[47]

There are two streams of thought that have been put forward to further specify a potential new standard for these weapons: "meaningful human control" and "appropriate levels of human judgement."[48]

---

[46] Chris Jenks, *False Rubicons, Moral Panic & Conceptual Cul-De-Sacs: Critiquing & Reframing the Call to Ban Lethal Autonomous Weapons*, 44 PEPPERDINE LAW REVIEW 1, 1 (2016).

[47] U.N. Doc. CCW/GGE.2/2018/WP.7, Proposal for a Mandate to Negotiate a Legally Binding Instrument that Addresses the Legal, Humanitarian and Ethical Concerns Posed by Emerging Technologies in the Area of Lethal Autonomous Weapons Systems (LAWS) (Austria, Brazil & Chile) (Aug. 30, 2018).

[48] Meeting of the High Contracting Parties, *supra* note 15, ¶ 20; U.N. Doc. CCW/GGE.2/2018/WP.4, Human-Machine Interaction in the Development, Deployment and Use of Emerging Technologies in the Area of Lethal Autonomous Weapons Systems (United States) (Aug. 28, 2018).

3.1 "Meaningful Human Control"

The U.K. NGO Article 36 seeks adoption of an explicit requirement for "meaningful human control" over the operation of AI weapon systems, and specifically over every individual attack.[49] By requiring "meaningful human control,"[50] a legally binding instrument "would ensure humans can apply judgment to the selection and engagement of targets, be held accountable for their actions, and uphold the principles of humanity and dictates of public conscience."[51]

Numerous states support this standard, although the definitions of the term vary.[52] Austria supports this standard because it views LAWS as by their nature lying outside of "meaningful human control."[53] The problem with "meaningful human control" as a standard is that, like LAWS itself, there is not a single interpretation of the term. Some consider it as a concept that ensures human control during the operation of a weapon (throughout the duration of an attack). Many proponents argue there is a temporal link between the initial assessment of LOAC in the context of conditions that justify using a weapon, and the assessment that is ongoing throughout the duration of the attack. If this link is broken, it raises problems with the human control over implementation of the law of war—in particular, the principles of proportionality, distinction, and precautions. Austria questions whether a proportionality assessment made on the front end of the kill chain will be valid by the time the ordinance lands on the target.[54] The concern arises because the battlespace is dynamic. There is a risk that human-informed decisions programmed into LAWS before an attack will not be durable throughout the entire kill chain, as conditions quickly change.[55] The

[49] Austria, The Concept of "Meaningful Human Control" (Lethal Autonomous Weapons System, Expert Meeting, Geneva, April 13–17, 2015, Working Paper); see also Merel Ekelhof, *Autonomous Weapons: Operationalizing Meaningful Human Control*, HUMANITARIAN LAW & POLICY: BLOG (online), Aug. 15, 2018.

[50] Meaningful human control could encompass different elements, including but not limited to: (1) necessary time for human deliberation and action; (2) sufficient access to information about the context in which force might be used and the machine's process for selecting and engaging target objects; and (3) predictable, reliable, and transparent technology. Docherty Statement, *supra* note 31.

[51] *Id.*

[52] Sandra de Jongh, Policy Officer, Ministry of Foreign Affairs, Netherlands, Statement delivered at Group of Governmental Experts on LAWS (Apr. 26, 2019).

[53] Laura Boillot, Program Manager for Article36, Statement at the 2015 Informal Meeting of Experts on Lethal Autonomous Weapons Systems (LAWS): On the Way Forward (Apr. 17, 2015).

[54] Austria, The Concept of "Meaningful Human Control," *supra* note 49.

[55] *Id.*

principle of proportionality requires an unbroken temporal link between the plan and the lethal strike so that proportionality is re-evaluated at each step of the chain.

The related concept of precautions in attack may also be difficult for LAWS to implement without human intervention because it is unclear whether the initial plans reviewed by humans and executed by the machine would be capable of adjusting to dynamic battlefield conditions.[56] Michael C. Horowitz and Paul Scharre defined meaningful human control as a three-part test, which has become another influential standard for the term:

- Human operators are making informed, conscious decisions about the use of weapons;
- Human operators have sufficient information to ensure the lawfulness of the action they are taking, given what they know about the target, the weapon, and the context for action;
- The weapon is designed and tested, and human operators are properly trained, to ensure effective control over the use of the weapon.[57]

The Campaign to Stop Killer Robots states that attacks that lack "meaningful human control" are unethical because they undermine human dignity by delegating "life-and-death decisions to inanimate machines" unable to comprehend the value of human life.[58] This approach finds it repugnant that targeting during armed conflict could be done without control by a "true moral agent in the form of a human," who has a "conscience and the faculty of moral judgment," even if human judgment is inherently flawed.[59] Machines would be worse, they suggest, because LAWS are incapable of the judgment required to comply with the LOAC, such as weighing the proportionality of an attack. For example, Austria suggests that it is problematic to delegate to a robot weapon the assessment of whether an enemy soldier is "*hors de combat.*"[60] In this view, it is unrealistic that LAWS could distinguish whether an enemy soldier was wounded or in the process of surrendering.[61]

---

[56] *Id.*

[57] MICHAEL C. HOROWITZ AND PAUL SCHARRE, MEANINGFUL HUMAN CONTROL IN WEAPON SYSTEMS: A PRIMER 4 (online), Mar. 2015.

[58] CAMPAIGN TO STOP KILLER ROBOTS, KEY ELEMENTS OF A TREATY ON FULLY AUTONOMOUS WEAPONS 3 (2019).

[59] Kenneth Anderson & Matthew Waxman, *Law and Ethics for Robot Soldiers*, 176 POLICY REVIEW (online), 2012.

[60] Austria, The Concept of "Meaningful Human Control," *supra* note 49.

[61] *Id.*

Nonetheless, 30 years ago five Iraqi soldiers attempted to surrender to an un-armed U.S. Pioneer UAV without incident.[62]

Proponents of the standard for "meaningful human control" suggest "'meaningful,' 'effective,' or 'appropriate' human control would be the type and degree of control that preserves human agency and upholds moral re-sponsibility in decisions to use force."[63] "Control," advocates say, is a higher and broader standard than alternatives, such as "judgment." "Meaningful" control qualifies that such control must be more than superficial and is "less specific or outcome driven" than alternatives, such as "appropriate" or "ef-fective" control.[64] This standard requires a sufficiently direct and close con-nection to be maintained between the human intent of the user and the eventual consequences of the operation of the weapon system in a specific attack. A human must always be "in the loop," particularly for selecting and engaging targets. But this position arguably bans LAWS, since such systems cease to be autonomous.[65]

More human control, however, does not necessarily mean more mean-ingful human control. If LAWS have greater accuracy than humans, for example, they may be able to better identify and more accurately strike a spe-cific location on a target with a smaller munition, such as a vulnerable hatch on an armored vehicle, with a reduced blast radius, minimizing collateral damage. In that case, less direct human control over the weapon could pro-duce greater realization of the intention of the commander and compliance with LOAC, which is to destroy the target while minimizing collateral effects. The United States believes that concerns expressed through human control can be better addressed by ensuring that LAWS are subject to "appropriate levels of human judgment."

3.2 "Appropriate Levels of Human Judgment"

Current DoD policy is consistent with this requirement. When using le-thal or non-lethal, kinetic or non-kinetic force—"autonomous and

---

[62] Ted Shelsby, *Iraqi Soldiers Surrender to AAI's Drones*, BALTIMORE SUN (online), Mar. 2, 1991.

[63] U.N. Doc. CCW/GGE.1/2018/WP.5, Ethics and Autonomous Weapon Systems: An Ethical Basis for Human Control? ¶ 8.1 (International Committee of the Red Cross) (Mar. 29, 2018); U.N. Doc. CCW/GGE.1/2017/CRP.1, *supra* note 21, annex II.

[64] CAMPAIGN TO STOP KILLER ROBOTS, KEY ELEMENTS OF A TREATY ON FULLY AUTONOMOUS WEAPONS, *supra* note 58, at 3, n. 3.

[65] William Boothby, Article 36, Address at the Meeting of Experts on Lethal Autonomous Weapons Systems (LAWS): Weapons Reviews and Autonomous Weapons (13 to 17 April 2015).

semi-autonomous weapon systems shall be designed to allow commanders and operators to exercise appropriate levels of human judgment over the use of force."[66] Such systems will also undergo a "rigorous hardware and software verification and validation . . . and realistic system developmental and operational test and evaluation . . .," and "training, doctrine, and tactics, techniques, and procedures . . . will be established" for their use.[67]

Additionally, all intended acquisitions of new weapon systems are subject to a legal review (consistent with article 36 of AP I) to ensure the systems are consistent with applicable domestic and international law, including the LOAC.[68] These measures will help ensure autonomous and semi-autonomous weapon systems:

(a) Function as anticipated in realistic operational environments. . . .
(b) Complete engagements . . . consistent with commander and operator intentions and, if unable to do so, terminate engagements or seek additional human operator input before continuing the engagement.
(c) Are sufficiently robust to minimize failures that could lead to unintended engagements or to loss of control of the system. . . .[69]

Commanders and operators who authorize or direct the use of, or operate, autonomous and semi-autonomous weapon systems will apply appropriate care to comply with LOAC, other applicable treaties, weapon system safety rules, and relevant rules of engagement. These weapon systems may employ lethal or non-lethal, kinetic or non-kinetic force. The systems include manned or unmanned platforms, munitions, or submunitions that function as semi-autonomous weapon systems or as subcomponents of them. However, such systems will be designed so that they cannot "autonomously select and engage individual targets or specific target groups that have not been previously selected by an authorized human operator" if communications are degraded or lost.[70]

Human-supervised autonomous weapon systems may be used to select and engage targets, except human targets, "for local defense to intercept

---

[66] DoD Directive 3000.09, *supra* note 6, at 2–3.
[67] *Id.* at 2.
[68] DEPARTMENT OF DEFENSE PUBLICATION NO. 5000.01, THE DEFENSE ACQUISITION SYSTEM 3 (2003).
[69] DoD Directive 3000.09, *supra* note 6, at 2.
[70] *Id.* at 3.

attempted time-critical or saturation attacks for (a) static defense of manned installations; and (b) onboard defense of manned platforms."[71]

It is important to note, however, that the DoD position requiring some degree of human control or intervention over the use of force during the targeting process is based on policy, not the law. Given the divergent positions advocated at the GGE in Geneva and in state practice, it is apparent that the law does not require human control over critical combat functions. In this regard, the only thing that LOAC requires is that the decision maker, human or machine or a combination thereof, is capable of compliance with the principles of military necessity, proportionality, distinction, and precaution in attack. If a fully autonomous weapon is outfitted with the necessary technology and AI that enable it to comply fully with LOAC requirements, the law does not require that there be a human in (or on)-the-loop before a target can be selected or engaged.[72]

The DoD requires that autonomous and semi-autonomous weapon systems shall be designed to allow commanders and operators to exercise "appropriate levels of human judgment over the use of force."[73] The United States has offered this standard during discussions at the GGE, noting that there is no single metric for determining the correct level of human control or judgment to be exercised over the use of force in LAWS.[74] Human judgment over the use of force is different than human control over the use of force. For example, if the operator is reflexively pressing a button to approve strikes recommended by the weapon system, it could be argued that there is control, but little judgment is being exercised.[75]

"Appropriate levels of human judgment" is viewed as a holistic standard that includes the totality of the circumstances in the employment of a weapon. There is neither a single metric for what constitutes "appropriate levels" of judgment, just as there is not for what type of control would be "meaningful." Factors that are considered in determining the appropriate level of human judgment include the characteristics and features of the weapon system, how it will be employed in a specific physical operating

[71] Id.
[72] Eric Talbot Jensen, *The (Erroneous) Requirement for Human Judgment (and Error) in the Law of Armed Conflict*, 96 INTERNATIONAL LAW STUDIES 26 (2020).
[73] DoD Directive 3000.09, *supra* note 6, at ¶ 4(a).
[74] U.N. Doc. CCW/GGE.2/2018/WP.4, *supra* note 44, ¶ 1.
[75] Id.

environment, and the tactical context of applicable operational concepts and rules of engagement.[76]

3.3 The Fruitless Quest for a Common Standard

The terms under debate at the GGE are semantic, and labels only gain importance once they are defined or explained.[77] The disconnect between the two competing standards of human-machine integration is widened by additional concepts offered for consideration. Australia suggests that any use of force by LAWS must be executed through a "system of control," which it defines as "an incremental, layered approach," to exercise human control over the weapons, from "design through to engagement."[78] France has claimed that there is "no way to define the contours" of each actor's responsibility—the political and military decision makers, manufacturers, programmers, and operators of LAWS.[79] It is apparent many participants in the debate over autonomous weapons are talking past each other.[80] This dysfunctional dynamic of the negotiations is evident in the array of terms represented in the table below used during discussions of human-machine interaction in the development, deployment, and use of LAWS.

Notice that the terms in the table, all of which were derived from GGE discussions, seek to link some level of human interaction with the use of LAWS. Reading left to right, GGE delegations have proposed various action verbs (e.g., "Maintaining," "Ensuring," "Exerting," or "Preserving") with a threshold level of human attention or oversight (e.g., "Substantive," "Meaningful," "Appropriate," "Sufficient, "Minimum level of…" or "Minimum indispensable extent of . . .") of human direction or decision (described as "Participation," "Involvement," "Responsibility," "Supervision," "Validation," "Control," "Judgment," or "Decision"). Yet each of these terms, except for "human," is highly subjective. It is virtually impossible, for example, to

---

[76] Chairman of the Joint Chiefs of Staff Instruction CJCSI 3121.01B, Standing Rules of Engagement (SROE)/Standing Rules for the Use of Force (SRUF) for U.S. Forces (2005).

[77] Merel Ekelhof, *Moving Beyond Semantics on Autonomous Weapons: Meaningful Human Control in Operation*, 10 GLOBAL POLICY 343, 344 (Table 1) (2019).

[78] U.N Doc. CCW/GGE.1/2019/WP.2/Rev.1, Australia's System of Control and Applications for Autonomous Weapon Systems ¶¶ I.3, II, (Mar. 26, 2019).

[79] France, Legal Framework for Any Potential Development and Operational Use of Future Lethal Autonomous Weapons Systems (LAWS) 2 (2016 Meeting of Experts on LAWS, Working Paper, Apr. 2016).

[80] McDougall, *supra* note 20, at 60.

identify a practical difference or impact between the action verbs, such as "Maintaining" and "Ensuring," within the context of LAWS. Likewise, it is meaningless to discern the distinction between "Human Participation" and "Human Involvement" in a LAWS activity, let alone "Human Judgment" or "Human Decision." The terms listed non-exhaustively by the GGE Chair for further discussion demonstrate the inability of states to objectively agree on how to think about human involvement with or interaction with autonomous weapons.[81]

Table: LAWS terms listed non-exhaustively by the Chair

	Substantive		Participation
	Meaningful		Involvement
Maintaining	Appropriate		Responsibility
Ensuring	Sufficient	Human	Supervision
Exerting	Minimum level of		Validation
Preserving	Minimum indispensable extent of		Control
			Judgment
			Decision

The quest to develop a standard for human-machine integration in LAWS is motivated by the desire to ensure that humans, who are responsible under LOAC for decisions on the battlefield, are held accountable for the results of those decisions. Human control over AI systems will be exercised in a different manner than conventional weapons because it changes the tasks that humans do in armed conflict, but it does not take away the responsibility of humans or create a gap in accountability. But no matter what terms or standards are used, for some observers, if there is a gap it can never be closed for AI systems because the machine has an informational advantage over the operator, whether it is in navigation of autonomous vehicles or radar-based flight control.[82] Humans are too slow, incapable of sifting through enough data quickly enough to control the analytical process. This perspective concludes that the designer of the machine gradually loses control over it, transferring control from the human to the machine itself.[83] Humans in

---

[81] U.N. Doc. CCW/GGE.1/2018/3, *supra* note 20, ¶ 22.
[82] Andreas Matthias, *The Responsibility Gap: Ascribing Responsibility for the Actions of Learning Automata*, 6 ETHICS & INFORMATION TECHNOLOGY 176, 182 (2004).
[83] *Id.*

the loop are not just redundant, as illustrated by the Aegis system, they are disadvantageous.[84]

In this respect, it is difficult not to conclude that it will be impossible to assign human responsibility for the actions of LAWS through some type of globally accepted standard.[85] As Russia stated, attempts to develop certain universal parameters of the so-called critical functions, for the wide variety of anticipated systems, "can hardly give practical results."[86] In the end, the CCW GGE process likely will be disappointing. Any agreement that emerges from the GGE is likely to be too vague to provide meaningful guidance.

4. Military Accountability

Regardless of the standards for human involvement or oversight of LAWS that may be adopted by the GGE, the law binds humans, not machines.[87] Military commanders bear the burden of full accountability for the entire scope of their prosecution of the war effort, including employment of appropriate weapons during the conflict, how those weapons are applied in the operational environment, and the consequences for their successes and their failures, both anticipated and unforeseen. Commanders are required to select appropriate and lawful weapons under the circumstances. The key for accountability is that someone is held to account for every employment of a method or means of warfare, and that person is the military commander.

Commanders are said to be "in command," meaning they have authority over the armed forces, and the "power to give orders and enforce obedience."[88] Commanders are the agents of the state, they exercise authority to control the forces under their command, and implement and enforce LOAC.[89] With the vast authority of commanders comes great responsibility while they serve in

---

[84] Robert Sparrow, *Killer Robots*, 24 JOURNAL OF APPLIED PHILOSOPHY 62, 68 (2007).

[85] *Id.*

[86] U.N. Doc. CCW/GGE.1/2018/WP.6, *supra* note 42, ¶ 9.

[87] Marco Sassóli, *Autonomous Weapons and International Humanitarian Law: Advantages, Open Technical Questions and Legal Issues to be Clarified*, 90 INTERNATIONAL LAW STUDIES 308, 323 (2014).

[88] Rome Statute of the International Criminal Court art. 28, July 17, 1998, 2187 U.N.T.S. 90.

[89] OFFICE OF THE GENERAL COUNSEL, U.S. DEPARTMENT OF DEFENSE, LAW OF WAR MANUAL § § 18.4 (rev. ed., Dec. 2016); *see* Convention (I) for the Amelioration of the Condition of the Wounded and Sick in the Armed Forces in the Field, art. 45, Aug. 12, 1949, 6 U.S.T. 3114, 75 U.N.T.S. 31; Convention (II) for the Amelioration of the Condition of the Wounded, Sick, and Shipwrecked Members of Armed Forces at Sea, art. 46, Aug. 12, 1949, 6 U.S.T. 3217, 75 U.N.T.S. 85; and Convention No. X for the Adaptation to Maritime Warfare of the Principles of the Geneva Convention, art. 19, Oct 18, 1907, 36 Stat. 2371, T.S. No. 543.

command. These leaders have authority commensurate with their responsibilities, exercised through intermediate subordinate commanders.[90]

4.1 Command Accountability

By whatever title they exercise leadership—commander, commanding officer, commandant—officers who lead units of the armed forces are accountable for the performance of the forces subject to their authority.[91] In U.S. joint force doctrine, the term "command" is all-encompassing, to include the authority and responsibility to organize, direct, coordinate, and control military forces to accomplish missions.[92] It also includes responsibility for health, welfare, morale, and discipline of all subordinates. The art of command flows from the commander's ability to use leadership to maximize performance.[93] "Clear commander's guidance and intent, enriched by the commander's experience and intuition, enable joint forces to achieve objectives."[94] Historically, the most senior military officers were held accountable for the general performance of their troops in combat. The commander leads through a combination of "courage, ethical leadership, judgment, intuition, situational awareness, and the capacity to consider contrary views. . . ."[95] In the U.S. Navy, commanders are required to observe the principles of international law.[96] In order to fulfill that responsibility, if there is a conflict between international law and other Navy regulations, commanders are authorized to uphold international law.[97] The Hague Regulations hold commanders directly and individually responsible for the methods and means of warfare they direct during the conduct of hostilities.[98]

In the aftermath of the First and Second World Wars, states recognized that any person, including heads of state or commanders-in-chief, is subject

[90] U.S. Department of Navy, United States Navy Regulations ¶ 0702 (Rev. Ed., 1990) (Responsibility and Authority of Commanders).

[91] Id. ¶ 0802 (Responsibility).

[92] Chairman, Joint Chiefs of Staff, Joint Publication 3-0 CH1, Joint Operations ¶ II-2 (rev. ed., Oct. 2018).

[93] Id.

[94] Id.

[95] Id.

[96] U.S. Department of the Navy, United States Navy Regulations art. 0705 (1990) (Observance of International Law).

[97] Id.

[98] Regulations Respecting the Laws and Customs of War on Land, annexed to Convention No. IV Respecting the Laws and Customs of War on Land art. 1, Oct. 18, 1907, 36 Stat. 2227, T.S. No. 539.

to LOAC and liable to criminal prosecution for their violation.[99] Military commanders are accountable for violations of LOAC that they personally commit or that they order their subordinates to commit.[100] Leaders may be held personally accountable for committing an offense, even when subordinates physically fulfill the material elements of the crime they have directed.[101] For example, commanders are directly liable for a range of international criminal acts that they commit during the conduct of hostilities: crimes against peace (planning and initiating war of aggression); war crimes (violations of the laws or customs of war); and crimes against humanity, including murder, extermination, and enslavement.[102] The commander's direct or individual accountability includes genocide and crimes against humanity that are committed by their forces at their direction, and for the consequences of decisions they have made or authorized for the employment of weapons, including LAWS, on the battlefield.

In all cases, commanders are accountable for the operational and legal judgments inherent in warfighting. Commanders employing an AI weapon system are no different. They would have an obligation to understand what LAWS can do in a particular environment in which it is used, like any other weapon.[103] They must know how the system responds in the field or at sea, where it excels and what are its limitations. They are not required to understand the intricacies of how the weapon works—the science and technology behind its performance—only appreciate how it functions and performs in the battlespace in which it is employed. In the event a LAWS proves to be indiscriminate the commander would be held to account. Every weapon system in the combat zone and every method of training—tactics, techniques, and procedures—falls within the remit of the commander's direct or individual accountability.

<hr>

[99] *Commission on the Responsibility of the Authors of the War and on Enforcement of Penalties*, reprinted from Pamphlet No. 32, Division of International Law, Carnegie Endowment for International Peace, 14 AMERICAN JOURNAL OF INTERNATIONAL LAW 95, 117 (1920) and Agreement for the Prosecution and Punishment of the Major War Criminals of the European Axis, Aug. 8, 1945, art. 7, 59 Stat. 1544, 1548, 82 U.N.T.S. 280, 288 [hereinafter Nuremburg Charter].

[100] United States v. Calley, 48 C.M.R. 19, 27 (1973-74); Prosecutor v. Milošević, IT-98-291/1-T (Dec. 12, 2007), ¶ 966 (the accused was in "command and control of his troops"); art. 1, Hague Regulations.

[101] ICTY, Prosecutor v, Delalic et al., (Judgment), Case No. IT-96-21-T, Trial Chamber (Nov. 16, 1998); Prosecutor v. Jadranko Prlić, Case No. IT-04-74-T, Judgement (TC), May 29, 2013, Vol. 1 ¶ 239.

[102] Nuremberg Charter, *supra* note 99, art. 6(c).

[103] DoD Directive 3000.09, *supra* note 6, at ¶ 4(a)(3)(a).

Human Rights Watch worries that it is "arguably unjust" to hold commanders accountable for the action of machines "over which they could not have sufficient control."[104] "These weapons' autonomy creates a 'responsibility gap,'" making it "arguably unjust to hold people responsible where they "could not have sufficient control."[105] This notion of responsibility, however, is too narrow, swallowed in practice by military accountability. Although it may seem "unfair" to impose liability on commanders for incidents occurring beyond their immediately control, and to sanction them even for mishaps they sought to avoid, the armed forces routinely do just that.[106] The U.S. armed forces, for example, consistently holds commanders accountable for literally everything that occurs throughout their entire force, from sexual harassment to peacetime ship collisions to battlefield disasters. The "fairness" of unbridled responsibility, and the unique exposure to perhaps unfair liability, is simply part of direct or individual command accountability—the burden of command—and it is subsumed by the duty owed by commanders to the armed forces and to the nation they serve.

As Marco Sassóli states, "it is as fair to hold a commander of a robot accountable as it would be to hold accountable a commander who instructs a pilot to bomb a target he describes as a military headquarters, but which turns out to be a kindergarten."[107] The commander's accountability, in this regard, is complete, even if some outsiders view it as "unfair"—even if the commander had no way of personally intervening to ensure a better outcome, indeed even if the commander optimized training and preparation of his or her forces to avoid such an outcome. This approach is used in warship collisions and other operational mishaps in order to hold leaders accountable and to develop "lessons learned" to avert future incidents. In the culture of direct accountability within the armed forces, loss of faith or confidence in the individual commander can result in criminal or administrative sanctions. For example, after the June 2017 collision by the USS *Fitzgerald* with the Motor Vessel *Acx Crystal*, which killed seven sailors, the commanding officer and the officer in charge of the combat information center were issued letters of censure.[108] The evidence was deemed insufficient to

[104] HUMAN RIGHTS WATCH, LOSING HUMANITY: THE CASE AGAINST KILLER ROBOTS 42 (2012).
[105] *Id.*
[106] Sparrow, *supra* note 84, at 74.
[107] Sassóli, *supra* note 87, at 324.
[108] Geoff Ziezulewicz, *Worse Than You Thought: Inside the Secret* Fitzgerald *Probe the Navy Doesn't Want You to Read*, NAVY TIMES (online), Jan. 13, 2019.

prevail against them in a criminal trial, even though the investigation uncovered ineffective command and control and deficiencies in training and
navigational skill.[109] In cases in which LOAC violations do not rise to the
level of war crimes, states typically pursue administrative mechanisms of accountability, initiating investigations and imposing nonjudicial punishment
or administrative censure.[110]

As a supplement to the criminal process, "administrative procedures,
inquiries, sanctions, and reforms" may be used to respond to violations of
LOAC, such as negligent actions that lack criminal culpability.[111] For example, the investigation of the shootdown by the USS *Vincennes* of Iran Air
flight 655 on July 3, 1988, exonerated the commanding officer of the warship.
In that case, the commanding officer gave the order to target what he thought
was an Iranian F-14 aircraft inbound to attack his warship—a calculation that
proved tragically wrong. Two hundred and 90 civilian lives were lost. After
an investigation, the Secretary of Defense concluded that the captain acted
prudently, given the high threat environment and previous demonstrations
of hostile intent and hostile acts by the Iranian Revolutionary Guard Corps
Navy against U.S. warships.[112] The investigating officer, a rear admiral,
recommended that no administrative or criminal action should be taken
against the captain.[113] This recommendation was endorsed by the Secretary
of Defense.[114]

Similarly, Laura Dickinson recounts administrative findings of a U.S.
Army investigation on the errant U.S. airstrike on October 3, 2015, against
a hospital in Kunduz, Afghanistan, operated by the humanitarian organization *Medecins Sans Frontieres* (MSF). The attack killed 24 patients, 14 staff

[109] The investigation determined that the collision and fatalities resulted from: (1) Failure to
plan for safety; (2) Failure to adhere to sound navigation practice; (3) Failure to execute basic watch
standing practices; (4) Failure to properly use available navigation tools; and (5) Failure to respond
deliberately and effectively when in extremis. *See* Memorandum from Office of the Chief of Naval
Operations, Department of the Navy, to Distribution, Collision Report for USS Fitzgerald and USS
John S. McCain Collisions (undated).
[110] Laura A. Dickinson, *Lethal Autonomous Weapons Systems: The Overlooked Importance of
Administrative Accountability, in* THE IMPACT OF EMERGING TECHNOLOGIES ON THE LAW OF ARMED
CONFLICT 69, 84–85 (Ronald T.P. Alcala & Eric Talbot Jensen eds., 2019).
[111] *Id.* at 71.
[112] Memorandum from Secretary of Defense to Secretary of the Navy, Formal Investigation into
the Circumstances Surrounding the Downing of Iran Air Flight 655 on 3 July 1988, at 61 (Aug.
19, 1988).
[113] *Id.* at 51.
[114] *Id.*

members, and four caretakers.[115] A cascade of errors led to the tragic airstrike. Some of those involved in the decision to attack received administrative penalties or disciplinary action, although they were not charged with a crime.[116] A comprehensive review of tactical directives, pre-deployment training, and rules of engagement followed.[117] The Secretary of Defense took corrective action to avoid another such incident. The military departments were directed to review command-and-control systems to ensure that they could maintain a "unified understanding of the battle space and enhance interoperability."[118] In another incident, this one in Iraq in 2003, Lieutenant Colonel Allen West was fined $5,000 and retired after he was found to have threatened the life of an uncooperative Iraqi detainee by discharging a firearm as an interrogation technique.[119] These cases demonstrate that DoD investigates mishaps and reviews decisions during hostilities, and takes administrative action as a supplement to criminal prosecution. These measures hold military leaders accountable through nonjudicial and administrative processes in cases lacking criminal culpability necessary to obtain convictions at trial.

Commanders may also be held responsible for violations of LOAC committed by their subordinates if they have failed to properly train their force, exercise appropriate oversight, or establish guidance and expectations in command environment conducive to compliance with the law.[120] The international law doctrine of command responsibility is a subset of the military doctrine of command accountability.

5. Conclusion

The unmanned systems of tomorrow, particularly autonomous and semi-autonomous systems, will fundamentally change the way nations conduct

---

[115] Dickinson, *supra* note 110, at 84–85; Alissa J. Rubin, *Airstrike Hits Doctors Without Borders Hospital in Afghanistan*, N.Y. TIMES (online), Oct. 3, 2015; Missy Ryan, Thomas Gibbons-Neff, & Mohammad Sharif, *Doctors Without Borders Says U.S. Airstrike Hit Hospital in Afghanistan; at least 19 Dead*, WASHINGTON POST (online), Oct. 3, 2015.

[116] Jim Garamone, *Centcom Commander: Communications Errors, Human Error Led to Attack on Afghan Hospital*, U.S. DEPARTMENT OF DEFENSE NEWS (online), Apr. 29, 2016.

[117] Memorandum from the Secretary of Defense to the Secretaries of the Military Departments et al., Secretary of Defense Guidance (Apr. 28, 2016).

[118] *Id.*

[119] Allen West went on to serve one term in the U.S. House of Representatives, representing Florida's 22nd congressional district from 2011 to 2013. *U.S. Officer Fined for Harsh Interrogation Tactics*, CNN (online), Dec. 13, 2003.

[120] NWP 1-14M, *supra* note 14, § 6.1.3.

naval operations. Their use and mission sets will continue to expand as new technologies, including greater stealth, persistence, autonomy, and durability, are developed and employed that not only reduce operational risk and cost, but exceed the capabilities of manned platforms. For example, by 2025, worldwide military UAV production will grow from $2.8 billion to $9.4 billion.[121] As these systems proliferate and are enhanced by new technologies, including AI and machine learning, unmanned systems capable of conducting offensive strikes, or conducting swarm attacks that deny access to a given area or overwhelm air defense systems, increasingly will be within the reach of states and nonstate actors alike.

Take, for example, the Iranian-sponsored precision attack on Saudi oil fields in September 2019. Despite Saudi Arabia's extensive and sophisticated air defense capabilities, Iran and its Houthi proxies were able to use inexpensive drones and cruise missiles to take out 50 percent of Saudi crude production—5.7 million barrels per day—resulting in a 20 percent spike in oil prices. On September 14, 18 drones struck the Abqaiq oil production facility damaging 11 spheroid separation tanks, five stabilization towers, and two tanks used to hold water removed from crude oil. Four stabilization towers were damaged at the Khurais facility by four cruise missiles.[122]

5.1 Raising the Risk of War

Inevitably, despite the legal and ethical concerns, autonomous systems will become more "intelligent." Will the proliferation of unmanned systems have the unintended consequence of lowering the threshold for an armed conflict? For example, U.S. Special Mission Ships (SMS) routinely conduct hydrographic surveys and military marine data collection in China's exclusive economic zone (EEZ). China objects to these operations, claiming that they pose a threat to China's national security interests and violate both international and Chinese domestic law. In most cases, the People's Liberation Army Navy (PLAN), China Coast Guard, and/or China Maritime Militia ships routinely challenge and harass U.S. survey ships and order them to leave the EEZ or "suffer the consequences." U.S. survey ships are lawfully exercising

---

[121] Jon Walker, *Unmanned Aerial Vehicles (UAVs): Comparing the USA, Israel, and China*, EMERJ. COM (online), Feb. 3, 2019 (Emerj is an AI research and advisory company).

[122] *Saudi Arabia Oil Attacks: UN "Unable to Confirm Iranian Involvement*," BBC (online), Dec. 11, 2019.

high seas freedoms in accordance with international law and continue on their mission.[123] To date, China has not attempted to board or seize any U.S. survey ships, which are protected by sovereign immunity. If the military survey ships were unmanned, however, China may attempt to board or seize them.

Compare China's response to SMS ships with its actions in 2016 toward a U.S. Navy "ocean glider" that was collecting oceanographic data in the South China Sea. On December 16, a PLAN *Dalang-III*-class submarine rescue vessel illegally seized a U.S. Navy UUV in international waters about 50 nautical miles northwest of Subic Bay. The unclassified, commercial off-the-shelf "ocean glider" system was being used to collect "military oceanographic data such as salinity, water temperature, and sound speed." In this case, the UUV had just completed a pre-programmed military oceanographic survey route and was returning to the USNS *Bowditch* (T-AGS 62).[124] As the crew of the *Bowditch* was attempting to recover the glider and a second UUV, the PLAN vessel launched a small boat and retrieved the glider.[125]

At the time of the incident, the *Bowditch* was legally conducting routine operations in international waters in full compliance with international law. The glider was clearly marked as U.S. Navy property. The *Dalang-III* ignored repeated calls from the *Bowditch* to return the UUV and departed the area, indicating she was "returning to normal operations"[126] Using diplomatic and military channels, the U.S. government immediately demanded that China return the unlawfully seized sovereign immune UUV. Three days later, on December 20, a PLAN Type 056 *Jiangdao*-class corvette 510 returned the glider to the USS *Mustin* (DDG 89).[127]

Under the U.S. Standing Rules of Engagement (SROE), "unit commanders . . . retain the inherent right and obligation to exercise unit

---

[123] *See* Raul Pedrozo, *Preserving Navigational Rights and Freedoms: The Right to Conduct Military Activities in China's Exclusive Economic Zone*, 9 CHINESE JOURNAL OF INTERNATIONAL LAW 9, 28–29 (March 2010); Raul Pedrozo, *Coastal State Jurisdiction over Marine Data Collection in the Exclusive Economic Zone: U.S. Views, in* MILITARY ACTIVITIES IN THE EEZ: A U.S.-CHINA DIALOGUE ON SECURITY AND INTERNATIONAL LAW IN THE MARITIME COMMONS 23, 33–34 (Peter Dutton ed., 2010); and Raul Pedrozo, *Military Activities in the Exclusive Economic Zone: East Asia Focus*, 90 INTERNATIONAL LAW STUDIES 514, 540 (2014).

[124] Terri Moon Cronk, *Chinese Seize U.S. Navy Underwater Drone in South China Sea*, DEPARTMENT OF DEFENSE NEWS (online), Dec. 16, 2016.

[125] *Id.*

[126] *Id.*

[127] Press Release, Peter Cook, Press Secretary, U.S. Department of Defense, Statement by Pentagon Press Secretary Peter Cook on Return of U.S. Navy UUV (online), Dec. 19, 2016.

self-defense in response to a hostile act or demonstrated hostile intent."[128] "Hostile act" is defined to include, not only an attack or other use of force against the United States, U.S. forces or other designated persons or property, but also "force used directly to preclude or impede the mission and/or duties of U.S. forces, *including the recovery of U.S. personnel or vital USG property* (emphasis added)."[129] Similarly, "hostile intent" includes "the threat of imminent use of force against the United States, U.S. forces or other designated persons or property," as well as "the threat of force to preclude or impede the mission and/or duties of U.S. forces, *including the recovery of U.S. personnel or vital USG property* (emphasis added)."[130] What if, rather than demand the return of the stolen U.S. government property, the embarked Security Detachment on board the USNS *Bowditch*, consistent with the SROE, used force to prevent the *Dalang-III* small boat from seizing the UUV? In such case, the *Dalang-III* might retaliate, leading to an armed confrontation by a nearby U.S. destroyer assigned to protect the *Bowditch*. Such a scenario is feasible: an unintended consequence of unmanned systems emboldening states to act in ways that escalate into a broader armed conflict.

Another example of potential miscalculation is Iran's June 20, 2019, shootdown of an unmanned U.S. Navy MQ-4C Triton in the Persian Gulf. The Triton was the airborne element of the Broad Area Maritime Surveillance Unmanned Aircraft System, a surveillance platform. The Triton was shot down by Iran's Islamic Revolution Guards Corps (IRGC). Brigadier General Amir Ali Hajizadeh, commander of the IRGC's aerospace force, claimed that the MQ-4C was downed by an Iranian missile while it was collecting intelligence in Iran's national airspace. U.S. officials denied wrongdoing and countered that the attack was unprovoked. The Triton was legally operating in international airspace. President Donald Trump called off a retaliatory strike against the Iranian missile launch sites and radar installations that had been involved in the MQ-4C shootdown just 10 minutes before execution because he concluded the strike was "not proportionate to shooting down an unmanned drone."[131] The president stated, "I imagine someone made a

---

[128] SROE, *supra* note 76.

[129] *Id.*

[130] *Id.*

[131] Richard Sisk, *Iran Chose to Take Out Drone Instead of Manned Navy Jet, Iranian General Says*, MILITARY.COM, (online), June 21, 2019; *Iran's IRGC Force Shoots Down Intruding US Spy Drone*, PRESSTV (online), June 20, 2019.

mistake. We didn't have a man or woman in the drone. It would have made a big, big difference."[132]

General Hajizadeh stated that Iran knew a Navy P-8 Poseidon aircraft was operating in the area where the MQ-4C was shot down, but Tehran purposely refrained from shooting down the manned aircraft to avoid escalation by the United States. The presence of manned U.S. aircraft in the area was confirmed by U.S. Central Command representative Captain William Urban, who stated there were "six different occasions where Iranian air defense stations queried or warned U.S. aircraft . . . in the 12 hours prior to and following the shootdown. . . ."[133] Thus, while the Iranians did not hesitate to shoot down an unmanned drone, they were reluctant to engage a manned U.S. aircraft for fear of a substantial U.S. response.

Perhaps General Hajizadeh recalled how the United States reacted to Iranian attacks on American forces in the Persian Gulf during the Iran-Iraq War. In response to continued aggression against U.S. merchant ships and naval forces in the Persian Gulf, the United States launched Operation Praying Mantis (October 1988 to April 1988). The operation was designed to neutralize Iranian oil platforms that were being used by the IRGC as logistics and staging bases to launch attacks against neutral merchant shipping in the Gulf. By the end of the operation—the Navy's largest surface naval engagement since the Second World War—three IRGC command-and-control platforms—Reshadat 4 and 7, Sassan and Sirri—were destroyed; six Iranian naval vessels, including the frigate *Saband* (F 74) and the missile patrol boat *Joshan* (P 225), were sunk; and the frigate *Sabalan* (F 73) was severely damaged.[134]

Nonetheless, these incidents reflect what could become a trend in times of increasing tensions. As nations increasingly rely on unmanned systems to conduct ISR operations against their adversaries in coastal areas or on the high seas, the potential for war also increases. The U.S. failure to respond with overwhelming kinetic force against China and Iran in these cases may encourage other nations to take similar measures against unmanned systems based on an assumption that the operator of a drone will not respond if there

---

[132] Michael R. Gordon, Sune Engel Rasmussen, & Siobhan Hughes, *U.S. Planned Strike on Iran After Downing of Drone but Called Off Mission*, WALL STREET JOURNAL (online), June 21, 2019.

[133] Oriana Pawlyk, *CENTCOM: Iran Never Warned RQ-4 Drone Before Shootdown*, MILITARY.COM (online), July 30, 2019.

[134] JAMES KRASKA & RAUL PEDROZO, THE FREE SEA: THE AMERICAN FIGHT FOR FREEDOM OF NAVIGATION 212–17 (2018).

is no loss of life. Other states may react differently to such hostile actions albeit against an unmanned system. While there may not be a pilot in the cockpit, unmanned and autonomous craft are imbued with sovereignty immunity and the trappings of national honor. This fact alone ensures the use of ever more intelligent or autonomous systems will generate legal and political fallout.

5

Submarine Warfare

1. Undersea Warfare

During the American Revolutionary War, the submersible *Turtle* became the world's first combat submarine. Initially designed by David Bushnell, a Yale College student, the *Turtle* was meant to break the British blockade of Boston Harbor. The submersible conducted its first, albeit unsuccessful, attack in September 1776 against a British warship anchored in New York Harbor. Two later attacks also failed. The *Turtle* was lost at sea on October 9, 1776, when the Royal Navy sank the colonial sloop-of-war that was transporting the submersible.[1]

Nearly one hundred years later, the U.S. Navy bought its first submarine, the USS *Alligator*, in 1862. Designed by French inventor Brutus de Villeroi, the *Alligator* never saw action and was lost off Cape Hatteras, North Carolina, on April 2, 1863, while it was being towed from Washington, D.C., to Charleston, South Carolina, to engage Confederate forces.[2] The Confederate submersible *H. L. Hunley*, however, was more effective, becoming the first submarine to sink an enemy warship. Under cover of darkness, on February 17, 1864, the *Hunley* rammed the USS *Housatonic* below the water line with an explosive-laden torpedo bolted to a 16-foot spar. The explosion tore a hole in the hull of the 16-gun sloop-of-war, sinking the Union warship four miles off the entrance to Charleston Harbor. Although the attack succeeded, the *Hunley* and her crew of eight perished during the engagement.[3]

It was not until the First World War, however, that the devastating effect and potential military advantage of submarine warfare became evident. German

---

[1] Frank Uhlig, Jr., *The Submarine, 1776–1918*, 57 NAVAL WAR COLLEGE REVIEW 146, 147 (2004); *The Submarine Turtle: Naval Documents of the Revolutionary War*, NAVAL HISTORY & HERITAGE COMMAND (online), undated.

[2] G. T. Reader & I. J. Potter, *Early Submarine Engine Development*, 106 SAE TRANSACTIONS: JOURNAL OF ENGINES 1921, 1922 (1997); Louis H. Bolander, *The Alligator, First Federal Submarine of the Civil War*, 64 U.S. NAVAL INSTITUTE PROCEEDINGS 845 (1938); Von Kolnitz, *The Confederate Submarine*, 63 U.S. NAVAL INSTITUTE PROCEEDINGS 1453 (1937).

[3] Eric A. Powell, *Hunley Decoded*, ARCHEOLOGY 46, 47 (2013); Reader & Potter, *supra* note 2, at 1922; H. L. Hunley Wreck (1864), NAVAL HISTORY & HERITAGE COMMAND (online), 2020.

Disruptive Technology and the Law of Naval Warfare. James Kraska and Raul Pedrozo, Oxford University Press.
© James Kraska & Raul Pedrozo 2022. DOI: 10.1093/oso/9780197630181.003.0006

Unterseeboots (U-boats) sank over 13 million gross tons of allied merchant shipping, some 5,000 ships, as well as 119 warships.[4] More than 15,000 merchant seamen lost their lives in these attacks. During the Second World War, with just 57 submarines, Germany sank 519 allied ships during the first six months after the United States entered the war. Ultimately, the U-boats were challenged by effective Allied convoys and sank only 290 allied merchant ships and 262 warships. In the Pacific Ocean, American submarines sank 686 Japanese warships of 500 gross tons or more, 628 smaller warships, and 2,346 merchant vessels, totaling 10.5 million gross tons.[5]

The increasing distance, lethality, and accuracy of stand-off weapons make surface ships vulnerable in high-end naval conflict. Naval operations are moving to relative safety underwater to escape advanced sensors and missiles that make surface operations so perilous. The most advanced naval forces, including the United States, China, Japan, the United Kingdom, and Russia are leading the way, developing a range of submarine and seabed capabilities that seek to leverage stealth, survivability, and maneuver with new weapons. This shift into the depths reintroduces legacy legal issues about submarine duties in the law of naval warfare and poses new questions about submarine operations in the littoral seas and on the continental shelf and deep seabed.

1.1 Submarine Fleets

More than 40 countries operate submarines.[6] The top-10 navies with the largest submarine fleets are: North Korea, China, the United States, Russia, Iran, Japan, India, South Korea, Turkey, Greece, and the United Kingdom.[7] Among these, the United States, Russia, and China have the most powerful and innovative submarine forces. Six countries—the United States, China, Russia, France, the United Kingdom, and India—operate ballistic missile

---

[4] Karl Lautenschlager, *The Submarine in Naval Warfare, 1901–2001*, 11 INTERNATIONAL SECURITY 94, 111–14 (1987) [hereinafter Lautenschlager].

[5] U.S. National Park Service, *The Silent Service: Submarines in the Pacific, in* WAR IN THE PACIFIC: THE PACIFIC OFFENSIVE, NPS.GOV (online).

[6] Countries with a sizable submarine fleet include North Korea (83 boats), China (74), the United States (66), Russia (62), Iran (34), South Korea (22), Japan (20), India (13), Turkey (12), Colombia (11) Greece (11), the United Kingdom (10), France (9), Pakistan (8), Italy (8), Egypt (8), Australia (6), Brazil (6), Germany (6), Vietnam (6), Norway (6), Algeria (6), Israel (6), Indonesia (6), and Sweden (6). Taiwan, Spain, Canada, and South Africa. Global Firepower, *Submarine Fleet Strength by Country (2020)*, GLOBALFIREPOWER.COM (online).

[7] *Id.*

submarines (SSBNs).[8] The French Navy operates four Triumphant-class SSBNs, and the Royal Navy runs four Vanguard-class SSBNs, which provide an independent European-based nuclear deterrent. India's Arihant-class SSBN is the first such boat launched by a state other than a permanent member of the UN Security Council.

For the major powers, submarines are a cornerstone of strategic deterrence and the most survivable leg of the nuclear triad, comprised of land-based ballistic missiles, nuclear-armed aircraft, and SSBNs. The permanent members of the UN Security Council, joined by India, all operate fast attack nuclear submarines that offer unmatched endurance and stealth. The Royal Australian Navy plans to acquire at least eight nuclear submarines under the trilateral Australia-UK-US (AUKUS) pact.

The Japan Maritime Self Defense Force has a fleet of 22 diesel-electric attack submarines (SSKs), more than half equipped with air-independent propulsion. India, Vietnam, Australia, Indonesia, Singapore, South Korea, and Vietnam are all expanding their fleets to balance the Chinese People's Liberation Army (Navy) (PLAN). China has provided Pakistan with eight Type 039B submarines to try to "contain" India, with the first entering service in 2022.[9] North Korea has some 80 submarines, consisting mostly of aging boats and miniature submarines, plus a fledgling SSBN program.[10]

1.2 U.S. Submarine Forces

The U.S. Navy submarine force includes 51 attack submarines (SSNs), four guided missile submarines (SSGNs), and 14 Ohio-class SSBNs. By 2028, the force will shrink to 42 attack boats and about a dozen SSBNs, as the Navy retires aging *Los Angeles*-class boats and replaces them with a fewer number of *Virginia*-class vessels. (In comparison, the Royal Navy has six SSNs and four SSBNs). Of the 35 *Los Angeles*-class SSNs, 30 are equipped with 12 Vertical

---

[8] China, France, India, Russia, United Kingdom, United States, and possibly North Korea, operate SSBNs. *See United States Strategic Weapon Systems, in* JANE'S SENTINEL: SECURITY ASSESSMENTS (2020); Minnie Chan, *China's Navy Has Put 2 New Nuclear-Powered Ballistic-Missile Subs into Service,* SOUTH CHINA MORNING POST (online), Apr. 30, 2020; *China Strategic Weapon Systems, in* JANE'S SENTINEL: SECURITY ASSESSMENTS (online), 2020; *Russian Federation Navy, in* JANE'S SENTINEL: SECURITY ASSESSMENTS (online), 2020; Tim Fish, *Sub-surface Ambitions: Indo-Pacific Submarine Programmes,* JANE'S DEFENCE WEEKLY (online), Oct. 6, 2020.

[9] H. Sutton, *Pakistan's New Type-039B AIP Submarines,* NAVAL NEWS (online), Oct. 6, 2020.

[10] Gabriel Dominguez, *North Korea Says It Test-Fired a New Type of Submarine-Launched Ballistic Missile,* JANE'S DEFENCE WEEKLY, Oct. 9, 2019, at 6.

Launch System (VLS) tubes loaded with Tomahawk cruise missiles.[11] Most of the *Virginia*-class boats are equipped with new Virginia Payload Modules (VPM), an additional 84-foot-long, mid-body section outfitted with four large-diameter, vertical launch tubes for cruise missiles or future weapons. Beginning in 2027, 12 *Columbia*-class submarines will replace the *Ohio*-class SSBNs—the Navy's top priority.[12] The three *Seawolf*-class SSNs are equipped with sophisticated sensors and are exceptionally quiet and fast.

1.3 Russian Submarine Forces

The Russian submarine fleet includes 62 boats of all classes, including nine SSGNs; 14 SSNs; and 22 conventional attack submarines.[13] Russia operates 10 SSBNs, and the new *Dologorukiy*-class SSBN is armed with the SS-N-32 Bulava SLBM.[14] All Russian SSBNs carry missiles that can reach the United States.[15] New and extremely quiet, the *Severodvinsk* SSGN is armed with a wide range of anti-ship cruise missiles (ASCM).

The Russian Navy has a global reach, with patrols in the Mediterranean Sea, the Arctic Ocean, the Western Hemisphere, and the Indian Ocean. The Northern Fleet is the most capable force, with seven ballistic missile submarines providing the bulk of the national undersea deterrent.[16] The Pacific Fleet submarine force includes attack submarines based mostly in Vladivostok and SSBNs in Petropavlovsk-Kamchatskiy. The Black Sea Fleet was in slow decline until Russia's invasion of Crimea in 2014. Now as many as six new attack submarines will enter the Black Sea Fleet in the coming years.

1.4 Chinese Submarine Forces

Beginning in May 2002, when China signed a contract with Moscow for eight Russian *Kilo*-class submarines, China has created an entirely new and

---

[11] CONGRESSIONAL RESEARCH SERVICE, PUBLICATION NO. R32418, NAVY *VIRGINIA* (SSN-774) CLASS ATTACK SUBMARINE PROCUREMENT: BACKGROUND AND ISSUES FOR CONGRESS 4 (2019).

[12] CONGRESSIONAL RESEARCH SERVICE, PUBLICATION NO. R41129, NAVY'S *COLUMBIA* (SSBN-826) CLASS BALLISTIC MISSILE SUBMARINE PROGRAM: BACKGROUND AND ISSUES FOR CONGRESS 5 (2020); *see also* Joseph Trevithick, *Navy Plans For "Large Payload Subs" Based on New* Columbia *Class to Take on SSGN Role and More*, THE DRIVE: THE WAR ZONE (online), Nov. 9, 2018.

[13] David Axe, *Is Russia's Submarine Force Dying?*, NATIONAL INTEREST (online), Jan. 20, 2020.

[14] U.S. DEFENSE INTELLIGENCE AGENCY, RUSSIA MILITARY POWER 30 (2017).

[15] *Id.* at 68–69.

[16] *Id.* at 67.

potent submarine force structure from the ground up. Qualitatively, China's submarines are inferior to U.S. and Russian boats, but they have improved in recent years. China originally began to develop submarines to target U.S. carrier battle groups.[17] Today China operates six (soon to be eight) SSBNs, six SSNs, and some 50 diesel-electric boats.[18]

The PLAN will likely maintain between 65 to 70 submarines through the 2020s, replacing legacy systems with advanced platforms, including as many as 25 or more of the new *Yuan*-class diesel-electric air-independent-powered attack submarines (SSP) by 2025.[19] The *Shang*-class is China's newest SSN. Two of the six *Jin*-class SSBNs entered into service in 2020. Each *Jin*-class ballistic missile submarine carries 12 SLBMs, China's first credible sea-based nuclear deterrent.[20] By 2030, China is expected to have 76 submarines, including eight SSBNs, 13 SSNs, and 55 SSKs and SSPs.[21]

2. The Law of Submarine Warfare

These underwater forces are increasingly important for war planning because they are more survivable than surface ships. Like all naval forces, submarines must comply with the law of armed conflict (LOAC). The right of a belligerent to adopt means or methods of warfare is not unlimited.[22] The most basic rule of LOAC for submarines is that they must be able to distinguish between lawful military objectives and civilian or protected vessels. Customary international law prohibits the use of indiscriminate weapons which, by their nature, cannot distinguish between military objectives and civilians or civilian objects.[23] Indiscriminate attacks are prohibited. Additional Protocol I to the Geneva Conventions defines indiscriminate attacks as the following:

---

[17] Wang Jiasuo, *Aircraft Carriers: Suggest You Keep Out of the Taiwan Strait*, JUNSHI WENZHAI [MILITARY DIGEST] (online), Apr. 1, 2001.

[18] SECRETARY OF DEFENSE, ANNUAL REPORT TO CONGRESS: MILITARY AND SECURITY DEVELOPMENTS INVOLVING THE PEOPLE'S REPUBLIC OF CHINA 45 (2020).

[19] *Id.*

[20] *Id.*

[21] CONGRESSIONAL RESEARCH SERVICE, CHINA NAVAL MODERNIZATION: IMPLICATIONS FOR U.S. NAVY CAPABILITIES—BACKGROUND AND ISSUES FOR CONGRESS 8–9 (Mar. 9, 2021).

[22] Convention and Customs of War on Land (Hague, II) art. 22, July 29, 1899, 32 Stat. 1803, T.S. 403; Protocol Additional to the Geneva Conventions of 12 August 1949, and relating to the Protection of Victims of International Armed Conflicts, art. 35(1), June 8, 1977, 1125 U.N.T.S. 3 [hereinafter AP I]; SAN REMO MANUAL ON INTERNATIONAL LAW APPLICABLE TO ARMED CONFLICTS AT SEA ¶ 38 (Louise Doswald Beck ed., 1995) [hereinafter SAN REMO MANUAL].

[23] SAN REMO MANUAL, *supra* note 22, ¶ 42(b); 1 INTERNATIONAL COMMITTEE OF RED CROSS, CUSTOMARY INTERNATIONAL HUMANITARIAN LAW r. 71 (Jean-Marie Henckaerts & Louise Doswald-Beck eds., 2005) [hereinafter 1 ICRC CUSTOMARY LAW STUDY].

a. those which are not directed at a specific military objective;
b. those which employ a method or means of combat which cannot be directed at a specific military objective; or
c. those which employ a method or means of combat the effects of which cannot be limited [. . . and] are of a nature to strike military objectives and civilians or civilian objects without distinction.[24]

Weapons, material, or methods of warfare that are designed to cause superfluous injury or unnecessary suffering are also prohibited.[25] Some weapons, such as chemical or biological weapons, are unlawful per se, while others may be rendered unlawful if they are altered—for example, coating an otherwise lawful munition with a poison.[26] Furthermore, a lawful weapon or weapon system, such as a submarine, may be used unlawfully if it is directed or used against noncombatants, civilians, or other protected persons and property.[27]

International efforts to regulate or prohibit the use or construction of submarines during armed conflict dates to the First Hague Peace Conference in 1899. Despite continuous negotiations over the intervening decades, there remains only one international agreement that regulates submarine warfare—the 1936 London Protocol.[28]

[24] AP I, *supra note* 22, art. 51.4; Rome Statute of the International Criminal Court, art. 8.2(b)(xx), July 17, 1998, 2187 U.N.T.S. 90 (defining "war crimes" as "Other serious violations of the laws and customs applicable in international armed conflict, within the established framework of international law, namely, any of the following acts: . . . (xx) Employing weapons, projectiles and material and methods of warfare which are of a nature to cause superfluous injury or unnecessary suffering or which are inherently indiscriminate in violation of the international law of armed conflict, provided that such weapons, projectiles and material and methods of warfare are the subject of a comprehensive prohibition and are included in an annex to this Statute, by an amendment in accordance with the relevant provisions set forth in articles 121 and 123."); SAN REMO MANUAL, *supra note* 22, ¶ 42(b) ("In addition to any specific prohibitions binding upon the parties to a conflict, it is forbidden to employ methods or means of warfare which: . . . (b) are indiscriminate, in that: (i) they are not, or cannot be, directed against a specific military objective; or (ii) their effects cannot be limited as required by international law as reflected in this document.").
[25] AP I, *supra note* 22, art. 35.2 ("It is prohibited to employ weapons, projectiles and material and methods of warfare of a nature to cause superfluous injury or unnecessary suffering."); SAN REMO MANUAL, *supra* note 22, ¶ 42(a) ("In addition to any specific prohibitions binding upon the parties to a conflict, it is forbidden to employ methods or means of warfare which: (a) are of a nature to cause superfluous injury or unnecessary suffering. . . .").
[26] 1 ICRC CUSTOMARY LAW STUDY, *supra* note 23, rr. 72–74.
[27] U.S. NAVY, U.S. MARINE CORPS, & U.S. COAST GUARD, NWP 1-14M/MCTP 11-10B/COMDTPUB P5800.7A, THE COMMANDER'S HANDBOOK ON THE LAW OF NAVAL OPERATIONS § 9.12 (2017) [hereinafter NWP 1-14M].
[28] Procès-Verbal Relating to the Rules of Submarine Warfare Set Forth in Part IV of the Treaty of London of April 22, 1930, Nov. 6, 1936, 173 L.N.T.S. 353, 3 Bevans 298, *reprinted in* 31 AMERICAN JOURNAL OF INTERNATIONAL LAW SUPPLEMENT 137 (1937); DIETRICH SCHINDLER & JIŘÍ TOMAN, THE LAWS OF ARMED CONFLICTS 883–84 (1988).

2.1 Pre-First World War

By the turn of the 20th century, several maritime states were experimenting with submarines. The United Kingdom had resisted development of the submarine from the time of its invention because it threatened the superiority of British sea power.[29] On December 30, 1898, Tsar Nicolas II of Russia invited world leaders to participate in a disarmament conference to address a number of issues, including the "prohibition of the use in naval battles of submarine or diving torpedo boats, or of other engines of destruction of the same nature. . . ."[30] States with weaker navies refused to eliminate U-boats as a cost-effective way to counter larger surface fleets.

The regulation of submarines in armed conflict was taken up at the second and third meetings of the Naval Sub-commission of the First Commission. Captain Alfred Thayer Mahan, America's preeminent naval strategist of the time, represented the United States at the meeting. The prohibition of submarines or diving torpedo boats was put to a vote at the fourth meeting of the Naval Sub-commission on June 23, 1899, but it lacked the votes for further consideration. Five states—Belgium, Greece, Persia, Siam, and Bulgaria— voted in favor of the proposal to ban submarines, with reservations. Five other states—Germany, Italy, Great Britain, Japan, and Romania—voted in favor of the proposal to ban submarines, but only if it received unanimous support from all participating states. Ten states—the United States, Austria-Hungary, Denmark, Spain, France, Portugal, Sweden, Norway, the Netherlands, and Turkey—opposed any prohibition on submarines.[31] Russia, Serbia, and Switzerland abstained from voting.

The 1898 proposal to prohibit the use of submarines was not resurrected at the Second Hague Peace Conference in 1907. Rather, the conference discussed bombardment of ports, cities, and villages by a naval force, and the use of torpedoes as means and method of naval warfare.[32] The issue of

[29] D. P. O'CONNELL, THE INFLUENCE OF LAW ON SEA POWER 25 (1975).

[30] Program Proposed by the Imperial Government of Russia to the Governments Invited to the First Peace Conference, Circular of December 30, 1898/January 11, 1889, in INDEX TO THE PROCEEDINGS OF THE HAGUE PEACE CONFERENCES, THE CONFERENCES OF 1899 AND 1907, at 1 (James Brown Scott ed., 1921).

[31] THE PROCEEDINGS OF THE HAGUE PEACE CONFERENCES, THE CONFERENCE OF 1899, at 274–75, 296, 299, 367–68 (James Brown Scott ed., 1920); W. T. Mallison, Jr., *Submarine Warfare in International Law*, 58 INTERNATIONAL LAW STUDIES 1, 13–14 (1966).

[32] Other topics discussed included the following: the transformation of merchant vessels into warships; the private property of belligerents at sea; the length of time to be granted to merchant ships for their departure from ports of neutrals or of the enemy after the opening of hostilities; and the rights and duties of neutrals at sea, among others, the questions of contraband, the rules

144 DISRUPTIVE TECHNOLOGY AND NAVAL WARFARE

submarine use was also not debated during the negotiations of the 1909 London Declaration, which focused on identifying generally recognized rules of international law relative to naval prize that would be applied by a new International Prize Court to be established by Hague Convention XII of 1907.[33] (The London Declaration was never ratified by any of the signatories; consequently, Hague XII never entered into force.)

2.2 First World War

In the years preceding the First World War, Admiral Tirpitz aggressively expanded the German surface fleet in the hopes of defeating the Royal Navy in a decisive engagement.[34] Barring this possibility, Germany wanted the submarine to place the British fleet at such risk in an engagement that its grip on its empire would be imperiled. The Royal Navy proved too powerful to confront directly. Germany turned to the submarine to attempt to impose on the United Kingdom the same type of blockade that the Royal Navy was inflicting on the continent. Germany prepared for years for such action. In 1910, Germany commissioned the U-9, the Imperial Navy's first effective offensive sea platform.[35] The U-9 had a submersible range of 3,200 nautical miles and was armed with six fairly reliable torpedoes. Germany also made a breakthrough transition from gasoline to diesel engines, as gasoline power was extremely dangerous and emitted large clouds of black smoke that revealed the submarine's position. By 1914, Germany had 10 diesel U-boats, with 17 more under construction.[36]

applicable to belligerent vessels in neutral ports; destruction, in cases of *force majeure*, of neutral merchant vessels captured as prizes. Program Proposed by the Imperial Government of Russia to the Governments Invited to the Second Peace Conference, Circular of March/April 1906, *in* INDEX TO THE PROCEEDINGS OF THE HAGUE PEACE CONFERENCES, THE CONFERENCES OF 1899 AND 1907, *supra* note 30, at 2.

[33] At the invitation of the United Kingdom, 10 major sea powers participated in the Conference. Declaration Concerning the Laws of Naval War, Feb. 26, 1909, 208 T.S. 338; Convention Relative to the Creation of an International Prize Court, Oct. 18, 1907, *reprinted in* SCHINDLER & TOMAN, *supra* note 28, at 825–36.

[34] Paul M. Kennedy, *The Development of German Naval Operations Plans Against England, 18961914, in* THE WAR PLANS OF THE GREAT POWERS 171, 188 (Paul M. Kennedy ed., 1979).

[35] Lautenschlager, *supra* note 4, at 102–03; BRYAN CLARK ET AL., SUSTAINING THE UNDERSEA ADVANTAGE: DISRUPTING ANTI-SUBMARINE WARFARE 15–18 (2020).

[36] Lautenschlager, *supra* note 4, at 102–03; BERNARD & FAWN M. BRODIE, FROM CROSSBOW TO H-BOMB: THE EVOLUTION OF THE WEAPONS AND TACTICS OF WARFARE 181 (1962); *see also* James Kraska, *Fear God and Dread Nought: Naval Arms Control and Counterfactual Diplomacy Before the Great War*, GEORGIA JOURNAL OF INTERNATIONAL & COMPARATIVE LAW 43, 88–89 (2006).

On August 4, 1914, Great Britain declared war on Germany and began enforcing a "hunger blockade" against the Central Powers. Britain tightened its stranglehold on the continent on November 3, 1914, by declaring the North Sea a "military area" and warning neutral nations that it would be mined. Neutral ships bound for Norway, the Baltic Sea, Denmark, and Holland would be escorted through the mine field by the Royal Navy only after they put into a British port for inspection and any contraband destined for Germany and its allies was removed.[37]

Germany responded by establishing its own war zone on February 4, 1915. Germany protected its surface fleet as a "fleet in being" while relying on submarine warfare, mines, and torpedo boats in hit-and-run attacks to whittle away at the Royal Navy. Framed as a reprisal for the November 3 mining of the North Sea, the German Admiralty proclamation provided that "the waters surrounding Great Britain and Ireland including the whole English Channel are hereby declared to be compromised within the seat of war and that all enemy merchant vessels found in those waters [after February 18] . . . will be destroyed although it may not always be possible to save crews and passengers."[38] Germany also warned neutral vessels transiting the zone that they would be exposed to danger within the war zone given the misuse of neutral flags by the British. The "contingencies of maritime warfare" meant that neutral vessels that found themselves in between belligerents were at risk from attacks intended to strike enemy ships.[39] Unrestricted submarine warfare became the primary method used by Germany to enforce the war zone. The submarine had become Germany's capital warship.[40]

Washington expressed grave concern over the German proclamation indicating that "to declare or exercise a right to attack and destroy any vessel entering a prescribed area of the high seas without first certainly determining its belligerent nationality and the contraband character of its cargo would be an act . . . unprecedented in naval warfare. . . ."[41] Secretary of State William

[37] *North Sea Closed by British Order; German Mine Laying Moves Admiralty to Declare It a Military Area*, N. Y. TIMES, Nov. 3, 1914, at 1.

[38] German Declaration of a Naval Zone, February 4, 1915, and Announcement of the German Admiralty Declaring the Waters Around Great Britain a War Zone, February 4, 1915, *in* PAPERS RELATING TO THE FOREIGN RELATIONS OF THE UNITED STATES 1915 SUPPLEMENT 93–94 (1915) [hereinafter FRUS 1915].

[39] *Id.*

[40] 2 ARTHUR J. MARDER, FROM THE *DREADNOUGHT* TO SCAPA FLOW: THE ROYAL NAVY IN THE FISHER ERA, 1904–1919, at 69–71 (1965).

[41] Letter from W. J. Bryan, Secretary of State, to Secretary of State W. J. Bryan to J. W. Gerard, U.S. Ambassador to Germany (Feb. 10, 1915), *in* FRUS 1915, *supra* note 38, at 98–99.

Jennings Bryan instructed Ambassador James W. Gerard to seek assurances from the German government that U.S. ships would not be "molested by the naval forces of Germany otherwise than by visit and search. . . ."[42] Warships are entitled to enforce the belligerent right of visit and search to determine the enemy character of the ship and its cargo, but submarines were ill-suited for the mission. The small size of the submarine crew meant that they could not place a prize crew on a merchant ship, nor could they bring the merchant crew onto the submarine to ensure their safety prior to sinking the ship.

At the same time, Great Britain was arming merchant vessels and instructing crews to forcibly resist visit and search by German submarines in the war zone.[43] In an effort to negotiate an acceptable compromise, the United States proposed that Germany and Great Britain agree to prohibit the use of submarines to attack merchant vessels of any nationality except to enforce the right of visit and search.[44] Great Britain responded that Germany's method of warfare was "entirely outside the scope of any of the international instruments regulating operations against commerce in time of war."[45] Germany countered that the extraordinary circumstances of the war and the defensive measures implemented by Great Britain to resist submarines compelled it to deviate from the "ordinary methods of warfare at sea."[46]

On May 7, 1915, a German U-boat sank the British passenger ship *Lusitania*, killing 1,200 people, including 94 children and 128 Americans. The United States demanded that Germany provide assurances that it would comply with the principles of international law regarding neutral merchant ships and safeguard American lives and ships.[47] On September 1, 1915, Ambassador J. Bernstorff informed Secretary of State Lansing that German submarines would not sink ocean liners without warning and without providing for the safety of the non-combatants, provided that the ships did not try to escape or offer resistance.[48] The following March, two U.S. citizens

---

[42] *Id.*

[43] Letter from J. Bernstorff, Germany Ambassador to the U.S., to W. J. Bryan, Secretary of State (Feb. 15, 1915), *in* FRUS 1915, *supra* note 38, at 104–05.

[44] Letter from W. J. Bryan, Secretary of State, to W. H. Page, U.S. Ambassador to the U.K. (Feb. 20, 1915), *in* FRUS 1915, *supra* note 38, at 119–20.

[45] Letter from C. S. Rice, U.K. Ambassador to the U.S., to W. J. Bryan, Secretary of State (Mar. 1, 1915), *in* FRUS 1915, *supra* note 38, at 127–28.

[46] Letter from W. J. Bryan, Secretary of State, to J. W. Gerard, U.S. Ambassador to Germany (May 13, 1915), *in* FRUS 1915, *supra* note 38, at 394–95.

[47] Letter from R. Lansing, Secretary of State ad interim, to J. W. Gerard, U.S. Ambassador to Germany (June 9, 1915), *in* FRUS 1915, *supra* note 38, at 438.

[48] Letter from J. Bernstorff, Germany Ambassador to the U.S., to R. Lansing, Secretary of State (Sept. 1, 1915), *in* FRUS 1915, *supra* note 38, at 531.

were among 80 passengers killed in the destruction of the cross-Channel passenger steamer *Sussex* by a German submarine, without summons or warning.[49] The United States complained to Germany on April 18, 1916, that it was violating U.S. neutral rights by prosecuting a "relentless and indiscriminate" war against commercial vessels by submarines, without regard for the "sacred and indisputable rules of international law and the universally recognized dictates of humanity."[50]

Germany issued the "*Sussex* Pledge" on May 4, 1916, caving to President Wilson's demands. The German Empire promised it would henceforth act "in accordance with the general principles of visit and search and destruction of merchant vessels recognized by international law." Merchant ships "both within and without the area declared as a naval war zone" would not be attacked without warning or ensuring the crew and passengers were left in a place of safety, unless they tried to escape or resist.[51]

On December 30, 1916, Germany's offer to negotiate a peace settlement was rebuffed by the Entente.[52] As a result, Germany resumed unrestricted submarine warfare on February 1, 1917.[53] Germany continued to insist submarines lacked the practical space and means to take on a large merchant crew or passengers before it sank an enemy ship even when it had submitted to visit and search. Therefore, submarines were not subject to the normal rules because they were vulnerable to attack when on the surface and unable to fulfill the customary duty of placing the crew and passengers in a "place of safety" before sinking a ship. The United Kingdom and the United States rejected this view, with jurist Pearce Higgins writing:

> But this is entirely contrary to all the principles of war. If a belligerent is allowed to use force against his adversary, it is not for him to complain if the weapon employed is of insufficient strength. It is for him to assure himself

---

[49] Letter from J. W. Gerard, U.S. Ambassador to Germany, to R. Lansing, Secretary of State (Apr. 11, 1916), *in* Papers relating to the Torpedoing of the S.S. *sussex* 5 (1916).

[50] Letter from R. Lansing, Secretary of State, to J. Bernstorff, Germany Ambassador to the U.S. (Feb. 3, 1917), *in* Papers Relating to the Foreign Relations of the United States 1917 Supplement 1, The World War 106–08 (1917) [hereinafter FRUS 1917].

[51] *Id.*

[52] *Says German Offer Halted Peace Plans; Bernstorff Asserts Berlin Move of December 1916, Spoiled Project of Wilson Peace*, N. Y. Times, Oct. 22, 1919, at 19; *Peace Overtures of the Central Powers and Reply of Entente Powers*, 11 American Journal of International Law Supplement: Diplomatic Correspondence Between the United States and Belligerent Governments Relating to Neutral Rights and Commerce 272–87 (1917).

[53] Memorandum from J. Bernstorff, Germany Ambassador to the U.S., to R. Lansing, Secretary of State (Jan. 31, 1917), *reprinted in* 11 American Journal of International Law 333 (1917).

that the weapon he uses will be strong enough to overcome all possible resistance. The attempt to change existing rules to the advantage of the party
that is not in command of the surface of the sea is an attempt to avoid the
consequence of naval weakness.[54]

Two days after the resumption of unrestricted submarine warfare, the United
States severed diplomatic relations with Germany.[55] Germany attempted to
forestall U.S. entry into the war, pledging once again that its submarine campaign would respect neutral rights. But President Woodrow Wilson asked
Congress for authority "to use any means that may be necessary for the protection of our seamen and our people in the prosecution of their peaceful
and legitimate errands on the high seas."[56] Two weeks later, Britain revealed
the contents of the Zimmerman Telegram to the U.S. ambassador in London.
The intercepted and decoded message revealed that upon the resumption
of unrestricted submarine warfare, Germany proposed an alliance with
Mexico in a war with America. The resumption of submarine warfare and
the Zimmerman Telegram brought the United States into the war on April
6, 1917.[57] The war effectively ended with the signing of the Armistice of
Compiègne on November 11, 1918. The ensuing Treaty of Peace prohibited
Germany from acquiring submarines, even for commercial purposes.[58]

2.3 Interwar Period

The end of the Great War brought renewed efforts to regulate submarine warfare.[59] The first of these efforts arose in the Washington Naval Conference of
1921–1922. The Conference succeeded in its goal of a naval arms limitation
program for the major maritime powers. Just five states participated in the

[54] A. Pearce Higgins, Defensively Armed Merchant Ships and Submarine Warfare 30
(1917).
[55] Letter from R. Lansing, Secretary of State, to J. Bernstorff, Germany Ambassador to the U.S.
(Feb. 3, 1917), in FRUS 1917, supra note 50, at 106–08.
[56] Woodrow Wilson, President, U.S., Address of the President of the United States to Congress
(Feb. 3, 1917), in FRUS 1917, supra note 50, at 109–12.
[57] Woodrow Wilson, President, U.S., Address of the President of the United States to Congress
(Apr. 2, 1917), in FRUS 1917, supra note 50, at 195–203; Proclamation of April 6, 1917, of the
Existence of a State of War between the United States and Germany, in FRUS 1917, supra note 50, at
207–08.
[58] Treaty of Peace with Germany art. 191, June 28, 1919, T.S. No. 1 [hereinafter Treaty of Versailles].
[59] W. Hays Parks, Making Law of War Treaties: Lessons from Submarine Warfare Regulation, 75
International Law Studies 339, 341–42 (2000).

negotiations—the United States, which hosted the meetings, and the United Kingdom, Japan, France, and Italy. On February 6, 1922, the states adopted the "Limitation on Naval Armament," but it did not apply to submarines.[60] The agreement placed limitations on cumulative warship tonnage for capital warships and aircraft carriers, and individual restrictions on the size and armaments of surface vessels in each class. The treaty entered into force the following year. Moreover, a supplemental Treaty Relating to the Use of Submarines and Noxious Gases in Warfare, which would have prohibited unrestricted submarine warfare, failed to enter into force because France did not ratify it.[61]

Five years later, Japan, the United Kingdom, and the United States met in Geneva to discuss the possible extension of the Five Power Treaty to other classes of warships, such as cruisers, destroyers, and submarines.[62] Japan rejected a U.S. proposal to apply the 5:5:3 ratios of the Five Power Treaty to other vessels, preferring a 10:10:7 ratio.[63] As a result of these negotiations, in October 1929, the United Kingdom invited France, Italy, Japan, and the United States to participate in a third naval disarmament conference, which convened in London on January 21, 1930. A British proposal, supported by the United States, to ban submarines failed to achieve consensus. Nonetheless, the Conference adopted the London Naval Treaty. The agreement limited individual submarine displacement to 2,000 tons, total tonnage of 52,700 tons each for the United Kingdom, Japan, and the United States, and the maximum gun caliber (5.1 inches).[64] Each party, however, was entitled to three

[60] The Five Power Treaty placed limitations on capital ships and aircraft carriers. U.S. and U.K. warship tonnage could not exceed 525,000 tons each. Japan was limited to 315,000 tons, and France and Italy were limited to 175,000 tons each (Art. IV). Capital ships were limited in size to 35,000 tons (Art. V) and no guns in excess of 16 inches (Art. VI). The total tonnage for aircraft carries for each of the Parties was 135,000 tons each for the United States and the United Kingdom, 81,000 tons for Japan, and 60,000 tons each for France and Italy (Art. VII). With some exceptions, aircraft carrier tonnage could not exceed 27,000 each, and no aircraft carrier could be fitted with guns in excess of 8 inches (Art. X). Also, the Parties were prohibited from acquiring warships, except capital ships and aircraft carriers, exceeding 10,000 tons (Art. XI) or fitted with guns in excess of 8 inches (Art. XII). Limitation of Naval Armament, arts. 4, 5, 6, 7, 10, 11, 12, Feb. 6, 1922, 43 Stat. 1655, T.S. No. 671.

[61] Article 1 prohibited submarine attacks on merchant vessels unless the vessel refused to submit to visit and search or failed to proceed as directed after seizure. In any event, merchant vessels could not be destroyed unless the crew and passengers were first place in safety. Article 4 further prohibited the use of submarines as commerce destroyers. Treaty Relating to the Use of Submarines and Noxious Gases in Warfare, Feb. 6, 1922, 25 L.N.T.S. 202.

[62] France and Italy participated as observers.

[63] Kichisaburo Nomura, *Japan's Demand for Naval Equality*, FOREIGN AFFAIRS 196, 196–97 (1935); W. Hays Parks, *supra* note 59, at 352.

[64] Limitation and Reduction of Naval Armament art. 7, Apr. 22, 1930, 46 Stat. 2858, T.S. No. 830 [hereinafter London Naval Treaty]; W. T. Mallison, *Studies in the Law of Naval Warfare: Submarines in General and Limited Wars*, 58 INTERNATIONAL LAW STUDIES 191 (1966); W. Hays Parks, *supra* note 59, at 353–54.

submarines not exceeding 2,800 tons armed with guns not above 6.1 inches. The London Naval Treaty reaffirmed the rules of international law with respect to attacks on merchant ships. Submarines must conform to the rules of international law applicable to surface vessels—the "cruiser rules." Article 22 of the agreement confirmed the existing rules of submarine warfare:

The following are accepted as established rules of International Law:

(1) In their action with regard to merchant ships, submarines must conform to the rules of International Law to which surface vessels are subject.

(2) In particular, except in the case of persistent refusal to stop on being duly summoned, or of active resistance to visit or search, a warship, whether surface vessel or submarine, may not sink or render incapable of navigation a merchant vessel without having first placed passengers, crew and ship's papers in a place of safety. For this purpose, the ship's boats are not regarded as a place of safety unless the safety of the passengers and crew is assured, in the existing sea and weather conditions, by the proximity of land, or the presence of another vessel which is in a position to take them on board.

Efforts by the League of Nations between 1932 and 1934, during the World Disarmament Conference, similarly did not alter the use or construction of submarines. Midway through the Conference, on October 14, 1933, Germany withdrew from the League of Nations and the Conference because its demands that it be permitted to increase its armaments or that the allies reduce theirs were dismissed.[65] Nine months after the Conference adjourned, on March 16, 1935, *Reichsführer* Adolf Hitler denounced the military clauses of the Versailles Treaty, citing the failure of other nations to disarm.[66]

Rather than object, Great Britain's response to Hitler's action was to exchange diplomatic notes on June 18, 1935, regarding limitations on naval armaments. Britain lacked popular support or military readiness for war and hoped limited concessions would constrain Hitler and buy time to better

[65] Harold A. Peters, *Germany Withdraws from League of Nations, Disarmament Pact*, UNITED PRESS INTERNATIONAL (online), Oct. 14, 1933.

[66] *Hitler Orders Military Conscription in Germany*, UNITED PRESS INTERNATIONAL (online), Mar. 16, 1935.

prepare should war come. The agreement provided, in part, that the total tonnage of the German fleet would not exceed 35 percent of the aggregate tonnage of the British fleet. Additionally, contrary to the provisions of the 1919 Treaty of Peace, the agreement allowed Germany to possess a submarine tonnage equal to Great Britain. Germany agreed, however, to limit its submarine tonnage to 45 percent of British total tonnage unless Germany determined that it was necessary to exceed the cap.[67] Four years later, on April 27, 1939, Germany denounced the Anglo-German Naval Agreement, arguing that British policy toward Germany had diluted the original premise of the accord, and that the British government now believed that impending war with Germany was "a capital problem of English foreign policy."[68]

A second naval disarmament conference hosted by the United Kingdom in London between December 1935 and March 1936 also failed to abolish the submarine as a means of warfare. Only Australia, Canada, France, India, New Zealand, the United Kingdom, and the United States signed the resulting treaty, the Second London Naval Treaty. Japan withdrew from the conference, and Italy refused to sign the agreement. Article 7 of the treaty limited the standard displacement of submarines to 2,000 tons and prohibited submarines from carrying a gun exceeding 5.1 inches in caliber.[69] The treaty also prohibited States Parties from transferring their submarines to a foreign navy.[70]

Also in 1936, given that the First London Naval Treaty of 1930 was due to expire in December 1936, the parties signed a *procès-verbal* on the 6th of November incorporating verbatim the provisions of article 22 of the Treaty of 1930, "which sets forth rules as to the action of submarines with regard to merchant ships as being established rules of international law, and remains in force without limit of time."[71]

The following year, nine states—Bulgaria, Egypt, France, Greece, Romania, Turkey, the Soviet Union, the United Kingdom, and Yugoslavia—participated in a diplomatic conference in Nyon, Switzerland, to address concerns over unrestricted submarine warfare, presumably conducted by Italy, against

[67] *Exchange of Notes Between His Majesty's Government in the United Kingdom and the German Government Regarding the Limitation of Naval Armaments*, Doc. No. A5462/22/45 (June 18, 1935), *in* 46 BRITISH DOCUMENTS ON FOREIGN AFFAIRS 181–83 (Jeremy Noakes ed., 1994).

[68] Memorandum from the German Government Denouncing the Anglo-German Naval Agreement (Apr. 27, 1939).

[69] Limitation of Naval Armament, art. 7, Mar. 25, 1936, 50 Stat. 1363, T.S. No. 919.

[70] *Id.*, art. 22.

[71] Procès-Verbal Relating to the Rules of Submarine Warfare Set Forth in Part IV of the Treaty of London of 22 April 1930 (Nov. 6, 1936), *reprinted in* SCHINDLER & TOMAN, *supra* note 28, at 883–84.

neutral merchant shipping in the Mediterranean during the Spanish Civil War. The parties agreed that submarines attacking neutral merchant ships in violation of international law could be counterattacked and, if possible, destroyed.[72] In order to protect neutral merchant ships and enforce the Nyon Agreement, the parties divided the Mediterranean Sea into patrol zones. British and French fleets would patrol the western Mediterranean and the Malta Channel, except for the Tyrrhenian Sea, which would be patrolled by Italy if it chose to join the agreement.[73] In the eastern Mediterranean, the other participating Powers would operate in their own territorial waters, and the British and French would patrol the high seas (with the exception of the Adriatic Sea) up to the entrance to the Dardanelles.[74]

The Parties also agreed that they would not deploy submarines to the Mediterranean, and that their submarines would pass through the Mediterranean after notice to the other Parties, provided that the vessels sailed on the surface and were accompanied by a surface ship.[75] Additionally, all Parties agreed to bar foreign submarines from their respective territorial waters, except in case of urgent distress or mere passage with prior permission, provided the submarine sailed on the surface and was accompanied by a surface ship.[76] Each Party would also advise their merchant fleets to follow certain shipping routes in the Mediterranean as agreed between the Parties.[77]

2.4 Second World War

The Second World War saw a resurgence of unrestricted submarine warfare by the major Axis and Allied Powers. On September 28, 1939, the Reich government sent a note to neutral governments requesting that "they warn their merchant ships against any suspicious conduct, such as changes in course and the use of wireless upon sighting German naval forces, blacking out, noncompliance with the request to stop, et cetera."[78] Neutral ships engaged in suspicious or hostile conduct would be treated like enemy ships.

---

[72] The Nyon Agreement, art. II, Sept. 14, 1937, 181 L.N.T.S. 137.
[73] Id. art. IV.1.
[74] Id. art. IV.2.
[75] Id. art. V.a–b.
[76] Id. art. V.c.
[77] Id. art. VI.
[78] 18 Trials of the Major War Criminals before the International Military Tribunal 327 (1947).

On October 3, 1939, one month after Germany and the Soviet Union invaded Poland, the United States and 20 Latin American republics adopted the Panama Declaration, asserting that the Western Hemisphere was off-limits to belligerent operations.[79] The agreement set forth a "zone of security" that encircled North, South, and Central America, and extended at some points as much as 300 miles into the ocean in which "all the normal maritime routes of communication and trade between the countries of America" were protected.[80] The declaration purported to limit Germany's belligerent rights on the high seas; Germany rejected it.[81]

On October 4, 1939, Germany ordered its U-boats to attack all armed enemy merchant vessels without warning.[82] Less than two weeks later, on October 17, 1939, Germany ordered its U-boats to attack *all* enemy merchant ships without warning.[83] On November 24, 1939, the Reich government sent a second note to all seafaring neutral states indicating enemy merchant ships were being used for aggressive purposes and acknowledging that the United States had barred U.S. shipping from operating within a carefully defined naval zone around the central European coast known as the U.S. Combat Zone. Based on these facts, the German government warned "anew and more strongly that . . . the waters around the British Isles and near the French coast . . . can no longer be considered safe for neutral shipping."[84]

On January 1, 1940, Germany ordered its U-boats to sink all Greek merchant ships in the U.S. Combat Zone and all merchant ships regardless of nationality in the Bristol Channel.[85] A few days later, on the 6th of January, Germany extended unrestricted submarine warfare to the North Sea; and on January 18, Berlin authorized U-boat commanders to sink without warning all ships in enemy coastal waters where mines could be used.[86] After the fall of France in the summer of 1940, Germany issued a declaration to neutral governments on August 17, 1940, designating the zone around the British

[79] Declaration Adopted by the Meeting of the Foreign Ministers of the American Republics at Panama (Oct. 3, 1939), *in* 34 AMERICAN JOURNAL OF INTERNATIONAL LAW: OFFICIAL DOCUMENTS 17–18 (1940); William E. Masterson, *The Hemisphere Zone of Security and the Law*, AMERICAN BAR ASSOCIATION JOURNAL 861 (1940).

[80] GREEN HACKWORTH, 7 DIGEST OF INTERNATIONAL LAW 702–09 (1943).

[81] SAMUEL ELIOT MORISON, THE TWO-OCEAN WAR: A SHORT HISTORY OF THE UNITED STATES NAVY IN THE SECOND WORLD WAR 27 (1963).

[82] *Id.* at 322.

[83] *Id.* at 323.

[84] *Id.* at 327–28.

[85] 1 TRIALS OF THE MAJOR WAR CRIMINALS BEFORE THE INTERNATIONAL MILITARY TRIBUNAL 312 (1947).

[86] *Id.*

Isles as an operational area where every ship is vulnerable to destruction from mines and "other combat means."[87]

Germany justified these measures in response to Great Britain's 1938 Defense of Merchant Shipping Handbook, which instructed British shipping to report the location of German submarines and use naval artillery and depth charges against them.[88] The Admiralty supplemented these instructions on October 1, 1939, calling on merchant vessels to ram all German submarines.[89] Then in early April 1940, after Germany invaded Norway, the Admiralty ordered British submarines operating in the Jutland area—the Heligoland Bight, the Skagerrak, and the Kattegat—to attack all German vessels, combatants *and* merchant ships, without warning during the daytime, and all vessels (including neutrals) at night.[90] On April 12, the Admiralty extended the zone north, all the way to Bergen.[91]

The following year, on February 5, 1941, the British Admiralty authorized its submarines to attack all ships south of 35° 46' north without warning. Then, on July 15, 1940, "British submarines were authorized to attack all vessels operating within thirty miles of the Italian coast."[92] Finally, on July 17, the Admiralty extended the Mediterranean sink-on-sight operational area to include the area between Italy and Libya, or within 30 miles of the Libyan coast.[93]

The United States likewise engaged in unrestricted submarine warfare in the Pacific following the Japanese abrogation of the 1936 *procès-verbal* and attack on Pearl Harbor on December 7, 1941. Following the attack, Washington declared the Pacific Ocean a theater of operations. With the exception of hospital ships and other vessels under "safe conduct" voyages for humanitarian purposes, Washington ordered U.S. submarines to attack enemy merchant ships without warning.[94] The United States justified these measures, in part, on intelligence that indicated that Japan had ordered its merchant ships to report any sighted U.S. submarines to the Japanese Armed Forces, and to attack U.S. submarines by any means available, such as ramming,

---

[87] 18 Trials of the Major War Criminals before the International Military Tribunal 328–29 (1947).

[88] *Id.* at 321.

[89] *Id.* at 322.

[90] *Id.* at 327, 453–54.

[91] W. Hays Parks, *supra* note 59, at 360.

[92] *Id.*

[93] *Id.*

[94] 60 Trials of the Major War Criminals before the International Military Tribunal 109 (1947).

gunfire, or depth charges.[95] The unrestricted submarine and air warfare that the Chief of Naval Operations ordered on December 7 was justified by "the Japanese attacks . . . on U.S. bases, and on both armed and unarmed ships and nationals, without warning or declaration of war."[96]

Contrary to existing international law, following an engagement, Washington did not require U.S. submarines to "rescue enemy survivors if undue additional hazard to the submarine resulted or the submarine would thereby be prevented from accomplishing its further mission."[97] The Navy determined that it would have been unsafe to pick up many survivors given the limited space on board the submarine for passengers and the "known . . . suicidal character of the enemy."[98] Nonetheless, U.S. submarines sometimes rescued enemy merchantmen after an attack, and submariners frequently gave survivors rubber boats and/or provisions.[99]

Grand Admiral Karl Dönitz was tried and convicted at Nuremberg for war crimes relating to unrestricted submarine warfare committed while he served as the Commander-in Chief of the German Navy. The International Military Tribunal (IMT) found that Dönitz's order to sink neutral vessels without warning when found within declared operational areas violated the Washington Conference of 1922, the London Naval Agreement of 1930, and the 1936 Procès-Verbal.[100] The IMT also found Dönitz guilty of violating the rescue provisions of the Protocol, finding that "if the commander cannot rescue, then under its terms he cannot sink a merchant vessel and should allow it to pass harmless before his periscope."[101]

However, because of the British practice of arming merchant ships during the war, the IMT did not find Admiral Dönitz guilty for his conduct of submarine warfare against them.[102] Furthermore, in view of the British Admiralty's order of May 8, 1940, that "all vessels should be sunk at night in the Skagerrak," and the fact that the United States admitted to conducting

[95] *Id.* at 109–10.
[96] *Id.* at 111.
[97] 40 TRIALS OF THE MAJOR WAR CRIMINALS BEFORE THE INTERNATIONAL MILITARY TRIBUNAL 110 (1947).
[98] *Id.*
[99] *Id.*
[100] 1 TRIALS OF THE MAJOR WAR CRIMINALS BEFORE THE INTERNATIONAL MILITARY TRIBUNAL 312–13 (1947) [hereinafter IMT]; Treaty Relating to the Use of Submarines and Noxious Gases in Warfare, *supra* note 61; London Naval Treaty, *supra* note 64; and Procès-Verbal Relating to the Rules of Submarine Warfare Set Forth in Part IV of the Treaty of London of April 22, 1930, *reprinted in* SCHINDLER & TOMAN, *supra* note 28, at 883–84.
[101] IMT, *supra* note 100, at 313.
[102] *Id.*

unrestricted submarine warfare in the Pacific from the first day it entered the war in 1941, Dönitz was not punished for his breaches of the international law of submarine warfare.[103] The IMT found, however, that neutral ships may not be sunk without warning—regardless of whether they are in a declared war zone.[104]

3. Contemporary Submarine Warfare

Given the effectiveness of the submarine as a weapon of war during the two world wars, the major maritime powers abandoned efforts to prohibit their use during armed conflict. While the U.S. submarine operations against Japanese shipping were effective, Germany's campaign in the Battle of the Atlantic was largely inadequate to stop the flow of forces into Europe, but thwarted at great cost to the allies. Submarines, therefore, retain their status as a lawful means of warfare, and their crews enjoy combatant status under the law of armed conflict.

Submarines are stealthy platforms which use torpedoes, missiles, and mines to attack enemy armed forces during armed conflict, targeting enemy submarines, surface ships, and naval auxiliaries. Hundreds or even thousands of enemy combatants may perish in these attacks.[105] When it comes to merchant ships, however, historical lessons persist. Resort to methods and means of warfare are not unlimited, and submarines must comply with the same rules of war as surface ships and aircraft.[106] Submarines may not sink or render incapable of navigation an enemy merchant vessel without having first placed the passengers, crew, and ship's papers in a place of safety.[107] The ship's lifeboats are not regarded as a place of safety unless the safety of the passengers and crew is assured, in the prevailing sea and weather conditions,

---

[103] *Id.*

[104] *Id.* at 304; YORAM DINSTEIN, CONDUCT OF HOSTILITIES UNDER THE LAW OF ARMED CONFLICT 263 (3d ed. 2016).

[105] DINSTEIN, *supra* note 104, at 129.

[106] Procès-Verbal Relating to the Rules of Submarine Warfare Set Forth in Part IV of the Treaty of London of April 22, 1930, *reprinted in* SCHINDLER & TOMAN, *supra* note 28, at 883–84; UNITED KINGDOM MINISTRY OF DEFENCE, THE MANUAL OF THE LAW OF ARMED CONFLICT 356–57, ¶¶ 13.24, 13.31 (2004); Wolff Heintschel von Heinegg, *The Law of Armed Conflict at Sea* § 17.46 *in* THE HANDBOOK OF INTERNATIONAL HUMANITARIAN LAW (Dieter Fleck ed., 4th ed. 2021).

[107] SAN REMO MANUAL, *supra* note 22, ¶ 139.

by the proximity of land, or another nearby vessel in a position to take them on board.[108] Submarines are ill-suited to fulfill the legal obligation to protect merchantmen and civilian passengers during armed conflict.

Since the end of the Second World War, submarines have sunk only three warships—a frigate, a cruiser, and a corvette—and no merchant vessels. In 1971, a Pakistani submarine sank an Indian frigate; during the Falklands conflict in 1982, a British submarine sank an Argentinian cruiser; and in 2010, a North Korean submarine destroyed a South Korean corvette.

3.1 Sinking of the INS *Khukri*

On December 9, 1971, the Pakistani submarine PNS *Hangor* sank the Indian anti-submarine warfare frigate INS *Khukri* off the coast of Diu, Gujarat. The Pakistani submarine tracked the Indian ship and fired a homing torpedo into its hull—the first time since the Second World War that a submarine sank another ship.[109] The *Khukri* sank in two minutes, with the loss of 18 officers and 176 sailors. Six officers and 61 men survived the attack. The stern of the INS *Kirpan* was also badly damaged in the attack.

The successful strike turned around Pakistan's flailing war effort at sea.[110] Until sinking of the *Khukri*, the Pakistani Navy had suffered two missile attacks by India against ships in Karachi harbor. In the first assault, Indian forces struck and sank the PNS *Muhafiz* and PNS *Khaiber*. In the second attack, Indian forces struck the replenishment tanker PNS *Dacca*, along with two merchant ships lying at anchorage. India canceled a third missile strike planned for December 10 after the loss of the *Khukri*. The Indian Navy launched a massive hunt for the *Hangor*, but the Pakistani submarine returned safely to Karachi on December 18.

---

[108] Procès-Verbal Relating to the Rules of Submarine Warfare Set Forth in Part IV of the Treaty of London of April 22, 1930, *reprinted in* SCHINDLER & TOMAN, *supra* note 28, at 883–84; NWP 1-14M, *supra* note 27, § 8.6.2.2.

[109] Rachel Chitra, *The Tale of INS* Khukri, *and Its Brave Captain, Mahendra Nath Mulla*, TIMES OF INDIA (online), Aug. 15, 2018; *Heroics and Act of Valour by PNS/M Hangor in 1971 War*, DAILY TIMES (Pakistan) (online), Dec. 8, 2019.

[110] Arshad Rahim, *Hangor Hits Hard: The Story of Pakistan Navy Submarine Hangor Which Changed the Course of the 1971 War at Sea*, DEFENSE JOURNAL (Karachi), Dec. 2019, at 19–20.

3.2 Sinking of the ARA *General Belgrano*

The second submarine attack since the Second World War occurred during the Falklands campaign in 1982, which began after Argentina invaded the British-claimed territory on April 2. On April 7, the United Kingdom declared that, beginning on April 12, Argentine warships and naval auxil-iaries in a 200-mile exclusion zone around the Falkland Islands "will be treated as hostile and are liable to be attacked by British forces."[111] The fol-lowing day, Argentina adopted a 200-nautical-mile exclusion zone off its coastline and around the Falklands Islands. On April 23, Britain informed the Argentine government that "any approach on the part of Argentine warships, submarines, naval auxiliaries or military aircraft which would amount to a threat to interfere with the mission of British forces in the South Atlantic would encounter the appropriate response."[112] All Argentine vessels, including merchant ships and fishing vessels, apparently engaged in surveil-lance or gathering intelligence against the Royal Navy in the South Atlantic would also be regarded as hostile. On April 28, Prime Minister Margaret Thatcher authorized enforcement of a total exclusion zone (TEZ) around the islands beginning on April 30. The British announcement stated that the zone applied to Argentine warships and naval auxiliaries and "any other ship . . . operating in support of the illegal occupation of the Falkland Islands." Any ship or any aircraft found within the TEZ was "regarded as hostile and liable to be attacked by British forces."[113] A belligerent state that declares an exclusion zone may to some extent (although not completely) presume that ships or aircraft in the area are more likely to be hostile.[114]

On May 1, the British nuclear-powered submarine *Conqueror* sighted the Argentine warship ARA *General Belgrano* and began to shadow.[115] The *Belgrano* was a light cruiser with a crew of 1,093. The next day, the *Conqueror* put two torpedoes into the *Belgrano*, sending her to the bottom. The *Belgrano*'s crew let away lifeboats in orderly fashion, and over the next two days Argentine and Chilean ships rescued 772 Argentine sailors from

---

[111] R. W. Apple, Jr., *Britain Imposing War Zone Around Falkland Islands; Haig Plans Mediation Trip*, N.Y. TIMES, Apr. 8, 1982, at A1.
[112] 2 LAWRENCE FREEDMAN, THE OFFICIAL HISTORY OF THE FALKLANDS CAMPAIGN: WAR AND DIPLOMACY 194 (2005) [hereinafter FREEDMAN].
[113] *Id.* at 202.
[114] SAN REMO MANUAL, *supra* note 22, at 1818–3, r. 106.
[115] FREEDMAN, *supra* note 112, at 235.

the sea. Low temperatures and wind gusts made the rescue difficult, and 323 Argentine sailors perished. The Argentine Navy returned to base and played no further role in the conflict. The *Belgrano* is the only ship to have been sunk by a nuclear-powered submarine.

The *Belgrano* was some 35 miles outside the TEZ as it headed toward Argentina. The British government report that the *Belgrano* was closing in on the British task force caused confusion, and later some observers suggested that the ship was outside of the TEZ and fleeing the battle. The sinking of the vessel created the greatest controversy of the war.[116] It appears that any change in course by the *Belgrano*, however, was merely tactical; and the warship was still engaged in the fight.[117] Despite the controversy, the *Belgrano* was a lawful target even though it was attacked outside the TEZ, and even if it was returning to Argentina. Enemy warships are lawful targets unless they have surrendered.[118]

Although geographically more limited than the 1939 Panama Declaration issued by the members of the Organization of American States, the TEZ went even further in asserting jurisdiction to infringe on freedom of navigation. Yet states generally complied with the order.[119] Britain decided against briefing the United States in advance.

Argentina also conducted submarine torpedo attacks on the British Fleet in the Falklands but these were ineffective due to poor torpedo settings. Several Argentine and British vessels were sunk during the Falklands campaign, including the Liberian-flag oil tanker *Hercules*. When the owner, Amerada Hess Corporation, later sued Argentina in the United States, the Supreme Court dismissed the case under the Foreign Sovereign Immunities Act.[120]

Exclusion zones remain useful for separating neutral from enemy shipping and thereby may safeguard merchant ships and crews, even though they may infringe on freedom of navigation.[121] The *San Remo Manual* accepts that belligerents may declare an exclusion zone as an "exceptional measure"

---

[116] *Id.* at 633–35.

[117] *Belgrano Crew "Trigger Happy": Argentine Commander Casts New Light on Falklands War Controversy*, THE GUARDIAN (London) (online), May 24, 2003.

[118] SAN REMO MANUAL, *supra* note 22, ¶ 47(i).

[119] R. R. CHURCHILL & A. V. LOWE, THE LAW OF THE SEA 424–25 (1999).

[120] Argentine Republic v. Amerada Hess Shipping Corp., 488 U.S. 428 (1989).

[121] *See* W. J. Fenwick, *The Exclusion Zone Device in the Law of Naval Warfare*, 24 CANADIAN YEARBOOK OF INTERNATIONAL LAW 91 (1986); R. Leckow, *The Iran–Iraq Conflict in the Gulf: The Law of War Zones*, 37 INTERNATIONAL & COMPARATIVE LAW QUARTERLY 629 (1988).

during armed conflict.[122] This rule means that protected ships and aircraft, such as merchant ships, do not lose their protection merely because they operate inside the zone. An exclusion zone may not become a "free fire" zone.[123] Belligerents may establish an exclusion zone, but the same law applies inside the zone that applies outside the zone.[124] Likewise, military platforms, such as warships, may be attacked whether they are inside or outside of an exclusion zone.

3.3 Sinking of the ROKS *Cheonan*

On March 26, 2010, a North Korean submarine torpedoed ROKN *Cheonan* (PCC-772) a South Korean Navy corvette in the Yellow Sea.[125] The sinking took place only two kilometers off Baengnyeong Island, South Korea's northwesternmost territory, and near the coastline of North Korea. Salvage operations confirmed that a North Korean heavy torpedo armed with a 200-kilogram warhead had struck the South Korean warship.[126] Forty-six Republic of Korea (ROK) Navy sailors were killed. The attack was the deadliest encounter on the Korean Peninsula in two decades.[127] Analysts believe the attack was to avenge the ROKN sinking of a North Korean ship four months earlier that had crossed the Northern Limit Line (NLL).

Pyongyang disputes the waters, which are a flashpoint where the two nations have clashed. In October 2009, the North Korean Navy reported that 16

---

[122] SAN REMO MANUAL, *supra*, note 22, at 181–83, r. 106, at 181–183; H.P.C.R. MANUAL ON INTERNATIONAL LAW APPLICABLE TO AIR AND MISSILE WARFARE 239–40, r. 107 (2013).

[123] DINSTEIN, *supra* note 104, at 263.

[124] Wolff Heintschel von Heinegg, *The Law of Armed Conflict at Sea* § 17.50, *in* THE HANDBOOK OF INTERNATIONAL HUMANITARIAN LAW (Dieter Fleck ed., 4th ed. 2021).

[125] Attribution of the attack to North Korea was unanimous among 50 South Korean investigators and 24 experts from the United States, Australia, Britain and Sweden. *See* Blaine Harde Sebastian, *S. Korea Jettisons Doubt About Sinking; Report Says Evidence of North's Involvement is Overwhelming*, WASHINGTON POST, May 20, 2010, at A11; Sebastien Falletti, *Investigation Attributes Cheonan Sinking to North Korean Torpedo*, JANE'S NAVY INTERNATIONAL (online), May 21, 2010; *Final Cheonan Report*, KOREA HERALD (online), Sept. 15, 2010.

[126] Choe Sang-Hun, *South Korea Publicly Blames the North for Ship's Sinking*, N.Y. TIMES (online), May 19, 2010; Choe Sang-Hun, *Sinking of Ship Feeds South Korea's Fears of the North*, N.Y. TIMES (online), Mar. 29, 2010; Neil Macfarquhar, *Draft Avoids Condemning North Korea in Ship Attack*, N.Y. TIMES (online), July 9, 2010.

[127] *Seoul Reacts to North Korean Cheonan Attack*, JANE'S INTELLIGENCE REVIEW (online), May 24, 2010; *Sinking Feeling—North and South Korea's Growing Divide*, JANE'S INTELLIGENCE REVIEW (online), June 11, 2010; Leon V. Sigal, *Primer on North Korea, South Korea, and the United States: Reading Between the Lines of the Cheonan Attack*, BULLETIN OF THE ATOMIC SCIENTISTS 35–44 (2010).

ROKN warships were operating in contested waters.[128] North Korean naval excursions across the declared NLL sea boundary have ignited numerous skirmishes, including deadly encounters in 1999, 2002, 2004, and June and November 2009.[129] The two navies exchanged hostile fire on November 15, 2009, when a flotilla of North Korea patrol boats crossed the NLL. The NLL marks an operational area regarded as the seaward extension of the armistice separation line between North and South Korea, rather than an official boundary. The ROKN "bumped" and then fired warning shots at North Korean vessels, which returned fire. The incident turned into a full-fledged engagement with machine gun and cannon fire on both sides. At least one North Korean vessel was sunk and another badly damaged. Three days later, the Communist Party newspaper, *Rodong Sinmun*, suggested the attack should be avenged.[130] Soon afterward, Kim Jong-il visited a naval base with his military high command and ordered a "do or die" mission to restore national honor.[131] The attack on the *Cheonan* accomplished that mission. The UN Security Council failed to act, although a presidential statement from the Council deplored and condemned the attack.[132]

4. Poseidon Nuclear Drone and Environmental Modification

Russia reportedly has developed an underwater drone with a two-megaton nuclear warhead that when detonated at the coastline could generate a tsunami powerful enough to destroy enemy port cities and naval bases.[133] The Poseidon, also called the "doomsday drone," is an autonomous submersible and is launched from two special-purpose submarines, the *Belgorod* and the *Khabarovsk*.[134] Powered by a small nuclear reactor, the drone can silently

[128] *Halt to Intrusion of S. Korean Warships in to DPRK Waters Demanded*, KOREAN CENTRAL NEWS AGENCY (online), Oct. 15, 2009.
[129] Tim Fish & Trefor Moss, *S. Korea Deploys Attack Craft to Maritime Border*, JANE'S DEFENSE WEEKLY, June 10, 2009, at 6.
[130] *S. Korea Will be Forced to Pay Dearly for Armed Provocations*, KOREAN CENTRAL NEWS AGENCY (online), Nov. 12, 2009.
[131] Sigal, *supra* note 127, at 44.
[132] U.N. Security Council Presidential Statement 2010/13 (July 9, 2010).
[133] Dave Makichuk, *Russia to Test "Doomsday Drone" in High Arctic*, ASIA TIMES (online), May 26, 2020; Franz-Stefan Gady, *Russia (Once Again) Announces Start of Sea Trials of "Doomsday Weapon,"* THE DIPLOMAT (Tokyo) (online), Dec. 27, 2018.
[134] Tim Ripley, *Moscow's New "Drone Mothership" Submarine Launched in Severodvinsk*, JANE'S DEFENSE WEEKLY, May 1, 2019, at 4.

traverse 10,000 kilometers underwater at speeds of up to 70 knots. Setting aside the issue of the legality of nuclear weapons, in this case the desired effects are to inject a massive amount of energy into the ocean to precipitate a destructive tsunami. A weapon that so dramatically unleashes environmental forces, however, appears incompatible with the law of war.[135]

The *San Remo Manual* defines "collateral casualties" or "collateral damage," as ". . . damage to or the destruction of the natural environment."[136] The *ICRC Customary Law Study* declares that "no part of the environment may be attacked" unless it is a military objective.[137] The principle of distinction forms the foundation of this rule. "Military objectives" are defined in AP I as those objects which, "by their nature, location, purpose or use make an effective contribution to military action and whose total or partial destruction, capture or neutralization, in the circumstances ruling at the time, offers a definite military advantage."[138] While the *ICRC Customary Law Study* also states that destruction of the environment is prohibited unless required by "imperative of military necessity," it caveats this allowance by prohibiting attacks that are expected to cause incidental damage to the environment that would be excessive in relation to the "concrete and direct military advantage anticipated."[139] Furthermore, Rule 45 of the *ICRC Customary Law Study* states, "[t]he use of methods of warfare that are intended, or may be expected, to cause widespread, long-term and severe damage to the natural environment is prohibited."[140] The norm against attacks on the environment applies in international and non-international armed conflicts.[141] In the past, customary international law concerning protection of the environment during armed

---

[135] DEPARTMENT OF THE ARMY, U.S. MARINE CORPS, FM 6-27/MCTP 11-10C, THE COMMANDER'S HANDBOOK ON THE LAW OF LAND WARFARE ¶ 2-139 (2019) [hereinafter FM 6-27].

[136] SAN REMO MANUAL, *supra* note 22, 87, r. 13.

[137] 1 ICRC CUSTOMARY LAW STUDY, *supra* note 23, r. 43; *see also Guidelines for Military Manuals and Instructions on the Protection of the Environment in Times of Armed Conflict, reprinted in* 311 INTERNATIONAL REVIEW OF THE RED CROSS 230 (1996).

[138] AP I, *supra* note 22, art. 52(2) and CDDH, Official Records, Vol. VI, CDDH/SR.41, 26 May 1977, p. 168. *See also* OFFICE OF THE GENERAL COUNSEL, U.S. DEPARTMENT OF DEFENSE, LAW OF WAR MANUAL § 5.5 (rev. ed., Dec. 2016) [hereinafter DoD LAW OF WAR MANUAL]; FM 6-27, *supra* note 135, ¶ 2-29 (Military Objective).

[139] 1 ICRC CUSTOMARY LAW STUDY, *supra* note 23, r. 43.

[140] The U.S. position is that this first sentence of Rule 45 does not reflect customary international law with regard to either conventional or nuclear weapons. *Id.* at 151; John B. Bellinger, III & William J. Haynes II, *A US Government Response to the International Committee of the Red Cross Study Customary International Humanitarian Law*, 89 INT'L REV. OF THE RED CROSS 443, 455 (2007).

[141] SAN REMO MANUAL, *supra* note 22, ¶¶ 44, 46(c); *see also* 1 ICRC CUSTOMARY LAW STUDY, *supra* note 23, rr. 43–45.

conflict has focused on destruction of forests and other plant cover used as concealment or camouflage of combatants.

The ENMOD treaty prohibits environmental modification techniques that have "widespread, long-lasting or severe effects" as the means of destruction.[142] The text was negotiated after U.S. congressional revelations of Army programs during the Vietnam War for defoliation to reduce cover along the Ho Chi Minh Trail and attempts to manipulate the weather to flood the same routes to make them impassable.[143]

The term "environmental modification techniques" is defined as "deliberate manipulation of natural processes, the dynamics, composition, or structure of the earth, including its biota, lithosphere, hydrosphere, and atmosphere. . . ."[144] Unlike a nuclear weapon designed to destroy enemy forces, the Poseidon uses the natural environment as an intervening cause of destruction, while also erasing the distinction between the enemy's armed forces and the civilian population.

The ENMOD was transmitted by the UN Conference of the Committee on Disarmament (CCD) to the UN General Assembly in 1976, accompanied by four understandings produced by a Consultative Committee of Experts. The first understanding, which defined the meaning of "widespread, long lasting or severe" effects, was the most critical of the four addendums. This text shall be interpreted as meaning "an area on the scale of several hundred square kilometers" ("widespread"); "lasting for period of months, or approximately a season" ("long-lasting"); and, "involving serious or significant disruption or harm to human life, natural and economic resources . . ." ("severe").[145] Any effects produced by a nuclear detonation from the Poseidon drone likely meets any of these three elements, and since they are listed in the alternative, any one of them would suffice.

The second CCD understanding includes a non-exhaustive list of phenomena that could be caused by environmental modification techniques under article 2. Tsunamis are specifically mentioned, along with earthquakes, weather, and attempts to alter climate patterns, ocean currents, and the

---

[142] Convention on the Prohibition of Military or Any Hostile Use of Environmental Modification Techniques, art. I(1), May 18, 1977, 31 U.S.T. 333, 1108 U.N.T.S. 151 [hereinafter ENMOD].
[143] Prohibiting Military Weather Modification: Hearing on Senate Resolution 281 Before the Senate Subcommittee on Oceans and International Environment of the Senate Committee on Foreign Relations, 92d Cong. (1972).
[144] ENMOD, *supra* note 142, art. II.
[145] Report of the Committee on Disarmament, at 91–92, U.N. Doc. A/31/27 (1976)

atmosphere.[146] These interpretative declarations are not themselves legally binding although they should be considered in interpretation.[147]

The United States was a principal advocate of ENMOD and is party to the convention.[148] The other major maritime powers are also states party to ENMOD.[149]

Additional Protocol I (AP I) fused two streams of the law of armed conflict—the Hague law on methods and means of warfare and the Geneva law on protection of civilians and civilian objects.[150] One example of this merger is AP I's proscription against "methods or means of warfare" that are intended, or may be expected, to cause "widespread, long-term and severe damage to the natural environment," contained in article 35(3).[151] The protection covers the environment at large, and not only the environment of parties to the conflict.[152] Further, Major-General A. V. P. Rogers adds that article 55 of AP I prohibits methods or means of warfare that are "intended or may be expected to cause such damage to the natural environment and thereby to prejudice the health or survival of the population."[153] This rule applies to protect the civilian population, individual civilians, and civilian objects in attacks on land (or attacked on land from the sea or air forces) in accordance with article 49(3), whereas article 35(3) protects the environment at large.[154] The *ICRC Commentary* summarizes these criteria to mean that any "method or means of warfare which are planned to cause, or may be expected (albeit without the intention) to cause serious damage to the natural environment, even if this effect is incidental, are prohibited."[155] This definition expands the meaning of the original text. The United States, for example, does not accept this approach because it is overly broad and ambiguous.[156] Not a party to AP I, the United States suggests the provisions do

---

[146] *Id.*

[147] Rep. of the International Law Commission § 1.2, U.N. Doc. A/66/10/Add.1 (2011); *see also* Christian Walter, *Reservations, in* VIENNA CONVENTION ON THE LAW OF TREATIES: A COMMENTARY 263–64 (Oliver Dörr & Kirsten Schmalenbach eds., 2018).

[148] *See also* FM 6–27, *supra* note 135, ¶ 2–135 (prohibiting wanton destruction of the environment).

[149] China (June 8, 2005), Japan (June 9, 1982), Russia (May 30, 1978), the United States (Jan. 17, 1980), and the United Kingdom (May 16, 1978) are parties.

[150] Emily Crawford, *Geneva Conventions Additional Protocol I (1977), in* MAX PLANCK ENCYCLOPEDIA OF PUBLIC INTERNATIONAL LAW (2015).

[151] AP I, *supra* note 22, art. 35(3).

[152] A. P. V. ROGERS, LAW ON THE BATTLEFIELD 166 (2d ed. 2004).

[153] AP I, *supra* note 22, art. 55(1).

[154] WILLIAM H. BOOTHBY, WEAPONS AND THE LAW OF ARMED CONFLICT 95 (2d ed. 2016).

[155] COMMENTARY ON THE ADDITIONAL PROTOCOLS OF 8 JUNE 1977 TO THE GENEVA CONVENTIONS OF 12 AUGUST 1949, ¶ 1440 (Yves Sandoz, Christophe Swinarski, & Bruno Zimmermann eds., 1987) [hereinafter AP I COMMENTARY].

[156] DoD LAW OF WAR MANUAL, *supra* note 138, § 6.10.3.1; FM 6–27, *supra* note 135, ¶ 2-143.

not acknowledge that the employment of weapons is prohibited only if they cause incidental injury to the civilian population that is clearly excessive "in relation to the concrete and direct overall military advantage anticipated."[157] Upon ratification, France stated that it considers the risk of damage in articles 35 and 55 to be "objectively analyzed on the basis of information available." AP I and the *ICRC Commentary* depart from this approach and recognize that any act on the battlefield that exceeds some very high level of environmental damage is a violation of the law of war regardless of the importance of the military mission or objective. The threshold requires that the damage pose a risk to the health of the entire population, not individual members.[158]

The *ICRC Commentary* also states that methods or means of warfare are prohibited if the "direct effects would last more than three months or a season," for one of the parties, produce effects that are "widespread and severe," regardless of duration, or generate collateral effects that "would cause widespread and severe damage over a period of decades."[159] The *San Remo Manual* states that methods and means of warfare should have "due regard" for the natural environment, "taking into account" rules of international law.[160] In this context, the "due regard" standard is relatively unhelpful, borrowed as it is from the international law of the sea and airspace law. As a peacetime rule, "due regard" merely requires respect for the legitimate rights of other actors in the shared space, without identifying the rules to be respected or the relative weight accorded to each if they are in conflict. Perhaps more constructively, the *San Remo Manual* declares that damage or destruction to the natural environment that is not justified by military necessity and "carried out wantonly" is prohibited.[161] The criteria for "military necessity" is the start of the analysis further developed in the ICRC Study and AP I. "Wanton" destruction means destruction that is malicious unjust and inhumane or reckless and careless. Certainly, this level of recklessness falls within the remit of "widespread, long-term and severe damage to the natural environment," contained in AP I.[162]

[157] DoD LAW OF WAR MANUAL, *supra* note 138, § 6.10.3.1
[158] Reservations and Declarations, Republic of France ¶ 6 (online), Apr. 11, 2001, AP I, ICRC (online); BOOTHBY, *supra* note 154 at 96.
[159] AP I COMMENTARY, *supra* note 155, ¶ 1453(c).
[160] SAN REMO MANUAL, *supra* note 22, ¶ 44.
[161] *Id.*
[162] AP I, *supra* note 22, art. 35(3).

The temporal element (long-term) is prominent in the analysis, with damage to the environment measured in decades.[163] It is widely assumed that collateral damage incidental to conventional warfare would not normally be covered by this provision. For example, Iraq's calamitous policy to ignite 700 Kuwaiti oil wells in January 1991 generated significant atmospheric effects on local agriculture and undermined the health of civilians.[164] Yet, it is debatable whether the environmental consequences of such appalling action met the threshold in either ENMOD or AP I. Only damage that risks major health problems over the long-term or the continued survival of the civilian population would meet the test. The Gulf War showed that, at the very least, there was an emerging rule forbidding the use of the marine environment as an instrument of warfare or making it an object of attack.[165]

A tsunami is an incredibly destructive series of waves caused by the displacement of a large volume of water. If the positive peak of the wave strikes the land first, it will cause flooding. If the negative peak or trough strikes land first, the water recedes, often hundreds of meters, before it snaps back, repeating the process in successive waves. The result is complete inundation along the coast that submerges civilization. A tsunami is all-encompassing, leaving survivors stunned and homeless amidst virtually complete destruction.[166] In 2011, a tsunami with 30-foot waves struck northern Japan, killing nearly 20,000 people.[167] The third largest earthquake ever recorded caused the Boxing Day tsunami off the coast of Sumatra in 2004 and may have killed 230,000 people across 14 countries.[168]

The *Lieber Code* forbids "wanton devastation."[169] Similarly, the Preamble to the *St. Petersburg Declaration* notes that the only legitimate aim of military action is to subdue the enemy's military force.[170] The proscription

---

[163] Rapporteur's Report CDDH/215/Rev.1, ¶, *in* ICRC Commentary, ¶ 1454; FM 6–27, *supra* note 135, ¶ 2-137.

[164] Donatella Lorch, *After the War: The Environment; Burning Wells Turn Kuwait into Land of Oily Blackness,* N.Y. TIMES, Mar. 6, 1991, at A1; Youssef M. Ibrahim, *Most Oil Fires Are Out in Kuwait, but Its Environment is Devastated,* N.Y. TIMES, Oct. 19, 1991, at A1.

[165] SAN REMO MANUAL, *supra* note 22, at 119–21, r. 44.

[166] Martin Fackler & Mark McDonald, *Death Toll Estimate in Japan Soars as Relief Efforts Intensify,* N.Y. TIMES (online), Mar. 13, 2011; Martin Fackler & Mark McDonald, *Need Overwhelms Japan After Quake and Tsunami,* N.Y. TIMES (online), Mar. 14, 2011.

[167] Hiroko Tabuchi, *An Anniversary of "Heartbreaking Grief" in Japan,* N.Y. TIMES (online), Mar. 11, 2012.

[168] *Boxing Day Ttsunami: How the Disaster Unfolded 10 Years Ago,* ABC NEWS (Aus.) (online), Dec. 23, 2014.

[169] U.S. DEPARTMENT OF WAR, GENERAL ORDINANCE NO. 100, INSTRUCTIONS FOR THE GOVERNMENT OF ARMIES OF THE UNITED STATES IN THE FIELD (1863).

[170] Declaration Renouncing the Use, in Time of War, of Explosive Projectiles Under 400 Grammes Weight, Dec. 11, 1868, *reprinted in* SCHINDLER & TOMAN, *supra* note 28, at 102.

against wanton or unlimited use of force is reflected in the *Oxford Manual* of 1880.[171] The rule is codified in the regulations annexed to Hague Convention II of 1899 and Regulations annexed to Hague Convention IV of 1907.[172] Although there is no history to suggest that these provisions were considered to form the basis for specific protection of the natural environment during armed conflict, their broad reach suggests that they may offer a secondary protective effect.[173] The Martens Clause declares that "inhabitants and the belligerents" are protected by the law of war even in cases that are not specifically identified.[174] Originally developed to protect resistance groups, it has been interpreted more broadly, although it remains uncertain how far residual protections might extend.[175]

Setting aside the unlawful design to produce a tsunami to devastate an enemy coastline, there is also debate over the legality of the use of nuclear weapons themselves in light of the obligation to protect the environment. The United Kingdom, for example, issued a reservation upon ratification of AP I that it understood the protocol applying exclusively to conventional weapons and did not alter rules of international law applicable to other types of weapons, including nuclear weapons.[176]

[171] Project of an International Declaration concerning the Laws and Customs of War, art. 12, Aug. 27, 1874, *reprinted in* SCHINDLER & TOMAN, *supra* note 28, at 22–34; Laws of War on Law, art. 4, Sept. 9, 1880, *reprinted in* SCHINDLER & TOMAN, *supra* note 28, at 36–48.

[172] Convention No. II with Respect to the Laws and Customs of War on Land, art. 23(a), July 29, 1899, 32 Stat. 1803, T.S. No. 403; Regulations Respecting the Laws and Customs of War on Land, art. 23(a), Oct. 18, 1907, 36 Stat. 2227, T.S. No. 539.

[173] Adam Roberts, *The Law of War and Environmental Damage, in* THE ENVIRONMENTAL CONSEQUENCES OF WAR: LEGAL, ECONOMIC AND SCIENTIFIC PERSPECTIVES 52 (Carl E. Bruch & Jay E. Austin eds., 2005).

[174] Convention No. IV Respecting the Laws and Customs of War on Land pmbl. ¶ 9, Oct. 18, 1907, 36 Stat. 2227, T.S. No. 539.

[175] BOOTHBY, *supra* note 154, at 89.

[176] United Kingdom of Great Britain and Northern Ireland, Reservation, Protocol Additional to the Geneva Conventions of 12 August 1949, and relating to the Protection of Victims of International Armed Conflicts (Protocol I), 8 June 1977, 2020 U.N.T.S. 75 (28 Jan. 1998).

6

Seabed Warfare

Advances in undersea technology have made the seabed more accessible to human activity. Understanding the seabed was important from the very beginning of maritime navigation to determine the depth of the water under the keel. For most of human history this measurement was made using a lead line extended into the water down to the bottom. Over the course of four millennia only two breakthroughs contributed to the accuracy of soundings.[1] First, the shift from hemp rope to piano wire made the line more stable and created less drag from the water current, enabling a more accurate reading. Second, the addition of tallow (or peanut butter) to the end of the line collected soil and provided objective evidence that the line had reached the bottom. In the early 20th century, for the first time, the depth of the seabed could be determined remotely. The single beam echo sounder was invented in 1913, and it accurately gauged water depth without physical contact with the seabed. Sound travels well in water and at a rate of about 1,500 meters per second, so mariners could obtain more accurate depth readings by measuring the time it takes for sound to bounce off the bottom and return. By the 1970s, multi-beam side-scan sonars made this method even more effective. Today just five states—the United States, China, Russia, France, and Japan—have the capability to operate below an ocean depth of 1,000 meters. American and Chinese submersibles have reached depths of 10,927 and 10,909 meters, respectively diving in the deepest known point of the Marianas Trench, Challenger Deep.

---

[1] Thank you to Larry Mayer for this observation. *New Chinese Submersible Reaches Earth's Deepest Ocean Trench*, PHYS.ORG (online) Nov. 20, 2020; Kinling Lo, *Underwater Station Could Be a Game Changer, Chinese Scientist Says*, SOUTH CHINA MORNING POST (online), Sept. 29, 2017.

Disruptive Technology and the Law of Naval Warfare. James Kraska and Raul Pedrozo, Oxford University Press.
© James Kraska & Raul Pedrozo 2022. DOI: 10.1093/oso/9780197630181.003.0007

1. Warfare from the Continental Shelf and the Deep Seabed

1.1 The Deep Seabed and the International Seabed Area

The international deep seabed area ("the Area") may be used for military activities. Neither the International Seabed Authority (ISA) nor individual coastal states have jurisdiction over foreign military activities on the seabed beyond the territorial sea. The (International Seabed) Area lies beyond areas of national jurisdiction. States may not claim or exercise sovereignty or sovereign rights over the Area or its resources.[2] Concerning the ISA's authority over the deep seabed, the United Nations Convention on the Law of the Sea (UNCLOS) states that "[t]he Area and its resources are the common heritage of mankind."[3] This remit, however, does not limit use of the deep seabed for activities other than mineral extraction. Mineral resource development in the Area shall be conducted only through applications to the ISA and "for the benefit of mankind as a whole."[4] Although the Area (like all parts of the ocean) are reserved for "peaceful purposes," this provision does not restrict peacetime military activities, or belligerent naval operations conducted in self-defense or in accordance with the authorization of the UN Security Council.[5]

Coastal States enjoy resource rights and jurisdiction in their exclusive economic zone (EEZ) and on their continental shelf—encompassing not just minerals, but all living and nonliving resources. Although coastal states have exclusive sovereign rights and jurisdiction over the resources in the EEZ and on the continental shelf, potentially including the outer or extended continental shelf beyond the outer limits of the EEZ, they have no authority to restrict military activities in these areas.

1.2 Artificial Islands, Installations, and Structures on the Continental Shelf

Coastal States have sovereign rights and jurisdiction over artificial islands on their continental shelf. This rule was demonstrated in the 2016 South China

---

[2] United Nations Convention on the Law of the Sea, art. 137, Dec. 10, 1982, 1833 U.N.T.S. 397 [hereinafter UNCLOS].
[3] *Id.* art. 136.
[4] *Id.* art. 140.
[5] *Id,* art. 141.

Sea arbitration. The tribunal held that China's artificial island construction on Mischief Reef was an unlawful violation of Philippine sovereign rights and jurisdiction over its continental shelf.[6] China failed to seek and receive Philippine consent for construction of its artificial island on Mischief Reef.[7]

While coastal States have exclusive sovereign rights and jurisdiction over artificial islands on their continental shelf, their right to regulate seabed structures and installations is more limited to those structures or installations that are for a purpose related to resources, marine scientific research, or marine environmental protection. Coastal States do not enjoy such rights or jurisdiction over military installations and structures on their continental shelf. Instead, coastal States enjoy sovereign rights and jurisdiction only over those seabed installations and structures that are "for the [economic] purposes provided for in article 56," or that "interfere with the exercise of the rights of the coastal State" over its resources.[8] In short, while coastal States have complete authority over construction of artificial islands on their continental shelves, they have a more limited right with regard to the emplacement of installations and structures thereon. This interpretation suggests that all States may engage in military operations and activities on the seabed anywhere beyond the territorial sea of neutral States.

The plain text of UNCLOS, however, has not stopped states from purporting to limit military activities on the continental shelf. India, for example, states explicitly that "other countries cannot use its continental shelf for military purposes."[9] India asserts a right to "verify, inspect, remove or destroy" any weapon or military device on its continental shelf, or to "take such other steps" it deems necessary to safeguard its security. Similarly, Canada states that paragraph 1 of the Seabed Nuclear Treaty "cannot be interpreted as indicating that any state has a right to implant or emplace any weapons not prohibited under Article 1, paragraph 1, on the seabed. . . ."[10] Canada asserts that the coastal state enjoys "exclusive sovereign rights" to the continental shelf that empower it to "verify, inspect, or effect the removal of" any weapon or associated device or installation on the continental shelf.[11] As is clear from

---

[6] South China Sea Arbitration (Phil. v. China), Case No. 2013-19, Award, ¶ 1016 (Perm. Ct. Arb. 2016).

[7] UNCLOS, *supra* note 2, arts. 56(1)(b)(i), 60(1), 80.

[8] *Id.* arts. 60(1)(b)–(c), 80.

[9] THE LAW OF NAVAL WARFARE: A COLLECTION OF AGREEMENTS WITH DOCUMENTS AND COMMENTARIES 605 (Natalino Ronzitti ed., 1988).

[10] *Id.* at 603.

[11] *Id.*

the text of article 56, however, there is nothing in UNCLOS to support such a claim.

Despite these pronouncements, UNCLOS suggests that foreign States may use the seabed in the EEZ and on the continental shelf beyond the territorial sea for military installations and structures since their purpose does not relate to exploring, exploiting, managing, and conserving the living or nonliving natural resources, or the coastal state's right to consent to marine scientific research or fulfill its duties to protect the marine environment. Installations and structures that are emplaced for purposes other than these purposes fall outside of the remit of coastal state jurisdiction.

In the South China Sea arbitration, China constructed an artificial island on Mischief Reef, which is a low-tide elevation (LTE) and therefore part of the Philippine continental shelf. While China's construction was unlawful, it would have acted lawfully if it had merely landed a military unmanned underwater vehicle (UUV) on the reef or erected a military structure or installation that is under the threshold of what constitutes an artificial island. In such case, however, the military activity still must have due regard for the resource rights of the Philippines, so there is a practical limit to the scope and extent of military operations that might have been lawfully conducted on a protrusion of the Philippine continental shelf, such as Mischief Reef. What, then is the practical limit of foreign military activities on the continental shelf of a coastal state? Only those military activities that are of such scale or impact that they fail to observe "due regard" for the coastal state's rights to living and nonliving resources of the EEZ and continental shelf are impermissible. For example, the deployment of nuclear weapons or other weapons of mass destruction on the continental shelf of the coastal state may trigger the "due regard" standard (in addition to violating the Seabed Arms Control Treaty). Likewise, military activities that inflict wanton destruction of large coral communities residing on the continental shelf might also be inconsistent with the "due regard" standard. Furthermore, the "due regard" provisions in article 58(3) of UNCLOS that apply to foreign operations in the EEZ (and on the continental shelf within the EEZ) during peacetime do not apply in armed conflict since they are displaced by the more specific *lex specialis* regime of the law of naval warfare. Although military activities are permitted on the continental shelf and deep seabed, the placement of weapons of mass destruction beyond the territorial sea is prohibited by the Seabed Arms Control Treaty and its status as reflective of customary law.

1.3 Seabed Arms Control Treaty

When Ambassador Arvid Pardo delivered a spirited call to action on governance of the seabed in the UN General Assembly in 1967, he set in motion the process that would produce UNCLOS.[12] At the same time, concern over military uses of the seabed was increasing as the oceans became a fulcrum for Cold War competition. The first nuclear submarine, USS *Nautilus* (SSN-571), had been launched in 1954. Many developing states feared that the vast undersea domain was becoming an arena of strategic nuclear competition. The superpower race for undersea technology would also permit the developed states to monopolize mineral development of the deep seabed. While Pardo's speech provided the impetus for reservation of minerals of the deep seabed as the common heritage of mankind, it also spurred action on a separate but related set of negotiations between the superpowers to limit the emplacement of nuclear weapons on the seabed.[13]

The Seabed Nuclear Arms Treaty was adopted in 1971.[14] The treaty prohibits the planting or emplacing on the seabed or ocean floor or in the subsoil thereof, beyond the 12-nautical-mile territorial sea, any nuclear weapons or any other types of weapons of mass destruction (WMD) or structures, launching installations, or any other facilities specifically designed for storing, testing, or using such weapons.[15] The term "weapons of mass destruction" was clarified by the Commission on Conventional Armaments of the Security Council of the United Nations in 1948 as meaning, "atomic explosive weapons, radioactive material weapons, lethal chemical and biological weapons," and those with "similar characteristics."[16] The treaty does not, however, prohibit the use of nuclear weapons in the water column, such as nuclear armed depth charges and torpedoes, provided they are not affixed to the seabed.[17]

[12] U.N. Doc. A/C.1/PV.1515, U.N. GAOR, 22nd Sess., 1515th mtg. at 1–15 (Nov. 1, 1967).
[13] U.N. Doc. A/AC.135/28, Arvid Pardo, Malta Ambassador to the U.N., Address at the U.N. Gen. Assembly, U.N. GAOR, 22d Sess., 1515th mtg. at 1 (Nov. 1, 1967).
[14] Treaty on the Prohibition of the Emplacement of Nuclear Weapons and other Weapons of Mass Destruction on the Seabed and the Ocean Floor and in the Subsoil thereof, May 18, 1972, 955 U.N.T.S. 115 [hereinafter Seabed Treaty].
[15] *Id.* arts. I–II.
[16] Res. S/C3/32/Rev.1, Commission for Conventional Armaments at 2 (Aug. 18, 1948).
[17] U.S. NAVY, U.S. MARINE CORPS & U.S. COAST GUARD, NWP 1-14M/MCTP 11-10B/ COMDTPUB P5800.7A, THE COMMANDER'S HANDBOOK ON THE LAW OF NAVAL OPERATIONS § 10.2.2.1 (2017) [hereinafter NWP 1-14M].

To ensure compliance with the treaty, State Parties may verify through "observation" the activities of other State Parties, provided the monitoring does not interfere with such activities. If reasonable doubt remains after such observation, the State Parties may consult and agree on further procedures for verification, including inspections. If doubt remains after consultation and cooperation, a State Party may refer the matter to the Security Council for action in accordance with the Charter. Verification activities "shall be conducted with due regard for rights recognized under international law, including the freedoms of the high seas and the rights of coastal States with respect to the exploration and exploitation of their continental shelves."[18]

Given that the treaty only applies to WMD, the emplacement of sensors or conventional weapons on the seabed or ocean floor, like the Hydra Distributed Undersea Network or Upward Falling Payloads, is therefore permissible. One such system, the U.S. Sound Surveillance System (SOSUS), has been operating for decades.

1.4 Sound Surveillance System (SOSUS)

The SOSUS system sprang from progress in anti-submarine warfare (ASW) technology during the Second World War.[19] The seabed network was originally designed as a distributed global system of some 1,000 underwater microphones to listen for Soviet submarines.[20] Since its inception, the United States and Japan (and presumably other nations) have jointly maintained underwater sound systems. The first experimental station was established at the Soya (La Perouse) Strait at the north-western tip of Hokkaido in 1957.[21] The networks gradually were upgraded and expanded to the United Kingdom.[22]

[18] Seabed Treaty, *supra* note 14, art. III.

[19] Edward C. Whitman, *SOSUS: The Secret Weapon of Undersea Surveillance*, UNDERSEA WARFARE (2005) (online).

[20] William J. Broad, *Scientists Object as Navy Retires Ocean Listening System*, N.Y. TIMES, June 12, 1994, at 1; *see also*, GARY E. WEIR, AN OCEAN IN COMMON 298–315 (2001); BRYAN CLARK ET AL, SUSTAINING THE UNDERSEA ADVANTAGE: DISRUPTING ANTI-SUBMARINE WARFARE USING AUTONOMOUS SYSTEMS 25–28 (Sept. 2020).

[21] DESMOND BALL & RICHARD TANTER, THE TOOLS OF OWATATSUMI: JAPAN'S OCEAN SURVEILLANCE AND COASTAL DEFENCE CAPABILITIES 51 (2015).

[22] THOMAS S. BURNS, THE SECRET WAR FOR THE OCEAN DEPTHS: SOVIET-AMERICAN RIVALRY FOR MASTERY OF THE HIGH SEAS 157–58 (1978).

Japanese and U.S. cooperation on underwater sound detection continued throughout the 1960s.[23] During the 1970s during the debates at the Third UN Conference on the Law of the Sea, the United States sought to protect its legal right to maintain the SOSUS network located on the continental shelves of other states.[24]

By the 1980s, the hydrophone network was supplemented by an enormous magnetic anomaly detection (MAD) system spanning key waterways, such as the Tsushima and Tsugaru straits.[25] Working in conjunction with the United States, the Japan Maritime Self Defense Force operates a network of seabed passive sonar running along the western coastline of the country.[26] Although the precise location of the persistent SOSUS network is not public, scholars and media suggest it may extend from Korea and Japan, through Sasebo and Kagoshima on Kyushu, across the Osumi Channel to Okinawa, further south to Miyako-jima and Yonaguni, and due south across the Bashi Channel to the Philippines, and possibly across the Java Sea and Andaman Sea to India's Andaman and Nicobar Islands, forming a massive "fishhook" of sensors.[27] India has discussed participating in the last section of the U.S.-Japan "fishhook," which would complete the maritime enclosure of mainland China.[28] Russia and China have developed SOSUS-like systems as well. At an exhibition in late 2015, the China State Shipbuilding Corporation displayed a model of a seabed acoustic array network with associated weapons.[29]

1.5 Hydra and Upward Falling Payloads

The seabed is also becoming an area of operations. Advances in computer modeling and processing will allow for the increased use of low-frequency

---

[23] Memorandum from W. W. Rostow, National Security Advisor, to Lyndon B. Johnson, President of the U.S. on Navy Exercise in the Sea of Japan (May 23, 1968), *in* 6 FOREIGN RELATIONS OF THE UNITED STATES (Kent Sieg ed., 2002); BALL & TANTER, *supra* note 21, at 51.

[24] Proposed Instructions for the Third United Nations Conference on the Law of the Sea (25 March 1974) CIA-RDP80801495R000800130001-9 (Secret; declassified on Sept. 5, 2001).

[25] Joel S. Wit, *Advances in Antisubmarine Warfare*, 244 SCIENTIFIC AMERICAN 31, 36–37 (1981); BALL & TANTER, *supra* note 21, at 48.

[26] BALL & TANTER, *supra* note 21, at 55–78.

[27] *U.S. and Japan Work Together*, BEIJING DAILY (online), July 10, 2013; BALL & TANTER, *supra* note 21, at 53.

[28] ABHIJIT SINGH, INDIA'S "UNDERSEA WALL" IN THE EASTERN INDIAN OCEAN (2016); Abhijit Singh, *Militarising Andamans: The Costs and the Benefits*, HINDUSTAN TIMES (online), July 29, 2020.

[29] Andrew Tate, *Unmanned Submarines: The Case for the Prosecution*, JANE'S NAVY INTERNATIONAL (online), Feb. 10, 2017; *Seabed Sonar Surveillance System*, JANE'S INTELLIGENCE REVIEW (online), July 1, 1989.

sonar, which currently lacks the precision of med-frequency sonar, as a tactical long-range ASW sensor. "Big data" computer processors, capable of running detailed models that can identify small changes in the marine environment "by comparing expected ambient noise from marine life, waves, and seismic events to measured noise fields," will be used to detect quiet submarines.[30] Emergent non-acoustic techniques, which are capable of detecting small changes on the surface or underwater caused by a submarine's wake, or that can "detect radiation or chemicals emitted by a submarine," are also under development.[31] Other non-acoustic ASW techniques include the use of lasers and light-emitting diodes, "precisely tuned to wavelengths in which the light energy suffers smaller losses," which bounce light off a submarine's hull.[32] At the same time, submarines are becoming more stealthy. Advances in technology, such as sound-absorbing materials and shapes, active sound cancellation, and the proliferation of decoys make submarines quieter and help them to avoid detection.

These increased risks of survival on the surface of the water and the cost equation drives the development and use of unmanned systems to accomplish missions previously performed by manned submarines. New fuel cell and battery technology, such as lithium-ion batteries, is being developed to increase the endurance of unmanned systems to support long-duration operations, such as intelligence, surveillance, and reconnaissance (ISR) or Electronic Warfare (EW), in the enemy's littorals. To avoid detection, these unmanned systems will be equipped with active (e.g., acoustic jamming) and passive (e.g., sound emissions that radiate noise or deployment of decoys that create false targets) counter-detection systems to enhance their survivability.[33]

Seabed instruments and devices are giving way to larger installations and structures, and networks of seabed infrastructure that offer the benefit of a persistent, close-in presence off an adversary's coast. DARPA's "Hydra" program is indicative of this approach to maximize the battlespace by utilizing the seabed, especially on the continental shelf, for cost-effective, scalable, distributed undersea networks. The network of seabed installations could house unmanned payloads resting on the seabed as a complement to submarines

---

[30] CLARK, THE EMERGING ERA IN UNDERSEA WARFARE 8 (2015).
[31] *Id.* at 9–10.
[32] *Id.* at 10.
[33] *Id.* at 10, 12–13.

and surface vessels.[34] This approach acknowledges the cost of a large surface fleet in a climate of budget austerity, expanding capabilities without relying on new warships. Pre-positioning the nodes on the deep seabed enhances concealment and security at less cost, especially when compared with operating manned warships. The undersea battle network will connect long-range sensors and undersea communications with fire control systems and weapons, utilizing swarms of unmanned or autonomous aerial vehicles (UAVs) or unmanned underwater vehicles (UUVs).[35] The Hydra system delivers unmanned submarines or aircraft into shallow coastal waters with manned ships, submarines, or airplanes.

Hydra's modular payloads enable fast and stealthy prepositioning and deployment of ISR and strike assets in high-threat coastal environments. Communication among the various nodes in the network could be done through encrypted data through underwater cables or ambient acoustic, electromagnetic, or optical signals.[36] The network could seamlessly connect platforms below the water, on the surface, and in the air to increase the operational reach of capabilities over the horizon. The modular enclosures serve as the storage and launch platforms for the unmanned payloads, autonomously supporting and sustaining them for extended periods of time. The modular enclosure will be outfitted with a ballast for descent and ascent of the payload through the water column and will be mobile throughout the littoral environment. The UAV payload, for example, would contain an individual aircraft or swarm of UAVs in capsules. Upon activation, the payload is released from the seabed and "floats" to the surface ("falling upward") and launches into the air. These Upward Falling Payloads (UFPs) make the Hydra network an effective underwater battle network. The pre-positioned containers lie on the ocean floor and wait until activation, at which time they "fall upward" or drift buoyantly upward through the water column to the surface. Activation could be done by either a physically tethered cable or an acoustic

---

[34] *Network of Unmanned Undersea Platforms Would Assist Manned* Vessels, DEFENSE ADVANCED RESEARCH PROJECTS AGENCY NEWS & EVENTS (online) Aug. 22, 2013; Andrew Nuss, *Hydra*, DEFENSE ADVANCED RESEARCH PROJECTS AGENCY PROGRAM INFORMATION (online), undated; Rajesh Uppal, *DARPA Hydra Developed a Distributed Undersea Network of UUVs and AUVs to Operate Independently for Weeks or Months*, INTERNATIONAL DEFENSE, SECURITY, & TECHNOLOGY (IDST) (online), Jan. 4, 2020.

[35] BRYAN CLARK, THE EMERGING ERA IN UNDERSEA WARFARE 16 (2015); *Stop, Collaborate and Listen: The Technologies Enabling Underwater Naval Communications*, NAVY LOOKOUT (online), June 16, 2021.

[36] Huw Williams, *DARPA to Develop Unmanned Undersea Network*, JANE'S INTERNATIONAL DEFENCE REVIEW (online), Oct. 24, 2014.

signal transmitted through the water. These missiles pre-positioned on the continental shelf would be closer to the targets of the adversary, so they could be smaller and shorter range and arrive at their targets more quickly than intercontinental missiles.

UUVs could be released and enter the water column and disperse. Submarine-launched unmanned aerial vehicles (SUAVs), for example, could be released from a submarine and rise buoyantly to the surface, as the SUAV booster engine ignites and the round or ISR platform is released airborne. Lockheed Martin tested the gull-wing titanium *Cormorant*, essentially a "swimming spy plane," for this mission.[37] Hydra may house UAVs such as Raytheon's *Switchblade* that could be forward deployed to the seabed near an adversary and then wait until activated. (The *Switchblade* is a loitering munition for use against targets beyond visual range).

Modular payloads may provide theater commanders with key capabilities, such as mine countermeasures (MCM), ASW, and targeting and strike solutions for cruise missiles and hypersonic missiles.[38] The payload modules are held secure in containers that could be easily transported and fixed to the seabed. Secure in water-tight containers, their functionality would be preserved for weeks or even months. The scalable network could be rapidly reconfigured to add or substitute modules to address emerging threats. Hydra provides capabilities for seamless operations on, above, and below the ocean surface. Some modules in the network could contain recharging hubs for other UAVs or UUVs.

The deep seabed networks could lie 4,000 meters below the surface of the water, safe from adversaries until they are needed. The UFP system could be deployed by surface ships or ballistic missile submarines (SSBNs). The U.S. Navy's four large, guided missile submarines (SSGNs) could also serve as logistics and command centers to emplace packages and control the seabed network.[39] The 12 *Columbia*-class boats replacing the 14 *Ohio*-class vessels will be capable of carrying a wide variety of large payloads, and may be able to launch networked swarms of UUVs or emplace UFPs.

Once the containers reach the surface, they execute naval warfare missions, such as powering other unmanned systems or launching submersibles,

[37] Bill Sweetman, *The Navy's Swimming Spy Plane*, POPULAR SCIENCE (online), Feb. 21, 2006.
[38] *Id.*
[39] Joseph Trevithick & Tyler Rogoway, *Ohio Guided Missile Submarines Were Designed to Be Drone-Carrying Clandestine Command Center*, THE WAR ZONE (online), Nov. 21, 2019.

missiles, or aircraft.[40] The waterproof containers may lie submerged on or anchored to the seabed for years. Prototypes can remain on the seabed until it is remotely triggered and deploys payloads into the water column.

The UFP system consists of three subsystems: (1) The "payload," which executes waterborne or airborne applications after being deployed to the surface. (2) The UFP "riser," which provides pressure tolerant encapsulation and launch of the payload. (3) The UFP "communications" triggers the UFP riser to launch. The program is undergoing at sea demonstrations of integrated riser and communications systems including the deployment of different payloads.

The once indisputable U.S. advantage in undersea warfare is eroding as peer adversaries develop their underwater capabilities with quieter submarines, improved detection technologies, autonomous UAVs and UUVs, and increased ability to distribute their sensors and weapons and send them below the water or onto the seabed. For example, China is working on a manned underwater station that could serve as a nerve center for a network like Hydra. These new technologies will fundamentally change the nature of future force architecture and naval warfare.

2. Submarine Cables in Armed Conflict

The importance of safeguarding the undersea cable network for civilian and military communications cannot be overemphasized. Satellites can only handle a fraction of the transmissions carried through cables.[41] Notwithstanding its critical importance to the world economy, national security, and governmental communications, the global submarine cable system is vulnerable to peacetime accidents, mishaps, and purposeful damage and exposed to attack during time of war. Some measures that can be taken to harden the submarine cable infrastructure from attack include installing sensors along cable routes to detect underwater vehicles, increasing the

---

[40] See Grace Jean, *DARPA's "Upward Falling" Payload Explores Future Maritime ISR Concept*, JANE'S DEFENCE WEEKLY (online), May 12, 2016; *Nodes, Networks and Autonomy: Charting a Course for Future ASW*, INTERNATIONAL DEFENCE REVIEW (online), Oct. 30, 2014; Allen McDuffee, *DARPA's Plan to Flood the Sea with Drones, Carrying More Drones*, WIRED (online), Sept. 13, 2013; and *Upward Falling Payloads Advances Deep-Sea Payload Technology*, DEFENSE ADVANCED RESEARCH PROJECTS AGENCY NEWS & EVENTS (online), Mar. 26, 2014.

[41] Doug Tsuruoka, *How World War III Could Start: Cut the "Cable,"* NATIONAL INTEREST (online), Jan. 7, 2018.

geographic diversity of submarine cables by avoiding choke points at sea and increasing the number of landing sites (and enhancing security at them), and installing backup and redundant cable systems to increase resiliency.[42] Peacetime adversaries or belligerents during armed conflict could degrade, damage, or sever submarine cables, or use them to launch cyberattacks.[43]

2.1 The Undersea Cyber Network

The first submarine cable linking Great Britain and France was laid in 1850. Two years later, a transatlantic cable 2,300 miles long (about twice the distance from Florida to New York City) connected Ireland with Newfoundland and Labrador. Between 1870 and 1872, cables were laid between Britain, India, and Australia. In 1902, the entire world became interconnected after a 6,000-mile-long cable linked the Philippines with California.

Today, a vast network of some 750,000 miles of seabed cables crosses the oceans' depths.[44] The interdependence of global submarine communication systems means that a break in one cable can have cascading effects on Internet access in distant states.[45] The global submarine cable network consists of 213 independent systems of fiber-optic cables and is recognized as one of the world's most indispensable infrastructure. The network carries 97 percent of all global communications.[46] The Internet facilitates $10 trillion in international financial transactions daily; submarine cables are the backbone of this distributed, global network.[47] Sabotage of the system could generate follow-on economic and security effects beyond the targeted state.[48]

The isolated location of cables on the deep seabed provides a modicum of security for their physical safety. Yet cables are concentrated in international choke points and straits, and their landfall locations are well known. To

---

[42] Rishi Sunak, *Undersea Cables: Indispensable, Insecure*, POLICY EXCHANGE 34–36 (Dec. 1, 2017) [hereinafter *Undersea Cables: Indispensable, Insecure*].

[43] Rob Wittman, *The Greatest Risk to National Security You've Never Heard Of*, DEFENSE NEWS (online), Jan. 30, 2020.

[44] *Submarine Cable Map*, TELEGEOGRAPHY (online) (2020).

[45] Eric Geller, *Russian Threat Has Senators Demanding Answers about Undersea Internet Cables*, DAILY DOT (online), Feb. 29, 2020.

[46] *Undersea Cables: Indispensable, Insecure*, *supra* note 42, at 12.

[47] *Id.*; Tim Johnson McClatchy, *Undersea Cables: Too Valuable to Leave Vulnerable?*, GOVERNMENT TECHNOLOGY (online), Dec. 12, 2017.

[48] *Undersea Cables: Indispensable, Insecure*, *supra* note 42, at 5.

prevent unintended damage to the network during peacetime by commercial fishers and merchant ships, the location of submarine cables is publicly available. The general transparency of the sprawling undersea cable network presents a challenge to the private communications companies and government authorities trying to protect them.[49]

Submarine cables are owned and operated by multinational consortia consisting of from four to as many as 40 stakeholders, each with a percentage ownership stake in the cable. Google, for example, has partial stakes in more than a dozen submarine cables.[50] These ownership consortia handle construction and maintenance of the cable based on control over a divided percentage of the capacity. The entities that own the cables typically are based in tax havens, such as Bermuda, even if the actual ownership is by a company located in the United States or Germany. There is no global registry of ownership for submarine cables, so it is virtually impossible to find all the actual owners. Each cable obtains a landing license in each state that it physically touches, and the landing state obtains information on all the owners. But, here it gets even more complicated because the owners often sublease part or all of their stake to another company found in another state, and this subdivision, called an "indefeasible right of use," is usually not subsequently reported afterward to landing states. Thus, states with an interest in the cable would not be known to either landing states or belligerent states that propose to use the cable during hostilities.

The critical importance of cables underscores the reluctance by nations to work with the Chinese communications conglomerate formerly named Huawei Marine Networks, now called HMN Technologies. HMN is one of the leading submarine cable companies. Russia and China view submarine cables as strategic assets and could either tap them, sever them, or disrupt them through cyberattack in a future conflict.[51] Western naval forces shadow Russia's surface ship *Yantar*, for example, because it is outfitted with cable-cutting gear and deep-sea submersibles that can be used to tap cables on the seabed.[52]

[49] *Id.* at 5–6, 9, 13.

[50] Winston Qiu, *Complete List of Google's Subsea Cable Investments, Insights, Submarine Cable Networks*, SUBMARINE CABLE NETWORKS (online), July 9, 2019.

[51] Jonathan Barrett & Yew Lun Tian, *Pacific Undersea Cable Project Sinks After U.S. Warns Against Chinese Bid*, REUTERS (online), June 17, 2021; Meaghan Tobin, *US-China Tech War's New Battleground: Undersea Internet Cables*, SOUTH CHINA MORNING POST (online), Dec. 14, 2019.

[52] David E. Sanger & Eric Schmitt, *Russian Ships Near Data Cables Are Too Close for U.S. Comfort*, N.Y. TIMES (online), Oct. 25, 2015; McClatchy, *Undersea Cables*, *supra* note 47.

2.2 Protection of Submarine Cables in Peacetime

All states have the right to lay submarine cables on the high seas, as well as in the exclusive economic zone (EEZ) and continental shelves of costal states.[53] In peacetime, the 1884 Protection of Submarine Cables Convention, the 1958 High Seas Convention, and UNCLOS protect submarine cables on the high seas from intentional damage. There is no right to land a cable on the territory of a state. Coastal states may regulate the protection of submarine cables in their territorial sea.[54] The territorial sea and internal waters are under the sovereignty of the coastal state, and there is no explicit right of foreign states to run submarine cables through those waters. There is an implied right to do so, however, if the coastal state adopts and enforces laws for their protection.

2.2.1 1884 Submarine Cables Convention
The 1884 Convention prohibits the breaking or injury of a submarine cable through willful or culpable negligence, which results in a total or partial interruption of telegraphic communication.[55] This provision does not apply, however, to situations of accidental damage, such as by fishers. Parties are exempt from the provision if they cause cable damage while trying to protect their lives or vessels and have taken "all necessary precautions" to avoid damaging cables.[56] If a warship on the high seas has "reason to believe" that a ship (other than a warship) has violated the provisions of the 1888 Convention, it may board the suspect vessel to examine the ship's documents and verify its nationality.[57] The inspecting officer shall draw up a report, which may be used as evidence in a court of competent jurisdiction over the case, presumably in the flag state or the coastal state.[58] The warship may not, however, seize the vessel and its crew. This type of boarding occurred only once, in 1959, when a U.S. Navy officer and four enlisted sailors from the USS *Roy O. Hale* boarded the Soviet fishing trawler *Novorossiisk* off the coast of Newfoundland. The U.S. Navy suspected the *Novorossiisk* of cutting five submarine cables.[59] The investigation on board the warship revealed that the Soviet ship had been

---

[53] UNCLOS, *supra* note 2, arts. 58, 79(1).

[54] *Id.* arts. 21(1)(c), 79(4).

[55] Protection of Submarine Cables Convention, art. 2, Mar. 14, 1884, 24 Stat. 989, T.S. 380 [hereinafter Submarine Cable Convention].

[56] *Id.* art. 2.

[57] *Id.* art. 10.

[58] *Id.*

[59] 40 U.S. DEPARTMENT OF STATE, DEPARTMENT OF STATE BULLETIN No. 1034, at 555–58 (1959) [hereinafter DEPARTMENT OF STATE BULLETIN No. 1034].

operating in the immediate vicinity of all five cable breaks at the time the lines were cut. The shipboard visit lasted 70 minutes, and the United States later stated to the U.S.S.R. that the evidence showed the boarding was "justified in every respect" in accordance with international law, and that there was a "strong presumption" the Soviet ship cut the cables.[60]

Domestic courts competent to prosecute violations of the 1884 Convention shall be those of the flag state of the vessel accused of committing the infraction.[61] If the flag state does not assert jurisdiction, courts "in each of the contracting States, in the case of its subjects or citizens," shall have jurisdiction "in accordance with the general rules of penal competence established by the special laws of those States, or by international treaties."[62] To facilitate criminal prosecution, the Parties are also required to enact domestic legislation implementing the penal provisions of the 1888 Convention.[63]

2.2.2 1958 High Seas Convention

Article 27 of the High Seas Convention mirrors the prohibition in article 2 of the Submarine Cables Convention. States must adopt domestic legislation that makes it a punishable offense for a ship flying its flag or a person subject to its jurisdiction to willfully or through culpable negligence break or injure a submarine cable beneath the high seas, which interrupts or obstructs telegraphic or telephonic communications.[64] An exception applies if the break or injury occurs while the ship or person "acted merely with the legitimate object of saving their lives or their ships, after having taken all necessary precautions to avoid such break or injury."[65]

Article 30 of the 1958 Convention states that prior agreements already in force shall continue. This provision suggests that article 10 of the 1884 Treaty, which specifies that warships and other government vessels have a right to verify the nationality of a merchant vessel if it is suspected of having broken a submarine cable, remains in effect. This provision is a departure from the concept of exclusive flag state jurisdiction over ships embodied in article 92 of UNCLOS. Yet article 10 persists by virtue of article 30 of the 1958 Convention and as a matter of customary international law and state

---

[60] *Id.* at 557.
[61] Submarine Cable Convention, *supra* note 55, art. 8.
[62] *Id.*
[63] *Id.* art. 12.
[64] Convention on the High Seas, art. 27, Apr. 29, 1958, 13 U.S.T. 2312, T.I.A.S. No. 5200, 450 U.N.T.S. 11 [hereinafter High Seas Convention].
[65] *Id.*

practice, as demonstrated by the 1959 U.S. boarding of the Soviet fishing trawler *Novorossiisk*.[66]

2.2.3 1982 Law of the Sea Convention

States have a right to lay cables on the deep seabed beyond national jurisdiction under articles 87(1)(c) and 112 of UNCLOS.[67] States also may lay cables in the EEZ and on the continental shelves of coastal States in accord with articles 58(1) and 79 of UNCLOS, subject to the duty to exercise "due regard" for the resource rights of the host coastal States, as set forth in article 56. In these areas coastal states may adopt "reasonable measures" concerning foreign cables to protect their right to develop seabed mineral resources or to protect the marine environment, under article 79(2).

The 1884 Cable Convention, 1958 Geneva High Seas Convention, and UNCLOS have corresponding provisions for the protection of submarine cables.[68] Article 113 of UNCLOS repeats verbatim the text of article 27 of the High Sea Convention. Article 113 prohibits "conduct calculated or likely to result in such breaking or injury."[69] Any "break or injury caused by persons who acted merely with the legitimate object of saving their lives or their ships, after having taken all necessary precautions to avoid such break or injury," is exempt.[70] Articles 114 and 115 of UNCLOS reflect the long-standing regime of liability and indemnity and are derived from the 1884 treaty.

2.3 Tapping or Cutting Submarine Cables

Neither the 1958 nor the 1982 conventions regulate belligerent acts during an armed conflict. During armed conflict, the *lex specialis* regime of the law of naval warfare suspends the High Seas Convention and UNCLOS among the belligerents and modifies the relationship between belligerent states and neutral states. Likewise, article 15 of the 1884 treaty states that the rules on submarine cables do not "affect the liberty of action" of belligerent states during

---

[66] DEPARTMENT OF STATE BULLETIN No. 1034, *supra* note 59, at 555–58.

[67] UNCLOS, *supra* note 2, arts. 87(1)(c), 112–15.

[68] DOUGLAS R. BURNETT & LIONEL CARTER, INTERNATIONAL SUBMARINE CABLES AND BIODIVERSITY OF AREAS BEYOND NATIONAL JURISDICTION: THE CLOUD BENEATH THE SEA 10 (2017); UNCLOS, *supra* note 2, arts. 113 to 115; High Seas Convention, *supra* note 64, arts. 27 to 29, and Submarine Cable Convention, *supra* note 55, arts. 2, 4, and 7.

[69] UNCLOS, *supra* note 2, art. 113.

[70] *Id.*

armed conflict.[71] The 1907 Hague IV convention prohibits belligerents from seizing or destroying submarine cables that connect an occupied territory with a neutral territory except in cases of "absolute necessity."[72] This prohibition, however, only applies on land; it does not apply to the destruction of submarine cables at sea.[73]

The 1913 *Oxford Manual* states that cables in neutral waters connecting neutral states with an enemy state may not be cut.[74] Such cables may be cut on the high seas only if the belligerent state doing so is conducting an effective blockade of the enemy state. Even the *Oxford Manual* cautions, however, that seizure or destruction of a submarine cable may not be done unless there is an "absolute necessity." This rule applies without discrimination as to nationality of the owner of the cable, whether a natural person or corporate entity. These rules are amplified by the U.S. Navy's 1955/1974 manual, *Law of Naval Warfare* and the *San Remo Manual*. The 1955/1974 Manual states that submarine cables between points in an enemy's territory or between an enemy and a neutral state are subject to "such treatment as the necessities of war may require." The *San Remo Manual* states that parties to a conflict shall "take care" to avoid damaging submarine cables and pipelines laid on the seabed that serve neutral states.[75] More recently, the *Oslo Manual* recognizes that states that have laid submarine cables, or whose nationals have done so, are "entitled to take protective measures" to prevent or terminate "harmful interference" of them.[76] It is unclear, however, the extent to which the rules set forth in these manuals reflects state practice, since states have physically cut cables during armed conflict, with the Spanish-American War providing a vivid example.

---

[71] Submarine Cable Convention, *supra* note 55, art. 15.

[72] Convention No. IV Respecting the Laws and Customs of War on Land, art. 54, Oct. 18, 1907, 36 Stat. 2227, T.S. No. 539.

[73] JAMES BROWN SCOTT, THE PROCEEDINGS OF THE HAGUE PEACE CONFERENCES: CONFERENCES: III THE CONFERENCE OF 1907, at 13 (1921).

[74] Institute of International Law, The Laws of Naval War Governing the Relations Between Belligerents, art. 54, Aug. 9, 1913 (Oxford Manual of Naval Warfare), *reprinted in* DIETRICH SCHINDLER & JIŘÍ TOMAN, THE LAWS OF ARMED CONFLICTS 858–75 (4th ed. 2004).

[75] OFFICE OF THE CHIEF OF NAVAL OPERATIONS, U.S. NAVY, LAW OF NAVAL WARFARE, NAVAL WARFARE INFORMATION PUBLICATION (NWIP) 10-2 § 520 (1955), *reprinted in* 50 INTERNATIONAL LAW STUDIES 359 (1955) [hereinafter NWIP 10-2]; SAN REMO MANUAL ON INTERNATIONAL LAW APPLICABLE TO ARMED CONFLICTS AT SEA 111, r. 37 (Louise Doswald Beck ed., 1995) [hereinafter SAN REMO MANUAL].

[76] YORAM DINSTEIN & ARNE WILLY DAHL, OSLO MANUAL ON SELECT TOPICS ON THE LAW OF ARMED CONFLICT 61–62, r. 67 (2020).

2.3.1 Spanish-American War

During the Spanish-American War, the United States set the precedent for the belligerent right to cut neutral cables serving the enemy that lie outside neutral waters. On May 1, 1898, Commodore Dewey entered Manila Bay and destroyed or captured the Spanish fleet. The following day, he cut the Manila-Hong Kong cable owned by a British company and laid down under Spanish concession. Ten days later and half-way around the world, the U.S. cruiser *Marblehead* and gunboat *Nashville* cut the underwater telegraph cables on the eastern side of the Colorado Point at the entrance to Cienfuegos Harbor and destroyed the cable house at Punta de la Colorados on the island of Cuba.

On July 11, U.S. auxiliary cruisers *St. Louis* and *Yankee*, and the cruiser *Marblehead* cut the submarine cable in the San Juan Channel that connected Santa Cruz del Sur, Trinidad, Cienfuegos, and La Habana with the Spanish stronghold of Manzanillo on the east side of the island. Both operations took place within the territorial sea of Cuba. Afterward, First Lord of the Treasury Balfour remarked in parliament that article 15 of the 1884 treaty recognized the right of belligerents to cut cables used by the enemy.[77] The United States also severed cables in Puerto Rico that were owned by a British company.

After the war, the British government, on behalf of the Cuba Submarine Telegraph Company Limited, filed a claim against the United States for £8,175, the amount spent by the British corporation to restore the cable. The case went before an international tribunal that disallowed the claim.[78] Under the circumstances of armed conflict, the tribunal ruled, "the right of the United States to take measures of admittedly legitimate defense against these means of enemy communication was fully justified."[79]

2.3.2 First World War

The day after Great Britain declared war on Germany, the cable ship CS *Alert*, commanded by Superintendent Bourdeaux, cut all but one of Germany's submarine telegraph cables in the English Channel.[80] The operation effectively denied Germany the ability to communicate with nations outside of continental Europe, including its African colonies and the United States. The

---

[77] *Right to Cut Cables in War; Admiral Dewey Created a New Precedent Under the Law of Nations in Manila Bay*, N.Y. TIMES, May 24, 1898, at 2.

[78] Cuba Submarine Telegraph Co. v. United States (Gr. Brit. v. U.S.), 6 R.I.A.A. 118 (Perm. Ct. Arb. 1923).

[79] *Id.*

[80] Gordon Corera, *How Britain Pioneered Cable-Cutting in World War One*, BBC NEWS (online), Dec. 15, 2017.

only telegraph cable available to the Germans was part of the "All-Red Line," which was under British control. Thus, any German telegraph messages transmitted through the cable could be intercepted and deciphered by British censors.[81] The "Zimmermann Telegram" was one such message that the British intercepted, and its publication helped draw the United States into the war. In the cable, Germany proposed an alliance with Mexico to counter U.S. intervention in the First World War, as well as the provision of German military supplies to Mexico to recoup Texas, New Mexico, and Arizona. British intelligence passed the message to Washington, contributing to American ire over unrestricted submarine warfare. Within five weeks, the United States declared war on Germany.[82]

Germany responded to British cable-cutting operations with their own attacks on British telegraph facilities. In September 1914, a raiding party from the German cruisers SMS *Nürnberg* and SMS *Titania* cut the telegraph cable and destroyed the Eastern Telegraph Company's central Pacific telegraph relay station on Fanning Island in the Pacific Ocean. Two months later, on November 9, a landing party from the German light cruiser SMS *Emden* destroyed the Eastern Telegraph Company's telegraph and wireless station on Direction Island in the Indian Ocean. Finally, in July 1915, the Germans successfully severed the telegraph cable connecting Newbiggin-by-the-Sea in Northumberland, England to Arnedal, Norway.[83]

2.3.3 The Cold War

During the Cold War the United States conducted submarine espionage to penetrate Soviet submarine cables under the name "Operation Holystone." The program was also known as "Operation Barnacle" and "Operation Bollard," and later renamed "Operation Pinnacle."[84] These missions lasted about 90 days each.[85] Operation Holystone tapped U.S.S.R. submarine cables over which secure military communications were sent.[86] President Dwight D. Eisenhower approved of the mission in 1959.[87]

---

[81] *Id.; see also* ELIZABETH BRUTON, FROM AUSTRALIA TO ZIMMERMANN: A BRIEF HISTORY OF CABLE TELEGRAPHY DURING WORLD WAR ONE 5 (2013) [hereinafter BRUTON, FROM AUSTRALIA TO ZIMMERMANN].

[82] U.S. National Security Agency, *The Zimmermann Telegram*, CRYPTOLOGIC QUARTERLY 43 (online), undated.

[83] BRUTON, FROM AUSTRALIA TO ZIMMERMANN, *supra* note 81, at 6–10.

[84] Seymour Hersh, *A False Navy Report Alleged in Sub Crash; Ex-Crew Members on U.S. Vessel Tell of Collision with Russian Craft Off Soviet Union*, N.Y. TIMES, July 6, 1975, at 1.

[85] *Id.*

[86] *Id.*; SHERRY SONTAG, BLIND MAN'S BLUFF 171–98 (1998).

[87] 145 Cong. Rec. 5234, 5235, 1999 (Additional Statements: The 1999 James Madison Prize).

Operation Holystone used specially equipped submarines to gather intelligence on the configuration and capabilities of the Soviet submarine fleet and helped to verify Soviet compliance with nuclear arms control agreements. The Chief of Naval Operations directed the program, which used specially equipped Sturgeon 637-class submarines to collect intelligence within the Soviet Union's territorial sea on the noise patterns and missile-firing capabilities of Soviet submarines.[88] Specifically, Navy divers tapped underwater cables on the seabed to intercept messages and communications that the Soviets deemed too sensitive to transmit via radio or other less secure means.[89]

Because the missions required U.S. clandestine submarine operations close to the Soviet shoreline, they resulted in two known and up to six suspected collisions with Soviet submarines.[90] One U.S. submarine went aground (and then refloated and escaped) inside the territorial sea of the Soviet Union.[91] In another incident, the USS *Gato* collided with a Soviet submarine while on a Holystone mission in 1969.[92] The event occurred 15 to 25 miles off the entrance to the White Sea near the Barents Sea.[93] The U.S. submarine had approached (inadvertently, according to the captain of the boat) within one mile of the Soviet Union.[94]

Operation Ivy Bells succeeded Operation Holystone in 1971. The Navy had reconfigured the USS *Halibut* (SSGN- 587) in 1970 to accommodate deep-water saturation divers.[95] The following year, the modified fast-attack submarine deployed to the Sea of Okhotsk. *Halibut*'s mission was to tap the submarine cable that connected the Soviet Navy's Pacific Fleet headquarters at Vladivostok with the ballistic missile submarine base at Petropavlovsk on the Kamchatka Peninsula.[96] Navy divers from the *Halibut* dropped waterproof recording pods on the cable, and every few weeks they would return and retrieve the tapes and send them to the National Security Agency (NSA)

---

[88] Hersh, *supra* note 84, at 1.
[89] *Id.*
[90] PETER SASGEN, STALKING THE RED BEAR: THE TRUE STORY OF A U.S. COLD WAR SUBMARINE'S COVERT OPERATIONS AGAINST THE SOVIET UNION 73 (2009).
[91] Hersh, *supra* note 84, at 1.
[92] *Id.*
[93] *Id.*
[94] One member of the crew reported that the submarine was under orders to remain beyond three miles, which the United States recognized at the time as the lawful extent of the territorial sea. *Id.*
[95] Kyle Mizokami, *How a Super-Secret U.S. Navy Submarine Tapped Russia's Underwater Communications Cables*, THE NATIONAL INTEREST (online), June 29, 2017.
[96] *Id.*

for analysis.[97] The operation was compromised in 1981 after Ronald Pelton, an NSA employee, sold information about the project to the Soviet Union for $35,000.[98]

2.3.4 Submarine Cables in Great Power Competition

Submarine cables are the information highways through which the cyber dimension of great power competition play out among the United States, China, and Russia. Since cables land on the shores of so many states, bad actors have relatively easy access to them. Many countries also operate submarines, remotely operated vehicles, and deep-diving submersibles that can be used to interfere with submarine cable communications. Russia and China maintain powerful cyber capabilities that they use in peacetime and may employ in armed conflict. In 2005, the Associated Press reported that U.S. submarine *Jimmy Carter* was specially designed to tap submarine cables.[99] The vessel is reportedly modified with an enormous "moon well," a floodable chamber to permit robots and machinery to move between the interior of the submarine and the water column or seabed. In recent years, the NSA and British GCHQ reportedly vacuum up terabytes of data from submarine cables each day.[100] Russia and China appear to have capabilities to cut, disrupt, or tap undersea cables by coming into physical contact with the seabed infrastructure or through nonmaterial, cyber intrusion or attack.

2.3.4.1 Russia

During the 2014 annexation of Crimea, Russia disrupted Ukraine's communications infrastructure. Moscow also appears to be responsible for massive disruptions that hit Estonia's cyber networks in 2007 and brought down Georgian cyber networks during the brief invasion in 2008.[101]

---

[97] Olga Khazan, *The Creepy, Long-Standing Practice of Undersea Cable Tapping*, THE ATLANTIC (online), July 16, 2013.

[98] Fred Kaplan & Walter V. Robinson, *Pelton's "Top-Secret" Intelligence Not So Secret*, BOSTON GLOBE, June 5, 1986, at 1; *Reports on U.S. Submarine Spying on Soviets 25 Years Old*, ASSOCIATED PRESS (online), May 21, 1986.

[99] *New Nuclear Sub Is Said to Have Special Eavesdropping Ability*, ASSOCIATED PRESS, Feb. 20, 2005, at 29; *New Nuclear Sub Is Said to Have Special Eavesdropping Ability*, N.Y. TIMES (online), Feb. 20, 2005; David Axe, *The Navy's Underwater Eavesdropper*, REUTERS (online), July 19, 2013.

[100] Khazan, *supra* note 97; Craig Timberg, *NSA Slide Shows Surveillance of Undersea Cables*, WASHINGTON POST (online), July 10, 2013; *GCHQ Taps Fibre-Optic Cables for Secret Access to World's Communications*, THE GUARDIAN (online), June 23, 2015.

[101] Steven Lee Myers, *Cyberattack on Estonia Stirs Fear of "Virtual War."* N.Y. TIMES (online), May 18, 2007; John Markoff, *Web Becomes a Battleground in Russia-Georgia Conflict*, N.Y. TIMES (online), Aug. 12, 2008; John Markoff, *Before the Gunfire, Cyberattacks*, N.Y. TIMES (online), Aug. 12, 2008; and JEFFREY CARR, INSIDE CYBER WARFARE: MAPPING THE CYBER UNDERWORLD 183–85 (2d ed. 2012).

Similarly, Russia is believed to have launched cyberattacks against Chechnya, Kyrgyzstan, Lithuania, Ingushetia, and the United States.[102]

Russia's *Yantar*-class intelligence ship is equipped with two three-person mini-submarines that can be used to cut or tap into undersea cables. Russia has developed the auxiliary nuclear submarines *Losharik* and *Nelma,* and self-propelled deep submersibles *Rus* and *Consul,* which can interact with cables on the seafloor.[103] In addition to modern submarines, Russian naval activities have been observed in the vicinity of submarine cables in the North Atlantic.[104] Senior NATO commanders have stated that the alliance is unprepared to deal with a Russian attack on undersea cable networks.[105] While Russia maintains naval capabilities to damage or tap submarine cables of other countries, it is among the best positioned to avoid a major disruption of its own systems. Spanning the Eurasian landmass, the Russian Federation is among the least vulnerable states to breaks in submarine cables because none of the cables land in Russia. All of Russia's major information pathways are continental and internal lines of communication.

2.3.4.2 China

China is likewise a cyber great power and a leader in laying and repairing submarine cables worldwide. Increasingly, the world is dividing into two distinct but connected Internet systems—one led by the United States, with Facebook, Amazon, and Google in the lead; and one led by China, with Alibaba, Baidu, and Tencent.[106] China's HMN, for example, has laid and improved nearly 100 undersea cables globally.[107] The Huawei cable network is the principal communications node for China's key foreign policy effort, the New Silk Road. The New Silk Road is part of the Belt Road Initiative (BRI) and consists of pipelines, ports, and railroads surrounding 63 countries that produce one-third of the world's GDP.[108] BRI is the key element in China's

---

[102] CARR, *supra* note 101, at 183–85.

[103] There was a fire on board the *Losharik* (AS-12) in July 2019 which killed 14 of its 25-man crews. Alexandra Ma & Ryan Pickrell, *The Russian Submarine that Caught Fire and Killed 14 May Have Been Designed to Cut Undersea Internet Cables,* BUSINESS INSIDER, (online), July 3, 2019.

[104] *Undersea Cables: Indispensable, Insecure* (2017), *supra* note 42, at 28–33.

[105] Jonathan Beale, *Russia a "Risk" to Undersea Cables, Defence Chief Warns,* BBC NEWS (online), Dec. 15, 2017.

[106] Interview by Leslie P. Norton with Haim Israel, Managing Director of Research, Bank of America (Dec. 27, 2019), *in* Leslie P. Norton, *The 2020s Will Bring Massive Change: Why Society Might Not Be Ready,* BARRON's (online), Dec. 30, 2019.

[107] James Stavridis, *China's Targeting Underwater Internet Cables,* BLOOMBERG (online), Apr. 9, 2019.

[108] Norton, *supra* note 106.

mercantilist economic policy and is designed to move beyond U.S.-China trade disputes to dominate a larger competition over not just leadership in technology, but global economic governance.[109]

In any cross-strait conflict, Taiwan's telecommunications cables would be at risk of attack by the Chinese Navy. At least 10 undersea cables and six cable landing stations connect Taiwan with the outside world. The Yilan station at Toucheng in northeastern Taiwan connects Taipei with the states in the North Pacific and North America, while the Pingtung station at Fangshan in the south connects Taiwan with Southeast Asia and Australia. Damaging these strategic cables and landing stations would not only significantly disrupt Taiwan's economy and communications with its major trading and security partners but would also have a devastating effect on international business and financial markets in Japan, Singapore, Indonesia, and Australia.[110]

2.3.4.3 United States

The United States has demonstrated powerful cyber capabilities in apparent retaliation against the Russian power grid in response to Russian interference in the 2018 U.S. midterm elections and attacks on American electrical systems.[111]

No single U.S. department or agency oversees U.S. submarine cable policy or activities. Instead, there are some 14 agencies, including the Maritime Administration, Coast Guard, Army Corps of Engineers, and the Federal Communications Commission, that meet at a National Security Council Task Force on Submarine Cable Vulnerability to resolve interagency disputes.

There are no U.S.-flagged cable ships, although some cable ships flagged in the Republic of the Marshall Islands are owned by U.S. companies. Congress has authorized a cable ship security program with the Military Sealift Command that could be activated in a national emergency. This authorization is a $5 million "firetruck" that is supposed to respond in a crisis, but Congress has never appropriated funds for it.

---

[109] William W. Priest, *A Long Winter for the U.S. and China*, BARRON's, Dec. 30, 2019, at 26.

[110] *Taiwan Undersea Cables "Priority Targets" by PLA in War*, ASIA TIMES (online), Dec. 6, 2017.

[111] Andrew E. Kramer & Michael R. Gordon, *Ukraine Reports Russian Invasion on a New Front*, N.Y. TIMES (online), Aug. 27, 2014; David E. Sanger & Nicole Perlroth, *U.S. Buries Digital Land Mines to Menace Russia's Power Grid*, N.Y. TIMES, June 16, 2019, at A1; David E. Sanger, *Russian Hackers Train Focus on U.S. Power Grid*, N.Y. TIMES, July 28, 2018, at A11.

2.4 Submarine Cables and Cyberattack

Coastal states exercise control over submarine cables in their archipelagic waters, territorial sea, and internal waters (and through straits used for international navigation), as though they were cyber infrastructure on their land territory.[112] Consequently, States may regulate the laying, maintenance, repair, and replacement of submarine communication cables and adopt laws and regulations concerning their protection, in the territorial sea.[113] Such laws may not impede innocent passage, transit passage, or archipelagic sea lanes passage.[114]

All States enjoy the right to lay submarine cables on the high seas and in the EEZ and on the continental shelves of coastal States as a high seas freedom.[115] This right is subject to due regard for the sovereign rights and jurisdiction of the coastal state.[116] The delineation or course laid for submarine cables in these areas, however, is not subject to coastal state consent.[117] China and India, however, purport to control the laying of submarine cables on their continental shelves and in their EEZ.[118] Under article 79 of UNCLOS, however, coastal states may regulate foreign submarine cables on the continental shelf only to the extent that such actions are "reasonable measures for the exploration . . . [or] exploitation of its natural resources."[119] The *Tallinn Manual 2.0* suggests that it is unreasonable for coastal States to impede the laying of submarine cables based upon this provision. This interpretation is correct because cables—measuring only a few inches in diameter—have only a *de minimis* effect on the natural resources of the EEZ.

States laying cables also may exercise a right to maintain and repair them. Some observers question whether the right extends to replacing outdated cables since UNCLOS only specifies that replacement of cables is authorized in archipelagic waters and is silent on the right to replace cables in the EEZ and on the continental shelf.[120] Yet, UNCLOS broadly recognizes the right to

---

[112] TALLINN MANUAL 2.0 ON THE INTERNATIONAL LAW APPLICABLE TO CYBER WARFARE 253, r. 54 (Michael N. Schmitt ed., 2017) [hereinafter TALLINN MANUAL 2.0].

[113] *See* UNCLOS, *supra* note 2, art. 58(3).

[114] *Id.* art. 17(1).

[115] UNCLOS, *supra*, note 2, arts. 58, 87, 112.

[116] *Id.* arts. 58(1)–(3), 79(1), (4); *see also* NWP 1-14M, *supra* note 17, §§ 1.6.2; 1.7.

[117] TALLINN MANUAL 2.0, *supra* note 112, at 254.

[118] CHINA MINISTRY OF COMMERCE, GOVERNING THE LAYING OF SUBMARINE CABLES AND PIPELINES art. 4 (1989); INDIA, TERRITORIAL WATERS, CONTINENTAL SHELF, EXCLUSIVE ECONOMIC ZONE AND OTHER MARITIME ZONES ACT art. 7 (1976).

[119] UNCLOS, *supra* note 2, art. 79(2); *see id.*, art. 56(2).

[120] TALLINN MANUAL 2.0, *supra* note 112, at 256.

lay new cables in any event, so whether they are replacement cables or new cables is legally immaterial.

The group of experts that produced the *Tallinn Manual 2.0* agreed that inflicting purposeful damage on cables by a state during peacetime is prohibited as a matter of customary law since it is counter to the "object and purpose" of the 1884 Convention and UNCLOS.[121] This understanding is also consistent with the right to lay cables, as it would be incongruent to recognize a right to lay them without a corresponding obligation on the part of the coastal state to respect them once they are on the seabed.[122]

Rather than physically cutting cables, adversaries may use cyber means to remotely disrupt or disable them. Cyber operations may be considered as tantamount to a kinetic attack when they produce injurious or destructive consequences.[123] The *Tallinn Manual 2.0* adopts the standard set forth in the 1986 Nicaragua decision at the International Court of Justice that an act of violence must reach some threshold in terms of "scale and effects" before it is considered an "armed attack."[124] States may exercise the inherent right of self-defense if they are subject to an armed attack. During an armed conflict, submarine cables may be attacked if they are determined to be a valid military objective.[125] Generally, civilian objects that are not military objectives shall not be the object of an attack.[126] As submarine cables generally are dual-use infrastructure, the determination of whether they constitute "military objectives" is fraught with subjective ambiguity.

Military objectives are defined in Additional Protocol I as "those objects which by their nature, location, purpose, or use make an effective contribution to military action and whose total or partial destruction, capture or neutralization, in the circumstances ruling at the time, offers a definite military advantage."[127] Nonetheless, an attack that "may be expected to cause incidental loss of civilian life, injury to civilians, damage to civilian objects, or a combination thereof, which would be excessive in relation to the concrete and direct military advantage anticipated," is prohibited.[128] The question

---

[121] *Id.*

[122] *Id.*

[123] Tallinn Manual 2.0, *supra* note 112, at 341 r. 71; Michael N. Schmitt, *Cyber Operations and the Jus in Bello: Key Issues*, 41 Israeli Yearbook of Human Rights 113, 119 (2011).

[124] Military and Paramilitary Activities in and against Nicaragua (Nicar. v. U.S), Judgment, 1986 I.C.J. Rep. 14, ¶ 191 (June 27); Tallinn Manual 2.0, *supra* note 112, at 341 r. 71.

[125] San Remo Manual, *supra* note 75, r. 60(a).

[126] Protocol Additional to the Geneva Conventions of 12 August 1949, and Relating to the Protection of Victims of International Armed Conflicts, art. 52, June 8, 1977, 1125 U.N.T.S. 3.

[127] *Id.*

[128] *Id.* art. 51.

is, therefore, whether submarine cables qualify as military objectives and, if so, whether their destruction or damage would cause excessive collateral damage to the civilian population in relation to the military advantage anticipated from the attack. Determining whether an object is a valid military objective involves a two-part test: (1) the nature, location, purpose, or use of the object must make an effective contribution to military action; and (2) destroying, capturing, or neutralizing the object must offer a definite military advantage.[129]

"Nature" refers to the "type of the object and may . . . refer to objects that are per se military objectives," such as military equipment and facilities.[130] A submarine cable that is used exclusively by the armed forces, by its nature, makes an effective contribution to military action (e.g., command and control, communications, intelligence gathering, precision targeting, etc.) and would be a valid military objective. "Use" refers to an "object's present function."[131] A civilian submarine cable that carries both civilian and military transmissions would result in providing an effective contribution to military action, which makes it targetable as a valid military objective. "Purpose" refers to the intended or possible use of the object in the future.[132] A civilian submarine cable that could be used to back up or supplement a military submarine cable that is damaged or destroyed during a conflict could qualify as a military objective. Even though it is not currently providing an effective contribution to military action, it could do so in the future if used to support an adversary's military operations. Finally, an object must effectively contribute to the enemy's warfighting, war-supporting, or war-sustaining capability.[133] Using submarine cables, for example, to provide command and control of military forces participating in an attack or targeting data to an unmanned aerial vehicle to conduct a precision strike against the enemy, would effectively contribute to military action. Communications objects like submarine cables that can be used for command and control of military operations or intelligence gathering are normally considered legitimate military objectives during an international armed conflict.[134] There is no requirement, however,

---

[129] OFFICE OF THE GENERAL COUNSEL, U.S. DEPARTMENT OF DEFENSE, LAW OF WAR MANUAL § 5.6.5 (rev. ed., Dec. 2016) [hereinafter DoD LAW OF WAR MANUAL]; NWP 1-14M, *supra* note 17, § 5.3.1.
[130] DoD LAW OF WAR MANUAL, *supra* note 129, § 5.6.6.1.
[131] *Id.*
[132] *Id.*
[133] *Id.* § 8.2.
[134] *Id.* § 5.6.8.2.

that the contribution be direct or provide immediate tactical advantages to the enemy, so long as the object makes an effective contribution to the opposing state's effort.[135]

The second prong of the test requires that the damage, destruction, capture, or neutralization of the object, "in the circumstances ruling at the time," offer a definite military advantage.[136] "Neutralization" refers to denying the use of an object to the enemy without destroying it, such as a cyberattack that affects the information flow through the cable without physically damaging or destroying the cable. Military advantage "in the circumstance ruling at the time" could include preventing the future use of an object.[137] Moreover, the military advantage offered by the attack does not have to be immediate if it contributes to the attacker's war strategy.[138]

The military advantage resulting from the attack must be "definite."[139] In other words, it must be "concrete and perceptible" rather than merely hypothetical or speculative.[140] However, the advantage gained need not be immediate. Severing a submarine cable, for example, that is used for command and control, even if it is not being used for that purpose at the time of the attack, would still present a direct military advantage because it would deny the enemy the ability to use the means to communicate in future military operations. Additionally, the military advantage anticipated from the attack must be considered as a whole, not in isolation. Military advantage is not "restricted to immediate tactical gains," but may be assessed more broadly within the "full context of the war strategy."[141]

Destroying a submarine cable that is being used for military purposes would also provide a military advantage if it improved the security of the attacking force (for example, degrading the ability of unmanned systems to target the attacking forces) or harms the morale of enemy forces. However, "diminishing the morale of the civilian population" in and of itself, "does not provide a definite military advantage."[142] Nonetheless, an otherwise lawful attack is not rendered unlawful simply because it diminishes the morale of the civilian population. For example, destroying a dual-use submarine cable

[135] *Id.* § 5.6.6.2.
[136] *Id.*
[137] *Id.*
[138] *Id.*
[139] *Id.*
[140] *Id.* § 5.6.7.3.
[141] *Id.*
[142] *Id.*

that degrades the enemy's targeting capabilities, but also takes out the civilian Internet, is likely to be lawful. Dual-use submarine cables that are used by both the military and civilian population are legitimate military targets. However, before executing such an attack, the commander should consider the expected harm to the civilian population that may result from the attack.

2.5 Maritime Neutrality and Submarine Cables

Submarine cables that lie on the continental shelf in the internal waters, archipelagic waters, or territorial sea of a coastal state are under the sovereignty of the coastal state and are physically inviolable during armed conflict. Neutral states are those that have elected not to take part in an armed conflict and instead seek to maintain friendly, impartial relations with all states.[143] The law of neutrality regulates the relationship between states that are party to a conflict and those that are not engaged in armed conflict.[144] Neutral states strive to balance two conflicting interests: the right of belligerents to prosecute the war effort by isolating the enemy and destroying opposing armed forces, and the right of neutral states to be free from the adverse effects of armed conflicts to which they are not a party. As President Thomas Jefferson decreed in 1793 as French warships sought refuge in American ports during the war between revolutionary France and the First Coalition, "the law of nations and the rules of neutrality" prevent the United States from taking sides.[145]

We may expect that belligerent states would use, damage, or even destroy neutral submarine cables during armed conflict. There are few restrictions on using or destroying neutral submarine cables in the law of naval warfare. Belligerents may lawfully use the entire global network of submarine cables as a domain of virtual warfare without any material restraint from the law of neutrality.

The law of neutrality applies during armed conflict and protects the rights of neutral states not party to the conflict, including the inviolability of submarine cables in their waters from physical attack by belligerents. This right, however, neither protects neutral cables lying outside neutral territorial

[143] *Id.* §§ 15.1.2.2., 15.1.3.
[144] *Id.* § 15.1.1.
[145] *George Washington, President of the United States* (Apr. 22, 1793), *reprinted in* 12 THE PAPERS OF GEORGE WASHINGTON 472–74 (Christine Sternberg Patrick & John C. Pinheiro eds., 2005).

waters from destruction by belligerents nor prevents belligerents from using neutral cable infrastructure for cyberattacks against another belligerent. The automatic routing of cable traffic (done instantly and without human decision) in today's global submarine cable systems means that belligerents engaged in cyberattack are unable to avoid neutral cables. It is virtually impossible to direct (or restrict) a cyberattack through a particular cable, which means that cyber operations are likely to use submarine cables owned or operated by neutral states. At the same time, neutral states are absolved of their traditional obligation under the law of neutrality to ensure that their cables are not (mis)used by a belligerent when communications travels through cables located in the neutral state.

2.5.1 Rights of Neutral States and Submarine Cables

The law of neutrality largely has focused on the right of neutral states on the high seas to engage in trade with one another, and separately, with belligerent states (except for contraband), as set out in the *British Declaration on Neutrals and Letters of Marque* of March 28, 1854, and the 1856 *Paris Declaration Respecting Maritime Law*.[146] These provisions were further codified in the U.S.-U.K. 1871 *Treaty of Washington*.[147] Neutral states have the right to engage in commerce, protected from the worst effects of armed conflict to which they are not a party.[148]

Neutral territory is inviolable by belligerents under Hague Convention V.[149] At sea, neutral space extends to the waters under the sovereignty of coastal states, including ports, internal waters, and the territorial sea of a state in accordance with Hague Convention XIII.[150] Similarly, article 3 of the 1928 *Convention on Maritime Neutrality* requires that belligerents shall "refrain from acts of war" in neutral waters.[151] This rule extends logically to archipelagic waters under Part IV of UNCLOS, as recognized in Part II, rules 23 to 30, of the *San Remo Manual*.[152] The *Helsinki Principles* take the same

---

[146] British Declaration on Neutrals and Letters of Marque, March 28, 1854, *reprinted in* 46 BRITISH & FOREIGN STATE PAPERS 36–37 (1865); Paris Declaration Respecting Maritime Law, Apr. 16, 1856, *reprinted in* 46 BRITISH & FOREIGN STATE PAPERS 26–27 (1865).

[147] Amity (Treaty of Washington), U.K.-U.S., art. 6, May 8, 1871, 17 Stat. 863, T.S. 133.

[148] DoD LAW OF WAR MANUAL, *supra* note 129, § 15.1.3

[149] Convention No. V Respecting the Rights and Duties of Neutral Powers and Persons in Case of War on Land, art. 1, Oct. 18, 1907, 36 Stat. 2310, T.S. 540.

[150] Convention No. XIII Concerning the Rights and Duties of Neutral Powers in Naval War, arts. 2, 5, Oct. 18, 1907, 36 Stat. 2415, T.S. No. 545.

[151] Convention on Maritime Neutrality, art. 3, Feb. 20, 1928, 135 L.N.T.S. 187.

[152] SAN REMO MANUAL, *supra* note 75, at r. 23–30.

approach.[153] Belligerent warships and auxiliaries may enter neutral territorial seas for mere transit but may not conduct operations in excess of simple innocent passage, archipelagic sea lanes passage, or transit passage through straits, as appropriate.

The law of neutrality has always been complex—even unsettled—and submarine cables make analysis even more challenging. Belligerent states are forbidden from using neutral waters as a base of naval operations against the enemy. This proscription includes using neutral waters to refuel, resupply, repair, or rearm warships (beyond what is minimally required to get underway) in accordance with article 6 of Hague XIII. Belligerent warships may not remain in neutral waters longer than 24 hours under the 1928 *Convention on Maritime Neutrality*.[154] Article 5 of Hague XIII prohibits belligerents from erecting on neutral territory "wireless telegraphy stations or any apparatus" used in military communications with "belligerent forces on land or sea." This rule is amplified in article 4 of the 1928 Convention: belligerents may not install in neutral waters "radio-telegraph stations or any other apparatus" to communicate with military forces, or to "make use" of such installations established before the war and "which have not been opened to the public."[155] These rules on the neutral inviolability of the physical domain of waters under coastal state sovereignty also apply to submarine cables physically present in those areas.

A 1902 exercise at the U.S. Naval War College concluded that belligerent states acting on the high seas could interrupt or cut submarine cables between belligerents and neutrals "if the necessities of war require," although cables connecting neutral states only were inviolable.[156] The U.S. cable cutting during the Spanish-American War resulted in a U.S.-U.K. arbitration tribunal in 1923, the "Eastern Extension Case," which considered compensation for British companies that owned the cables.[157] The tribunal denied compensation, ruling that cutting the cables was consistent with the law of naval warfare and "fully justified." The holding in the Eastern Extension Case concluded that belligerents could damage or cut neutral submarine cables "if

---

[153] Committee on Maritime Neutrality, *Helsinki Principles on the Law of Maritime Neutrality*, in INTERNATIONAL LAW ASSOCIATION REPORT OF THE 68TH CONFERENCE TAIPEI, at § 1.1 (1998), *reprinted in* DIETRICH SCHINDLER & JIŘÍ TOMAN, *supra* note 74, at 1425.

[154] Convention on Maritime Neutrality, *supra* note 151, at arts. 5, 12.

[155] *Id.* art. 3.

[156] *Situation I: Submarine Telegraphic Cables in Time of War*, 2 INTERNATIONAL LAW STUDIES 7–20 (1902).

[157] Eastern Extension, Australasia, and China Telegraph Co. v. United States (Gr. Brit. v. U.S.), 6 R.I.A.A. 112 (Perm. Ct. Arb. 1923).

the necessities of war require." The *Tallinn Manual 2.0* commentary is more restrictive, stating that such attacks are prohibited if the belligerent realizes that such action would generate foreseeable spillover effects on the neutral state. The *Tallinn Manual 2.0* also asserts that the exercise of belligerent rights by cyber means "directed against" neutral submarine infrastructure, such as submarine cables, is prohibited.[158] This proscription applies to cables inside the territorial waters of the coastal state, as well as those owned by companies of the neutral state that span the globe. Furthermore, the *Tallinn Manual 2.0* states that "the exercise of belligerent rights by cyber means" are prohibited in neutral territory.[159] This approach incorrectly analogizes cyber data as akin to physically transporting munitions or supplies of war through a neutral power, which would be a violation of Hague V.[160]

Between the more restrictive *Tallinn Manual 2.0* commentary and the permissive 1923 arbitration, the arbitration is the more realistic and compelling standard, as it reflects state practice. In the exigencies of war, belligerents will utilize cables and conduct cyberattacks through them, particularly when the law is less than certain. The 1923 arbitration and the practicalities driven by cable operations today suggest that belligerents may resort to using—or even cutting—submarine cables as a method of naval warfare. This approach is consistent with article 54 of the 1907 Hague IV Regulations, which provides that cables connecting an occupied territory with a neutral territory are protected from seizure or damage "except in the case of absolute necessity." The exception seems to swallow the rule. The upshot is that virtual cyberspace within submarine cables, like the airwaves, constitutes a global electromagnetic domain that is open to belligerents. Neither the black letter law nor the actual technology supports more aspirational cyber protections for cable networks of neutral states, and indeed state practice suggests that international law does not shield cyber infrastructure on the seabed (or land territory) from the vagaries of armed conflict.

Submarine cables located in neutral states are themselves physically inviolable, but their usage as information conduits is not protected during armed conflict. Belligerents may utilize submarine cables as part of their cyberattack against the enemy. The nature of submarine cables today means there is no alternative to this view because the seabed infrastructure is no

---

[158] TALLINN MANUAL 2.0, *supra* note 112, at 555.
[159] *Id.* r. 151, at 556.
[160] Convention No. V Respecting the Rights and Duties of Neutral Powers and Persons in Case of War on Land, art. 2, Oct. 18, 1907, 36 Stat. 2310, T.S. 540.

longer bi-polar, in which data serves only two states physically connected. Consequently, implementation of the *Tallinn Manual 2.0* rules appears to presume a level of control required by belligerents to avoid cables lying in neutral waters or neutral cables on the deep seabed that is unrealistic.

2.5.2 Duties of Neutral States and Submarine Cables

Not only may neutral states have very little or no expectation that belligerents will refrain from using their submarine cables, it is also largely impractical to expect neutral states to attempt to prevent such use. These factors have absolved neutral states of their traditional duties of neutrality in armed conflict when it comes to cyberwarfare in submarine cables.

Rule 152 of the *Tallinn Manual 2.0* suggests that neutral states have a due diligence requirement to ensure their submarine cables are not utilized for belligerent purposes. Yet the amorphous nature of the electromagnetic data traveling through submarine cables, while exposing neutral states to belligerent activity, also mitigates their duty to ensure belligerents do not use their cables. Neutral states have an obligation to ensure that belligerents do not use their territory or waters under their sovereignty to prosecute the war effort.[161] The *British Wireless Telegraphy (Foreign Ships) Regulations* of 1908, for example, authorized the postmaster general and the Admiralty to "control transmissions of messages by wireless telegraphy" by foreign ships in the territorial waters. The United States had the same policy, which rankled Germany and Austria during the First World War, since there was no similar restriction on submarine cable messages.[162] The U.S. rationale to distinguish censoring radio transmissions in the territorial sea, but not submarine cable messages, was that radio waves broadcast in the open cannot be interrupted and may be received and utilized by anyone—including belligerent warships on the high seas.[163] The U.S. position was based on the fact that submarine cables could not be used as a means of direct communication from its neutral territory with belligerent warships on the high seas, whereas wireless

[161] Memorandum from Frank L. Polk, Counsel, U.S. Department of State to John J. Fitzgerald, U.S. Rep. (Aug. 18, 1916), *in* U.S. Department of State, Foreign Relations of the United States: 1916 Supplement: The World War (Joseph V. Fuller ed., 1929).

[162] Letter from Robert Lansing, Counsel, U.S. Department of State, to William Jennings Bryan, Secretary of State (Jan. 1, 1915), *in* 1 U.S. Department of State, Papers Relating to the Foreign Relations of the United States, The Lansing Papers, 1914–1920 (J. S. Beddie ed., 1939).

[163] Letter from William Jennings Bryan, Secretary of State, to Walter Hines Page, U.S. Ambassador to the U.K. (Jan. 9, 1915), *in* U.S. Department of State, Papers Relating to the Foreign Relations of the United States: 1915 Supplement: The World War (Joseph V. Fuller ed., 1929).

telegraphy could serve that purpose. Furthermore, undersea cables could always be cut by belligerents, as the German cruiser SMS *Nürnberg* did in its 1914 attack on the cable relay station at Fanning Island in the central Pacific Ocean.[164]

Article 8 of Hague V states that neutral powers need not "forbid or restrict the use on behalf of the belligerents of telegraph or telephone cables or of wireless telegraphy apparatus belonging to it or to companies or private individuals." Utilizing submarine cables, like telephone and wireless transmissions, does not involve physical entry into the neutral state. Thus, neutral states are not under an obligation to ferret out and stop the (mis)use of their submarine cables by belligerent states, and by not doing so, they do not jeopardize their neutral status. Regardless of either approach, however, if a neutral state restricts or prohibits belligerents from using its submarine cables, it must do so in a manner that is impartial to all parties to a conflict.

[164] Peter R. Jensen, Wireless at War 50–81 (2013).

7

Missile Warfare and Nuclear Weapons

1. Missile Warfare

Missiles are self-propelled, unmanned weapons that pass through the medium of airspace and outer space.[1] They may be launched from fixed or mobile sites on land; surface ships; submarines; aircraft; and potentially, from outer space.[2] Missiles serve either a tactical or theater role or a strategic purpose (particularly when armed with nuclear weapons or other weapons of mass destruction). Three broad categories of missiles are common today: cruise missiles, hypersonic missiles, and ballistic missiles. Numerous caveats apply, however. "Rockets," for example, include small tactical systems, such as the Multiple Launch Rocket System (MLRS) or the massive Saturn V, leading to a long-standing debate over the difference between a rocket and a missile. Most "rockets" are unguided after launch, whereas missiles are guided. While some hypersonic missiles are lofted by a ballistic missile (Boost Glide Vehicle or BGV), others feature sustained aerodynamic flight with scramjet propulsion, which makes them more like cruise missiles. Thus, the three general categories of missiles are a loose but useful point of departure. All three classes of weapons may be launched from mobile carriers or platforms, so they provide flexible strike options and complicate defensive responses in naval warfare. Mobility complicates the defenders' "left of launch" option (killing the archer) and can also thwart detection and calculation of the trajectory of the incoming missile, which counters both active and passive defenses.

Cruise missiles are air breathing (or at least travel through the atmosphere) and in the past have done so mainly at subsonic speed. Ballistic missiles are

---

[1] PROGRAM ON HUMANITARIAN POLICY AND CONFLICT RESEARCH AT HARVARD UNIVERSITY, MANUAL ON INTERNATIONAL LAW APPLICABLE TO AIR AND MISSILE WARFARE ¶ 1(z) at 50 (2009) [hereinafter HPCR MANUAL ON AIR AND MISSILE WARFARE]. A Commentary for the HPCR Manual was published in February 2010.

[2] The United States and Russia have experimented with air-launched ballistic missiles as well. Thomas Newdick, *Air Force Fighters Almost Got an Air-Launched Ballistic Missile 40 Years Ago, Now They're a Hot Item*, THE WAR ZONE (online), Jan. 26, 2021.

Disruptive Technology and the Law of Naval Warfare. James Kraska and Raul Pedrozo, Oxford University Press.
© James Kraska & Raul Pedrozo 2022. DOI: 10.1093/oso/9780197630181.003.0008

powered by rocket engines that draw on liquid or solid fuel propellants to form a high-speed propulsive jet, usually high-temperature gas that produces enormous thrust. The thrust propels a classic ballistic missile into outer space, where it follows a predictable arc or trajectory as it returns to earth, re-entering the atmosphere and approaching the target zone. More advanced ballistic missiles, however, have lofted or depressed trajectories, and can also dispense maneuverable re-entry vehicles or MaRVs. Even these trajectories, however, fall within certain predictable limits. While ballistic missiles traditionally were nuclear-armed, serving a strategic function, the proliferation of ballistic missile technology has gradually meant more of them are deployed in a conventional role. Ballistic missiles may serve as conventional theater weapons in long-range, precision strike (LRPS), a term that encompasses any class of weapon where range is independent of accuracy. The United States seeks an LRPS capability called Conventional Prompt Strike (CPS) to quickly and accurately hit targets worldwide, although not all LRPS systems are necessarily fast.[3]

Traditional ballistic missiles re-enter the atmosphere at greater than Mach 5, so they also are hypersonic at some point in their flight. Once boosted into space on a ballistic missile bus or BGV, hypersonic glide vehicles (HGVs) ride their own shockwave into the target at speeds in excess of Mach 5.[4] Some cruise missiles are also capable of hypersonic speeds. These advanced hypersonic weapons are in development and would rely on scramjet technology to maintain hypersonic cruise without the boost from a ballistic missile. The U.S. Navy intends to deploy hypersonic CPS capabilities on board its three *Zumwalt*-class destroyers by 2025, although this timeline appears ambitious.[5]

There are great variations among cruise, ballistic, and hypersonic missiles, with distinctions mixing and blurring. Technology has increased the range and performance of missiles at the same time horizontal proliferation has made them available to more states and even nonstate actors. Hamas, for example, launched more than 4,000 rockets into Israel in May 2021.[6] Iran and Syria have supplied Hamas with some 7,000 missiles. Hezbollah possesses

[3] CONGRESSIONAL RESEARCH SERVICE PUBLICATION NO. R41464, CONVENTIONAL PROMPT GLOBAL STRIKE AND LONG-RANGE BALLISTIC MISSILES: BACKGROUND AND ISSUES REPORT 7–8 (Dec. 16, 2020).

[4] DEFENSE INTELLIGENCE BALLISTIC MISSILE ANALYSIS COMMITTEE, BALLISTIC AND CRUISE MISSILE THREAT 2 (2017).

[5] Megan Eckstein, *US Navy Conducts First Live-Fire Test of Hypersonic Missile Motor*, DEFENSE NEWS (online), May 28, 2021.

[6] Isabel Debre, *How Hamas Amassed Thousands of Rockets to Strike at Israel*, L.A. TIMES (online), May 20, 2021.

more firepower than 95 percent of the world's conventional militaries, and more rockets and missiles than all European NATO members combined.[7] The weapons have little accuracy and are area saturation/terror weapons, but the scale of Hezbollah's missile force is nonetheless alarming. Iran has some 2,500 to 3,000 ballistic missiles.[8]

1.1 Evolution of Strike Technology

Missiles are the primary weapon for contemporary naval warfare, as they permit the strike of enemy forces with fine precision from great distances. The weapons have had a transformative effect on tactical, operational, and strategic levels of armed conflict at sea by solving the challenge of how to close with the enemy without exposing one's own forces to danger. As self-propelled projectiles, missiles are part of the larger evolution in strike warfare. In the ancient world, arrows were used to strike the enemy from a distance, and these were replaced by firearms during the Middle Ages. Advances in firearm technology, and eventually rifled guns, gradually increased the strike distance between opposing naval forces.

During their naval engagement in the Yellow Sea in August 1904, the Japanese and Russian navies fought at a distance of about eight miles. This range held relatively constant for naval battles throughout the First World War. Despite improvements in the accuracy of naval gunfire, however, hit percentages were abysmal in this period. During the Spanish-American War, for example, of the 9,500 naval shots fired at various but close ranges, only 121 found their mark.[9] Aircraft were first used during armed conflict in the Italian Tripoli campaign of 1911 to 1912 but did little damage. By 1915 to 1916 aircraft were an essential feature of warfare. During the Second World War, the range of naval gunfire doubled to about 20 miles, just as aircraft displaced surface warships as the primary means of delivering kinetic effects at great distances. As aircraft became effective platforms for delivery of bombs, the distance at which naval engagements were fought shifted from dozens of

---

[7] Richard Natonski & Jonathan Ruhe, *Learn from Gaza, Prepare for Hezbollah*, BREAKING DEFENSE (online), May 24, 2021.

[8] Jeremy Binnie, *Iran Has 2,500-3,000 Ballistic Missiles, Says CENTCOM Commander*, JANE'S DEFENCE WEEKLY, Mar. 18, 2020, at 18.

[9] ELTING MORISON, MEN, MACHINES, AND MODERN TIMES 44 (2016).

miles to hundreds of miles. Aircraft carriers displaced battleships as the capital warship.[10]

Carrier aircraft strikes were decisive in turning back Japan's advance in the Pacific Theater. During the Battle of the Coral Sea, and especially the Battle of Midway from June 4 to 7, 1942, the aircraft carrier became the world's first integrated battle network, with radar and command and control combined with organic aircraft for defense and attack.[11] At Midway, three U.S. aircraft carriers, *Enterprise, Hornet,* and *Yorktown,* confronted four Japanese carriers, *Hiryu, Akagi, Kaga,* and *Soryu.* The USS *Hornet* and *Enterprise* launched Devastator torpedo bombers against the Japanese fleet, but nearly all of them were shot down by Japanese fighter aircraft. As the Japanese fighters refueled on *Akagi, Kaga,* and *Soryu,* however, their decks were exposed to attack from U.S. carrier aircraft. American bombers sank all three Japanese carriers. In turn, aircraft from the remaining Japanese carrier, *Hiryu,* successfully attacked the USS *Yorktown,* which was so heavily damaged it was abandoned (and later sunk by a Japanese submarine). Meanwhile, U.S. dive-bombers set the *Hiryu* ablaze, sinking it. The Imperial Japanese fleet was forced to withdraw. The Battle of Midway underscores how carrier-based bomber and torpedo aircraft replaced surface ships and foretold the transition from manned aircraft to missiles.

1.2 Transition to Missiles

The Japanese "Baka Bombs" were the bridge from aircraft to missiles. These rocket-powered kamikaze aircraft were piloted cruise missiles that devastated U.S. naval forces near the end of the war. In the battle of Okinawa from April to June 1945, the Baka Bomb proved to be Japan's most effective weapon of the war against the U.S. Navy, sinking 26 of the 28 warships destroyed by the Japanese during the campaign.[12] Even the Kamikaze, however, had

---

[10] John Keegan regarded the aircraft carrier "the supreme instrument of command of the sea." JOHN KEEGAN, THE PRICE OF ADMIRALTY: THE EVOLUTION OF NAVAL WARFARE 267 (1989). *But see* James R. FitzSimonds, *Aircraft Carriers versus Battleships in War and Myth: Demythologizing Carrier Air Dominance at Sea,* 84 JOURNAL OF MILITARY HISTORY 843, 844 (July 2020) (Battleships proved more resilient than many believe, with aircraft carriers unable to prevent them from accomplishing their missions).

[11] JONATHAN PARSHALL & ANTHONY TULLY, SHATTERED SWORD: THE UNTOLD STORY OF THE BATTLE OF MIDWAY xxv (2007); Malcolm A. LeCompte, *Radar and the Air Battles of Midway,* NAVAL HISTORY 28, 29–32 (Summer 1992).

[12] ROY E. APPLEMAN, OKINAWA: THE LAST BATTLE 190 (1948).

extremely poor hit rates. Nevertheless, as a "guided" missile, the piloted bombs were something of a harbinger of where we are today.

Germany was the first state to develop a true, unmanned cruise missile, the V1 "flying bomb." The V1 was an air breathing pulse jet with a range of 285 to 370 km.[13] About 30,000 of the notoriously inaccurate V1 rockets were fired between June 1944 and June 1945. The more advanced V2 was the first long-range ballistic missile.[14] Germany launched some 4,300 V2 rockets between September 1944 and March 1945, but like the V1 they also failed to produce strategic effect. The Circular Error of Probability or CEP of the V2 was about 5 km. Gradually, missile accuracy increased. Germany also employed the Fritz-X and Henschel Hs 293 rudimentary glide bombs as anti-ship weapons during 1943–44. The weapons were launched from a bomber and steered into their targets over a radio link by the bombardier in the launching aircraft. The Allies attacked and destroyed narrow wood railway bridges in Burma with a similar weapon, the VB-1 (Vertical Bomb 1).[15]

After the war, guided missiles continued to replace guns and aircraft. Battleships were retired, except for brief appearances in the Korean War and the Vietnam War, and their refurbishment during the 1980s as cruise missile platforms. Torpedoes launched from submarines, and bombs (and missiles) from aircraft, had a much longer range and were more accurate than naval gunfire.[16] Torpedoes had extremely short ranges. Even modern homing torpedoes are generally not employed beyond about 5–6 nm. The real shift in precision reach came in the 1970s with the AS-4 Kitchen anti-ship cruise missile (ASCM) that could be launched from the Backfire bomber against U.S. aircraft carrier battle groups from more than 200 nm—well outside of ship defenses. The turning point came when the ship needed to defend itself from the missile and could no longer survive by engaging the delivery aircraft. Missiles defeat aircraft, but missiles do not easily defeat missiles. That is the bottom line for LRPS. The AS-4 changed the game, as did the Soviet introduction of long-range surface- and submarine-launched missiles like the SS-N-12 and SS-N-19.

After the Second World War, missiles largely replaced manned aircraft as the most effective means of delivery for a warhead because they offered

---

[13] UN Doc. A/57/229, The Issue of Missiles in all its Respects, July 23, 2002, ¶ 8.

[14] Id. ¶ 9.

[15] Jacob Neufeld, *Early Experimental Guided Missiles*, AIR POWER HISTORY 28, 33 (Spring 2011).

[16] BERNARD & FAWN M. BRODIE, FROM CROSSBOW TO H-BOMB: THE EVOLUTION OF THE WEAPONS AND TACTICS OF WARFARE 290 (1962).

long-range strike without exposing a pilot to enemy fire. But aircraft-delivered weapons without ample standoff range still gave the advantage to the defender since air defenses generally prevailed over manned aircraft. (The Fritz-X was guided, but the delivering aircraft needed a line of sight (and be within the missile's radio range) to guide the weapon, making the aircraft vulnerable to counterfire.) Autonomous missiles allow the aircraft to avoid this problem. Missiles have a longer reach than naval guns, and they are more accurate and have a heavier payload. On the downside, missiles are generally larger and more costly than gun projectiles, so ships carry fewer missile rounds in their magazine than gun shells. Missiles that rely on guidance systems also may be more easily spoofed than naval gunfire. There is at least some prospect of shooting missiles down in flight or denying the missile seeker its targeting data through jamming or obscurants. It remains to be seen whether a future short-range gun might prove more viable if passive defenses gain an advantage over the guided missile. Nonetheless, whereas missiles require only the most minimal of launch systems, guns are quite an investment within the platform itself.

1.3 Missiles in Naval Warfare

Warships are vulnerable to missiles and a single strike will put most of them out of action.[17] This has to do with the penetrating power of missiles that has tended to render ship armor moot. But that was also largely true for shells. The SS-N-2 Styx from the 1950s could penetrate four feet of armor. The thickest armor ever installed on a combatant was two feet on the HMS *Inflexible* in the 1870s. Modern warships are more vulnerable, with fragile radar and computers on board they may be put out of action by a single strike. The Russians were the first to integrate this thinking into their force structure. The Soviet Union led the way on anti-ship missile development in the 1950s by terminating their major ship programs in favor of missiles and submarines as their primary weapons to neutralize the U.S. fleet. Moscow was ahead of the United States in recognizing the potential of anti-ship missiles and were unencumbered by a cultural attachment to increasingly obsolete aircraft carrier delivery of ordnance close-in. The United States did

---

[17] WAYNE P. HUGHES JR., FLEET TACTICS AND NAVAL OPERATIONS 143 (3d ed. 2018) [hereinafter HUGHES, FLEET TACTICS].

not introduce a standoff guided anti-ship weapon until the Harpoon missile in the mid-1970s and even then, the delivery aircraft were vulnerable to surface-to-air (SAM) missiles. Four decades later, the United States is just beginning to field follow-on missiles to the Harpoon, after countless variants of anti-ship weapons from Russia and China.

The first successful anti-ship missile attack in history occurred in 1967, when Egyptian forces fired six Russian Styx ASCMs at the Israeli destroyer *Eilat*.[18] The destroyer sank in just two minutes, with the loss of 47 crew members.[19] The attack demonstrated the utility of missiles against surface ships, and more strikes followed. During the Indo-Pakistan War of 1971, India used Styx missiles against Pakistani warships and merchant vessels. Two years later, Styx and Gabriel missiles were used in the Yom Kippur War. In 1974, a Chinese *Komar*-class boat sank a Vietnamese destroyer escort with Styx missiles during the Battle of the Paracel Islands.[20]

In the Falklands Campaign in 1982, Argentinian forces destroyed the British warship HMS *Sheffield* with air-launched Exocet ASCMs. In another engagement, on May 25, two Argentinian jet fighters launched Exocet missiles that homed in on the HMS *Ambuscade*. The *Ambuscade* launched chaff, successfully diverting the inbound missiles, which continued onward searching for a target. Eventually the missiles slammed into the British navy ship, SS *Atlantic Conveyor*. The converted commercial ship previously had disembarked Harriet jets and was ferrying helicopters to the fight.[21] Separately, the Royal Navy struck two Argentinian patrol boats with Sea Skua air-to-surface missiles.

1.4 Long-Range Precision Strike

Advances in technology have extended the range, precision, and lethality of missiles. Naval forces are developing and employing LRPS options to reach enemy forces hundreds or even thousands of miles away. The First Gulf

[18] D.P. O'Connell, *The Legality of Cruise Missiles*, 66 AMERICAN JOURNAL OF INTERNATIONAL LAW 785, 785 (Oct. 1972).

[19] D.P. O'Connell, *International Law and Contemporary Naval Problems*, BRITISH YEARBOOK OF INTERNATIONAL LAW 19, 28–30 (1970); Robert D. Colvin, *Aftermath of the Eilat*, 95 U.S. NAVAL INSTITUTE PROCEEDINGS (Oct. 1969), at 60, 62.

[20] Yann-Huei Song, *China and the Military Use of the Ocean*, 20 OCEAN DEVELOPMENT & INTERNATIONAL LAW 213, 225, 228 (1990).

[21] Commander-in-Chief Fleet, Board of Inquiry Report, Loss of the SS Atlantic Conveyor, July 21, 1982, at 1–5; *Iran Said to Fortify Key Strait*, N.Y. TIMES, July 1, 1988, at A2.

War in 1991 provided a glimpse of nascent precision strike capabilities, as U.S. forces systematically dismantled Iraq's military forces and hunted (unsuccessfully) for Scud missile tractor-erector-launchers (TELs). The "Scud hunt" appears to have failed to eliminate a single TELs pre-launch, and debatably a single one post-launch. The unique U.S. capability and the nation's position at the pinnacle of unipolar power created quiet admiration, embarrassment, and resentment abroad.[22] China, in particular, took notice of how U.S. technological superiority in the tactical kill chain produced a quick strategic victory in Iraq. China realized that U.S. power projection hinged upon aircraft penetration of integrated air defense systems (IADS) for delivery of relatively short-range strike weapons in large numbers. In response, China improved its IADS, but also focused heavily on holding at risk tactical air bases ashore (for example, U.S. bases in Japan and Korea) and at sea (aircraft carriers) with a massive inventory of missiles of increasing range and accuracy.

LRPS missiles now can penetrate active defenses at extended range in operationally relevant numbers to produce lethal results. Passive countermeasures, such as camouflage, making weapon systems mobile, and hardening or deeply burying key facilities degrades the effectiveness of precision strikes.[23] Sufficient numbers of missiles (in the hundreds or thousands) appear capable of surviving attack through a combination of mobility, stealth, and range. These surviving forces may overmatch traditional surface naval forces if they can be targeted accurately and in a timely manner. In defense, surface forces need to employ counter-targeting and counter-seeker measures. Part of this equation may include stealth technologies to reduce the prospect of long-range targeting. Much like the DDG-1000 *Zumwalt*-class surface ships or the Lockheed *Sea Shadow*, mobile launchers on land or at sea may be "hiding" among the clutter of broken terrain or underwater, or in "plain sight" among civilian infrastructure. Russia's Club-K missile launcher, for example, may be secreted in a commercial shipping container. The *Sea Shadow* and *Zumwalt*-class of three ships were configured to have an extremely low radar cross section. *Sea Shadow* has low electro-optical visibility; *Zumwalt* does not. The vessels are engineered to reduce the wake, heat, and acoustic signatures as well. All that technology raises the costs considerably. The three *Zumwalt* ships cost about $22 billion without any combat

---

[22] Charles Krauthammer, *The Unipolar Moment*, FOREIGN AFFAIRS (1990/1991), at 23, 25.
[23] MARK GUNZINGER & BRYAN CLARK, SUSTAINING AMERICA'S PRECISION STRIKE ADVANTAGE 2 (2015)

systems. One alternative to making a traditional combatant stealthy is to build an unmanned arsenal ship, where weapons afloat are targeted by some offboard process. The downside of this is that the enemy might declare a kill zone and simply shoot at anything that has a signature, increasing the chance that protected civilian objects might be inadvertently destroyed.

The sensor-to-shooter connectivity also has to be sufficiently survivable to complete the LRPS kill chain. C4ISR satellites are becoming inexpensive and too numerous to jam or kill. For example, SpaceX's Starlink portends constellations of tens of thousands of small satellites in low earth orbit replacing dozens of large satellites. They will likely become too cheap to kill, although it is still an open question whether they can be effectively blinded or jammed. Satellites have to maintain sensor-to-shooter connectivity, but if the sensor is blind, the connectivity to the shooter becomes irrelevant. Meanwhile, direct ascent anti-satellite (ASAT) missiles hold C4ISR at risk to negate the LRPS complex. But, when modern micro-, nano- and pico- satellites become so numerous, kinetic ASAT may cost more than the satellites. High-speed, high-altitude drones, including China's DR-8, could supplement satellites in this role. Perhaps the earliest attempt to do this was the D-21 supersonic reconnaissance drone introduced in 1969 and the SR-71 Blackbird that flew from the 1960s through the 1990s.

In East Asia, the current U.S. strike complex relies on precision strike from combat aircraft forward deployed to bases in Japan and aboard aircraft carriers. China has concluded that this force structure and basing is the U.S. "Achilles Heel." In any future conflict, China plans to destroy U.S. air bases and aircraft carriers and thereby eliminate the primary U.S. strike capability. Over the past 20 years, China has invested heavily to develop the largest and most active LRPS program, and the largest arsenal of intermediate-range conventional and nuclear missiles in the world.[24] China conducts more ballistic missile live-fire launches every year than the rest of the world combined.[25] China now has more than 1,250 ground-launched ballistic missiles (GLBMs) and ground-launched cruise missiles (GLCMs) with ranges between 500 and 5,500 kilometers.[26] The conventional and nuclear systems

[24] Statement by Adm. Harry B. Harris, U.S. Navy, Commander, U.S. Indo-Pacific Command, House Armed Services Committee Meeting on U.S. Pacific Command Posture (online), Apr. 26, 2017.

[25] Statement of Admiral Philip S. Davidson, U.S. Navy, Commander, U.S. Indo-Pacific Command, before the Senate Armed Services Committee on U.S. Indo-Pacific Command Posture, Mar. 9, 2021, at 33 [hereinafter Davidson Statement 2021].

[26] DEPARTMENT OF DEFENSE, MILITARY AND SECURITY DEVELOPMENTS INVOLVING THE PEOPLE'S REPUBLIC OF CHINA 2020: ANNUAL REPORT TO CONGRESS vii (2020) [hereinafter DoD ANNUAL

are integrated into a single force architecture, reducing strategic stability.[27] Beijing's lead in missile technology and deployment has eroded conventional deterrence, weakened nuclear deterrence, and poses the greatest threat to U.S. and allied forces in East Asia.[28] China has pinned its strategy to control the Western Pacific Ocean on its dominance in theater ballistic, cruise, and hypersonic missiles.[29] Nevertheless, China has a much smaller nuclear force than the United States and claims to fear a disarming first strike by U.S. nuclear and/or precision conventional weapons. From this perspective, China seeks to mix their weapons in order to deny the United States of an "attractive" option of eliminating its assured second-strike capability. In China's view, the mixing of conventional and nuclear forces restores and maintains the stability that is threatened by is inferiority in numbers.

Unencumbered by the Intermediate Range Nuclear Forces (INF) Treaty, China has progressed more quickly than anticipated in medium-range ballistic missiles (MRBMs), such as the DF-26 anti-ship ballistic missile (ASBM) and the DF-17 HGV, which outrange U.S. land-based and carrier-based aviation.[30] The DF-21, for example, can reach over 900 nm farther than the 700 nm combat radius of the Joint Strike Fighter. Most tactical aircraft have a combat radius under 500 nm. These LRPS weapons will be able to reach U.S. forces in Guam or beyond. This strategy foretells an end to distance from the mainland providing any sanctuary for U.S. forces, exposing to enemy attack rear area port facilities, bases, runways, hangars, depots, energy, and transportation infrastructure.

1.4.1 Cruise Missiles

Cruise missiles are small, low-flying tactical or theater unmanned single-use weapons that may be launched from land, aircraft, ships, or submarines.[31]

CHINA REPORT 2020]; Andrew Tate, *China's Growing Missile Arsenal Challenges U.S. Operations*, JANE'S DEFENCE WEEKLY, Oct. 16, 2019, at 20–21.

[27] David Logan, *Are They Reading Schelling in Beijing?*, The Dimensions, Drivers, and Risks of Nuclear-Conventional Entanglement in China, JOURNAL OF STRATEGIC STUDIES 19, 24 (2020).
[28] Davidson Statement 2021, *supra* note 25, at 41.
[29] Richard Stone, *National Pride Is at Stake. Russia, China, United States Race to Build Hypersonic Weapons*, SCIENCE (online), Jan. 8, 2020; R. Jeffrey Smith, *Hypersonic Missiles Are Unstoppable. And They're Starting a New Global Arms Race*, N.Y. TIMES MAGAZINE (online), June 19, 2019.
[30] James E. Fanell, *China's Global Navy: Today's Challenge for the United States and the U.S. Navy*, 73 NAVAL WAR COLLEGE REVIEW 13, 37 (Autumn 2020). (U.S. misjudgments of Chinese capabilities systematically underestimated and downplayed the threat of China and the rise of the PLA Navy.)
[31] CONGRESSIONAL BUDGET OFFICE, CONGRESS OF THE UNITED STATES, THE U.S. MILITARY'S FORCE STRUCTURE 49 (July 2016).

Flying supersonic or subsonic speed, cruise missiles are autonomously guided to their terrestrial or surface naval targets. Internal digital terrain maps dramatically improved precision over earlier weapons. Onboard radar points toward the ground and compares the signal received with the internal maps to guide the missile to its target.[32]

The Soviet Union initially developed cruise missiles to counter U.S. aircraft carrier strike groups approaching its territory. By the 1980s, however, the U.S.S.R. had a preponderance of conventional and nuclear-armed missiles in Eastern Europe, weakening U.S. extended deterrence commitments and calling into question the U.S. doctrine of Flexible Response. The destabilizing element in this equation was the short time of flight and the prospect of a disarming first strike. With the nuclear balance destabilized, NATO approved the deployment of 464 U.S. nuclear-armed GLCMs and Pershing II intermediate-range ballistic missiles (IRBMs) to counter the Soviet missiles. The ground-based missiles began to enter service in Europe in 1983 and cruise missiles began to enter the U.S. fleet in the summer of 1984. The U.S. deployments led President Gorbachev to accept President Reagan's offer for a "zero-zero" option to eliminate intermediate nuclear forces in Europe.[33] The Intermediate Nuclear Forces (INF) Treaty banned cruise missiles and ballistic missiles with a range of between 500 to 1,000 km (short medium-range) and 1,000 to 5,500 km (intermediate-range).[34] The agreement stabilized intermediate-range missiles in Europe for three decades. The United States, however, withdrew from the INF Treaty in 2019 after years of alleged Russian noncompliance.[35] The INF Treaty only applied to ground-launched systems. It did not restrain ship or air-launched systems—thus Navy's Tomahawk Land Attack Missile (TLAM) and the Air-Launched Cruise Missile and Russian equivalents were exempt.

Cruise missiles also played a prominent role in the Tanker War of the 1980s. Some 400 commercial ships were attacked in the Persian Gulf during the conflict. In comparison, the Allies lost some 2,828 merchant ships in the Battle of the Atlantic.[36] About 80 percent of all Iraqi attacks on commercial

---

[32] William J. Broad, *Cruise Missiles: What They Are and Do*, N.Y. Times, Aug. 28, 1983, at A12.

[33] David Shipler, *Reagan and Gorbachev Sign Missile Treaty and Vow to Work for Greater Reductions*, N.Y. Times, Dec. 9, 1987, at A1.

[34] Treaty Between the United States of America and The Union of Soviet Socialist Republics on the Elimination of Their Intermediate-Range and Shorter-Range Missiles, art. I, Dec. 8, 1987, 1657 U.N.T.S. 2 [hereinafter INF Treaty].

[35] Michael R. Gordon, Russia Deploys Missile, Violating Treaty and Challenging Trump, N.Y. TIMES, Feb. 15, 2017, at A16.

[36] HUGHES, FLEET TACTICS, *supra* note 17, at 145.

ships were conducted using missiles, while Iran used a combination of missiles, mines, and naval gunfire. On May 17, 1987, the USS *Stark* (FFG 31) was struck by two Iraqi *Exocet* cruise missiles fired from a Mirage F-1 aircraft, apparently accidentally.[37] The U.S. warship was outside Iraq's and Iran's maritime exclusions zones. Thirty-seven crew members were killed in the attack. In Operation Praying Mantis near the end of the Tanker War, the United States fired 11 Harpoons and five Standard missiles; Iran fired one Harpoon.[38] The Tanker War illustrates how warships, civilian vessels, and commercial ships become intertwined in a complex maritime battle environment that increases the danger to neutral warships and merchant shipping. In the 1991 Gulf War, the USS *Missouri* (BB 63) was targeted by two Silkworm ASCMs launched from Iraqi-occupied Kuwait. Nearby, HMS *Gloucester* fired a Sea Dart that successfully downed one of the incoming missiles, while the other failed to reach its target.[39] This incident represents the sole evidently successful active defense engagement to shoot down a missile in recorded history.

Cruise missiles have become the optimal choice for theater strikes for the United States since it lacks theater ballistic missiles. In 1999, the United States used GPS to guide cruise missiles to destroy military targets in Belgrade.[40] Some 750 cruise missiles were used in the "shock and awe" campaign against Saddam Hussein in the 2003 coalition invasion of Iraq.[41] Connecting real-time intelligence to precision guidance, coalition forces surgically dismantled Baghdad's communications networks and governance capacity. Similarly, more than 130 cruise missiles supplemented aircraft in the first strikes on Libya in March 2011 to oust Muammar el-Qaddafi from power.[42]

Cruise missiles are becoming the principal weapon of naval warfare, as ubiquitous as cannon in the age of sail. In this regard, the U.S. Navy is still behind its rivals, as it has hundreds of legacy Harpoon ASCMs, the Joint Stand-Off Weapon (JSOW) C1, which suffer from a very short range, and a

---

[37] Steven V. Roberts, *Missile Toll on Frigate is 28; Ship Did Not Fire in Defense; U.S. Orders a Higher Alert*, N.Y. TIMES, May 19, 1987, at A1.

[38] HUGHES, FLEET TACTICS, *supra* note 17, at 147.

[39] Richard Pyle, *British Warship Destroys Iraqi Anti-Ship Missiles*, ASSOCIATED PRESS (online), Feb. 25, 1991.

[40] Joseph Fitchett, *Cruise Missiles Enhance NATO's Scope*, N.Y. TIMES (online), Apr. 5, 1999.

[41] John H. Cushman, Jr., & Thom Shanker, *A Nation at War: Combat Technology; A War Like No Other Uses New 21st-Century Methods to Disable Enemy*, N.Y. TIMES, Apr. 10, at B5.

[42] Elisabeth Bumiller & Kareem Fahim, *U.S.-Led Assaults Hit Tripoli Again; Objective Is Near*, N.Y. TIMES, Mar. 22, 2011, at A1.

small number of the new Long-Range Anti-ship Missile (LRASM). Only the LRASM offers standoff capability.

Both the United States and Russia have used cruise missiles to intervene in the war in Syria. In 2015, Russian warships in the Caspian Sea launched 26 cruise missiles at 11 targets in Syria, with additional strikes in 2016.[43] Two years later, two U.S. Navy warships launched 59 Tomahawk cruise missiles into Syria.[44] In June 2017, Russia warships fired six SS-N-30 *Kalibr* cruise missiles into Syria.[45] The *Kalibr* is more than twice as fast as the Iraqi *Exocet* that nearly sank the *Stark*. By deploying the missile on its newest class of frigate, the Russian Navy is distributing its firepower—"putting its eggs in more baskets."[46] In recent years, even nonstate actors are using sophisticated missiles in combat. Houthi rebels in Yemen, for example, launched ASCMs at oil tankers and U.S. and Saudi warships and fired short-range ballistic missiles into Saudi Arabia.[47]

In East Asia, the United States is studying the employment of distributed swarms of smaller ships armed with cruise missiles to replace expensive warships as a means to counter China's land-based LRPS complex that outranges U.S. carrier-borne aircraft.[48] Complementing this strategy, the U.S. Marine Corps is examining whether to disperse its units armed with ASCMs throughout the first island chain that stretches from Borneo to Kamchatka.[49] By 2023, the Marines could deploy to Japan and possibly Taiwan with Tomahawk cruise missiles with a range of some 1,500 miles.[50] Armed with ASCMs sprinkled throughout the small islands of East Asia, the Marine Corps could threaten enemy shipping hundreds of miles away.[51]

[43] Richard Johnson, *How Russia Fired Missiles at Syria from 1,000 Miles Away*, WASHINGTON POST (online), Oct. 23, 2015; Sam LaGrone, *Ship-Launched Russian Cruise Missile Strike Part of New Aleppo Offensive*, U.S. NAVAL INSTITUTE PROCEEDINGS (online), Nov. 15, 2016.

[44] Dan Lamothe, *Why the Navy's Tomahawk Missiles Were the Weapon of Choice in Strikes in Syria*, WASHINGTON POST (online), Apr. 6, 2017.

[45] Thomas Grove, *Russia Fires Cruise Missiles at Islamic State Weapons in Syria*, WALL STREET JOURNAL (online), June 23, 2017.

[46] *Russia: Russian Shipbuilders to Flout out Latest Frigate Armed with Kalibr Cruise Missiles*, ASIA NEWS MONITOR (online), May 11, 2020.

[47] Asa Fitch, *U.S. Probes Third Attack on Ship Off Yemen's Coast*, WALL STREET JOURNAL, Oct. 16, 2016; Gordon Lubold, *U.S. Ship Again Targeted by Apparent Houthi Missiles*, WALL STREET JOURNAL, Oct. 12, 2016; Matthew Rosenberg & Mark Mazzetti, *American Warship Fires Missiles at 3 Yemeni Rebel Installations*, N.Y. TIMES, Oct. 12, 2016, p. A1; *Houthi Ballistic Missiles Target Saudi Arabia, Says Coalition*, AL JAZEERA (online), Mar. 16, 2021.

[48] HUGHES, FLEET TACTICS, *supra* note 17, at 128.

[49] Joseph Trevithick, *Marines Set to Be the First to Bring Back Land-Based Tomahawk Missiles Post-INF Treaty*, THE DRIVE (THE WAR ZONE) (online), Mar. 5, 2020.

[50] David B. Larter, *To Combat the China Threat, US Marine Corps Declares Ship-killing Missile Systems its Top Priority*, DEFENSE NEWS (online), Mar. 5, 2020.

[51] *Id.*

Since its withdrawal from the INF Treaty, the United States is legally permitted to deploy theater missiles in East Asia. However, it is unlikely that there is sufficient political will in Tokyo and Washington to approve such deployments.

1.4.2 Ballistic Missiles

While cruise missiles have been a staple of naval warfare for more than 50 years, technological advances in ballistic missile and hypersonic weapons are rewriting LRPS battle plans. ASBMs can hit a moving warship at sea. Ballistic missiles are classified according to their range. Close-range ballistic missiles (CRBMs) have a range under 300 km; short-range ballistic missiles (SRBMs) have range of less than 1,000 km; medium-range ballistic missiles (MRBMs) have a range of from 1,000 to 3,000 km; intermediate-range ballistic missiles (IRBMs) range from 3,000 to 5,500 km; and intercontinental ballistic missiles (ICBMs) have a range beyond 5,500 km.

Ballistic missiles follow a ballistic trajectory through a relatively brief phase of powered flight along a generally predictable arc, usually entering outer space range dependent. Outer space is typically understood as 100 km altitude at the von Karman Line. In a standard ballistic trajectory, the missile apogee is one-third of the ground distance. Ballistic missiles exit the atmosphere before re-entering along a flight path to targets on land or at sea, except CRBMs or those fired on a depressed trajectory. Thus, a 300 km range SRBM will barely achieve exo-atmospheric flight before returning to earth at a fixed point or within a circular error of probability. Most of the flight is unguided (the entire flight of the V2 was unguided) and most ballistic missile travel is unpowered.

ICBMs may travel 10,000 km in 30 or 35 minutes.[52] Although legacy ballistic missiles can reach virtually any point on the globe, they are vulnerable to interception because their flight path is predictable, much like a baseball being thrown. It is unsettled as a matter of law whether the passage of ballistic missiles over neutral territory violates territorial airspace, as the boundary between national airspace and outer space is not explicit.

The United States, Russia, China, the United Kingdom, France, and India are capable of launching ballistic missiles able to strike virtually anywhere on earth.[53] These states are also the only ones with submarine-launched ballistic missiles (SLBMs) that can be fired from underwater, although North Korea is

---

[52] UN Doc. A/57/229, *supra* note 13, ¶ 27.
[53] Sergio Peçanha & Keith Collins, *Only 5 Nations Can Hit Any Place on Earth with a Missile. For Now*, N.Y. TIMES (online), Feb. 7, 2018; Rahul Bedi, *India Declares its Nuclear Triad Complete*, JANE'S

developing an SLBM capability as well. Ballistic missile submarines (SSBNs) are the most survivable leg of the nuclear triad of sea-based, land-based, and aircraft-armed platforms, and therefore are the most stabilizing. The U.S. Navy deploys low-yield nuclear warheads on its *Ohio*-class SSBNs.[54] A low-yield warhead might be less than 10 kilotons and is designed to deter limited nuclear employment by providing a flexible response option. The warhead is in response to Russia's strategy of "escalate (to nuclear weapons) to deescalate," by providing a lower yield strike option.[55] Detractors suggest that low-yield weapons make nuclear war more inviting.

Ballistic missiles are attractive because they offer an offensive LRPS "punch" that cannot be easily countered. The United States, France, Italy, the United Kingdom, Israel, Russia, China, and Taiwan operate rudimentary anti-ballistic missile (ABM) systems, but these are ineffective at best.[56] Furthermore, the cost exchange and technology favor ballistic missile offense over defense. The total original cost of U.S. ground-based interceptor (GBI) system was $44 billion featuring just 44 interceptors. Additional interceptors are being fielded at a lower price due to economies of scale, but the cost advantage of the offense is clear.

Even small states can field ballistic missiles arsenals numbering in the hundreds or even thousands. China's DF-26 is an example of this cost curve dynamic. First revealed by Beijing in 2015 and entered service in 2016, the missile is the most significant weapon in the past 40 years because it has a 2,500-mile range. The missile can strike U.S. bases and aircraft carriers within the first island chain (from Japan running south through the Philippines) and reach America's second line of defense in Guam at a fraction of the cost of any feasible American defense.[57]

Missiles become more expensive as their range increases, and the cost of the launcher must be added to the total. Nevertheless, defense costs much more than offense and is only marginally effective. The effective distance of the DF-26 exceeds the range of U.S. forward deployed combat aircraft, forcing

DEFENCE WEEKLY, Nov. 14, 2018, at 16. Japan has not built an ICBM but it could do so, as could any other state that has boosted a satellite into orbit.

[54] *U.S. Deploys Low-Yield Nuclear Warhead*, ARMS CONTROL TODAY 30 (online), Mar. 2020.
[55] CONGRESSIONAL RESEARCH SERVICE, A LOW-YIELD, SUBMARINE-LAUNCHED NUCLEAR WARHEAD: OVERVIEW OF THE EXPERT DEBATE (Jan. 5, 2021).
[56] Laura Grego, *The Faulty and Dangerous Logic of Missile Defense*, SCIENTIFIC AMERICAN (online), Apr. 24, 2018.
[57] DoD ANNUAL CHINA REPORT 2020, *supra* note 26, at 59.

them to refuel in mid-air to extend their reach forward. China possesses several hundred DF-26s, while the United States relies on tactical aircraft for weapons delivery. Yet the U.S. aircraft have shorter ranges than the missiles targeting their bases. Furthermore, active defense will be extremely challenging. Passive defense might be viable but is expensive and unproven. The alternative is to pull tactical aircraft even farther to the rear areas and refuel them in flight. But then the aircraft have a longer flight time into theater and their refueling bases will be at risk. The competition is playing out with China's array of missiles seizing the advantage.

1.4.3 Hypersonic Missiles

Hypersonic missiles add complexity to the mix of high-end ballistic and cruise missile capabilities in theater military strategy because currently there is no defense against them. Active defenses have been proposed, but they would be very expensive and of dubious utility. The key is still passive defense—deny targeting and/or defeat the seeker. Even medium-sized powers can deliver deep strikes.[58] The weapons fly at incredible rates of speeds, beginning at Mach 5.[59] Like a ballistic missile, a hypersonic weapon could traverse the Pacific Ocean in 90 minutes. At such high terminal velocities, hypersonic missiles evade air defenses and can strike targets with such force it obviates the need for an explosive payload.[60] HGVs present offensive advantage because they may be impossible to intercept.

One great advantage of HGVs is their ability to fly below the radar horizon of defenses. Another is the ability to maneuver without expending propellant. Low warning and unpredictable trajectories are what make HGVs hard to intercept, although the failure of current interceptors against ballistic missiles makes the advantage of HGVs relatively unimportant. Perhaps the greatest advantage, given that BMD is ineffective, is that HGVs get far more range out of a given "propulsion stack," so an SRBM booster may loft an HGV to IRBM ranges.

Ballistic missiles and HGVs may be so fast they can avoid radar detection, and if they are detected, may be impossible to shoot down. Speed is the new stealth. The SR-71 manned spy plane, for example, flies at Mach 3, and has outrun anti-aircraft missiles after being fired upon unsuccessfully hundreds

---

[58] Steve Simon, *Hypersonic Missiles Are a Game Changer* (online) (op. ed.) N.Y. TIMES, Jan. 2, 2020.
[59] Dan Gouré, *DoD Presses the Accelerator on Hypersonic Weapons*, REAL CLEAR DEFENSE (online), June 20, 2019.
[60] UN Doc. A/57/229, *supra* note 13, ¶ 22.

of times over previous decades.[61] An unmanned "SR-72" aircraft that can fly at Mach 6 in either reconnaissance or strike roles may be under development.[62] Ballistic missiles are exo-atmospheric and susceptible to intercept by the Standard Missile 3 (SM-3) at ranges exceeding over 350 km, but hypersonic weapons never enter the exo-atmosphere, negating the SM-3.[63] They can also maneuver to some extent (BGVs) or to a large extent (scramjet—if ever developed). The cruise altitude coupled with the speed makes hypersonic missiles especially lethal.

Hypersonic weapons may be either air-breathing hypersonic cruise missiles (HCMs) that use scramjet power to bob and weave through the stratosphere, surfing on their own shock waves. HGVs are boost-glide vehicles mounted on ballistic missiles, gliding or "skipping" along in the mesosphere at an altitude of 25 to 40 km before striking targets as far as 10,000 miles away. Sea-based HGVs can be launched from vessels. Land-based variants and may be distributed among roaming TELs.[64]

Active defenses against hypersonic weapons are severely challenged and likely untenable. Like a ballistic missile, the flight path for a hypersonic boost glide vehicle is rather predictable, but the weapons fly too high and too fast for endo-interceptors and too low for exo-interceptors. Passive defenses may work better but would require transformational changes to existing systems and operational concepts. Because hypersonic vehicles travel at low altitude through the atmosphere, they cannot be detected by ground-based radar until they are near the target. The high speed of approach compresses the timeline for a response to mere seconds, and their maneuverability makes them difficult to hit by area or point defense systems, such as the U.S. Terminal High-Altitude Area Defense (THAAD).[65] Thus, these weapons are destabilizing because the decision-making time for a defensive response is condensed.[66] Further complicating the defense is that, like ballistic missiles, HGVs may

---

[61] Gouré, *DoD Presses the Accelerator on Hypersonic Weapons, supra* note 59; Sebastien Roblin, *The Super Secret SR-72 Spy Plane (That Might Also Be a Stealth Bomber)*, NATIONAL INTEREST (online), Apr. 8, 2019.

[62] Gouré, *supra* note 59.

[63] U.S. successfully conducts SM-3 Block IIA Intercept Test against an Intercontinental Ballistic Missile Target, MISSILE DEFENSE AGENCY NEWS RELEASE (online) (Nov. 16, 2020).

[64] Dave Deptula, *Hypersonic Weapons Could Transform Warfare. The U.S. Is Behind*, FORBES (online), Oct. 5, 2018.

[65] CONGRESSIONAL RESEARCH SERVICE PUBLICATION No. R45811, HYPERSONIC WEAPONS: BACKGROUND AND ISSUES FOR CONGRESS 3–4 (Apr. 26, 2021) [hereinafter CRS PUB. R45811 HYPERSONIC WEAPONS].

[66] *But cf.* William J. Broad, *Analysis Raises Doubts about the Capabilities of Hypersonic Weapons*, N.Y. TIMES, Jan. 16, 2021, p. A17.

carry multiple independently targetable re-entry vehicles (MIRVs) as well as maneuverable vehicles (MaRVs), so one missile can strike several targets.

Because hypersonic weapons compress the reaction time of an opponent, they are destabilizing. Traditional ballistic missiles loft high, offering long-range radar detection. Traditional cruise missiles need to go high if they are supersonic, but that means they may be detected by radar at longer ranges. In contrast, HGVs cruise low, thus preventing radar detection until late in the flight. Nevertheless, an IRBM may have a 10-minute time of flight and the warning time might be only seven minutes, whereas a hypersonic weapon may offer just two-to-three-minute warning time. It is unclear whether this difference upsets the operational picture.

Legally, hypersonic weapons represent a change in degree, but not in kind, in missile capability.[67] The weapons pose no risk to aircrews, are likely unstoppable and as accurate as ballistic missiles or cruise missiles, and may carry either conventional or nuclear warheads. The principal effect of hypersonic missiles on the law of targeting is that their high speeds reduce the decision-making time available to meet the requirements of the law of armed conflict (LOAC).

China and Russia have embraced hypersonic weapons as the optimal LPRS weapon because they take U.S. SM-3 and any other exo-interceptors off the table. Missiles are high leverage for China because they can strike forward deployed U.S. combat aircraft on the ground or on ships and land bases in Asia well outside the range of carrier-based aircraft.

Because the United States is dependent on aircraft it lacks an effective stand-off strike capability and is slowly adopting hypersonic weapons. France, Germany, Japan, and India are also experimenting with hypersonic missiles.[68] Russia stepped up investment in hypersonic weapons after the U.S. withdrawal from the Anti-Ballistic Missile Treaty in 2001.[69] Then Russia feared that U.S. missile defense would completely devalue its ballistic missile force so Moscow turned toward hypersonic weapons to counter this strategic pitfall.

[67] UN Doc. A/57/229, *supra* note 13, ¶ 21.

[68] CRS PUB. R45811 HYPERSONIC WEAPONS, *supra* note 65, at 17; Kosuke Takahashi, *Tokyo Outlines Plan to Develop and Field Hypersonic Weapons*, JANE'S DEFENCE WEEKLY, Nov. 27, 2019, at 4; Kosuke Takahashi, *Japan Developing New Anti-Surface Warheads for Hypersonic Weapons*, JANE'S DEFENCE WEEKLY, Mar. 18, 2020, at 4; Liu Zhen, *Japan Is Working on a Hypersonic Anti-Ship Missile That May Be a Threat to Chinese Navy Activities*, SOUTH CHINA MORNING POST (online), Apr. 29, 2020. Tokyo's enhanced version is planned for anti-ship roles beginning in 2028, and its range would be limited to 500 km (310 miles) under Japan's defensive policy.

[69] CRS PUB. R45811 HYPERSONIC WEAPONS, *supra* note 65, at 10–11.

In the final week of December 2019, President Vladimir Putin announced that his country had deployed the Avangard Mihai, an HGV that strikes its target at up to an astonishing 27 times the speed of sound.[70] The boost-glide vehicle is lifted into space and then the Avangard is launched from a Sarmat ICBM rocket and can travel more than 20 times the speed of sound.[71] The missile is outfitted with countermeasures and is designed to carry a nuclear warhead. This method of launch gives the missile a theoretically unlimited range.[72] Any ballistic missile that can achieve orbit is also of unlimited range, resulting in FOBS and MOBS systems—Fractional and Multiple Orbital Bombardment.

Russia is also working on the air-to-ground Kinzhal, which can reach Mach 10 under its own power.[73] In 2018, the missile was test-fired from a modified MiG-31 Foxhound, striking a target at a distance of about 500 miles. The missile can maneuver in flight to avoid countermeasures. Russia intends to mount the system on long-range fighters and the Tu-22 Backfire strategic bomber.[74] Russia is also developing the hypersonic Zircon (or Tsirkon) missile, capable of speeds of up to Mach 9, for deployment on surface warships.[75] The Zircon will enter service in 2023 and can strike targets at land and sea. Russia's newest Project 22350 class frigates are outfitted with 16 to 24 vertical launch tubes that can carry the Zircon, as well as the Kalibr and Oniks missiles.[76]

China is also a leader in hypersonic missile development, adding HGVs to its inventory.[77] The first operational HGV, the DF-17, was introduced in late-2017 and appeared in the parade of the 70th anniversary of the People's Republic of China in 2019.[78] In August 2018, China successfully tested the

---

[70] *New Russian Weapon Can Travel 27 Times the Speed of Sound*, N.Y. TIMES (online), Dec. 27, 2019.

[71] Jonathan Marcus, *Russia Deploys Avangard Hypersonic Missile System*, BBC NEWS (online), Dec. 27, 2019.

[72] Nicholas Fiorenza, *Russia Declares First Avangard Regiment Operational*, JANE'S DEFENCE WEEKLY, Jan. 8, 2020, at 6.

[73] Stone, *National Pride Is at Stake*, *supra* note 29; Tom Demerly, *Russia Test Fires New Kh-47M2 Kinzhal Hypersonic Missile*, THE AVIATIONIST (online), Mar. 12, 2018.

[74] Dave Majumdar, *Russia: New Kinzhal Aero-Ballistic Missile Has 3,000 km Range if Fired from Supersonic Bomber*, THE NATIONAL INTEREST, July 18, 2018.

[75] Joseph Trevithick, *Russian Navy's Top Officer Says Shadowy Zircon Hypersonic Missile Has 'Childhood Diseases,'* THE DRIVE (THE WAR ZONE) (online), Jan. 21, 2020.

[76] *Russian Report Says New Frigates to Carry 24 Tsirkon Missiles*, BBC MONITORING (online), Apr. 17, 2020.

[77] DoD ANNUAL CHINA REPORT 2020, *supra* note 26, at 56; Andrew Tate, *China Testing Intercontinental-Range HGV, Says NORTHCOM Commander*, JANE'S DEFENCE WEEKLY, Feb. 26, 2020, at 4.

[78] Tetsushi Takahashi, *China Deploys New Missile Seen as "Guam Express" Beijing Projects Power as Washington Strengthens Ties with Taipei*, NIKKEI ASIAN REVIEW (online), Apr. 18, 2018.

Xingkong-2 (Starry Sky-2) HGV. Like Russia, China justifies its development of HGVs and other capabilities, including MaRVs, MIRVs, decoys, chaff, jamming, and thermal shielding, as necessary to counter U.S. and other countries' BMD and LRPS systems.[79] To test its growing fleet of missiles, China is developing a hypersonic wind tunnel capable of simulating flights at speeds of Mach 30.[80] Missiles at that speed may travel so fast that BMD is useless.

Although Russia, China, and the United States have made advances in hypersonic technology in recent years, Moscow and Beijing are ahead of Washington.[81] The United States is focusing mainly on conventionally armed hypersonic systems and eventually could deploy thousands of them.[82] In 2018, the Undersecretary of Defense for Research and Engineering identified hypersonic development as the first priority, yet since then Russia and China have surged ahead.[83] The United States has multiple lines of research and development for hypersonic vehicles by the Navy, Army, Air Force, and the Defense Advanced Research Projects Agency (DARPA).[84] By November 2021, the United States had completed nine hypersonic missile tests; China had completed hundreds.[85]

In 2020, the U.S. Army and Navy successfully tested their Common Hypersonic Glide Body at the Pacific missile test range off the coast of Hawaii.[86] LRPS is the top priority for the U.S. Army.[87] The service is analyzing options for theater deterrence and conflict, with a mix of hypersonic

[79] DoD ANNUAL CHINA REPORT 2020, *supra* note 26, at 87.

[80] Dave Makichuk, *Mach 30 "Tunnel" Will Put China Decades Ahead*, ASIA TIMES (online), June 2, 2021.

[81] Stone, *National Pride Is at Stake, supra* note 29.

[82] Jon Harper, *Pentagon to Spend Billions Mass-Producing Hypersonic Weapons*, NATIONAL DEFENSE (online), Mar. 4, 2020.

[83] Michael Griffin stated, "I'm sorry for everybody out there who champions some other high priority, some technical thing; it's not that I disagree with those. But there has to be a first [priority], and hypersonics is my first." Aaron Mehta, *3 Thoughts on Hypersonic Weapons from the Pentagon's Technology Chief*, DEFENSE NEWS (online), July 16, 2018.

[84] Programs include Conventional Prompt Strike (CPS) (Navy); Long-Range Hypersonic Weapon (LRHW) (Army), and AGM-183 Air-Launched Rapid Response Weapon (ARRW) (Air Force). DARPA is developing the Tactical Boost Glide (TBG) (with the Air Force), Operational Fires (OpFires), and the Hypersonic Air-breathing Weapon Concept (HAWC). *Id.*

[85] Ryo Nakamura, *Pentagon sounds alarm on China's 'hundreds' of hypersonic tests*, NIKKEI (online), Oct. 30, 2021.

[86] Sydney J. Freedberg, Jr., *Hypersonics: Army, Navy Test Common Glide Body*, BREAKING DEFENSE, Mar. 20, 2020. This second test followed a successful test of the C-HGB in October 2017, and earlier tests in 2011 and 2014. Megan Eckstein, *Navy Conducts Flight Test to Support Conventional Prompt Strike from Ohio-Class SSGNs*, U.S. NAVAL INSTITUTE NEWS (online), Nov. 3, 2017.

[87] Mandy Mayfield, *Army Examining Basing Options for New Weapons in Indo-Pacific*, NATIONAL DEFENSE (online), July 31, 2020.

missiles and ASCMs to bolster U.S. naval firepower in East Asia.[88] By 2023, the Army could field a battery of four truck-borne hypersonic missile launchers. The Marine Corps is also exploring options for LRPS strike in East Asia, including hypersonic missiles and ASCMs forward deployed to small islands to supplement U.S. naval power.[89] Basing will require host nation support, which is uncertain.

The Navy's hypersonic procurement receives the greater level of funding and is designed for surface combatants or the *Virginia*-class submarine.[90] The Air Force plans to field an operational prototype of a boost-glide system in the 2022–2023 time period.[91] If the United States develops nuclear-armed HGVs, they may be more accurate than their Chinese or Russian counterparts to comply with stricter U.S. collateral damage assessments.[92] There is an inverse relationship between accuracy and warhead size. Every nation is searching for the optimum combination, and both Russia and China can guide a missile to within a few meters of the target. Warhead size might be increased to mitigate terminal counter-targeting efforts.

1.4.4 Conventional-Nuclear Integration

In the past, states typically have differentiated between nuclear-armed missiles and conventionally armed missiles. Nuclear-armed ICBMs are strategic weapons, but conventionally armed ballistic missiles and hypersonic weapons are being studied for tactical or theater roles. Maintaining a hard-line distinction between conventional and nuclear weapons enhances strategic stability by ensuring that potential adversaries do not mistake the launch of a conventional warhead for a nuclear warhead. Yet, Russia and China, and possibly the United States, now envision at least some types of hypersonic weapons armed with conventional and nuclear warheads, making it difficult to distinguish between them.[93] China, Russia, and North Korea are developing the capability to swap conventional and nuclear warheads on the same type of cruise missiles, ballistic missiles, and HGVs to introduce "warhead ambiguity" to complicate an adversary's decision-making.[94] This

---

[88] *Id.*

[89] *Id.*

[90] CRS Pub. R45811 Hypersonic Weapons, *supra* note 65, at 5.

[91] John A. Tirpak, *The Great Hypersonic Race*, Air Force Magazine (online), June 27, 2018.

[92] CRS Pub. R45811 Hypersonic Weapons, *supra* note 65, at 1.

[93] Steve Trimble, *USAF Errantly Reveals Research on ICBM-Range Hypersonic Glide Vehicle*, Aviation Week & Space Technology (online), Aug. 18, 2020.

[94] Justin Anderson & James R. McCue, *Deterring, Countering, and Defeating Conventional-Nuclear Integration*, 15 Strategic Studies Quarterly 1, 12 (Spring 2021).

conventional-nuclear integration (CNI) is designed to dissuade the United States from defending its allies in Europe and Asia by introducing uncertainty into war planning.

2. Missiles as a Means of Warfare

Missiles, like other weapons, may be used mistakenly, as in the July 3, 1988, shootdown of Iran Air Flight 655 by a SM-2 surface-to-air missile fired from the USS *Vincennes*.[95] Similarly, the United States mistakenly targeted the Chinese embassy in an attack in Belgrade in 1999.[96] These imperfect attributes do not make missiles inherently unlawful or qualitatively different from other weapons. Like aircraft strikes, missiles may be supremely accurate or less accurate than gunfire, depending on their tactical employment, technical proficiency of the operator, and technological characteristics of the weapon. Missiles may be either guided or unguided and generally cannot be recalled, although they may be destroyed in flight.[97] Neither treaty law nor customary law prohibits the employment of missiles per se, and missiles may be used in lawful attacks.[98] "It is the way the weapon is used that poses the legal question."[99]

2.1 Air Warfare Areas of Operation

Belligerent naval operations may be conducted anywhere outside of the territory, territorial sea, or national airspace of neutral states. Unlike the international law of the sea that includes numerous geographic and functional maritime zones, airspace has just two legally distinct geographies.[100]

---

[95] William J. Fenrick, *Legal Aspects of Targeting in the Law of Naval Warfare*, 29 CANADIAN YEARBOOK OF INTERNATIONAL LAW 238, 276 (1991).

[96] Steven Lee Myers, *Crisis in the Balkans: The Overview; NATO Raid Hits China Embassy; Beijing Cites 'Barbarian Act'*, N.Y. TIMES, May 8, 1999, at A1.

[97] In 2002, a UN Panel of Government Experts on the issue of missiles defined them as "unmanned, self-propelled, self- contained, unrecallable, guided or unguided vehicle[s] designed to deliver a weapon or other payload." UN Doc. A/57/229, *supra* note 13, ¶ 19.

[98] O'Connell, *The Legality of Cruise Missiles, supra* note 18, at 793; Wolff Heintschel von Heinegg, *The Law of Armed Conflict at Sea* § 17.45, *in* THE HANDBOOK OF INTERNATIONAL HUMANITARIAN LAW (Dieter Fleck ed., 4th ed. 2021).

[99] O'Connell, *The Legality of Cruise Missiles, supra* note 17, at 793.

[100] U.S. Navy, U.S. Marine Corps & U.S. Coast Guard, NWP 1-14M/MCTP 11-10B/COMDTPUB P5800.7A, The COMMANDER'S HANDBOOK on the Law of Naval Operations § 1.9 (2017) [hereinafter NWP-14M].

Airspace is divided into two categories: national airspace and international airspace. National airspace includes airspace over the land territory, internal waters, lakes and rivers, archipelagic waters, and the territorial seas of a state. States have complete and exclusive sovereignty over their national airspace.[101] International airspace includes everything else—the airspace beyond the territorial sea. The airspace of the contiguous zone, exclusive economic zone (EEZ), and high seas are part of international airspace. Airspace above territory not subject to the sovereignty of any state, such as the *terra nullius* land territory of Antarctica or perhaps some features in the South China Sea, is also international airspace. Vertically, airspace extends to just below the lowest possible perigee of an earth satellite in orbit, at which point outer space begins.[102] Low earth orbit (LEO) is at 100 to 200 miles above the earth. Outer space is typically considered to start at 100 km, or 54 nm, or about 60 statute miles altitude. Consequently, the vast expanse of the oceans as a domain for operational maneuver and warfighting is surpassed only by international airspace and outer space.

During armed conflict, belligerent parties may conduct air and missile warfare anywhere in their own national airspace, enemy national airspace, and international airspace; and potentially outer space. Neutral airspace is inviolable. Belligerents are not entitled to launch missiles from or utilize neutral airspace to strike at the enemy. Neutral states have an obligation to act within their capabilities or means at their disposal to prevent their territory and airspace from being used to launch attacks on belligerent states. That said, a belligerent may violate neutral airspace if the neutral state is unwilling or unable to prevent its territorial airspace from being used to launch attacks against a belligerent.[103] In the air domain, third-party self-help may be more common, since many states lack the technological capability to control their airspace and effectively intercept transiting missiles. Furthermore, the proscription against using neutral airspace for belligerent missile operations

---

[101] Convention on International Civil Aviation, Dec. 7, 1944, arts. 1–2, 61 Stat. 1180, T.I.A.S. No. 1591, 15 U.N.T.S. 295.

[102] NWP -14M, *supra* note 99, § 1.10.

[103] *See* Abraham D. Sofaer, *Terrorism, the Law, and the National Defense*, 126 MILITARY LAW REVIEW 89, 108 (1989); Bill Richardson, letter dated Aug. 20, 1998, from the Permanent Representative of the United States of America to the U.N. addressed to the President of the Security Council, United Nations, U.N. Doc. S/1998/780 (1998); John B. Bellinger, III, Legal Advisor, U.S. Department of State, address at the London School of Economics: Legal Issues in the War on Terrorism, Address at the London School of Economics (Oct. 31, 2006); Michael N. Schmitt, *Preemptive Strategies in International Law*, 24 MICHIGAN JOURNAL OF INTERNATIONAL LAW 513, 541–43 (2003).

does not extend to the outer space above the atmosphere (national airspace). Despite the general rule on the inviolability of neutral airspace, aircraft of other states may exercise the right of transit passage through straits used for international navigation and archipelagic sea lanes passage (ASLP) through archipelagic sea lanes (although archipelagic waters outside such sea lanes are neutral and inviolable). Like aircraft, long-range UAVs and drones are entitled to transit passage through straits and ASLP.[104]

The Outer Space Treaty prohibits placement around the earth of missiles carrying weapons of mass destruction (WMD), the installation of WMD on celestial bodies, or the stationing of WMD in outer space in any other manner.[105] This prohibition does not affect the legality of conventionally armed missiles and suborbital missile systems, or the transit of nuclear-armed ballistic missiles through outer space since they are not orbiting around the earth. Similarly, the Moon Agreement prohibits the placement "in orbit around or other trajectory to or around the Moon," of missiles carrying weapons of mass destruction, including nuclear weapons.[106] Like the Outer Space Treaty, this rule leaves unaffected the right to launch military payloads into outer space and use space as a corridor temporarily for the delivery of warheads during armed conflict.

2.2 Law of Air and Missile Warfare

Like all weapons, missiles are subject to LOAC.[107] Unless restricted by international law, belligerents are legally permitted to use any means to conduct hostilities.[108] Yet, the right of parties to a conflict to adopt means of

---

[104] Michael R. Gordon, *Pentagon Details 2-Pronged Attack*, N.Y. TIMES, Apr. 15, 1986, at A1 (U.S. FB-111s from the United Kingdom flew over the Strait of Gibraltar on attack missions against military targets in Libya).

[105] Treaty on Principles Governing the Activities of States in the Exploration and Use of Outer Space, including the Moon and Other Celestial Bodies, art. 4, Jan. 27, 1967, 610 U.N.T.S. 205; UN Doc. A/57/229, *supra* note 13, ¶ 34.

[106] Agreement Governing the Activities of States on the Moon and Other Celestial Bodies, art. 3, May 12, 1979, 1363 U.N.T.S. 3.

[107] Respect for Human Rights in Armed Conflicts, UNGA Resolution 2444 (XXIII), 19 December 1968, *reprinted in* DIETRICH SCHINDLER & JIŘÍ TOMAN, THE LAWS OF ARMED CONFLICTS 263–64 (1988); Hays Parks, *Submarine-Launched Cruise Missiles and International Law: A Response*, 103 U.S. NAVAL INSTITUTE PROCEEDINGS 120, 123 (Sept. 1977) (The legal rules for the employment of submarine-launched cruise missiles are no different from any other weapon).

[108] Regulations Respecting the Laws and Customs of War on Land, annexed to Convention No. IV Respecting the Laws and Customs of War on Land, art. 22, Oct. 18, 1907, 36 Stat. 2227, T.S. No. 539 [hereinafter 1907 Hague Regulations].

injuring the enemy is not unlimited.[109] LOAC is based on key principles formed through treaties and customary international law. The use of force in armed conflict must comply with military necessity, humanity, proportionality, distinction, and honor or chivalry. Missiles are also subject to the proscription against unnecessary suffering, as reflected in the Preamble to the 1868 St. Petersburg Declaration.[110] Missiles are additionally subject to the rule of precautions in attack. The *Harvard Air and Missile Warfare Manual* states, "All feasible precautions must be taken to spare all persons and objects entitled to specific protection. . . ."[111] Given the speed and range of missiles, there is an imperative to ensure that feasible precautions in attack are observed.

Both guided and unguided weapons are lawful so long as they are capable of being directed with a reasonable degree of accuracy.[112] Accuracy in targeting is dependent on the technical capabilities of the missile, the quality of the intelligence that informed the strike, and the good faith efforts of commanders and their personnel to apply LOAC principles. While some weapons are inherently unlawful, such as non-detectable fragments,[113] even lawful weapons may be used in an illegal manner. Like all weapons, missiles may not be indiscriminate in their effects and may be used only to attack military objectives. An artillery round (or missile) that meets this test, but nonetheless fails to strike its target and causes incidental or collateral civilian casualties when directed at a lawful military objective, is not an indiscriminate weapon.[114] Only weapons that are incapable of being directed with a reasonable degree of accuracy are unlawful.[115]

---

[109] Office of the General Counsel, U.S. Department of Defense, Law of War Manual § 2.6.2.1 (rev. ed., Dec. 2016) [hereinafter DoD LAW OF WAR MANUAL]; NWP -14M, *supra* note 99, § 9.1.2.

[110] St. Petersburg Declaration Renouncing the Use, in Time of War, of Explosive Projectiles under 400 Grammes Weight, 1868, *reprinted in* DIETRICH SCHINDLER & JIŘÍ TOMAN, THE LAWS OF ARMED CONFLICTS 102 (1988).

[111] HPCR MANUAL ON AIR AND MISSILE WARFARE, *supra* note 1, ¶ 31 at 16 (2009).

[112] NWP 14M, *supra* note 99, § 9.1.2; United Kingdom, Conflict Department Briefing to UK Mission to the UN, June 25, 2012; UNSC Open Debate on Protection of Civilians Briefing, June 22, 2012; FOI Digest: Ref: 0155-13, Richard Moyes. ("When talking of air-delivery of weapons or heavy artillery in relation to populated areas, care should be taken not to imply that the air-delivery of weapons or the use of heavy artillery, or of any other weapons, projectiles or munitions, is less accurate or less capable of being carried out discriminately than all or any other means. We should avoid language which implies a weapon is inherently indiscriminate.)

[113] *See* Protocol on Non-Detectable Fragments, Oct. 10, 1980, 1342 U.N.T.S. 168.

[114] NWP-14M, *supra* note 99, § 9.1.2.

[115] 2 CUSTOMARY INTERNATIONAL HUMANITARIAN LAW 247 (Jean-Marie Henckaerts & Louise Doswald-Beck eds., 2005).

2.3 Over-the-Horizon and Beyond Visual Range

Missiles and other weapons that strike over-the-horizon (OTH) or beyond-visual-range (BVR) are lawful so long as they are equipped with internal sensors or employed with external guidance to ensure they can comply with the rule of distinction.[116] Missiles that are manufactured with a faulty guidance system that makes them intrinsically incapable of distinguishing between military and civilian objects may be considered unlawful per se.[117] Accuracy of the missile is key to its ability to discriminate.[118] The question of accuracy is compounded by the great distances that some missiles travel, sometimes providing ample opportunity for the military target to move out of harm's way or a civilian object to move into harm's way.

Most missiles are armed with a high explosive warhead. Missiles carrying weapons of mass destruction, such as biological weapons or chemical weapons, will be deemed to be unlawful per se due to the nature of the warhead.[119] Other types of warheads may be prohibited by agreement of States, such as the 2008 Dublin Convention on Cluster Munitions[120] and the 1997 Anti-Personnel Mine Convention.[121] Protocol II of the Conventional Weapons Convention restricts the use of mines and booby-traps, which could be delivered by missiles.[122] Possession of nuclear-armed missiles for deterrence is lawful, and even their use is not prohibited by any specific rule of international law.

The general rule that missiles must be technological capable or operationally employed to discriminate between lawful and unlawful targets

[116] NWP-14M, *supra* note 99, § 9.10; SAN REMO MANUAL ON INTERNATIONAL LAW APPLICABLE TO ARMED CONFLICTS AT SEA ¶ 78 at 167 (Louise Doswald Beck ed., 1995) [hereinafter SAN REMO MANUAL].
[117] Legality of the Threat or Use of Nuclear Weapons, Advisory Opinion, 1996 I.C.J Rep. 226, ¶ 226, 588–89 (July 8) (Dissenting Opinion of Judge Higgins) [hereinafter Nuclear Weapons Advisory Opinion]. *See also* Michael N. Schmitt, *Future War and the Principle of Discrimination*, 28 ISRAELI YEARBOOK ON HUMAN RIGHTS 51, 55 (1998).
[118] D.P. O'CONNELL, THE INFLUENCE OF LAW ON SEA POWER 89 (1975)
[119] Convention on the Prohibition of the Development, Production, and Stockpiling of Bacteriological (Biological) and Toxin weapons and on their destruction, Apr. 10, 1972, 1015 U.N.T.S. 163 and Convention on the Prohibition of the Development, Production, Stockpiling and Use of Chemical Weapons and on their Destruction, Jan. 13, 1993, 1974 U.N.T.S. 45 and 1975 U.N.T.S. 3.
[120] Convention on Cluster Munitions, May 30, 2008, 2688 U.N.T.S. 39.
[121] Convention on the Prohibition of the Use, Stockpiling, Production and Transfer of Anti-Personnel Mines and on their Destruction, Sept. 18, 1997, 2056 U.N.T.S. 211.
[122] Protocol on Prohibitions or Restrictions on the Use of Mines, Booby-Traps and Other Devices (Protocol II as amended on May 3, 1996), annexed to the Convention on Prohibitions or Restrictions on the Use of Certain Conventional Weapons which may be deemed to be Excessively Injurious or to have Indiscriminate Effects, Geneva, May 3, 1996, 2048 U.N.T.S. 93.

also applies in naval warfare. In October 1987, Iran's attack with Chinese-made Silkworm missiles on the U.S-flagged Kuwaiti oil tanker *Sea Isle City* demonstrates unlawful, indiscriminate attacks against merchant shipping.[123] Even when missiles lawfully target enemy warships or merchant vessels engaged in the fight, they may pose implications for collateral damage against nearby vessels. Unlike torpedoes, there is no requirement that missiles become harmless if they miss their target.[124] The *San Remo Manual* states: "missiles and projectiles, including those with over-the-horizon capabilities, shall be used in conformity with the principles of target discrimination . . . ."[125] Indeed, Nazi Germany's V1 and V2 rockets illustrate indiscriminate missiles that were used as terrorizing weapons against the civilian population in London, and were therefore unlawful.[126]

3. Nuclear Missiles

The speed and relative invulnerability of cruise, hypersonic, and ballistic missiles make them ideal delivery devices for nuclear weapons. Nuclear strikes still must comply with the principles of LOAC, such as necessity, proportionality, distinction, and the proscription against unnecessary suffering.[127] The effects of nuclear weapons make compliance with LOAC problematic. Blast, thermal radiation, and ionizing radiation is released in the initial flash. Eighty-five percent of the energy produced by a nuclear explosion is in the form of a blast (shock wave) that can destroy or damage structures, and thermal radiation (heat) that inflicts severe burns and ignites fires at great distances. Lingering radiation fallout continues to cause harm.

Shock waves produce changes in air pressure that pulverize buildings and other structures, and high winds knock down utility poles, trees, and people. The extent of the blast effect depends on the size of the warhead and the height of the burst above ground level. The remaining 15 percent of the

---

[123] *U.S. Destroys 3 Iranian Oil Platforms in the Gulf,* L.A. TIMES, Oct. 19, 1987, p. A1.

[124] Convention No. VIII Relative to the Laying of Automatic Submarine Contact Mines, art. 1(3), Oct 18, 1907, 36 Stat. 2332, T.S. No. 541; NWP-14M, *supra* note 99, § 9.4 ("Torpedoes must be designed to sink or otherwise become harmless when they have missed their intended target. This rule is based upon the premise that a torpedo that misses its target becomes a hazard to innocent shipping in the same manner as a free-floating mine.").

[125] SAN REMO MANUAL, *supra* note 115, ¶ 78 at 167.

[126] ICRC Commentary on the Additional Protocols of 8 June 1977 to the Geneva Conventions of 12 August 1949, ¶ 1958.

[127] Nuclear Weapons, Advisory Opinion, *supra* note 116, ¶ 86 et. seq.

energy of a detonation is comprised of initial radiation, gamma rays and neutrons, and residual radiation, such as fallout.[128] Thermal radiation in the form of extreme heat causes deadly burns in people close to the explosion, and intense light, which can cause temporary "flashblindness" or permanent retinal burn in people who view the explosion. A one-megaton bomb can cause first-degree burns at a distance of about 7 miles, second-degree burns at a distance of about 6 miles, and third-degree burns at a distance up to 5 miles, as well as "flashblindness" at a distance as far as 13 miles during the day and 53 miles at night. Half of the deaths at Hiroshima and Nagasaki were caused by severe burns that were not promptly treated. Thermal radiation causes fires either directly, through igniting flammable materials, or indirectly, through severed gas lines and ruptured gas infrastructure.

The explosive energy or yield that a nuclear weapon can produce is measured in terms of the amount of TNT required to generate the same amount of energy. A one megaton nuclear weapon is equivalent to an explosion of one million tons of TNT and can destroy objects within 80 square miles. A high-altitude nuclear detonation can create an electromagnetic pulse (EMP), which does not pose a physical harm to humans, but could destroy or cause physical damage to electrical or electronic systems, such as power lines or antennas. These attacks could damage communications systems or information technology for a long period of time. The follow-on physical effects of a detonation on dams, dykes, and nuclear power-generating stations are likely to release "dangerous forces" and therefore these protected civilian objects may not be attacked unless they are used as military objectives.[129]

3.1 Russian and Chinese Nuclear Warfighting Capabilities

As of March 2021, the United States and Russia have agreed to a five-year extension of the New START, which limits both parties to no more than 1,550 ICBM/SLBM warheads. Nonetheless, Russia's nuclear arsenal will grow significantly in the next decade, particularly with regard to non-strategic

---

[128] OFFICE OF TECHNOLOGY ASSESSMENT, CONGRESS OF THE UNITED STATES, THE EFFECTS OF NUCLEAR WAR Ch. 2 (1979).

[129] Protocol (I) Additional to the Geneva Conventions of Aug. 12, 1949, and Relating to the Protection of Victims of International Armed Conflicts, art. 56(1)–(2), June 8, 1977, 1125 U.N.T.S. 3 [hereinafter AP I]; YORAM DINSTEIN, THE CONDUCT OF HOSTILITIES UNDER THE LAW OF INTERNATIONAL LAW OF ARMED CONFLICT 226–27 (3d ed. 2016).

nuclear weapons—theater- and tactical-range systems—that can be employed by ships, aircraft, or ground forces. These new systems include short- and close-range ballistic missiles, cruise missiles, torpedoes, and depth charges, all with greater accuracy, longer ranges, and lower yields. Russia is modernizing every leg of its nuclear triad, to include road-mobile (SS-27) missiles and silo-based ICBMs (*Sarmat* and *Avanguard* hypersonic glide vehicles), SLBMs, improved strategic nuclear bombers, and a strategic air-launched cruise missile.[130] Putin announced in July 2020 that the Russian Navy would be armed with the *Tsirkon* hypersonic nuclear cruise missile and the Poseidon underwater nuclear drone, which will be able to strike targets anywhere in the world.[131] Russia has conducted nuclear weapons experiments that have created nuclear yields in violation of the "zero-yield" standard.[132]

Russia believes that first use of nuclear weapons or threat of nuclear attack can de-escalate or terminate a conventional conflict on favorable terms.[133] In 2020, President Vladimir Putin endorsed the nuclear deterrent policy—Basic Principles of State Policy of the Russian Federation on Nuclear Deterrence. The policy reaffirms that Russia can use nuclear weapons to respond to a nuclear attack or the use of other types of weapons of mass destruction, as well as an attack with conventional weapons in cases that threaten the "very existence of the state."[134] This "escalate to de-escalate" doctrine suffers from the misperception that a limited use of nuclear weapons would be acceptable to the United States and its allies.

China, however, officially maintains a "no first use" policy that prioritizes a survivable nuclear force that can retaliate "with sufficient strength to inflict unacceptable damage on an enemy."[135] This policy was reaffirmed in China's July 2019 Defense White Paper.[136] China also could "Launch on Warning,"

---

[130] Lt. Gen. Robert P. Ashley, Jr., Director Defense Intelligence Agency, *Russian and Chinese Nuclear Modernization Trends*, Remarks at the Hudson Institute (online), May 29, 2019.

[131] Andrew Osborn, *Putin says Russian Navy to Get Hypersonic Nuclear Strike Weapons*, REUTERS (online), July 26, 2020.

[132] U.S. DEPARTMENT OF STATE, ADHERENCE TO AND COMPLIANCE WITH ARMS CONTROL, NONPROLIFERATION, AND DISARMAMENT AGREEMENTS AND COMMITMENTS, Apr. 2020, at 8 [hereinafter DEPARTMENT OF STATE, ADHERENCE TO AND COMPLIANCE WITH ARMS CONTROL]; DoD ANNUAL CHINA REPORT 2020, *supra* note 26, at 87.

[133] Lt. Gen. Ashley Remarks at Hudson Institute, *supra* note 129.

[134] Vladimir Isachenkov, *Putin Signs Russia's Nuclear Deterrent Policy*, ASSOCIATED PRESS (online), June 2, 2020; Ankit Panda, *What's in Russia's New Nuclear Deterrence "Basic Principles"?*, THE DIPLOMAT (online), June 9, 2020.

[135] DoD ANNUAL CHINA REPORT 2020, *supra* note 13, at 86.

[136] THE STATE COUNCIL OF THE PEOPLE'S REPUBLIC OF CHINA, *China's National Defense in the New Era*, XINHUA (online), July 24, 2019.

a "preemptive second strike," if it were alerted to inbound missiles. The idea of "Launch on Warning" or "Launch Under Attack" requires an ability to release ICBMs from their silos within 30 minutes in order to use them before they are destroyed by a disarming first strike. If fully adopted by China or Russia, these nuclear warfighting concepts are terrifying and destabilizing. Beijing's lack of transparency concerning the scope and scale of its nuclear weapons program is a perennial challenge and raises questions regarding its intentions.[137] Nonetheless, if the U.S. nuclear threat increases dramatically or if the United States develops new counterforce technology that allows it to destroy most of China's retaliatory force in an initial nuclear attack, Beijing may rethink its current policy.[138] Coupled with this lack of transparency, Chinese military experts advocate an increase in the country's nuclear arsenal to 1,000 weapons to counter the U.S. defensive posture in the Indo-Pacific region.[139]

China is moving quickly to develop its nuclear forces. In recent years China's nuclear arsenal has grown faster than at any other time in its history.[140] China is expected to double the size of its nuclear arsenal, currently estimated at about 300 warheads, over the next decade, by adding more road-mobile ICBMs (CSS-10-class DF-31, DF-31A and DF-31AG), multi-warhead silo-based ICBMs (CSS-4 Mod 2 (DF-5A) and Mod 3 (DF-5B)), a new SLBM (JL-3), improving the H-6N long-range strategic bomber, and building the nuclear-capable H-20 strategic bomber.[141] The H-20 completes China's nuclear triad and doubles the PRC's nuclear strike range to include Australia, Japan, South Korea, and Guam.[142] The JL-3 SLBM has a range of 7,450 miles, which puts the United States within range even if the missile is launched off the Chinese coast.[143] Like Russia, China is developing

---

[137] OFFICE OF THE SECRETARY OF DEFENSE, DEPARTMENT OF DEFENSE NUCLEAR POSTURE REVIEW 11 (2018).

[138] Fiona Cunningham, *The Role of Nuclear Weapons in China's National Defence*, THE CHINA STORY (online), July 23, 2020.

[139] Liu Xuanzun, *China Urged to Expand Nuclear Arsenal to Deter US Warmongers*, GLOBAL TIMES (online), May 8, 2020.

[140] Peter Huessy & Bradley A. Thayer, *China's Nuclear Developments Reflect Its Growing Ambition*, THE HILL (online), Nov. 7, 2019.

[141] Gabriel Dominguez, *China Likely to "at Least Double" Its Nuclear Stockpile by 2030, Says US DoD Official*, JANE'S DEFENCE WEEKLY, Mar. 11, 2020; Richard D. Fisher, Jr., *Missile Investments Are Needed to Meet China's Nuclear Challenge*, THE DIPLOMAT (online), Apr. 25, 2020; DoD ANNUAL CHINA REPORT 2020, *supra* note 26, at 85, 87.

[142] Barnini Chakraborty, *China's Xian H-20 Stealth Bomber Completes Nuclear Triad, Could Make Debut This Year*, FOX NEWS (online), May 4, 2020.

[143] Liu Zhen, *China Fires Its Latest Underwater Nuclear Missile into Spotlight with Science Prize*, SOUTH CHINA MORNING POST (online), May 12, 2020.

theater-range precision-strike nuclear systems, like the roll-out-to-launch CSS-3 (DF-4) IRBM, the road-mobile CCS-5 Mod 2 and Mod 6 (DF-21) MRBM, and the DF-26 IRBM. China is also developing low-yield nuclear weapons to increase the deterrence value of its nuclear force. A lower-yield weapon is envisioned for use against campaign and tactical targets in theater, while reducing the potential for collateral damage.[144] This warhead would most likely be placed on the DF-26, China's first nuclear-capable missile system that can conduct precision strikes.[145]

3.2 Conventional-Nuclear Integration and the INF Treaty

Because nuclear weapons have such fearsome power, states use them for deterrence and integrate them into warfighting doctrine.[146] The strategic reality of conventional and nuclear "entanglement" suggests that nuclear weapons may play a role in future armed conflict.[147] The issue of integrating conventional and nuclear capabilities first became apparent during the late-1970s. In 1976, the Soviet Union began to deploy SS-20 medium-range missiles in Eastern Europe. With a 5,000-km range, the SS-20 was just short of the 5,500-range that would make it subject to the strategic arms limitations. NATO forces had nothing comparable to the SS-20, which could be outfitted with multiple warheads.

In 1983, in tandem with European allies, and especially West Germany, the United States and NATO deployed Pershing II IRBMs and GLCMs in Western Europe to provide a mobile nuclear deterrent against a short warning Soviet theater nuclear attack. The Pershing II was a particularly formidable weapon. Not unlike the SS-20, it could fly 1,000 miles in six to eight minutes, strike targets with high accuracy, and drill deep into hardened bunkers with a tungsten earth-penetrating warhead. In the aftermath of the NATO deployments, the United States and the U.S.S.R. successfully negotiated the INF Treaty to ban ground-launched missiles with a range of 500 to 5,500 km that were capable of carrying a nuclear warhead.[148] The ban

[144] DoD Annual China Report 2020, *supra* note 26, at 88.
[145] *Id.*
[146] Anderson & McCue, *supra* note 93, at 30–32.
[147] *Id.*
[148] INF Treaty, *supra* note 34. The term "intermediate-range missile" means a GLBM or a GLCM having a range capability in excess of 1,000 kilometers but not in excess of 5,500 kilometers. The term "shorter-range missile" means a GLBM or a GLCM having a range capability equal to or in

included all ground-launched missiles and launchers to such missiles, and all support structures and support equipment associated with such missiles and launchers were to be destroyed within three years after entry into force of the Treaty.[149] The parties were also prohibited from producing or flight-testing any intermediate-range missiles or produce any stages of such missiles or any launchers of such missiles, and producing, flight-testing or launching any shorter-range missiles or any stages or launchers of such missiles.[150] To ensure compliance, the treaty contained an extensive verification regime and data exchange mechanism, to include baseline, closeout, elimination, short-notice, and continuous portal monitoring inspections.[151] National technical means aided verification.[152] However, the right to conduct on-site inspections terminated on May 31, 2001.[153]

In 2014, the United States determined that Russia had violated its obligations under the INF Treaty by covertly developing and fielding a prohibited nuclear-capable missile system—the SSC-8 *Screwdriver* GLCM (formerly designated as the SSC-X-8).[154] The missile was determined to pose a direct threat to U.S. allies and troops in Europe and the Indo-Pacific region. After 30-plus meetings and a 60-day opportunity to return to compliance on February 2, 2019, the United States suspended its obligations under the Treaty, and withdrew from the agreement in August 2019.[155] Russia now fields multiple battalions of SSC-8s that pose a direct conventional and nuclear threat to most of Europe and parts of Asia.[156]

NATO allies supported the Trump administration's withdrawal from INF, acknowledging that Russia was in material breach of the treaty.[157] The United States and NATO cited Russia's SSC-8, also known as the 9M729 GLCM,

---

excess of 500 kilometers but not in excess of 1,000 kilometers. *Id.* art. II. The United States eliminated the Pershing II and the BGM-109G intermediate-range missiles, and the Pershing IA shorter-range missile and the Soviet Union eliminated the RSD-10 (SS-20), the R-12 (SS-4) and the R-14 (SS-5) intermediate-range missiles, and the OTR-22 (SS-12) and the OTR-23 (SS-23) shorter-range missiles. *Id.* art. III.

[149] *Id.* art. IV.
[150] *Id.* art. VI.
[151] *Id.* art. XII.
[152] *Id.*
[153] *Id.* art. XI.
[154] DEPARTMENT OF STATE, ADHERENCE TO AND COMPLIANCE WITH ARMS CONTROL, *supra* note 131, at 4, 10.
[155] INF Treaty, *supra* note 34, art. XV.
[156] Statement of Director of Intelligence Daniel Coats on Russia's Intermediate-Range Nuclear Forces (INF) Treaty Violation (online), Nov. 30, 2018.
[157] NATO Foreign Ministers, Statement on the Intermediate Nuclear Forces Treaty (online), 4 December 2018, updated Jan. 31, 2019.

which is hard to detect, mobile, and nuclear-capable.[158] The United States and NATO attempted to engage Russia on the SSC-8 on numerous occasions without success. Russia, nevertheless, claimed that armed American UAVs such as the Predator meet the definition of "ground-based cruise missiles" and should be regulated by the convention. Russia also asserts that the U.S. Mk-41 universal launchers that are part of the land-based Aegis complex, should be counted as launchers under the INF Treaty. Even though the launchers are for BMD, they can accommodate the combat use of Tomahawk medium-range cruise missiles and possibly SM-3 in a land-attack mode. After the U.S. withdrawal from the INF Treaty, Russia did so as well, with President Putin stating that Russia would "not be the first" to deploy new intermediate-range missiles in Europe.[159]

The U.S. withdrawal from the treaty is likely to remain in effect unless Russia reenters compliance by complete and verifiable destruction of its violating missiles, launchers, and associated equipment.[160] The U.S. move, however, was not just related to Russian deceit, and Russian cheating may be a function of its concerns in Asia rather than Europe. China and Iran, which are not parties to the INF Treaty, each possess over 1,000 intermediate-range missiles. Their arsenals are not regulated by any agreement. Accordingly, Russia's intermediate-range missile capabilities are now poised to balance China, as well as threaten the West. Likewise, since the United States is no longer a party to the INF Treaty it may develop intermediate-range missile systems to balance against the threat from China and Iran as well, invariably benefiting the strategic balance in Russia's favor vis-à-vis those states.[161] Ultimately, China may be the tail wagging the INF "dog," and the greatest loser in the dissolution of the treaty.

In the aftermath of the demise of the INF Treaty, the United States is on the cusp of developing its own intermediate-range missiles.[162] On May 19, 2019,

---

[158] Michael R. Gordon, On Brink of Arms Treaty Exit, U.S. Finds More Offending Russian Missiles, WALL STREET JOURNAL (online), Jan. 31, 2019.

[159] Nicholas Fiorenza, US Withdrawal from INF Treaty Takes Effect, JANE'S DEFENCE WEEKLY, Aug. 7, 2019, at 5; Talia Kaplan, Putin Signs Bill Withdrawing from Nuclear Arms Treaty with the United States, FOX NEWS (online), July 3, 2019.

[160] Michael R. Pompeo, U.S. Withdrawal from the INF Treaty, Press Statement (online), Aug. 2, 2019; Matthew Gross, The Future of the INF Treaty, HARVARD POLITICAL REVIEW (online) Mar. 24, 2021.

[161] United States Initiates Withdrawal from Intermediate-Range Nuclear Forces Treaty, Feb. 1, 2019, 113 AMERICAN JOURNAL OF INTERNATIONAL LAW 631 (2019); DEPARTMENT OF STATE, ADHERENCE TO AND COMPLIANCE WITH ARMS CONTROL, supra note 131, at 5.

[162] Rachel Cohen, DOD to Proceed with Cruise Missile Plans as US Prepares to Leave INF Treaty, AIR FORCE MAGAZINE (online), Feb. 1, 2019.

the United States tested its first ground-launched intermediate-range cruise missile since withdrawing from the INF treaty, launching a conventionally-configured missile from San Nicolas Island off the coast of California. China and Russia both condemned the test and urged the United States to not raise military tensions.[163] Beijing and Moscow additionally sought a Security Council meeting to discuss the U.S. plan to develop and deploy intermediate-range missiles in Europe and Asia as a possible threat to international peace and security.[164]

Chinese officials expressed "deep regret" over Washington's decision to withdraw from the INF Treaty, indicating that it would undermine regional and global stability.[165] China also pledged to counter any U.S. deployment of intermediate-range missiles in Asia, although it already has fielded such weapons and is developing missiles with both nuclear and conventional capabilities, such as the DF-26 IRBM and the DF-17 HGV.[166] China is unlikely to join any INF agreement since it would require it to give up 95 percent of its missile force.[167] Furthermore, China has pinned its strategy of sea control within its near seas on a land-based missile force that targets ships offshore and regional air bases in allied states that host U.S. aircraft.

While ambiguity enhances deterrence against first strikes, it also increases the danger that the launch of a conventional warhead might be mistaken for a nuclear attack and precipitate a nuclear exchange.[168] The United States and its allies in East Asia now face the prospect of balancing China's land-based strike complex to assure stability in East Asia, much as it deployed Pershing IIs and GLCMs to balance the SS-20 some 40 years ago.[169]

---

[163] Angus MacKinnon, *Russia Says U.S. Missile Test 'Escalation of Military Tensions'*, AGENCE FRANCE PRESSE (online), Aug. 19, 2019; Dong Zhaohui, *China Urges U.S. to Exercise Restraint on Armament Development After Missile Test*, XINHUA (online), Aug. 20, 2019.

[164] Michelle Nichols & David Brunnstrom, *Russia, China Seeks U.N. Security Council Meeting on U.S. Missile Developments*, REUTERS (online), Aug. 22, 2019.

[165] Fu Cong, Director General of the Department of Arms Control and Disarmament of Ministry of Foreign Affairs, People's Republic of China (online), Aug. 6, 2019.

[166] Michael Martina, *China Warns of Countermeasures if U.S. Puts Missiles on its Doorstep*, REUTERS (online), Aug. 5, 2019.

[167] Mike Yeo, *China Could Lose 95% of Ballistic, Cruise Missiles Under Strategic Arms Control Pact, Says New Analysis*, DEFENSE NEWS (online), June 5, 2020.

[168] Caitlin Talmadge, *Beijing's Nuclear Option: Why a U.S.-Chinese War Could Spiral Out of Control*, FOREIGN AFFAIRS 44 (Nov./Dec. 2018).

[169] C. Raja Mohan, *Biden, Asia, and the Politics of Nuclear Arms Control* (online), FOREIGN POLICY, Feb. 4, 2020.

3.3 Legality of Nuclear Weapons

The right of belligerents to adopt methods or means of warfare is not un-limited.[170] Weapons that are uncontrollable and unpredictable by design, and in all likelihood will cause injury without distinction to combatants and noncombatants are illegal.[171] Because the civilian population and civilian objects enjoy special protection against the dangers arising from military operations, belligerents are required to "distinguish between the civilian population and combatants and between civilian objects and military objectives . . ." and may only conduct military operations against military objectives.[172]

Unless they are taking a direct part in hostilities, civilians cannot be the object of attack. The use of a nuclear weapon with the specific intent to spread terror among the civilian population,[173] as well as indiscriminate attacks—those that strike military objectives and civilians or civilian objects without distinction—are similarly prohibited.[174] Examples of indiscriminate attacks include:

(a) an attack by bombardment by any methods or means which treats as a single military objective a number of clearly separated and distinct military objectives located in a city, town, village, or other area containing a similar concentration of civilians or civilian objects; and

(b) an attack which may be expected to cause incidental loss of civilian life, injury to civilians, damage to civilian objects, or a combination thereof, which would be excessive in relation to the concrete and direct military advantage anticipated.[175]

When conducting military operations, commanders are required to take certain precautions to ensure that the civilian population and civilian objects

---

[170] Regulations Respecting the Laws and Customs of War on Land, annexed to Convention (II) with Respect to the Laws and Customs of War on Land, art. 22, Jul. 29, 1899, 32 Stat. 1803, 1811; 1907 1907 Hague Regulations, *supra* note 107, art. 22; AP I, *supra* note 128, art. 35.

[171] DoD LAW OF WAR MANUAL, *supra* note 108, § 6.4.

[172] AP I, *supra* note 128, art. 48.

[173] *Id.* art. 51.

[174] Indiscriminate attacks include "(a) those which are not directed at a specific military objective; (b) those which employ a method or means of combat which cannot be directed at a specific military objective; or (c) those which employ a method or means of combat the effects of which cannot be limited as required by this Protocol. . . ." *Id.*

[175] *Id.*

are properly protected. Accordingly, when planning an attack, commanders must, inter alia:

(ii) take all feasible precautions in the choice of means and methods of attack with a view to avoiding, and in any event to minimizing, incidental loss of civilian life, injury to civilians and damage to civilian objects; and

(iii) refrain from deciding to launch any attack which may be expected to cause incidental loss of civilian life, injury to civilians, damage to civilian objects . . ., which would be excessive in relation to the concrete and direct military advantage anticipated.[176]

Willfully causing great suffering or serious injury to body or health not justified by military necessity and carried out unlawfully and wantonly is considered a grave breach of the Geneva Conventions.[177] Similarly, "making the civilian population or individual civilians the object of attack; [and] launching an indiscriminate attack affecting the civilian population or civilian objects in the knowledge that such attack will cause excessive loss of life, injury to civilians or damage to civilian objects . . ." are also considered grave breaches when committed willfully, in violation of the relevant provisions of AP I, and causing death or serious injury to body or health.[178]

Are nuclear weapons incapable of being used in accordance with the principles of distinction and proportionality, and should they therefore be considered inherently indiscriminate? Even if directed at a military objective, will nuclear weapons inevitably cause excessive incidental harm among the civilian population compared to the military advantages gained from their use?[179] The International Court of Justice addressed these issues at the request of the UN General Assembly (UNGA) in a 1996 advisory opinion.

Specifically, the UNGA requested that the ICJ urgently render an advisory opinion on the following question: "Is the threat or use of nuclear weapons in any circumstances permitted under international law?"[180] The ICJ did not

---

[176] *Id.* art. 57.

[177] Geneva Convention (I) for the Amelioration of the Condition of the Wounded and Sick in Armed Forces in the Field, art. 50, Aug. 12, 1949, 75 U.N.T.S. 31; Geneva Convention (IV) Relative to the Protection of Civilian Persons in Time of War, art. 147, Aug. 12, 1949, 75 U.N.T.S. 287.

[178] AP I, *supra* note 128, art. 85.

[179] DoD LAW OF WAR MANUAL, *supra* note 108, § 6.4

[180] G.A. Res. A/RES/49/75 K, Request for an advisory opinion from the International Court of Justice on the legality of the threat or use of nuclear weapons, Dec. 15, 1994.

find a "conventional rule of general scope, nor a customary rule specifically proscribing the threat or use of nuclear weapons per se."[181] Moreover, in view of the current state of international law, the Court could not then "conclude definitively whether the threat or use of nuclear weapons would be lawful or unlawful in an extreme circumstance of self-defense, in which the very survival of a State would be at stake."[182] It nonetheless found by seven votes to seven, "that the threat or use of nuclear weapons would generally be contrary to the rules of international law applicable in armed conflict, and in particular the principles and rules of humanitarian law."[183] The United States has long held that there was no specific rule of international law that precluded the use of nuclear weapons in warfare.[184] Nonetheless, recourse to nuclear weapons is reserved only to states that face perilous conditions of self-defense likely tantamount to self-preservation.[185]

---

[181] Nuclear Weapons Advisory Opinion, *supra* note 116, ¶ 74.

[182] *Id.* ¶ 105(2)E, p. 266.

[183] *Id.*

[184] OFFICE OF THE CHIEF OF NAVAL OPERATIONS, U.S. NAVY, LAW OF NAVAL WARFARE, NAVAL WARFARE INFORMATION PUBLICATION (NWIP) 10-2 § 513 (1955), *reprinted in* 50 INTERNATIONAL LAW STUDIES 359 (1955).

[185] YORAM DINSTEIN, WAR, AGGRESSION AND SELF-DEFENSE 183 (6th ed. 2017); Chris Greenwood, *Jus ad Bellum and Jus in Bello in the Nuclear Weapons Advisory Opinion, in* INTERNATIONAL LAW, THE INTERNATIONAL COURT OF JUSTICE AND NUCLEAR WEAPONS 247, 264 (L. Boisson de Chazournes & P. Sands eds., 1999).

8

Naval Operations in Outer Space

Outer space is a warfighting domain inextricably linked to contemporary armed conflict.[1] The vastness of the sea makes satellites especially valuable for naval operations.[2] Satellites and space objects are used in the targeting process; for positioning, navigation, and timing (PNT); to conduct intelligence, surveillance, and reconnaissance (ISR); for command and control (C2); and to facilitate communications. Without satellites, oceanic communications still would be conducted by high-frequency radio with limited capacity and range. During the Cold War, satellites were necessary to provide transparency and serve as a confidence-building measure to prevent nuclear miscalculation. The United States and Soviet Union developed reconnaissance radar satellites based on triangulation to track surface ship radar emissions. While satellites provided greater transparency, they also introduced new vulnerabilities. In the 1980s, states began to exploit satellite links from ground stations to track ships at sea.[3] The U.S. use of satellites during the First Gulf War demonstrated their utility for targeting and warfighting, with Global Positioning Satellites (GPS) supporting precision strikes that quickly dismantled the Iraqi armed forces.

After the Gulf War satellites were no longer considered strategic systems but were regarded as tactical support systems to provide real-time intelligence and precision targeting data to forces on the battlefield. While once reserved for collecting strategic intelligence, enforcing arms control treaties, and warning of an impending nuclear strike, satellites are required for accomplishing the most basic operational and tactical military missions. Consequently, states have turned toward counterspace operations to deny military use of this domain to the enemy.

---

[1] Brooks Tigner, *NATO Declares Space as Operational Domain and Looks to Raise Hybrid Attack Resilience*, JANE'S DEFENCE WEEKLY, Nov. 27, 2019, at 10.

[2] Norman Friedman, *Satellite Systems for Naval Warfare*, NAVAL FORCES (Jan. 2020, at 52.

[3] *Id.* at 51.

Disruptive Technology and the Law of Naval Warfare. James Kraska and Raul Pedrozo, Oxford University Press.
© James Kraska & Raul Pedrozo 2022. DOI: 10.1093/oso/9780197630181.003.0009

1. Counterspace Operations

Counterspace, or space control, includes both offensive and defensive capabilities or techniques to gain space superiority and deny its use to an adversary. Satellites are so important for naval operations that they have become a prime target during armed conflict. Defensive measures to protect space assets may include using expendable satellites or replacing satellites with substitutes if they are destroyed, making satellites less observable to the enemy, providing satellites with the means for evading attack, and placing escort satellites into position to fend off attacks.

Over limited areas, satellite functions can also be performed by substitute platforms, such as high-altitude unmanned aerial vehicles (UAVs), like the U.S. Navy's high altitude, long-endurance Triton, as well as manned maritime patrol aircraft, such as the P-8 Poseidon. In 2020, the first operational Triton deployed to Guam, but it cannot be launched from a ship.[4] While tactically useful, aircraft do not provide the theater-wide connectivity of satellites. In this respect, satellite communications and strike reconnaissance represent a leap forward in capability. If naval forces have to return to using aircraft to accomplish these missions, then airbase and aircraft carrier capacity and strike power will be diminished.[5]

Satellites move at a high rate of speed, but along predictable paths that facilitate targeting them.[6] This point was shown in 2008, when the USS *Lake Erie* (CG 70) used an SM-3 anti-ballistic missile to shoot down a failing U.S. satellite.[7] Low earth orbit (LEO) reconnaissance satellites are more vulnerable to attack than very high-altitude communication satellites in geosynchronous equatorial orbit (GEO) or intermediate-altitude GPS satellites in medium earth orbit (MEO).

The speed at which a satellite travels varies drastically depending on its altitude. Satellites farther away from earth travel more slowly. For example, the International Space Station (circa 400 km above Earth) travels at approximately 28,000 km/h. Communications satellites in geosynchronous orbit (circa 36,000 kilometers above earth) travel at approximately 11,000 km/h. In this respect, the launch technology to place satellites into orbit is similar

---

[4] Stefano D'urso, *The U.S. Navy Has Deployed the MQ-4C Triton for the First Time*, THE AVIATIONIST (online), Feb. 2, 2020.

[5] Friedman, *supra* note 2, at 52.

[6] *Id.*

[7] *Navy Uses Aegis/SM-3 To Take Down Dead Intel Satellite*, DEFENSE DAILY (online), Feb. 20, 2008.

to that used by ballistic missile boosters, and technologies designed for either mission often support the other. Nonetheless, ballistic missiles do not orbit the earth and only serve one function. Ballistic missile defense (BMD) and DA-ASAT leverage similar capabilities.

More states are developing offensive counterspace capabilities to deceive, disrupt, deny, degrade, or destroy rival space systems. In outer space, attack is easier than defense.[8] The development of offensive counterspace capabilities, including anti-satellite (ASAT) weapons, increases the possibility that armed conflict will spill over into outer space. These capabilities include direct-ascent anti-satellite weapons (DA-ASAT), co-orbital, electronic warfare (EW), directed energy weapons (DEW), and cyber means of attack. Direct-ascent weapons include ground-, air-, or sea-launched missiles with interceptors that kinetically destroy satellites on impact but are not placed into orbit themselves. Co-orbital weapons, however, are placed into orbit and maneuvered to approach and kill the target. The normative regime to inhibit the militarization of outer space has not constrained progress on developing these space warfare technologies, although it has for weapons of mass destruction (WMD).

Alternative or non-kinetic methods may also be used to destroy or degrade enemy space assets. Directed energy weapons (DEW) emit focused energy, such as lasers, particle beams, or microwave beams to interfere with or destroy space systems. Electronic warfare weapons employ radiofrequency energy to jam or disrupt satellite communications. Finally, cyber weapons using software or network techniques may be used to disrupt or destroy computer systems. The United States, China, Russia, and India lead the world in the technology of destructive earth-to-space attacks against satellites in orbit.[9]

1.1 China Counterspace Capabilities

In 2014, China placed its first ocean reconnaissance satellite into orbit.[10] At the same time, China seeks to exploit U.S. reliance on such systems by

---

[8] Friedman, *supra* note 2, at 51.

[9] Jeffrey Gettleman & Hari Kumar, India Shot Down a Satellite, Modi Says, *Shifting Balance of Power in Asia*, N.Y. TIMES (online), Mar. 27, 2019; Rahul Bedi, *India Approves New Agency to Develop Space-Based Weapons*, JANE'S DEFENCE WEEKLY, June 19, 2019, at 6.

[10] Friedman, *supra* note 2, at 52.

targeting American ISR satellites. China is developing a broad range of offensive space capabilities, some of which have military applications primarily for positioning, navigation and timing (PNT) and ISR.[11] China has tested technologies for rendezvous and proximity operations (RPO) in both LEO and GEO that presage a co-orbital ASAT capability.[12] China is also developing DA-ASAT capabilities that can be used as a counterspace system or in missile defense. Although DA-ASAT weapons for use against targets in both MEO and GEO are still in the experimental stage, China has operationally fielded a DA-ASAT capability against LEO targets from mobile launchers.[13]

On January 11, 2007, China used a ground-based medium-range ballistic missile (SC-19) launched from the Xichang Satellite Launch Center to destroy the Feng Yun 1C polar orbit weather satellite. The intercept occurred more than 537 miles above the earth and was the first successful ASAT test in more than 20 years. The destruction of the satellite produced a large debris field, which imperiled civilian and military satellites operating in the same orbit and put at risk everything in LEO.[14] Within minutes after the collision, a debris cloud formed around the satellite's original orbit. Within 10 days the debris had spread throughout the entire orbit, creating a "ring" of debris around the Earth. Five months later, the UN Committee on the Peaceful Uses of Outer Space adopted guidelines to mitigate space debris.[15] The Guidelines advise states to avoid intentional destruction of satellites because the debris created presents an increased risk to other space operations. "When intentional break-ups are necessary, they should be conducted at sufficiently low altitudes to limit the orbital lifetime of resulting fragments."[16]

The SC-19, which appears to be based on the DF-21 ballistic missile and HQ-19 missile defense system, was tested again in 2010 and 2013 from the

[11] OFFICE OF THE SECRETARY OF DEFENSE, MILITARY AND SECURITY DEVELOPMENTS INVOLVING THE PEOPLE'S REPUBLIC OF CHINA, ANNUAL REPORT TO CONGRESS 2020, at 63 [hereinafter CHINA ANNUAL REPORT 2020].
[12] SECURE WORLD FOUNDATION, GLOBAL COUNTERSPACE CAPABILITIES: AN OPEN-SOURCE ASSESSMENT (Brian Weeden & Victoria Samson eds., Apr. 2021), at 1–12 [hereinafter SWF SPACE ASSESSMENT 2021].
[13] CHINA ANNUAL REPORT 2020, supra note 11, at 65; National Air and Space Intelligence Center, Competing in Space (online), Dec. 2018; Statement of Daniel Coats, Director of National Intelligence, Worldwide Threat Assessment of the United States Intelligence Community: Hearing Before the Senate Select Committee on National Intelligence 94th Cong., 2d Sess., Senate Hearing 116–75 (Jan. 29, 2019).
[14] William J. Broad & David E. Sanger, China Tests Anti-Satellite Weapon, Unnerving U.S., N.Y. Times, Jan. 18, 2007; Concern Over China's Missile Test, BBC NEWS (online), Jan. 19, 2007; Brian Weeden, 2007 Chinese Anti-Satellite Test Secure World Foundation Fact Sheet (Nov. 23, 2010).
[15] United Nations, Office for Outer Space Affairs, Space Debris Mitigation Guidelines of the Committee on the Peaceful Uses of Outer Space (June 15, 2007), at 3.
[16] Id.

Korla Missile Test Complex, successfully intercepting a ballistic missile on each occasion.[17] On May 13, 2013, China conducted a DA-ASAT test from Xichang capable of reaching higher orbits. A second test was done in July 2014. China claimed that that launch was part of a land-based missile interceptor program, but State Department officials suggested that China completed a non-destructive ASAT test. The Americans called on China to cease developing such capabilities.[18] Tests conducted on October 30, 2015, July 22, 2015, and February 5, 2018, may also have been associated with China's ASAT program.[19]

On February 4, 2021, China's Ministry of Defense reported a land-based mid-course missile intercept technology test by the Space Systems Department of the People's Liberation Army Strategic Support Force (PLA/SSF).[20] Most likely, the event was an ASAT test like the "missile" test conducted by the PLA in July 2014. The PLA views mid-course ballistic missile defense ("space defense") and kinetic ASAT ("space control") as comparable or even synonymous capabilities under the umbrella of "space operations." Moreover, the PLA/SSF oversees the Army's strategic space mission. Because SSF played a role in developing the mid-course interceptors, the missiles are likely suitable for space missions as well.[21]

In addition to an active ASAT program, China is pursuing counterspace capabilities used to jam or spoof an adversary's space-based PNT capabilities. China has deployed PNT jammers on its man-made islands in the South China Sea, for example. Imagery of Mischief Reef reveals the presence of mobile military jamming trucks that are designed to interfere with GPS or other Global Satellite Navigations System (GNSS) assets that deliver PNT signals.[22] China is testing these capabilities. There have been numerous incidents of jamming and spoofing of GNSS signals used by the automatic identification system (AIS) to track commercial shipping near Shanghai.[23] In July 2019, an

[17] SWF SPACE ASSESSMENT 2021, *supra* note 12, at 1–10.
[18] Mike Gruss, *U.S. State Department: China Tested Anti-satellite Weapon*, SPACE NEWS (online), July 28, 2014.
[19] SWF SPACE ASSESSMENT 2021, *supra* note 12, at 1–16; Brian Weeden, Chinese Direct Ascent Anti-Satellite Testing Fact Sheet 3 (Apr. 2021).
[20] Roderick Lee, *China's Recent Ballistic Missile Defense Test May Have Actually Been an Anti-Satellite Test*, U.S. DEPARTMENT OF THE AIR FORCE, AIR WAR UNIVERSITY, CHINA AEROSPACE STUDIES INSTITUTE (online), Feb. 2021.
[21] SWF SPACE ASSESSMENT 2020, *supra* note 12, at 1–31.
[22] *Id.* at 1–20.
[23] Dana Goward, *GPS Jamming and Spoofing Reported at Port of Shanghai*, MARITIME EXECUTIVE (online), Aug. 13, 2019; SWF SPACE ASSESSMENT 2021, *supra* note 12, at 1–20.

attack spoofed the locations of more than 300 ships in the port of Shanghai and on the Huangpu River in a single day.

China's existing space situational awareness (SSA) capability allows it to maintain accurate orbital positions on and characterize most space objects in LEO, MEO, and GEO.[24] It is also "developing a sophisticated network of ground-based optical telescopes and radars" to detect, track and characterize an adversary's space objects for targeting by ASAT weapons.[25] On October 12, 2020, China successfully launched a new optical remote-sensing satellite—Gaofen-13—into orbit with a Long March-3B carrier rocket from the Xichang Center. The satellite will be used primarily for "land surveys, crop yield estimations, environmental protection, weather forecasting, early warning, [and] . . . disaster prevention and mitigation."[26] China is also constructing a new 27.6-ton spacecraft that will carry astronauts to the moon. The new rocket designed by the China Academy of Launch Vehicle Technology (CALT) is comparable to the U.S. SpaceX's Falcon Heavy rocket and United Launch Alliance's Delta IV Heavy.[27]

1.2 Russian Counterspace Capabilities

The Russian Federation has spent the past 20 years trying to regain many of its space capabilities that eroded after the Cold War and the breakup of the Soviet Union. Moscow now seeks to mitigate U.S. space superiority by developing and deploying ground-, air-, and space-based offensive capabilities. Russia is testing technologies for RPO in both LEO and GEO to support a co-orbital ASAT capability.[28] Since 2011, Russia's Central Scientific Research Institute for Chemistry and Mechanics (TsNIIKhM) has been developing a potential co-orbital ASAT program—Burevestnik (Petrel) or protect 14K168—supported by the Nivelir (Dumpy level) surveillance and tracking program. The U.S. Department of the Treasury has sanctioned TsNIIKhM for its involvement in Triton malware cyberattacks. Burevestnik involves ground-based infrastructure at Plesetsk Cosmodrome near Noginsk-9, the

---

[24] SWF Space Assessment 2021, *supra* note 12, at 1–28.

[25] *Id.* at 1–25

[26] *China Launches New Optical Remote-Sensing Satellite*, Xinhua (online), Oct. 12, 2020.

[27] Andrew Jones, *China Is Building a New Rocket to Fly Its Astronauts on the Moon*, Space.com (online), Oct. 1, 2020.

[28] Space Assessment 2021, *supra* note 12, at 2-2, 2-7, 2-8, 2-14, 2-15, 2-22.

location of the Soviet era IS co-orbital ASAT ground control center, which is near the Russian military space surveillance network headquarters.[29] TsNIIKhM also supplied an explosive fragmentation device for the Soviet era IS co-orbital ASAT, which was tested against Russian satellites to simulate attacks on LEO satellites. The Nivelir inspection satellites are similar to Burevestnik and provide tracking and targeting support. Given the high-velocity deployment of sub-satellites and multiple releases of orbital debris, it is clear that at least some of the LEO activities are weaponized.

Russia has three primary DA-ASAT programs with counterspace capabilities—the Nudol, Kontakt, and S-500. The Nudol missile defense system is a ground-launched ballistic missile that can intercept targets in LEO.[30] Both a short-range and a long-range missile are being develop by OKB Novator and the Moscow Institute of Thermal Technology, respectively, to support the Nudol system. The Kontakt air-launched interceptor is also designed for targets in LEO orbit.[31] In September 2018, images surfaced of a modified MiG-31 supersonic near-space interceptor loaded with a mock-up of an ASAT missile.[32] The system is believed to be operational.[33] Finally, the S-500 is a next-generation exo-atmospheric ballistic missile defense system being developed to engage ballistic missiles and targets in low LEO orbits.[34]

On July 23, 2020, USSPACECOM reported that Russia conducted a non-destructive test of a space-based ASAT weapon by releasing an object into orbit from Cosmos 2543 in proximity to another Russian satellite.[35] The test was similar to an on-orbit activity conducted by Russia in 2017, and inconsistent with the system's stated mission as an inspector satellite.[36] After a Russian satellite intentionally maneuvered near a U.S. government satellite in 2017, American officials expressed concern that the Kremlin was exercising its counterspace military doctrine.[37] Similar incidents occurred in 2018

---

[29] *Id.* at 2-2.

[30] *Id.* at 2-14 to 2-18; TODD HARRISON ET AL, CSIS SPACE THREAT ASSESSMENT 2021, Apr. 2021, at 21.

[31] SWF SPACE ASSESSMENT 2021, *supra* note 12, at 2-15, 2-19, 2-20 to 2-21.

[32] *Russians Alter MiG-31 for ASAT Carrier Roles*, AVIATION WEEK AND SPACE TECHNOLOGY, Aug. 17, 1992, at 63.

[33] Amanda Macias, *A Never-before-Seen Russian Missile Is Identified as an Anti-satellite Weapon and Will Be Ready for Warfare by 2022*, CNBC (online), Oct. 25, 2018.

[34] SWF SPACE ASSESSMENT 2021, *supra* note 12, at 2-15, 2-22.

[35] Robert Burns, *US Accuses Russia of Testing Anti-satellite Weapon in Space*, WASHINGTON POST (online), July 23, 2020.

[36] *Russia Conducts Space-Based Anti-satellite Weapons Test*, U.S. Space Command Public Affairs Office, U.S. Space Command (online), July 23, 2020.

[37] *Id.*

and in February 2020 that also looked like tests for a space-based weapon.[38] Russia successfully conducted another test on December 16, 2020.[39]

Like Chinese thinkers, Russian strategists consider modern warfare as a struggle for information dominance and network-centric operations.[40] Accordingly, integrating EW capabilities into military operations is a high priority. Russia has developed both fixed and mobile GPS jamming capabilities and is highly proficient in jamming the U.S. GPS network. Russia has deployed over 250,000 GPS [Pole-21] jammers on cell phone towers throughout the country that can be used to protect fixed installations by reducing the accuracy of foreign unmanned aerial systems, precision guided munitions, and cruise missiles.[41] The Pole-21 jammers have an effective range of 80 km.[42]

The Russian Army also deploys mobile EW systems, such as the R-330Zh *Zhitel* and the *Borisoglebsk-2*, which can jam specific satellite communications within tactical ranges.[43] Russia deployed mobile EW systems in support of military operations in Syria and Ukraine.[44] Jamming incidents attributed to Russia have also occurred near the Russian Black Sea port of Novorossiysk in 2017, in Norway and Finland in 2018 during a NATO military exercise, and at Israel's Ben Gurion International Airport in Tel Aviv in 2019.[45] Russia additionally appears to be working on high-powered space-based EW platforms powered by nuclear reactors.[46]

Russia's space situational awareness (SSA) capabilities are second only to the United States. These systems allow Russia to track, identify, and characterize objects from earth orbit larger than 10 centimeters. The Voronezh phased array radar can be used for both ballistic missile early warning and

---

[38] *Id.*

[39] Hanneke Weitering, *Russia Has Launched an Anti-satellite Missile Test, US Space Command Says,* SPACE.COM (online), Dec. 16, 2020; Nathan Strout, *Space Command Calls Out Another Russian Anti-satellite Weapon Test,* C4ISR.NET (online), Dec. 16, 2020.

[40] SWF SPACE ASSESSMENT 2021, *supra* note 12, at 2-39; QIAO LIANG & WANG XIANGSUI, UNRESTRICTED WARFARE 9 (1999) (Foreign Broadcast & Information Service, trans., Beijing: PLA Literature and Arts Publishing House, Feb. 1999).

[41] SWF SPACE ASSESSMENT 2021, *supra* note 12, at 2–24; Dana Goward, *Jammers at Dachas Add to Russia's Ability to Silence GPS,* GPS WORLD (online), June 19, 2019.

[42] SWF SPACE ASSESSMENT 2021, *supra* note 12, at 2-24.

[43] *Id.* at 2-24, 2-26, 2-41.

[44] Joseph Trevithick, *Ukrainian Officer Details Russian Electronic Warfare Tactics Including Radio "Virus,"* THE WAR ZONE (online), Oct. 30, 2109; Roger McDermott, *Russia's Electronic Warfare Capabilities as a Threat to GPS,* vol. 18 no. 40 EURASIA DAILY MONITOR (online), Mar. 10, 2021.

[45] SWF SPACE ASSESSMENT 2021, *supra* note 12, at 2-26.

[46] *Id.* at 2-28.

SSA missions, with the ability to track an object the size of a soccer ball at 8,000 km and track up to 500 objects simultaneously.[47]

1.3 U.S. Counterspace Capabilities

For now, the United States has the most advanced military space capabilities in the world.[48] For example, the United States has the technological capability to quickly develop a co-orbital ASAT capability and has demonstrated capabilities in missile defense, on-orbit inspections, and satellite servicing. On April 14, 2018, the United States launched multiple small satellites in GEO, including at least one that conducted rendezvous and proximity operations.[49] The United States does not have an (acknowledged) operational DA-ASAT capability, but it possesses operational mid-course missile defense interceptors that have demonstrated ASAT capabilities against satellites in LEO.[50] The United States has also developed dedicated conventional and nuclear-tipped DA-ASAT capabilities.[51]

The ASM-135 air-launched DA-ASAT missile was developed in 1984 to counter Soviet co-orbital ASAT capabilities without the need to use nuclear weapons. The ASM-135 could be launched from a modified F-15A fighter in a supersonic climb to intercept targets in LEO.[52] On September 13, 1985, the ASM-135 intercepted and destroyed the Solwind P78-1 satellite 290 miles above the Pacific Ocean, marking the first time a U.S. missile destroyed a satellite in space.[53]

The United States also developed mid-course missile defense systems that are designed to destroy long-range ballistic missiles, but also have inherent ASAT capabilities. American ground-based interceptors (GBIs) and ship-based Standard Missile 3 (SM-3) interceptors have latent DA-ASAT capabilities.[54] Although GBIs have the greater potential for DA-ASAT roles, only the

---

[47] *Id.* at 2-34.
[48] *Id.* at 3-1.
[49] *Id.* at 3-9.
[50] *Id.* at 3-11.
[51] *Id.* at 3-1, 3-11.
[52] NORMAN FRIEDMAN, SEAPOWER AND SPACE 196 (2000).
[53] Bill Keller, *Air Force Missile Strikes Satellite in First U.S. Test*, N.Y. TIMES, Sept. 14, 1985, at 1.
[54] Laura Grego, The Anti-Satellite Capability of the Phased Adaptive Approach Missile Defense System, Federation of American Scientists Public Interest Report 1-6 (Winter 2011); RONALD O'ROURKE, NAVY AEGIS BALLISTIC MISSILE DEFENSE (BMD) PROGRAM: BACKGROUND AND ISSUES FOR CONGRESS 9-10 (Apr. 19. 2011).

SM-3 has been used in a demonstrated DA-ASAT role. During Operation Burnt Frost in 2008, for example, an Aegis cruiser fired an SM-3 Block IA interceptor that destroyed an ailing U.S. reconnaissance satellite at an altitude of 240 km.[55]

The United States has deployed 44 GBIs in Alaska (Fort Greely) and California (Vandenberg Air Force Base), with an additional 20 planned for future deployment. The missiles could lift an exo-atmospheric kill vehicle (EKV), placing all satellites at risk that are either in LEO or in highly elliptical orbits with perigees that dip down into these altitudes.[56] Although SM-3 Block IA/IB interceptors are only capable of engaging satellites at or below 600 km altitude, the SM-3 Block IIA interceptor being developed jointly with Japan will be able to reach most, if not all, satellites in LEO. The SM-3 can be deployed at sea on Aegis warships configured for BMD or at Aegis Ashore land-based sites, like the operational site in Romania, and future sites in Poland (or possibly Japan).[57]

On November 17, 2020, a U.S. Navy warship using the Aegis BMD SM-3 Block IIA interceptor shot down an ICBM target missile in space that was launched from the Marshall Islands test range.[58] Previous successful shootdowns were conducted using GBIs in Alaska and California.[59] Although not developed as an ASAT weapon, the SM-3 Block IIA and GBIs provide the United States with a formidable and flexible DA-ASAT capability that may be used against enemy military satellites in LEO.[60]

Since 2003, the United States has operated the Counter Communications System (CCS) as an operational EW counterspace network. CCS can be deployed worldwide to provide uplink jamming capability against geostationary communications satellites (COMSATs).[61] The system provides space situational awareness and reversible offensive space control effects that prevent an adversary's use of satellite communications in an area of conflict.[62]

---

[55] Grego, The Anti-Satellite Capability, *supra* note 54, at 1–3.

[56] SWF SPACE ASSESSMENT 2021, *supra* note 12, at 3–15.

[57] Jen Judson, *Poland's Aegis Ashore Delayed to 2022 with New Way Forward Coming Soon*, DEFENSE NEWS (online), Feb. 18, 2020; *Navy Commissions Naval Support Facility Redzikowo, a Future Aegis Ashore Site*, SEAPOWER MAGAZINE (online), Sept. 3, 2020; Mike Yeo, *Japan Suspends Aegis Ashore Deployment, Pointing to Cost and Technical Issues*, DEFENSE NEWS (online), June 15, 2020.

[58] David B. Larter, *US Navy Destroyer Shoots Down an ICBM in Milestone Test*, DEFENSE NEWS (online), Nov. 17, 2020.

[59] Dave Aaro, *US Shoots Down ICBM in Space from Warship for First Time in Successful Test*, FOX NEWS (online), Nov. 17, 2020.

[60] SWF SPACE ASSESSMENT 2021, *supra* note 12, at 3-15 to 3-16.

[61] *Id.* at 3-17 to 3-18.

[62] Fact Sheet, 4th Space Control Squadron, Peterson Air Force Base (online), Oct. 2019.

For example, CCS can target enemy COMSAT to disrupt C2, transmission of intelligence information, and targeting links for unmanned aircraft.

The Navigation Warfare (NAVWAR) program protects U.S. and allied use of GPS during armed conflict using deliberate defensive and offensive action to assure and prevent PNT information through coordinated employment of space, cyberspace, and EW operations. NAVWAR can jam GPS, and similar services, such as the Russian GLONASS, and China's Beidou, within a local area of operation, while preserving GPS availability to friendly forces outside the area of conflict.[63] In the future, the United States may employ basing sensors and interceptors in outer space. Space-based sensors can leverage the larger viewable area of space to improve tracking and targeting against threats, such as hypersonic glide vehicles and hypersonic cruise missiles.[64] Space-based interceptors are especially advantageous in boost-phase defense.

The United States operates a robust SSA network of geographically dispersed ground-based radars and telescopes and space-based telescopes.[65] These capabilities are being upgraded with new radars and telescopes in the Southern Hemisphere, and data sharing agreements with strategic partners.[66] Since 2010, the United States has signed over 100 SSA data sharing agreements with other states, commercial satellite operators, and international nongovernmental organizations.[67] The agreements permit the Department of Defense to share data and analysis with other entities.

The United States also operates a Space Surveillance Network (SSN) consisting of phased array radars, mechanical (conventional) tracking radars, ground-based electro-optical telescopes, and space-based optical telescopes.[68] The space-based sensors include the Space-Based Space Surveillance (SBSS) satellites in LEO, the Canadian Sapphire

[63] SWF SPACE ASSESSMENT 2021, *supra* note 12, at 3-19 to 3-20.
[64] U.S. DEPARTMENT OF DEFENSE, OFFICE OF THE SECRETARY OF DEFENSE, MISSILE DEFENSE REVIEW XIV (2019).
[65] SWF SPACE ASSESSMENT 2021, *supra* note 12, at 3-25 to 3-26.
[66] *Id.* at 3-25, 3-28.
[67] DoD has signed SSA agreements with Australia, Japan, Italy, Canada, Finland, France, South Korea, the United Kingdom, Germany, Israel, Spain, the United Arab Emirates, Belgium, Norway, Denmark, Brazil, the Netherlands, Thailand, New Zealand, Poland, Romania, and Chile. *Id.* at 3-25, 3-27.
[68] Phased-array radars can track multiple satellites at the same time and are capable of scanning large segments of space in a split second. Conventional radars use moveable tracking antennas or fixed detection and tracking antennas to collect data on satellites. Electro-optical telescopes are linked to video cameras and computers, which allows images to be recorded and analyzed in real-time. *Id.* at 3-25 to 3-26.

military satellite, and four U.S. Air Force Geosynchronous Space Situational Awareness Program (GSSAP) satellites in GEO.[69]

1.4 Directed Energy Weapons

China, the United States, and Russia are also developing directed energy weapons (DEW) for offensive counterspace operations, including lasers, neutral particle beams, and radio frequency weapons. DEWs may be used to interfere or disable a satellite without generating a significant debris field. Depending on the effects they cause, the use of DEWs may fall under the definition of "attacks" in Additional Protocol I (AP I) as "acts of violence" against the adversary.[70] A minority of scholars and states would say that any use of DEW, regardless of effect, would constitute an attack.

Ground-based lasers can be used to dazzle or blind EO satellites, or even inflict thermal damage on most satellites in LEO.[71] China is a leader in this area.[72] Russia is reinvesting in its legacy DEW systems, to include an aircraft-borne laser system that can target optical sensors of imagery reconnaissance satellites.[73] The Sokol Echelon (Falcon Echelon) system will reportedly carry a 1LK222 airborne laser system and fitted on a modified Ilyushin IL-76MD-90A transport aircraft.[74] Russia can also use ground-based satellite laser ranging (SLR) facilities in the North Caucasus to dazzle the sensors of optical imagery satellites.[75]

The United States has also conducted research on the use of ground-based high energy lasers, neutral particle beams, and high-power directed radio frequency energy for counterspace and other military purposes. These weapons are being developed for defense against missiles, rockets, artillery, and unmanned systems. While none of these systems are being built for counterspace roles, the technology being developed could have counterspace applications. The Missile Defense Agency is conducting research into the use of space-based DEW to defend against ballistic missiles, which also

---

[69] *Id.* at 3-26.
[70] Protocol Additional to the Geneva Conventions of Aug. 12, 1949, and Relating to the Protection of Victims of International Armed Conflicts, art. 49(1), June 8, 1977, 1125 U.N.T.S. 3 [hereinafter AP I].
[71] SWF SPACE ASSESSMENT 2021, *supra* note 12, at 1-25.
[72] CSIS SPACE THREAT ASSESSMENT 2021, *supra* note 30, at 4.
[73] SWF SPACE ASSESSMENT 2021, *supra* note 12, at 2-29 to 2-33.
[74] *Id.*
[75] *Id.*

has a counterspace application. For example, the Mid-Infrared Advanced Chemical Laser (MIRACL) (deuterium fluoride) emits a multi-megawatt beam in the infrared spectrum. The laser was successfully used against a U.S. Air Force experimental satellite in October 1997.[76]

2. International Regulatory Regime

On October 4, 1957, the Soviet Union inaugurated the "Space Age" by launching Sputnik on an R-7 intercontinental ballistic missile (ICBM) boost vehicle from the Kazakh Republic.[77] The unexpected Soviet success in placing the first man-made object into earth's orbit galvanized American resolve to retake the lead in space exploration.[78] Sputnik also made tangible the debate over international law in outer space, and even legal claims to celestial bodies.[79]

On November 3, 1957, the Soviet Union achieved a second milestone, launching the first biological spacecraft—Sputnik 2—into orbit. The cone-shaped capsule carried an experimental dog named Laika, who is believed to have survived for only two days, yet the mission provided Soviet scientists with the first data on the behavior of a living organism in space.[80] The United States raced to catch up.[81]

Months later, on January 31, 1958, the United States launched its first satellite—Explorer 1—on an adapted Jupiter-C rocket. The satellite was developed under the supervision of the famed German rocket scientist Wernher von Braun. A second attempt to launch a satellite into orbit failed on March 5, 1958. That year the UN General Assembly (UNGA) adopted a resolution to encourage the peaceful uses of outers space.[82] On September 12, 1959, the Soviet Union successfully launched a spacecraft that landed on the Moon. Then, on April 12, 1961, Cosmonaut Yuri Gagarin, a Soviet Air Force pilot,

---

[76] *In Test, Military Hits Satellite Using a Laser*, N.Y. TIMES, Oct. 21, 1997, at A18; SWF SPACE ASSESSMENT 2021, *supra* note 12, at 3-21.

[77] William J. Jorden, *Soviet Fires Earth Satellite into Space; It Is Circling the Globe at 18,000 M.P.H.; Sphere Tracked in 4 Crossings Over U.S.*, N.Y. TIMES, Oct. 5, 1957, at 1.

[78] Robert Hartman, *Arms to Meet Space Challenge Ike's Plea: Request for Extra Billion Made at Congress Opening*, L.A. TIMES, Jan. 8, 1958, at 1.

[79] Monroe W. Karmin, *Up in the Air: Growing Space Race Spurs Drive for Laws on Planetary Claims*, WALL STREET JOURNAL, Nov. 25, 1959, at 1.

[80] *Id.*

[81] John G. Norris, *Dulles Says Russia Probably Leads U.S. in the Ballistic Missiles Race*, WASHINGTON POST, Oct. 17, 1957, at A1.

[82] G.A. Res. 1348 (XIII), Question of the Peaceful Use of Outer Space (Dec. 13, 1958).

became the first human in space, making a complete orbit of the Earth before re-entering the atmosphere one hour and 48 minutes later and safely returning to Kazakhstan.

As the Space Race intensified, Western powers made several proposals to ban the use of outer space for military purposes, to include a prohibition on orbiting and stationing WMD in outer space.[83] On September 22, 1960, President Dwight D. Eisenhower addressed the General Assembly and asked, "Will outer space be preserved for peaceful use and developed for the benefit of all mankind? Or will it become another focus for the arms race—and thus an area of dangerous and sterile competition?"[84] Eisenhower's proposed solution was to apply the model of the Antarctica Treaty to outer space. The Antarctic Treaty placed the continent off limits to military preparations or national conquest.[85]

In October 1963, the United States and the Soviet Union signed the Limited Test Ban Treaty, which bans explosive nuclear testing or other nuclear explosions in the atmosphere, outer space, and underwater.[86] One week later, the UNGA adopted a resolution that welcomed superpower commitments to refrain from stationing nuclear weapons or other WMD in outer space.[87]

In December 1963, the General Assembly adopted Resolution 1962, which sets forth nine principles for conducting activities in outer space.[88] The resolution states that space is reserved for the benefit and interests of all mankind. All States are free to explore and utilize celestial bodies, which are not subject to appropriation, on the basis of equality. The exploration and use of outer space shall be conducted in accordance with international law and the Charter of the United Nations. States are responsible for their space activities. States also shall have due regard to the interests of other states in outer

[83] WMD are defined as "atomic explosive weapons, radioactive material weapons, lethal chemical and biological weapons, and any weapons developed in the future which have characteristics comparable in destructive effect to those of the atomic bomb or other weapons mentioned above." U.N. Doc. S/C.3/32/Rev.1, Resolution adopted by the Commission for Conventional Armaments at it Thirteenth Meeting, Aug. 12, 1948 (Aug. 18, 1948), p. 2.

[84] *Address by Dwight D. Eisenhower at the Fifteenth General Assembly of the U.N., Sept. 22, 1960*, DEPARTMENT OF STATE PUBLICATION 7086, INTERNATIONAL ORGANIZATION AND CONFERENCE SERIES 7 (online), Oct. 17, 1960.

[85] *Id.* at 7–8.

[86] Treaty Banning Nuclear Weapon Tests in the Atmosphere, in Outer Space and Under Water, done at Moscow, Aug. 5, 1963, entered into force Oct. 10, 1963, art. I, 14 U.S.T. 1313, T.I.A.S. 5433, 480 U.N.T.S. 43.

[87] G.A. Res. 1884(XVIII), Question of General and Complete Disarmament (Oct. 17, 1963).

[88] G.A. Res 1962 (XVII), Declaration of Legal Principles Governing the Activities of States in the Exploration and Use of Outer Space (Dec. 13, 1963).

space. The state of registry retains jurisdiction and control over its space objects, and any personnel thereon, while in outer space, and such objects and component parts shall be returned to the state of registry. States are internationally liable for damage to a foreign state or to its natural or juridical person caused by an object launched into outer space. Finally, astronauts shall be regarded as envoys of mankind in outer space, and states shall render assistance if they need help, and quickly return them to the state of registry of their space vehicle in the event of distress. None of the UNGA resolutions, however, formed "instant" customary international law.

The subsequent codified law of outer space arises principally from four major peacetime treaties: (1) The Outer Space Treaty, (2) The Rescue Agreement, (3) The Liability Convention, and (4) The Registration Convention. These agreements form the bedrock of peacetime outer space law. In peacetime, jamming of another's state's military satellite is likely not an "attack," or even considered unlawful, provided the effects are not too harmful. This approach is consistent with interference in the context of cyber operations, as set forth in the *Tallinn Manual*.[89] Furthermore, some of the provisions in the space conventions may not apply between belligerents during international armed conflict.[90]

Generally, the law of armed conflict (LOAC) applies as a regime *lex specialis* during armed conflict.[91] In such case, the peacetime principle of noninterference with space systems may be displaced by the rules governing war. At the same time, however, the International Law Commission's Draft Articles on the Effects of Armed Conflicts on Treaties (Draft Articles), state that armed conflict does not ipso facto terminate or suspend peacetime treaties.[92] Article 6 of the Draft Articles states that the nature of the treaty, including its object and purpose, and the characteristics of the armed conflict, determine whether it continues to apply during armed conflict. Peacetime treaties apply only through their express wording and subject to normal rules of interpretation. The major outer space treaties set forth a framework that likely would exert a latent normative influence even during war in space.

---

[89] TALLINN MANUAL 2.0 ON THE INTERNATIONAL LAW APPLICABLE TO CYBER OPERATIONS r. 92, at 418 (Michael N. Schmitt gen. ed., 2017).

[90] Department of Defense, Office of the General Counsel, An Assessment of International Legal Issues in Information Operations (2nd ed. Nov. 1999), *reprinted in* 76 INTERNATIONAL LAW STUDIES 459, 494 (2002).

[91] Military and Paramilitary Activities in and against Nicaragua (Nicar. v. U.S), Judgment, 1986 I.C.J. Rep. 14, ¶ 25 (June 27).

[92] International Law Commission, The Draft Articles on the Effects of Armed Conflicts on Treaties (A/66/10), 2 Pt. 2 YEARBOOK OF THE INTERNATIONAL LAW COMMISSION ¶ 101, art. 3 (2011).

2.1 The Outer Space Treaty

To sustain the momentum to conclude an arms control agreement applicable to outer space, the United States and the Soviet Union submitted draft treaties to the United Nations on June 16, 1966. The U.S. proposal applied only to celestial bodies, while the Soviet proposal covered the entirety of outer space. The scope of the treaty was decided in favor of the Soviet broader draft, and by December outstanding issues had been resolved and a text was completed. On December 19, 1966, the General Assembly adopted a resolution commending the treaty and requesting that it be opened for signature and ratification.[93]

The Outer Space Treaty entered into force on October 10, 1967.[94] The agreement provides that outer space, the Moon, and other celestial bodies, are the province of all mankind.[95] Like the high seas, space is not subject to national appropriation or claims of sovereignty by means of use or occupation, or by any other means.[96] The exploration and use of outer space, including the moon and other celestial bodies, shall be carried out "in the interest of maintaining international peace and security" and promoting cooperation and understanding.[97] The Moon, other celestial bodies, and outer space are also "free for exploration and use by all states without discrimination of any kind, on a basis of equality and in accordance with international law, and there shall be free access to all areas of celestial bodies."[98]

2.1.1 Peaceful Purposes
Article IV of the Outer Space Treaty is the central arms control provision, which prohibits states from placing into "orbit around the Earth any objects carrying nuclear weapons or any other kinds of weapons of mass destruction, install such weapons on celestial bodies, or station such weapons in outer space in any other manner."[99] Article IV further requires that "the

---

[93] G.A. Res. 2222 (XXI), Treaty on Principles Governing the Activities of States in the Exploration and Use of Outer Space, Including the Moon and Other Celestial Bodies (Dec. 18, 1966).

[94] Treaty on Principles Governing the Activities of States in the Exploration and Use of Outer Space, Including the Moon and Other Celestial Bodies, Jan. 27, 1967, 18 U.S.T. 2410, T.I.A.S. No. 6347, 610 U.N.T.S. 205 [hereinafter Outer Space Treaty].

[95] *Id.* art. I.

[96] *Id.* art. II; United Nations Convention on the Law of the Sea, art. 89, Dec. 10, 1982, 1833 U.N.T.S. 397 [hereinafter UNCLOS].

[97] Outer Space Treaty, *supra* note 94, art. III.

[98] *Id.* art. I.

[99] *Id.* art. IV.

Moon and other celestial bodies shall be used . . . exclusively for peaceful purposes," and it prohibits the "establishment of military bases, installations and fortifications, the testing of any type of weapons and the conduct of military maneuvers on celestial bodies. . . ."[100]

The meaning of the term "peaceful purposes" in article IV remains the subject of contending interpretations. Given the plain meaning of the word "peaceful," some suggest the term could be interpreted to exclude all military activities in space. The United States and other space powers, however, interpret the term to allow for all military activities in space that are not specifically prohibited by treaty (e.g., stationing WMD in outer space) or are not inconsistent with article 2(4) (prohibition on the aggressive use of force) or article 51 (right of individual and collective self-defense) of the UN Charter.[101]

The U.S. position on "peaceful purposes" was first articulated in December 1962, well before the conclusion of the Treaty in 1966. Speaking before the Seventeenth Session of the First Committee of the UNGA, the U.S. representative, Senator Albert Gore, Sr., stated that "outer space should be used only for peaceful—that is, non-aggressive and beneficial—purposes." The test of any space activity "must not be whether it is military or non-military, but whether or not it is consistent with the . . . [UN] Charter and other obligations of law."[102] In 2006, the Bush administration committed itself to explore and use space for peaceful purposes, but clarified that "peaceful purposes" permits defense and intelligence-related activities.[103] Similarly, the Obama administration stated that "peaceful purposes" and international law allow outer space to be used for national security missions.[104] Both the 2010 U.S. National Space Strategy and 2020 U.S. Defense Space Strategy reinforce this position.

The same issue was debated in negotiations for the United Nations Convention on the Law of the Sea (UNCLOS). Article 88 of the Convention reserves the high seas for "peaceful purposes," while article 301 calls on states to "refrain from any threat or use of force against the territorial integrity or

---

[100] Id.

[101] Bing Cheng, *Properly Speaking, Only Celestial Bodies Have Been Reserved for Use Exclusively for Peaceful (Non-Military) Purposes, but Not Outer Void Space*, 75 INTERNATIONAL LAW STUDIES 81, 96 (2000) ("little doubt the world 'peaceful' means 'non-military' and not 'non-aggressive'").

[102] U.N. Doc. A/C. I/PV. 1289, International Cooperation in the Peaceful Uses of Outer Space (Dec. 3, 1962), at 13.

[103] DEPARTMENT OF HOMELAND SECURITY, U.S. NATIONAL SPACE POLICY (Aug. 31, 2006).

[104] OFFICE OF THE PRESIDENT, NATIONAL SPACE POLICY OF THE UNITED STATES OF AMERICA 3–7 (June 28, 2010); DEPARTMENT OF DEFENSE, DEFENSE SPACE STRATEGY 8 (June 2020).

political independence of any state. . . ."[105] Some states take the position that articles 88 and 301 prohibit all military activities in the oceans.[106] Maritime states oppose such a restrictive interpretation, however, arguing that whether an activity is considered "peaceful" is determined by the UN Charter and other obligations of international law.[107] The consensus position is that "articles 88 and 301 do not prohibit all military activities on the high seas and in exclusive economic zones, but only those that threaten or use force" in a manner inconsistent with article 2(4) of the Charter.[108]

To accept that all military activities in space are, by their nature, prohibited by the "peaceful purposes" provision of article IV would be inconsistent with long-standing state practice. The first military reconnaissance satellite was launched by the United States in 1959, almost a decade before the Outer Space Treaty was concluded.[109] The Soviet Union soon followed suit. By 2019, 19 nations were operating more than 300 military satellites in earth's orbit.[110] Three major powers accounted for 265 of them: the United States had 123, Russia 74, and China 68. Even middle powers operate military satellites and have a military space program. France and Israel each have eight military satellites; India, the United Kingdom, and Germany each have seven. In April 2020, Iran became the 20th nation to successfully launch a military satellite (Noor-1) into LEO.[111]

---

[105] UNCLOS, *supra* note 96, arts. 88, 301.

[106] Ecuador, for example, argued that "the use of the ocean space for exclusively peaceful purposes must mean complete demilitarization and the exclusion from it of all military activities." 3 UNITED NATIONS CONVENTION ON THE LAW OF THE SEA 1982: A COMMENTARY 88–89 (Satya N. Nandan & Shabtai Rosenne eds., 1995).

[107] *Id.* at 89–91. In response to Ecuador's proposal, the U.S. delegate stated, "The term 'peaceful purposes' did not, of course, preclude military activities generally. The United States has consistently held that the conduct of military activities for peaceful purposes was in full accord with the Charter of the United Nations and with the principles of international law. Any specific limitation on military activities would require the negotiation of a detailed arms control agreement. The Conference was not charged with such a purpose and was not prepared for such a negotiation. Any attempt to turn the Conference's attention to such a complex task would quickly bring to an end current effort to negotiate a law of the sea convention." *Id.* at 89. *See also* U.N. Doc. A/CONF.62/WS/67, V, Third U.N. Conference on the Law of the Sea, 67th Plenary Meeting, Official Records, p. 62 (1973–1982).

[108] UN Doc. A/40/535, Study on the Naval Arms Race: Report of the Secretary-General, Sept. 17, 1985, para. 188; Moritaka Hayashi, *Military and Intelligence Gathering Activities in the EEZ: Definition of Key Terms*, 29 MARINE POLICY 123–37 (2005); JAMES KRASKA & RAUL PEDROZO, INTERNATIONAL MARITIME SECURITY LAW § 10.4.3 (2013); JAMES KRASKA, MARITIME POWER AND THE LAW OF THE SEA 253–61 (2010).

[109] Albert D. Wheelon, *Corona: The First Reconnaissance Satellites*, PHYSICS TODAY 24, 29 (Feb. 1997).

[110] Joyce Chepkemoi, *Countries by Number of Military Satellites*, WORLD ATLAS (online), Mar. 16, 2018; *Here Are All the Satellites Orbiting the Earth in 2019*, ALL IN ALL SPACE (online), Mar. 25, 2019.

[111] *Iran Launches Military Satellite Amid Tensions with US*, ASIA NEWS MONITOR (online), Apr. 23, 2020; Amir Vahdat & Jon Gambrell, Iran Guard Reveals Secret Space Program in Satellite Launch, AP (online), Apr. 22, 2020.

Satellites are used for a variety of military purposes, including military communications, early warning systems, space-based navigation systems, ISR, and PNT operations. Regarding ISR operations in particular, the UN Security Council has determined that peacetime intelligence collection is not an act of aggression and does not violate article 2(4) of the Charter.[112] States have not challenged the presence and operation of these satellites for defense-related purposes. On the contrary, military satellites have elevated transparency and serve as a confidence-building measure contributing to international peace and security. Therefore, so long as the purposes are peaceful, the activity is non-aggressive.[113]

2.1.2 Military Activities in Outer Space

The prohibition on placement of WMD in orbit, as well as installing or stationing such weapons on celestial bodies or in outer space, does not prohibit using space as a medium for delivering a nuclear weapon.[114] The treaty does not ban WMD that go into a fractional orbit or engage in suborbital flight. Intercontinental ballistic missiles are permissible since they travel through space during only a portion of their trajectory and are there temporarily. States are also prohibited from establishing military bases, installations, and fortifications on celestial bodies, as well as testing any type of weapons or the conduct of military maneuvers on such celestial bodies.[115] These activities are prohibited only on the Moon and other celestial bodies, however, and not in the vast spaces among such bodies.

Conventional DA-ASAT capabilities are not prohibited, and even WMD tests (as opposed to emplacement in orbit) are not specifically proscribed. The United States, for example, conducted the Starfish Prime experiment in 1962 that tested the effects of nuclear weapons in high altitudes or lower outer space. The 1.45 megaton explosion took place 400 km above Johnston Atoll in the Northern Pacific Ocean. Consistent with the "Lotus Principle," sovereign states are free to conduct activities so long as they do not contravene an

---

[112] Oliver J. Lissitzyn, *Electronic Reconnaissance from the High Seas and International Law*, 61 INTERNATIONAL LAW STUDIES 563, 566–67, 574–75, 578–79.

[113] G.A. Res. 3314(XXIX), Definition of Aggression, art. 1 (Dec. 14, 1974) (Aggression is the use of armed force by a State against the sovereignty, territorial integrity or political independence of another State, or in any other manner inconsistent with the Charter of the United Nations, as set out in this Definition). Article 3 includes within the Defintion armed invasion, bombardment, blockade, attack on the land, sea, or air forces, use of armed forces in the territory of another State, sending by or on behalf of a State armed bands, groups, irregulars, or mercenaries. *Id.*

[114] Outer Space Treaty, *supra* note 94, art. IV.

[115] *Id.*

explicit prohibition in international law.[116] Similarly, the U.S. Department of Defense concluded that because the Partial Nuclear Test Ban Treaty does not specifically prohibit the use of nuclear weapons in wartime, it must therefore be presumed that no such prohibition would apply.[117] This position infers that the Outer Space Treaty does not apply during armed conflict, as the treaty is silent on the issue (other than to say that the UN Charter governs in outer space). The Outer Space Treaty also recognizes that military personnel, as well as equipment and facilities, may be used freely for peaceful purposes in outer space missions.[118]

States are responsible in international law for their activities in outer space, "including the Moon and other celestial bodies, whether such activities are carried on by governmental agencies or by non-governmental entities. . . ."[119] If a state launches an object into outer space, including to the Moon and other celestial bodies, it is internationally liable for damage to another state or its natural or juridical persons.[120] This provision would be trumped by the *lex specialis* of LOAC, however, between belligerents. It is uncertain whether it also applies as against third-party states whose satellites are harmed. States bear responsibility during armed conflict for violations of the law of war, which generate an obligation to compensate other states for violations.[121] States are additionally required to conduct all their activities in outer space, including on the Moon and other celestial bodies, with "due regard" to the corresponding interests of all other states.[122] To monitor compliance, all stations, installations, equipment, and space vehicles on the Moon and other celestial bodies shall be open to the representatives of other states on the basis of reciprocity if advance notice of the projected visit is provided.[123] If a state

[116] S.S. Lotus (Fr. v. Turk.), 1927 P.C.I.J. (ser. A) No. 10 (Sept. 7). ("Restrictions upon the independence of States cannot therefore be presumed.")

[117] U.N. Doc. A/CN.4/552, First Report on the Effects of Armed Conflicts on Treaties by Mr. Ian Brownlie, Special Rapporteur (Apr. 21, 2005), ¶ 67 at 221; Treaty Banning Nuclear Weapons Tests in the Atmosphere, in Outer Space, and Underwater: Hearing before Sen. Committee on Foreign Relations, 88th Cong., 1st sess. (1963) (statement of John T. McNaughton, General Counsel of the Department of Defense), at 177–78.

[118] Outer Space Treaty, *supra* note 94, art. IV.

[119] *Id.* See also *Report of the International Law Commission to the General Assembly*, 53 U.N. GAOR Supp. No. 10, U.N. Doc. A/56/10 (2001), *reprinted in* [2001] 2 YEARBOOK OF THE INTERNATIONAL LAW COMMISSION 32, U.N. Doc. A/CN.4/SER.A/2001/Add.1 (Part 2).

[120] *Id.* art. VII. See also Kieran Tinkler, *Rogue Satellites Launched into Outer Space: Legal and Policy Implications*, JUST SECURITY (online), June 17, 2018.

[121] OFFICE OF THE GENERAL COUNSEL, U.S. DEPARTMENT OF DEFENSE LAW OF WAR MANUAL § 18.9.1 (rev. ed., Dec. 2016) [hereinafter DoD LAW OF WAR MANUAL].

[122] Outer Space Treaty, *supra* note 94, art. IX.

[123] *Id.* art. XII.

cannot meet this obligation of reciprocity then it is presumptively not entitled to take advantage of visits under art. XII of the OST.

2.2 The Rescue Agreement

Astronauts are considered envoys of mankind. Accordingly, states shall
render all possible assistance to such personnel of a spacecraft "in the event
of accident, distress, or emergency landing on the territory of another State
Party or on the high seas."[124] Additionally, personnel of a spacecraft "shall be
safely and promptly returned to the State of registry of their space vehicle."[125]
Astronauts shall also render all possible assistance to other astronauts when
conducting activities in outer space and on celestial bodies.[126] The state of
registration maintains ownership over its space objects, wherever located,
and all states shall, upon request, provide assistance to the launching state in
recovering its space objects that return to earth.[127]

2.3 The Liability Convention

The Liability Convention elaborates on article VII of the Outer Space
Treaty.[128] Article II imposes absolute liability on the launching state "to
pay compensation for damage caused by its space object on the surface of
the earth or to aircraft flight."[129] For damages not on the earth's surface, the
launching state is "liable only if the damage is due to its fault or the fault of
persons for whom it is responsible."[130] A launching state may be exonerated
from absolute liability if it can establish that the damage resulted "from gross
negligence or from an act or omission done with intent to cause damage" by
the "claimant State or of natural or juridical persons it represents," unless the
damage results from activities conducted by the launching state that are inconsistent with international law, in particular the UN Charter and the Outer

---

[124] Agreement on the Rescue of Astronauts and the Return of Objects Launched in Outer Space,
art. V, Apr. 22, 1968, 19 U.S.T. 7570, 672 U.N.T.S. 119.
[125] *Id.*
[126] *Id.*
[127] *Id.* art. VIII.
[128] Convention on International Liability for Damage Caused by Space Objects, Mar. 29, 1972, 24
U.S.T. 2389, 961 U.N.T.S. 187.
[129] *Id.* art. II.
[130] *Id.* art. III.

Space Treaty.[131] A claim for compensation for damages "shall be presented to the launching state through diplomatic channels" or through the UN Secretary-General.[132] If the parties cannot settle the claim through diplomatic negotiations within one year, the dispute will be decided by a Claims Commission.[133]

2.4 The Registration Convention

The Registration Convention requires states to register their space objects launched into earth orbit or beyond in an appropriate registry maintained by the launching state.[134] The UN Secretary-General shall maintain a Register of the various state registries.[135] All states shall provide the Secretary-General information concerning each space object recorded in its registry, to include:

(a) name of launching State or States;
(b) an appropriate designator of the space object or its registration number;
(c) date and territory or location of launch;
(d) basic orbital parameters, including: (i) nodal period; (ii) inclination; (iii) apogee; (iv) perigee; and
(e) general function of the space object.[136]

States shall also inform the Secretary-General when a previously reported space object is no longer in earth orbit.[137]

2.5 ITU Regulations

More important than the Moon Agreement, the International Telecommunication Union (ITU) Radio Regulations are focused on space

---

[131] Id. art. VI.
[132] Id. art. VIII, IX.
[133] Id. art. XIV, XVIII, XIX.
[134] Convention on Registration of Objects Launched into Outer Space, art. II, Jan. 14, 1975, 28 U.S.T. 695, 1023 U.N.T.S. 15.
[135] Id. art. III.
[136] Id. art. IV.
[137] Id.

sustainability. Like the International Maritime Organization, the ITU is a specialized agency of the UN. The ITU helps states harmonize rules for the radio spectrum to ensure interoperability and global roaming. Radio frequencies and satellite orbits, including the geostationary-satellite orbit, are scarce natural resources requiring careful management.[138] The member states of the ITU develop international regulations and set global standards and guidelines for telecommunications, managing rights of access to the radio spectrum, promoting a rational, equitable, and economical use of the spectrum, and ensuring that operations are free from interference.[139] This latter provision, coupled with the Outer Space Treaty, may form a principle or norm of noninterference in peacetime activities in outer space.[140]

Article IX of the Outer Space Treaty requires States Parties to conduct "appropriate international consultations" before initiating any activity in space if it has reason to believe that it would cause "potentially harmful interference" with another state's peaceful use of space. A State Party that believes the activities of another state may interfere with its own activities may request such consultations. Similarly, the ITU Constitution and Convention (CS CV) embodies the principle of noninterference: "The Member States are bound to abide by the provisions of this Constitution . . . in all stations established or operated by them . . . which are capable of causing harmful interference."[141] Furthermore, Member States are "responsible to ensure that the stations duly authorized by them shall not cause harmful interference to radio services of other member states."[142] Yet, this provision has to be read in conjunction with article 48, which states that Member States "retain their entire freedom with regard to military radio installations."[143] "Nevertheless, [military] installations must, so far as possible, observe . . . provisions relative . . . to the measure to be taken to prevent harmful interference."[144] The

---

[138] Constitution of the International Telecommunication Union, *reprinted in* CONSTITUTION AND CONVENTION OF THE INTERNATIONAL TELECOMMUNICATION ADOPTED BY THE 2018 PLENIPOTENTIARY CONFERENCE, ITU Doc. CS/art. 44 (CS 196) (2019) [hereinafter ITU Constitution].

[139] *Id.* The special needs of developing countries and geographically disadvantaged state must also be taken into account.

[140] *See* NATIONAL SPACE POLICY OF THE UNITED STATES OF AMERICA 3–4 (Dec. 9, 2020) ("The United States considers the space systems of all nations to have the rights of passage through, and conduct of operations in, space without interference. Purposeful interference with space systems, including supporting infrastructure, will be considered an infringement of a nation's rights.").

[141] ITU Constitution, *supra* note 138, art. 6 (CS 37)

[142] *Id.* art. 45 (CS 197 to 198).

[143] *Id.* art. 48 (CS 202).

[144] *Id.* (CS 203).

application of the principle of noninterference concerning military operations in the Outer Space Treaty and the CS CV is fact dependent and uncertain since military installations appear bound to observe the principle "so far
as possible."

2.6 The Moon Agreement

The Moon Agreement elaborates on numerous provisions in the Outer Space
Treaty as applied to the Moon and other celestial bodies.[145] The Agreement
entered into force in June 1984 but has only 18 State Parties. None of the
five permanent members of the UN Security Council are a party to the
Agreement. This suggests that the Moon Agreement clearly does not reflect
customary international law.

The Agreement states that all activities on the Moon shall be carried out in
accordance with the UN Charter and with due regard for the interests of all
other states.[146] Moreover, the Moon and its natural resources shall be considered "the common heritage of mankind," and no state may purport to claim
sovereignty over the Moon.[147] When exploitation of the natural resources
of the Moon becomes feasible, the State Parties to the Agreement undertake to establish an international regime to govern the exploitation of such
resources.[148]

The Agreement requires that the Moon be used "exclusively for peaceful
purposes."[149] "Any threat or use of force or any other hostile act or threat of
hostile act on the moon is prohibited."[150] The use of the Moon to commit
any such act or engage in any such threat "in relation to the earth, the moon,
spacecraft, the personnel of spacecraft or man-made space objects" is likewise prohibited.[151] State Parties also agree not to place in orbit around the
Moon objects carrying nuclear weapons or any other WMD "or place or use
such weapons on or in the moon."[152] The Agreement further prohibits the
"establishment of military bases, installations and fortifications, the testing

---

[145] Agreement Governing the Activities of States on the Moon and Other Celestial Bodies, Dec. 18,
1979, 1363 U.N.T.S. 3 [hereinafter Moon Agreement].
[146] *Id.* art. 2.
[147] *Id.* art. 11.
[148] *Id.*
[149] *Id.* art. 3.
[150] *Id.*
[151] *Id.*
[152] *Id.*

of any type of weapons and the conduct of military manoeuvres on the moon...."[153] States may, however, "establish manned and unmanned stations on the moon" to conduct activities consistent with the Agreement.[154]

2.7 Draft PPWT

In 2002, China and Russia submitted a joint working paper to the Conference on Disarmament (CD) that contained "Possible Elements for a Future International Legal Agreement on the Prevention of the Deployment of Weapons in Outer Space, the Threat or Use of Force Against Outer Space Objects."[155] Basic obligations under the proposed treaty included:

- Not to place in orbit around the Earth any objects carrying any kinds of weapons, not to install such weapons on celestial bodies, or not to station such weapons in outer space in any other manner.
- Not to resort to the threat or use of force against outer space objects.
- Not to assist or encourage other States, groups of States, international organizations to participate in activities prohibited by this Treaty.[156]

China and Russia submitted a second joint working paper to the CD concerning "Transparency and Confidence-Building Measures in Outer Space Activities and the Prevention of Placement of Weapons in Outer Space" in May 2006.[157] In general, China and Russia proposed that transparency and confidence-building measures (CBM) could be divided into several categories:

- measures aimed at enhancing more transparency of outer space programs;

---

[153] Id.

[154] Id. art. 9.

[155] Letter dated June 27, 2002, from the Permanent Representative of the People's Republic of China and the Permanent Representative of the Russian Federation to the Conference on Disarmament addressed to the Secretary-General of the Conference transmitting the Chinese, English and Russian Texts of a Working Paper entitled "Possible Elements for a Future International Legal Agreement on the Prevention of the Deployment of Weapons in Outer Space, the Threat or Use of Force Against Outer Space Objects," CD/1679 (June 28, 2002).

[156] Id.

[157] The People's Republic of China and the Russian Federation Working Paper "Transparency and Confidence-Building Measures in Outer Space Activities and the Prevention of Placement of Weapons in Outer Space," CD/1778 (May 22, 2006).

- measures aimed at expansion of information on outer space objects in orbits; and
- measures related to the rules of conduct during outer space activities.[158]

The paper suggested different types of CBMs, such as exchanges of information, demonstrations, notifications, consultations, and thematic workshops.[159]

In February 2008, China and Russia introduced a draft "Treaty on Prevention of the Placement of Weapons in Outer Space and of the Threat or Use of Force against Outer Space Objects (PPWT)" to the CD.[160] Article II of the draft treaty obligates states:

(1) not to place in orbit around the Earth any objects carrying any kinds of weapons;
(2) not to install such weapons on celestial bodies;
(3) not to place such weapons in outer space in any other manner;
(4) not to resort to the threat or use of force against outer space objects; and
(5) not to assist or induce other States, groups of States or international organizations to participate in activities prohibited by this Treaty.[161]

The draft defines "use of force" or "threat of force" as any "hostile actions against outer space objects including, *inter alia*, actions aimed at destroying them, damaging them, temporarily or permanently disrupting their normal functioning or deliberately changing their orbit parameters, or the threat of such actions."[162] Nothing in the treaty, however, is intended to impede the right of self-defense under article 51 of the UN Charter.[163]

The United States criticized the joint proposal indicating that the draft "only bans the placement of weapons in space."[164] It does "not ban the

[158] *Id.*
[159] *Id.*
[160] Letter dated Feb. 12, 2008, from the Permanent Representative of the Russian Federation and the Permanent Representative of China to the Conference on Disarmament addressed to the Secretary-General of the Conference transmitting the Russian and Chinese Tests of the Draft "Treaty on Prevention on the Placement of Weapons in Outer Space and of the Threat or Use of Force Against Outer Space Objects (PPWT)" introduced by the Russian Federation and China, CD/1839 (Feb. 29, 2008).
[161] *Id.* art. II.
[162] *Id.* art. I.
[163] *Id.* art. V.
[164] Letter dated Aug. 19, 2008, from the Permanent Representative of the United States of America addressed to the Secretary-General of the Conference transmitting comments on the Draft "Treaty on Prevention of the Placement of Weapons in Outer Space and of the Threat or Use of Force Against

research, development, production, or storage of (orbital) anti-satellite systems."[165] Therefore, a "Party could build a breakout capability consistent with the provisions of the Treaty."[166] Moreover, the proposed draft would not "prohibit the testing of otherwise prohibited space-based weapons if they were tested against cooperative orbital targets by launching the test vehicle into a sub-orbital trajectory."[167] Specifically, the United States highlighted that

- The term "use of force" and "threat of force" only captures actions "taken against another country's satellite(s), which are not part of a mutually-agreed cooperation program."
- The definition of "use of force" "captures not only "hostile" counter-space activities against another country's space objects that result in permanent and irreversible damage, but also "hostile activities and actions that cause temporary and reversible effects, such as from radio frequency jamming and optical sensor dazzling."
- The definition of "use of force" also captures "the deliberate alteration of the orbit of another country's satellite."[168]

In addition, the right of self-defense under article V appears to be inconsistent with article II prohibitions.

Additionally, when read together with the definitions in article I, article II "prohibits the deployment or stationing of any weapons in space, regardless of the military mission, and regardless of the specific technologies employed by the weapon system in question."[169] For example, the draft "prohibits the deployment of space-based missile defense interceptors, lasers, and other missile defense-related weapon capabilities employing other physical principles," but it does not prohibit "research, development, production, and terrestrial storage of space-based, for example, anti-satellite or missile defense weapons."[170] Therefore, terrestrial-based anti-satellite weapons like "direct-ascent ASAT interceptors, ground-based lasers, and jammers" are

Outer Space Objects (PPTW)" as contained in Document CD/1839 of Feb. 29, 2008, CD/1847 (Aug. 26, 2008).

[165] Id.
[166] Id.
[167] Id.
[168] Id.
[169] Id.
[170] Id.

not prohibited.[171] Yet, the deployment of terrestrial-based ASATs "would un-dermine the object and purpose of the proposed draft treaty."[172]

Russia and China introduced a revised draft PPWT on June 10, 2014, to the CD to remove ambiguities in the initial draft.[173] In an explanatory note, Russia and China highlight the main amendments to the draft Treaty. The term outer space—"the space above the Earth in excess of 100 km above sea level"—was removed from article I.[174] The definitions of "outer space object," "weapon in outer space," "use of force," and "threat of force" were also clari-fied.[175] Article II was amended to add a new obligation—"not engage in outer space activities, as part of international cooperation, inconsistent with the subject matter and the purpose of this Treaty."[176] Article III of the initial draft was also incorporated into article II in the new draft. The revised article IV on self-defense recognizes the right of both individual and collective self-de-fense. Article V recognizes "the need for measures to control compliance with the . . . Treaty," but does not provide specific approaches to those measures.[177] Article VI establishes a "clear mandate for the Executive Organization to fa-cilitate implementation of the treaty."[178] A more robust dispute resolution mechanism has been included in article VII "considering the key elements of the dispute resolution mechanism provided by other international le-gally binding instruments. . . ."[179] Article VIII was "amended to include the conditions of international intergovernmental organizations participation in the Treaty."[180] The revised article X identifies the UN Secretary-General as the Depositary of the Treaty.[181] Article XI has been modified to require con-sensus of the Parties to amend the Treaty.[182] Finally, article XII was amended to require a State Party to provide the Secretary-General with a statement of

[171] Id.
[172] Id.
[173] Treaty on the Prevention of the Placement of Weapons in Outer Space, the Threat or Use of Force against Outer Space Objects (Draft), Permanent Mission of the People's Republic of China to the United Nations Office at Geneva and other International Organizations in Switzerland (online), June 5, 2014.
[174] Women's International League for Peace and Freedom (WILPF), Explanatory Note on the updated draft Treaty on the Prevention of the Placement of Weapons in Outer Space, the Threat or Use of Force against Outer Space Objects (online), undated.
[175] Id.
[176] Id.
[177] Id.
[178] Id.
[179] Id.
[180] Id.
[181] Id.
[182] Id.

the extraordinary events that have jeopardized its supreme interests when withdrawing from the Treaty.[183]

The U.S. response to the joint proposal expressed a willingness "to consider space arms control proposals and concepts that are equitable, effectively verifiable, and enhance the national security of international participants."[184] Nonetheless, the United States has yet to see "any legally-binding proposals that meet these criteria."[185] Specifically, the United States believes that any non-legally binding transparency and confidence-building measures for outer space activities should:

- be verifiable by other parties in their application, either independently or collectively;
- be clear, practical and proven, meaning that both the application and the efficacy of the proposed measure must be demonstrated by one or more actors; and
- reduce or even eliminate the causes of mistrust, misunderstanding and miscalculation with regard to the activities and intentions of States.[186]

A preliminary U.S. assessment of the revised PPWT concluded that the new draft "does not address the significant flaws in the 2008 PPWT."[187] The revised draft does not contain an "effective verification regime to monitor compliance, and terrestrially-based anti-satellite systems posing the greatest and most imminent threat are not captured."[188]

In 2019, the United States reiterated its opposition to the PPWT. In addressing the Plenary Meeting of the CD on August 14, Ambassador Robert Wood, U.S. Permanent Representative to the Conference on Disarmament, stated "the greatest threat to satellites is not from weapons in outer space, but rather from ground-based anti-satellite weapons that are designed to destroy, damage or disrupt the normal functioning of objects in outer space."[189]

[183] Id.

[184] Continuing Progress on Ensuring the Long-Term Sustainability and Security of the Space Environment, Conference on Disarmament Plenary, Frank A. Rose Deputy Assistant Secretary for Space and Defense Policy Bureau of Arms Control, Verification and Compliance Geneva, Switzerland (online), June 10, 2014.

[185] Id.

[186] Id.

[187] Id.

[188] Id.

[189] Statement by Ambassador Robert A. Wood, U.S. Permanent Representative to the Conference on Disarmament at the Conference on Disarmament Plenary Meeting on Agenda Item Three, "Prevention of an arms race in outer space" (online), Aug. 14, 2019. These concerns were reiterated

Even though China and Russia argue that article II of the draft PPWT would prohibit the use of ground-based threats, nothing in the agreement, including article II, "prohibits the development, testing, production, storage or deployment of . . . ground-based anti-satellite weapons."[190] Moreover, these are precisely the types of weapons that Russia and China are developing and deploying.[191]

Russia, for example, has acknowledged developing a ground-based laser weapon at Peresvet Combat Laser Complex that is designed to interfere with the normal functioning of another nation's satellites. Yet, President Putin has failed to explain how Russia's development of a ground-based laser that is designed to "fight satellites" is consistent with Moscow's "public-facing push for space arms control."[192] In 2006, China illuminated a U.S. spy satellite with a laser.[193] The following year, China intentionally destroyed a Chinese weather satellite with a ground-based missile designed to strike the satellite using kinetic force, creating 3,000 pieces of debris in orbit.[194] Most of the 3,000 fragments generated by the explosion remain in orbit today and pose an indiscriminate threat to spacecraft in LEO.[195] China has deployed the missile system, suggesting that it is willing to use it during an armed conflict. Like Russia, China has failed to reconcile the development and deployment of this debris-generating weapon "with its outward-facing push for space arms control."[196] Nothing suggests Russia and China will restrain their programs to develop ground-based ASAT missiles.[197]

These incidents demonstrate that Russia and China are testing their ability to attack satellites in orbit from the ground, whether through directed energy or missile strikes, while professing a concern about attacks on satellites and serve as the main proponents of PPWT.[198] Russia's anti-satellite test of April

on June 1, 2021: Statement by Ambassador Robert A. Wood for the Session on the Prevention of an Arms Race in Outer Space, Conference on Disarmament (online), June 1, 2021.

[190] Statement by Ambassador Robert A. Wood (2019), *supra* note 189.
[191] *Id.*
[192] *Id.*
[193] *NRO Confirms Chinese Laser Test Illuminated U.S. Spacecraft*, SPACE NEWS (online), Oct. 3, 2006.
[194] Statement by Ambassador Robert A. Wood (2019), *supra* note 189.
[195] *Id.*
[196] *Id.*
[197] *Id.*
[198] *Id.*

15, 2020, for example, further indicates Moscow is not serious about arms control in outer space.[199]

2.8 The Artemis Accords

In 2020, eight nations signed The Artemis Accords, which represent a political commitment to establish a set of principles, guidelines, and best practices to enhance the civil exploration and use of outer space.[200] South Korea, New Zealand, and Brazil signed the Accord on May 24, May 31, and June 15, 2021, respectively.[201]

Adherence to the Accords when conducting civil space activities on the Moon, Mars, comets, and asteroids will "increase the safety of operations, reduce uncertainty, and promote the sustainable and beneficial use of space for all humankind."[202] All cooperative activities under the Accords "should be exclusively for peaceful purposes and in accordance with relevant international law," including the Outer Space Treaty, Rescue and Return Agreement, Liability Convention, and the Registration Convention.[203] Scientific information resulting from space activities under the Accords will be shared with the public and international scientific community.[204] The Signatories intend to preserve outer space heritage that "comprise historically significant human or robotic landing sites (e.g., Apollo landing sites), artifacts, spacecraft, and other evidence of activity on celestial bodies."[205] Extraction and utilization of space resources, including any recovery from the surface or subsurface of the Moon, Mars, comets, or asteroids, should comply with the Outer Space Treaty and support safe and sustaining space activities.[206]

---

[199] Sandra Erwin, *U.S. Space Command Blasts Russia for Anti-satellite Missile Test*, SPACE NEWS (online), Apr. 15, 2020 (General John Raymond called the test, "further proof of Russia's hypocritical advocacy of outer space arms control proposals designed to restrict the capabilities of the United States while clearly having no intention of halting their counterspace weapons programs.").

[200] The Artemis Accords: Principles for Cooperation in the Civil Exploration and Use of the Moon, Mars, Comets, and Asteroids for Peaceful Purposes (online), Oct. 13, 2020. The states are Australia, Canada, Japan, Luxemburg, Italy, the United Kingdom, the United Arab Emirates, and the United States.

[201] *New Zealand Signs Artemis Accord*, NASA.gov (online), May 31, 2021; U.S. Department of State, Office of the Spokesperson, Media Note, *Brazil Signs Artemis Accords* (online), June 15, 2021.

[202] Artemis Accords, *supra* note 200, § 1.

[203] *Id.* § 3.

[204] *Id.* § 4, 8.

[205] *Id.* § 9.

[206] *Id.* § 10.

Additionally, exploration and use of outer space will be conducted with due regard for the rights of others and the Signatories will "refrain from any intentional actions that may create harmful interference with each other's use of outer space."[207] The Accords allow for the declaration of temporary safety zones to avoid harmful interference. Within these zones, the Signatories commit to provide notification of their activities and coordinate with any relevant actor to avoid harmful interference. Within a safety zone, the following principles will apply:

(a) The size and scope of the safety zone, as well as the notice and coordination, should reflect the nature of the operations being conducted and the environment that such operations are conducted in;

(b) The size and scope of the safety zone should be determined in a reasonable manner leveraging commonly accepted scientific and engineering principles;

(c) If the nature of an operation changes, the corresponding safety zone should be altered in size and scope as appropriate; and

(d) The Signatories should promptly notify each other and the UN Secretary-General of establishment, alteration, or end of any safety zone.[208]

Finally, as part of their mission planning process, the Signatories commit to plan for the mitigation of orbital debris, "including the safe, timely, and efficient passivation and disposal of spacecraft at the end of their missions, when appropriate. . . ."[209] Additionally, the Signatories "commit to limit, to the extent practicable, the generation of new, long-lived harmful debris released through normal operations, break-up in operational or post-mission phases, and accidents and conjunctions, by taking appropriate measures such as the selection of safe flight profiles and operational configurations, as well as post-mission disposal of space structures."[210]

3. Law of Armed Conflict in Outer Space

There is no international consensus on whether all, or even some, LOAC applies in space.[211] Nevertheless, the use of force in outer space during an

---

[207] *Id.* § 11.
[208] *Id.*
[209] *Id.* § 12.
[210] *Id.*
[211] Frans G. von der Dunk, *Armed Conflicts in Outer Space: Which Law Applies?*, 97 INTERNATIONAL LAW STUDIES 188, 191–92 (2021); Michael N. Schmitt, *International Law and Military Operations in*

armed conflict is constrained by existing treaty and customary international law, including the UN Charter and rules regulating means and methods of warfare.[212] The Geneva Conventions and AP I apply "to all cases of declared war or any other armed conflict which may arise between two or more of the . . . Parties."[213] Additionally, while the rules on the conduct of hostilities reflected in article 49(3) of AP I apply to air, land, or sea warfare that may "affect civilians on land," this may be considered as tantamount to actually covering all hostilities, including conflict in outer space.[214] The treaties and customary law governing armed conflict are "understood to regulate the conduct of hostilities . . . in outer space."[215] Thus, belligerents must respect LOAC rules governing the conduct of hostilities, to include the "principle of distinction, the prohibition against indiscriminate and disproportionate attacks, and the obligation to take precautions in attack against the effects of attack."[216] Belligerents likewise would be restricted in "attacking, destroying, removing, or rendering useless objects indispensable to the survival of the civilian population."[217] Whether satellites are "indispensable" to the survival of the civilian population is debatable, and depends on one's view of how essential are the services they provide to modern life.

There is no question that man-made space satellites are lawful military objectives if they carry weapons; are part of the enemy's kill chain (such as GPS); or are used for ISR, military communications, or command and control.[218] GPS satellites are dual-use space objects, however, with civilian uses. An attack on a GPS satellite directly or indirectly destroys or degrades safety-critical civilian activities, such as air traffic control, but may present a

---

Space, MAX PLANCK UN YEARBOOK (2006); Michael Schmitt & Kieran Tinkler, *War in Space: How International Humanitarian Law Might Apply*, JUST SECURITY (online), Mar. 9, 2020.

[212] INTERNATIONAL COMMITTEE OF THE RED CROSS, INTERNATIONAL HUMANITARIAN LAW AND THE CHALLENGES OF CONTEMPORARY ARMED CONFLICT 32 (Nov. 22, 2019) [hereinafter ICRC REPORT ON CONTEMPORARY ARMED CONFLICT]; DoD LAW OF WAR MANUAL, *supra* note 121, § 14.10.2.2.

[213] AP I, *supra* note 70, art. 1(3); *See also* Convention (I) for the Amelioration of the Condition of the Wounded and Sick in the Armed Forces in the Field art. 2, Aug. 12, 1949, 6 U.S.T. 3114, 75 U.N.T.S. 31; Convention (II) for the Amelioration of the Condition of the Wounded, Sick, and Shipwrecked Members of Armed Forces at Sea art. 2, Aug. 12, 1949, 6 U.S.T. 3217, 75 U.N.T.S. 85; Convention (III) Relative to the Treatment of Prisoners of War art. 2, Aug. 12, 1949, 6 U.S.T. 3316, 75 U.N.T.S. 135; and Convention (IV) Relative to the Protection of Civilian Persons in Time of War art. 2, Aug. 12, 1949, 6 U.S.T. 3516, 75 U.N.T.S. 287.

[214] AP I, *supra* note 70, art. 49(3); ICRC REPORT ON CONTEMPORARY ARMED CONFLICT, *supra* note 212, p. 34.

[215] DoD LAW OF WAR MANUAL, *supra* note 121, § 14.10.2.2. ("[L]aw of war treaties and the customary law of war are understood to regulate the conduct of hostilities, regardless of where they are conducted, which would include the conduct of hostilities in outer space.)

[216] REPORT ON CONTEMPORARY ARMED CONFLICT, *supra* note 212, p. 34.

[217] AP I, *supra* note 70, art. 54(2).

[218] YORAM DINSTEIN, THE CONDUCT OF HOSTILITIES UNDER THE LAW OF INTERNATIONAL ARMED CONFLICT 124 (3d ed. 2016) [hereinafter DINSTEIN, CONDUCT OF HOSTILITIES].

military advantage because it could aid the adversary.[219] Targeting GPS satellites requires a proportionality analysis to ensure that the anticipated military advantage outweighs expected incidental harm to civilians. Furthermore, attacks against purely military satellites and space vehicles may generate significant space debris that could affect civilian satellites, requiring an analysis of whether the attack is proportional in relation to the expected harmful effects and anticipated military advantage.[220] Such attacks also implicate the rights of neutral states that may own or operate satellites that are affected by debris.[221] Yoram Dinstein and William H. Boothby, therefore, suggest that cyberattacks against satellites are preferable to kinetic strikes since they do not generate new debris in outer space.[222]

During an armed conflict, enemy military satellites and other space objects are always lawful targets. Civilian and dual-use satellites or space objects may also be military objectives and subject to attack if they are used by the enemy to conduct or sustain operations, such as for PNT or ISR, and other war fighting or war sustaining activities.[223] A kinetic strike against a lawful target in space would clearly constitute an attack under LOAC. According to the International Committee of the Red Cross (ICRC), a non-kinetic operation, such as a directed energy or laser weapon or cyberattack, which only disables the space object, but does not physically damage it, is also considered an attack under LOAC.[224] Depending on the consequences of the loss of the space object, the ICRC position may be reasonable in light of the importance of satellites to a thriving and healthy society. However, in the context of cyber operations, numerous states have taken the position physical damage is required for an operation to amount to an "attack" under LOAC.[225] As such, the meaning of "attack" in outer space appears equally unsettled.

Proportionality and precautions in attack also apply in outer space. A civilian satellite or space object that is not making an effective contribution to

---

REPORT ON CONTEMPORARY ARMED CONFLICT, *supra* note 212, 32–35.

DINSTEIN, CONDUCT OF HOSTILITIES, *supra* note 218, at 124.

Michel Bourbonnière & Ricky J. Lee, *Jus ad Bellum and Jus in Bello Considerations on the Targeting of Satellites: The Targeting of Post-Modern Military Space Assets,* 44 ISRAELI YEARBOOK OF HUMAN RIGHTS 167, 200 (2014), *but cf* Wolff Heintschel von Heinegg, *Neutrality and Outer Space,* 93 INTERNATIONAL LAW STUDIES 526, 530 (2017).

DINSTEIN, CONDUCT OF HOSTILITIES, *supra,* note 218, at 124–25; W. H. BOOTHBY, LAW OF TARGETING § 17.7, 371–73 (2012).

AP I, *supra* note 70, art. 52(2); DoD LAW OF WAR MANUAL, *supra* note 121, § 5.17.2.3.

REPORT ON CONTEMPORARY ARMED CONFLICT, *supra* note 212, p. 34.

Roy Schöndorf, *Israel's Perspective on Key Legal and Practical Issues Concerning the Application of International Law to Cyber Operations,* 97 INTERNATIONAL LAW STUDIES 395, 400 (2021).

military action may not be attacked.[226] Moreover, in the event of a dual-use satellite or space object, belligerents must take into consideration the "expected incidental harm to civilians and civilian objects . . . while assessing the legality of the attack under the principles of proportionality and precautions."[227] Even temporarily disabling a commercial satellite may, in certain circumstances, impose severe consequences on the civilian population, such as loss of essential civilian services, like an electrical power grid.[228] When conducting a kinetic attack on a space object, belligerents must also consider the amount of space debris that will be created by the operation. Space debris resulting from an attack on a lawful military target in space has the potential to harm both protected civilian satellites and third-party neutral military satellites. There may be no practical way to eliminate these effects.

Another way to approach these issues is through the principle of discrimination in LOAC. Are attacks in space against enemy satellites by their nature indiscriminate? Indiscriminate attacks are defined in AP I and include those that "employ a method or means of combat the effects of which cannot be limited. . . ."[229] The United Kingdom Joint Service Manual provides that this form of indiscriminate attack covers two situations: (1) where the attacker is unable to control the effects of the attack, such as dangerous forces released by it; and (b) where the incidental effects are too great (i.e., a violation of the rule of proportionality).[230] While it is questionable whether a biological weapon, for example, releases "dangerous forces" per se, it manifests uncontrollable effects. The U.S. Department of Defense (DoD), however, seems to mix discrimination and proportionality, suggesting that a condition precedent for uncontrollable effects to arise is that the attack is expected to cause excessive harm to civilians.[231] In this view, LOAC does not prohibit weapons whose effects are uncontrollable unless the anticipated civilian harm in any particular case is expected to be excessive. Proportionality analysis would apply.

DoD asserts that the use of such weapons is not prohibited when they are necessarily required against a military target of such importance as to

[226] AP I, *supra* note 70, art. 52.

[227] *Id.* art. 57; REPORT ON CONTEMPORARY ARMED CONFLICT, *supra* note 212, p. 34.

[228] REPORT ON CONTEMPORARY ARMED CONFLICT, *supra* note 212, p. 35.

[229] AP I, *supra* note 70, art. 51(4)(c).

[230] UNITED KINGDOM MINISTRY OF DEFENCE, THE JOINT SERVICE MANUAL OF THE LAW OF ARMED CONFLICT § 5.23.1 (fn 93) (2004) [U.K. JOINT SERVICE MANUAL].

[231] DoD LAW OF WAR MANUAL, *supra* note 121, 6.7.4. (The authors thank Wing Commander Kieran Tinkler, RAF, for the comparison between the U.K. JOINT SERVICE MANUAL and the DoD LAW OF WAR MANUAL.)

"outweigh the inevitable, but regrettable, incidental casualties to civilians and destruction to civilian objects."[232] If disabling, rather than destroying, an enemy satellite will achieve a similar (or same) military advantage, the means selected to engage it should be the one that is least likely to cause danger to civilians and civilian objects.[233]

3.1 Restatements of Outer Space Law

The lack of consensus concerning the application of LOAC to outer space has generated efforts to restate, or progressively develop, this area of international law. Two prominent efforts are underway, yet they appear to disagree on a fundamental question—whether military operations in outer space are "peaceful," or whether the prescriptions reserving space for "peaceful purposes" set forth in article IV of the Outer Space Treaty ban military objects in space altogether.

Most nations agree that LOAC and law regarding the use of force contained in the UN Charter apply to military operations in outer space. However, there is no consensus on how these bodies of law should be interpreted in the context of military activities in outer space in times of peace and war. The Woomera Manual and McGill Manual aim to articulate and clarify the rules-based international legal order that applies to military activities in outer space.

3.1.1 The Woomera Manual

The *Woomera Manual on the International Law of Military Space Operations* (Woomera Manual), spearheaded by The University of Adelaide, The University of Exeter, the University Of Nebraska, and the University of New South Wales-Canberra, seeks to objectively articulate and clarify existing law that applies to military space operations, particularly during periods of tension (when states and nonstate actors may consider using force) or outright hostilities.[234] None of the five major space treaties expressly mention the initiation and conduct of hostilities in outer space, and there is little state

---

[232] J. Fred Buzhardt, *General Counsel, Department of Defense, Letter to Senator Edward Kennedy, Sept. 22, 1972, reprinted in* 67 AMERICAN JOURNAL OF INTERNATIONAL LAW 122, 124 (1973).

[233] AP I, *supra* note 70, art. 57; Schmitt & Tinkler, *supra* note 211. AP I uses the term "similar" military advantage but the United Kingdom Ministry of Defence interprets this to mean the "same" military advantage. U.K. JOINT SERVICE MANUAL, *supra* note 230, § 5.32 (2004).

[234] The Woomera Manual on the International Law of Military Space Operations (online).

practice on the subject. This "lack of normative clarity" presents the risk that a state or nonstate actor may engage in an activity in outer space "that might be misunderstood by others, or even characterized as unlawful."[235] Lack of clarity likewise allows states "to conduct hostile space operations . . . in a zone of uncertainty, which complicates responses by other States."[236]

The Woomera Project brings together legal experts that specialize "in the fields of international space law, international law on the use of force [jus ad bellum] and the law of armed conflict [jus in bello], together with technical experts."[237] Experts participate in their personal capacity, "independent of the official position or preference of any State or organization."[238] To support a stable, rules-based global order, for periods of both heightened tension and armed conflict, the Manual (1) examines the circumstances in which operations associated with space infrastructure would be considered unlawful as a violation of the law on the use of force; (2) consider the responses available to states in reacting to such operations; and (3) determine how the law of armed conflict governs operations that are conducted from, to or through outer space, should armed conflict break out.[239] The Woomera Manual also covers purely peacetime rules relevant to military space operations, such as the meaning of "due regard" in day-to-day operations with even friendly states.

3.1.2 McGill Manual

Launched in 2016 by the McGill Centre for Research in Air and Space Law, the *McGill Manual on International Law Applicable to Military Uses of Outer Space* (MILAMOS) also seeks to articulate and clarify extant law that applies to military activities in outer space during peacetime, as well as limitations that apply to the threat or use of force in outer space.[240] The drafters of the Manual suggest that, given the world's geopolitical polarization and renewal of great power competition, there is a possibility that hostilities between states or nonstate actors could occur in outer space.

International efforts to establish transparency and confidence-building measures related to outer space activities have not "adequately addressed

---

[235] *Id.*
[236] *Id.*
[237] *Id.*
[238] *Id.*
[239] *Id.*
[240] Manual on International Law Applicable to Military Uses of Outer Space, McGill Centre for Research in Air and Space Law, Montreal Quebec (online).

the legal nature of the range of military activities currently being conducted or . . . envisaged in outer space," or the extent to which the body of law that regulates the initiation (*jus ad bellum*) and conduct (*jus in bello*) of hostilities applies in outer space.[241] Therefore, the drafters strive for greater certainty on how to deter conflict in outer space, and to sustain present and future space activities and solidify governance of outer space.[242] The McGill Manual seeks to provide a clear and authoritative statement of the law, as well as a framework for regulating military activities in space.

[241] Id.
[242] Id.

Index

For the benefit of digital users, indexed terms that span two pages (e.g., 52–53) may, on occasion, appear on only one of those pages.

cables, submarine, damage to, in wartime
  efforts to recover damages for, 186,
    198–99
  known location of cables and, 180–81
  legality of, 198
  and *lex specialis* law of naval
    warfare, 184–85
  as practical reality, 199
  requirements for legal attacks, 193–96
  rules on, 184–85
  and rules *vs.* practice, 185
  in Spanish-American War, 186, 198–99
  vulnerability to, 179–80
  in World War I, 186–87, 200–1
cables, submarine, tapping of
  and great power competition, 189
  Russia and, 190
  U.S. tapping of Soviet cables in Cold
    War, 187–89
CALT. *See* China Academy of Launch
  Vehicle Technology
Campaign to Stop Killer Robots, 119–20
Canada
  and interwar naval disarmament
    conferences, 151
  military installations on continental
    shelf, prohibition on, 171–72
cannons
  advances in size and range, 5
  as first effective stand-off weapon, 3
  on galleasses, 2, 3
  on sail-powered ships, 2–3
Cape of Good Hope, 4–5
caravels, 3–4
carracks, 3–4
carrier strike groups, U.S., vulnerability to
  missiles, 9–10
CCW. *See* Convention on Certain
  Conventional Weapons (CCW)
  [United Nations]
CDM. *See* Clandestine Delivered Mine
Cheonan (South Korean warship), 160–61
Chicago Convention. *See* Convention on
  International Civil Aviation
Chief of Naval Operations (CNO), power
  to designate ships as warships, 97
China
  advanced weaponry, investment in,
    11, 12–13

  aggressiveness of, and neighboring
    states' increase of submarine
    fleets, 139
  anti-ballistic missile (ABM) systems,
    217, 244–45
  artificial island constructed on Mischief
    Reef, 170–71, 172
  Belt Road Initiative (BRI), 190–91
  capability for operations below depths
    of 1000 meters, 169
  CH-4B Fighter, as copy of U.S. F-35, 76
  conflict with, likely forms of, 11
  container missiles (YJ-18C), 68
  conventional-nuclear integration in
    missiles, 211–12, 223–24
  cyber capabilities, use in peacetime, 189
  deep-dive submersibles, 169
  Defense White Paper (2019), 231–32
  DF-26 ballistic missiles, 212, 217–18
  exertion of control over sea lanes, as
    existential threat to U.S., 14
  flag state responsibilities, violation
    of, 47–48
  harassment of U.S. Special Mission
    Ships, 131–32
  high-speed high-altitude drones, 211
  and hypersonic missiles, conventional-
    nuclear integration in, 223–24
  and hypersonic missiles, development
    of, 220, 221–22
  illegal seizure of U.S. UUV (2016), 132
  illegal use of laser weapons in
    peacetime, 29–30
  and international order, efforts to
    undermine, 11, 12–14
  Internet system of, and Belt Road
    Initiative (BRI), 190–91
  Internet system of, as separate from but
    connected to U.S. system, 190–91
  and LAWS, views on, 113
  leadership in technology and global
    governance as goal of, 190–91
  and long-range ballistic missiles, 216–17
  LRPS missiles, 211–12
  LRPS missiles, U.S. plans to
    counter, 215–16
  medium-range ballistic missiles, 244–45
  military-civic fusion, military
    advantages of, 13

Western Paracel Islands, China's seizure
from South Vietnam, 61–62
PAFMM in, 61
U.S.'s failure to respond to, 61–62
Wilson, Woodrow, 73, 147, 148
wireless telegraphy, by belligerents, neutral
nations' restriction of, 200–1
WMDs. *See* weapons of mass destruction
*Woomera Manual on the International Law
of Military Space Operations*, 276–77
World Disarmament Conference, and
submarine warfare law, 150
World War I
armed Allied merchant vessels in, 50–51
British blockade of Central Powers, 145
cutting of submarine cables in,
186–87, 200–1
end of, 148
German attacks on British telegraph
facilities, 187
German offer of peace negotiations, 147
and law of naval warfare, ignoring of, 10
peace treaty forbidding German
acquisition of submarines, 148
range and accuracy of naval gunfire
in, 205–6
ruses of war in, 25, 64–65
submarine warfare in, 137–38, 144–48
U.S. arming of merchant ships in, 73
U.S. entry into, 148, 186–87
use of merchant ships in conflict, 57–58
and Zimmerman Telegram, 148, 186–87
See also U-boats in World War I
World War II
aircraft carriers in Pacific War, 206
British use of merchant ships for
military purposes, 154
German glide bombs in, 207
German V1 and V2 rockets in,
207, 228–29
and law of naval warfare, ignoring of, 10

number of naval mines laid by U.S.
in, 85–86
and Panama Declaration, 153
Pearl Harbor attack, U.S. unrestricted
submarine warfare following, 10
range and accuracy of naval gunfire
in, 205–6
U.S. barring of U.S. shipping from
central European Coast, 153
use of merchant ships in conflict, 57–58
and U.S. neutrality rights, violation
of, 73–74
World War II, submarine warfare in,
137–38, 152–56
Britain's unrestricted submarine
warfare, 154
Germany's submarine warfare, as
largely ineffective, 156
Germany's submarine warfare, war
crimes conviction for, 155–56
Germany's unrestricted submarine
warfare, 152, 153–54
in Pacific, 137–38, 154–55
United States' unrestricted submarine
warfare, 154–55, 156
U.S. decision not to pick up
survivors, 155

Xingkong-2 (Starry Sky-2) missile, 221–22

Yantar (Russian ship), as cable cutting and
tapping ship, 181
Yugoslavia, and interwar naval
disarmament conferences, 151–52

Zimmerman Telegram, 148, 186–87
Zircon (Tsirkon) missile, 221
Ziyan, 79–80
Zumwalt class ships
cost of, 210–11
stealth technology of, 210–11